THE MUSIC OF ISRAEL

THE MUSIC OF ISRAEL

FROM THE BIBLICAL ERA
TO MODERN TIMES

Peter Gradenwitz

SECOND EDITION, REVISED AND EXPANDED

Amadeus Press
Reinhard G. Pauly, General Editor
Portland, Oregon

This edition, revised and expanded, is based on Peter Gradenwitz, *The Music of Israel: Its Rise and Growth Through
5000 Years,* W. W. Norton and Company, Inc., New York,
1949.

Music examples for this edition
rendered by Peter Huszagh.

ISBN 1-57467-012-3

Printed in Singapore

AMADEUS PRESS
The Haseltine Building
133 S.W. Second Avenue, Suite 450
Portland, Oregon 97204, U.S.A.

Library of Congress Cataloging-in-Publication Data

Gradenwitz, Peter, 1910–
The music of Israel : from the biblical era
to modern times / Peter Gradenwitz. —
2nd ed., rev. and expanded.
p.   cm.
Includes bibliographical references (p.   ) and index.
ISBN 1-57467-012-3
1. Music—Israel—History and criticism. I. Title.
ML345.I5G73   1996
780′.89′924—dc20   95-47994
CIP
MN

To
LEONARD BERNSTEIN
as a token of friendship
and sincere appreciation

Thus read the original (1949) dedication of the book.
Leonard Bernstein, who became a very dear friend, welcomed the prospect of a new, updated edition, and the
book is now dedicated

IN MEMORIAM LEONARD BERNSTEIN

CONTENTS

ILLUSTRATIONS

Music Examples

FOREWORD

During my first years in Israel (the late 1940s) I had the good fortune to come to know Peter Gradenwitz, whose love for music (of all kinds) and special insights into the music of the Jewish community impressed me deeply. He had a particular gift for the comparative analysis of so-called "Jewish" music of the European communities with the newly burgeoning developments in the musical life of the newly born State of Israel. The book that resulted from that gift was the first of its kind that I had known about, and I was proud indeed to be its dedicatee. I am even prouder now that the book has been expanded and updated; it has become an invaluable guide to a musical history that ranges from liturgical cantillation to the most sophisticated avant-garde music being written today by Jewish composers. Being a "Jewish" composer myself, in a number of senses, I am naturally attracted to this kind of well-organized overview of a very subtle and complicated subject, and I applaud Dr. Gradenwitz's scholarship and energies.

Leonard Bernstein

INTRODUCTION

The book *The Music of Israel* not only traces the rise and growth of Hebrew and Jewish music from the earliest beginnings to the present but also discusses the Jewish contributions to world music and proves that musical cross-relations have always existed both between the Jews of the Holy Land and their neighbors and between the Jews of the Diaspora and their host countries.

The new edition of this book is therefore timely not only in terms of our post-war murderous and warring world caught in the toils of mass confrontations on a scale which has reduced whole sections of humanity to the bitter rivalries of ancient city-states, but it is equally important in that it symbolically fulfills the role and mission of the Jew, and in particular of the Israeli, to reconcile the warring factions of related cultures. This is the Jew's supreme role, and any other will remain mere makeshift, a substitute which can only be an evasion of the higher Jewish destiny.

The irony is that no other people has established more conclusively the separateness of culture from state, no other people has proven so irrefutably that a culture can survive on a language, a religious faith and conviction, and a high moral tradition alone, without a state, for 2000 years. If now in

Israel, and everywhere else, the Jew is discovering an identity beyond that of the West's assimilated "exotic," it is surely to fulfill his God-given task, even at the expense of the curtailment of his vision of a Promised Land all to himself, and of an exclusive state. For the supreme justification of Israel can only be that, rediscovering and repossessing his ancient and genuine character—that of a Mosaic Middle Eastern people among their brethren, native to the land by the same religious, climatic, and regional attachments, bonds not only spiritual but cultural, psychological, and temperamental—the Jew in Israel *will* succeed in transforming swords into ploughshares, in translating fear into trust, and in teaching mankind the excitement, exultation, and reality of a challenge greater than war. For cultures are more precious than states: cultures can enrich one another; states can often only fight.

Today, as for thousands of years, the world's most important nerve center is the Middle East, and Jerusalem in particular—and the Jew will lead us all either into the light or into the darkness. Music is the most intimate and revealing expression of a culture. Therefore this excellent book should contribute markedly to a clearer perception of ourselves, of our neighbors, and of humanity at large within which sphere we must accomplish this, our higher mission—a mission of understanding, compassion, sacrifice, and love.

Yehudi Menuhin

AUTHOR'S PREFACE

Many books and essays have been written on the music of the ancient Hebrews as described in the books of the Bible and in the commentaries of rabbinical scholars, and many writers have studied the role of the Jew in the general history of the civilizations and the arts. Theologians, historians, sociologists, and literary and musical scholars have tried to analyze various aspects of Jewish history and to explain the singular case of a people who, after enjoying a few centuries of cultural prosperity and giving to the world a high code of laws and ethics, its greatest book, and some of its most magnificent poetry, were then dispersed among the nations of the globe and subjected to oppression and persecution for two millennia. Jewish history, it has been said, reads more strangely than fiction, and historians, swayed either by affection and compassion or by intolerance and agitation, have found it difficult to let the undistorted facts speak for themselves. In the field of music, too, the reader has hitherto had to choose between extremes of superlative praise and of vilification; only a very few aspects of Jewish musical history have been studied by scholars in a detached and truly scientific spirit.

A prominent scholar in the field of Jewish music, Eric Werner, rightly pointed out in the Prolegomenon to his anthology *Contributions to a His-*

torical Study of Jewish Music (by various authors, published in New York in 1976) that regrettably there is in "the scientific standard of our discipline . . . a clean demarcation between musicology, popular musical journalism, and a rather questionable music critique" (p. 19). He distinguishes between "popularizers . . . , scholars who do not limit themselves to strictly scientific methods, but who nonetheless know their subjects quite well," and those "whose enthusiasm for Jewish Music exceeds by far their knowledge or ability, scribblers who mainly compile their books or articles from learned sources without mentioning them . . . mainly bibliographers, and writers for popular encyclopedias or second-class newspapers" (pp. 25–26). Eric Werner cites as an example the widely praised and quoted book *The Cantillation of the Bible* (New York 1957) by Salomon Rosowsky, a leading figure in the St. Petersburg national Jewish music movement in the beginning of the century, as a work that shows "lack of historical knowledge and interest" (p. 14).

The present author may be proud that the critical scholar ranks him as a "meritorious popularizer . . . of special significance as an internationally known music-critic and as an indefatigable champion of contemporary music in Israel, whose modern composers must fight a stiff uphill battle, not only to be recognized, but even to be performed at all. His merits for the new generation of Israeli composers are considerable even if not always appreciated by them" (pp. 20–21).

In the new edition of this book, completed some forty-six years after its original publication, the author tries to live up to Eric Werner's classification as "meritorious," and to incorporate, as much as is possible within a single volume, the most recent historical discoveries and fruits of research. These come both from the work of Israeli and international scholars and from the author's own studies. The new edition also examines the background and state of musical life in Israel in our time and the streams and tendencies in the music of contemporary Israeli composers. Last but by no means least, this book considers those fields in which Israeli musicologists and scholars see the foremost tasks of research.

Since this book's first edition in 1949, hitherto unknown or hardly studied sources have been brought to light to add to our knowledge of ancient, medieval, and modern Hebrew liturgical and Jewish secular music.

Yet the serious student of the music of Israel is still confronted with various difficulties.

It is never easy to write the musical history of a particular nation or people, for the national character—like that of the individual personality—is composed not only of distinctive, seemingly inborn features but of a considerable number of foreign influences absorbed in one way or another. In the case of the Jews there is added the peculiar fact that throughout history their fate has been linked with that of other peoples. The ancient Hebrews had wandered from country to country before they were able to found their theocratic state in a land of their own, and on the way they adapted many foreign customs to their own way of living. Later, in the two millennia of their dispersion among the nations of the world, they were in close contact with the life and art of many different peoples, and though preserving their own ancient belief and spiritual values they could not but keep up with the spirit of the times and assimilate themselves to European thinking and ways of expression. In modern times, at last, Jews are again assembling in the land of the Bible from all corners of the globe, and from each country they bring different customs and different standards of culture to the land they are building anew.

It was the ancient Torah—their religious, legal, and moral canon—together with their prayer chant that kept the Jews united throughout the world and allowed them to maintain some of their ancient eastern character, however extensive became their westernization in later centuries. Law and music have been the fields traditionally cultivated by the Jews throughout the ages, and it is not to be wondered at that they excelled in these professions when European civilization permitted them to take part, like other citizens, in public and social life. The Jewish love for music and their specific musical talent are evidenced all the way from the earliest pages of Genesis—where the "invention of music" is attributed to the seventh generation of humankind—down to the era of high European cultural development, to which Jewry contributed many ingenious creators and performers of great music. In music, as well as in other fields, the Jew always held a position between tradition and progress; but it is not always easy to distinguish the Jew in general works of art, and in the case of assimilated composers it is well-nigh impossible.

Jewish musicology labors under difficulties. The ban on worldly science on the part of the rabbinical authorities—particularly in the early periods and in the eastern European sphere—forbade a detached study of the biblical sources and the notation of actual melodies. Moreover, the ancient commandment to refrain from the creation of images denies us a close knowledge of the music of the Hebrews; only a few representations of musical instruments but not original biblical melodies have come down to us, and the very names for the instruments used in biblical times have not all been completely explained as yet. The wholesale burning of Jewish books in the Middle Ages and again in modern times robbed us of a great many important theoretical sources and ancient manuscripts and added to the scarcity of material prevailing in our field. Comparative study and conjecture thus reign foremost in all investigations into the history of the music of Israel.

The present book is a survey extending from the music of ancient Israel to the new music in the modern state. It attempts to show the function of music in the ancient Temple and in Jewish life in the various centers of the Diaspora as well as the influence the ancient Hebrew culture and later Jewish achievements exerted on general music history, and to fix the historical position of the Jewish composers whose works have become part of the treasure of world music. The historical and general cultural background for all periods of musical development is provided, and the mutual influences shaping the music of the nations and of the Jews living within their midst are always examined.

The reader will note that the present book often varies from the generally accepted texts in its translations of well-known biblical sources and of talmudic passages; it must be understood that these variants constitute part of our research.

The author has been able to draw on a great many sources and monographs (listed in the bibliographical appendix) to offer a comprehensive study of most aspects of his theme. In his investigation of the ancient sources—biblical and talmudic—the author was greatly assisted by the late Mr. Ephraim Trochae (Dror), with whom he collaborated on a first short survey of this vast subject which was published in Jerusalem (in Hebrew) in 1945 and extended for the publication of the English (and the simultaneously published Spanish) book, *The Music of Israel,* of 1949.

A great many colleagues and friends have assisted the author in his re-search in many countries, and a number of composers and their publishers were good enough to make available their manuscripts and printed edi-tions and permitted the quotation of musical excerpts. I hope they will all accept the author's sincere thanks for their valuable help in this way—col-lectively—as individual acknowledgments would fill many pages.

In the Introduction to the first edition, I mentioned a few of the schol-ars to whom I was particularly indebted for their active interest and assis-tance while I prepared my study for publication. Among them were the late Dr. Paul Henry Lang, whose valuable suggestions and queries set me think-ing anew about many historical problems; and the late literary critic and author Dr. Paul Landau, who checked the general cultural aspects. Curt Sachs and Eric Werner, the two great scholars of the music of the ancient world whose work laid the foundations for all subsequent research, and Edith Gerson-Kiwi, who permitted me to read and quote from the manu-script of her book *Music of the Orient: Ancient and Modern* (which has not been published in its entirety), and read and commented upon my manu-script before publication. I was also grateful for the exchange of ideas with M. Leon Algazi of Paris, Mr. Samuel Alman of London, Mr. Arno Nadel of Berlin, Mrs. Alice Jacob-Loewenson of Jerusalem, and Mr. Joachim Stut-chevsky of Tel Aviv—all of them meanwhile lamentably deceased.

Needless to say, the author has also carefully read and studied reviews and serious critiques of the earlier book and sometimes either revised or queried earlier findings or opinions. I most gratefully remember Miss Katherine Barnard, who in the process of preparing the book for its publi-cation by W. W. Norton, excelled in offering all kinds of friendly assistance, good will and understanding, as well as wholehearted cooperation in the last, and decisive, stage of my original work.

For the present new edition the author enjoyed the devoted coopera-tion of Mrs. Suzanne Copenhagen, whose inspiring enthusiasm for the sub-ject helped to solve manifold problems arising during the process of com-pleting the preparations for the production of a book of this kind and scope.

Peter Gradenwitz
Freiburg-Breisgau and Tel Aviv

THE ETERNAL LAND

UNDER A SOLITARY PALM TREE on the edge of the wide desert of
the Southland a shepherd boy dreamily plays his pipe. Soon he
will leave the dry sands of the Negev for the friendlier North,
once the oasis has yielded its sparse treasures to his patient and placid flock.
The hollow yet piercing tones of his serene pastorale resound over the endless plains and from somewhere an echo faintly answers; is it another shepherd far away in the desert, is it a camel driver's plaintive song, or is it just
his own tune that returns to the friendly oasis from a futile journey across
the sands? We cannot tell, and the shepherd does not care. He is engulfed
in his own world, which is the welfare of his flock and the eternal question
whither to go next in search of pasture and food. His meditations, his joy,
and his sorrow ring through his tune. . . .

Over the rocky Judean mountains reverberate the mighty sounds of a
many-voiced chorus and an orchestra composed of a colorful variety of instruments. You can hear their solemn music far across the stony desert
down to the lowest valley of this earth, where the Jordan rushes its waters
into the Dead Sea, and it resounds in the olive and cypress groves on the
hills as well as in the lanes and alleys of the Holy City. You listen spell-

bound, and the magnitude of the Jerusalem scene and the loftiness of the music inspire you with awe. . . .

A light breeze carries the exquisite music of a small group of instruments over the gentle waters of the Sea of Galilee. In the cool night following a scorching day sweet chamber music refreshes and delights the company stretched out on the lawns adorning the shores of the beautiful lake. You can distinguish the flute and the violins singing a song of yearning and love, and again sounding a lively tune of hope and joy. . . .

This is the country holy to three great world religions, a land full of bold contrasts—the fertile valley bordering on barren desert, the sounds of feasts and rejoicing next to solitude and austerest calm, the building and planning for a bright future of the people that remembers with bitterness and sorrow what brutal rulers inflicted upon them in the past. The scenery and the atmosphere, the place names and the relics, the sound of the shepherd's pipe and the song of children, the prayers in recitation and psalmodic cantillation transport you back through almost two thousand years of history, to the time when a Nazarene rabbi preached a new ethos to the Jews of Galilee and Judea and ushered in a new era in the history of mankind, or even further back, to the splendors of King Solomon's Temple, the cultural center in Israel's Jerusalem. It was shortly after the painful death of the Nazarene that the Temple fell under the blow of the Romans, the mighty conquerors of Israel whose victory opened two millennia of Jewish dispersion and misery among the people of the world.

The shepherd now playing his tranquil tune in the southern desert knows more of the world now than did his forebears of ancient times, for there is television in the smallest tent or hut, and the onlooker's memory of the Palestine of three thousand years ago is abruptly disturbed by today's reality: the shepherd has stopped his playing and hurries to soothe his flock, which is frightened by a loud noise and by clouds of dust whirled up from the desert. The boy rubs his eyes and looks around—and here it is, the four-legged monster that has disturbed the calm of the oasis. It is a motor truck laden with young people, singing and laughing gaily as their car struggles its way through the dry sands and speeds them home from a hard day's work. They have built houses and huts in the midst of the desert, and the shepherd has often rested and refreshed himself in their spacious dining hall. Their song has little of the melancholy strains of his own plaintive pipe, but strange as it sounds to his ears he finds that theirs, too, is a song of the desert, a song of the common land. And they brought with them a little black box from which emanates a horrible noise in stamping rhythms, frightening to listen to.

So this is the twentieth century, with the motorcar usurping the camel's place and with the desert yielding soil and fruit to the Jews returning to their land of yore? Then what are the sounds ringing over the mountains of Judea, the music heard on the shores of the Sea of Galilee? The Temple has not been rebuilt, and Diaspora traditions and memories deny to observant Jews the use of music in the house of worship. But on one of the hills overlooking the Holy City there has risen a center of learning and study, the Hebrew University, and in its amphitheater there plays a symphony orchestra assisted by a large modern chorus. And music rises over the mountains just as it did when the trumpets of the Lord made the walls of Jericho crumble.

On the shores of the Kinnereth new life has risen from ancient ruins as well. The lake is surrounded by agricultural settlements, and the one most favored by natural beauty, Ein Gev, on the slopes of the Susita hill opposite the ancient city of Tiberias, invites music lovers all over the country once a year for a one-week music festival. Today, just as three millennia ago, there is singing and dancing on the romantic shores of the Sea of Galilee.

Time seems to have stood still in the Holy Country. Elsewhere empires have risen to mighty power and have rotted and perished. Men and women have loved and hated, succeeded to fame and vanished, have usurped power and were brought low. Genius has given to the world immortal treasures of thought, art, and music, and built magnificent edifices of marble and stone. Mankind has learned to traverse the wide world on land, on sea, and in the air, and magic machines have been created that allow us to watch and to listen to people speaking, acting, or singing hundreds or thousands of miles away. In this Holy Land many armies and nations have fought for possession of holy places and strategic positions, have devastated and again rebuilt the country. Little was left of the ancient glory, and few are the monuments telling of the splendors of old. Today the Jews continue to come back to the country they had made great in olden times;

they are bringing with them the experience and the knowledge they gathered in the two thousand years of their contact with the western world, a world whose ideas are diametrically opposed to those of the East but which has also absorbed much of eastern custom and thought. This continues a fascinating chapter in the long and exciting story of the fight between desert and land of plenty, between the unsteady and the settled, between a life of thrift and a life of luxury.

The music of modern Israel mirrors continuity as well as change: it has not fundamentally changed in character as it still sounds over the plains of the south, the Judean hills, and the waters of Galilee. The shepherd's song, played on the thousand-year-old pipe, is the calm and austere tune created by the son of the wide deserts; the sonorous music of the orchestral instruments belongs in the prosperous towns and the fertile valleys. These are the very same opposing forces acknowledged by ancient Greece, where they find expression in the temperate art of the Apollonian cult—with the soft-voiced cithara as the favorite instrument—and the orgiastic music of the worshipers of Dionysus who accompanied their song on the shrill-sounding aulos. Just as in classical Greece, geographic conditions created the life of the inhabitants of ancient Palestine and their social development; their music was a direct and simple expression of their soul in their life with nature, while in the wealthy urban centers it developed into an exuberant art. Today the soil of the desert is being reclaimed and forced to yield fruit, but the song of the plain is still shaping the tunes sung by the settlers. In the towns the chorus and orchestra created to sing and play unto the Lord have been replaced by choruses and orchestras serving the community of citizens, elevating their souls and adorning their hours of leisure just as they do in the great urban centers of other civilized continents. But the characteristic aspect of the country has not changed at all: the shepherd—Jewish or Arab—plays his flute just as he did in King Solomon's time, the Judean mountains reverberate to the sounds of a many-voiced chorus and orchestra, and the light breeze carries over the Sea of Galilee the exquisite music of a small group of flutes and violins. . . .

CHAPTER ONE

MUSIC OF THE DESERT

FROM THE DAWN of its history down to the beginning of the first millennium before the Common Era, Israel was a people of nomads and shepherd tribes; their patriarchs, their judges, and their first prophets and kings were sons of the land. It is only with the rise of their kingdom that urban civilization begins to develop and that pastoral poetry and song are rivaled by courtly art and music. But the parables and the proverbs, the verse and the song of Israel are living witness of the people's origin; they come forth from the mind and the heart of shepherd poets and singers, and it is the peasant and the shepherd whom they still glorify in their song:

> The Lord is my shepherd [sings David, the royal shepherd boy];
>   I shall not want.
> He maketh me to lie down in green pastures;
> He leadeth me beside the still waters.
> He restoreth my soul;
> He leadeth me in the paths of righteousness for his name's sake.
> Yea, though I walk through the valley of the shadow of death,
>   I will fear no evil:
> For thou art with me; thy rod and thy staff they comfort me.

Thou preparest a table before me in the presence of mine enemies:
Thou anointest my head with oil; my cup runneth over.
Surely goodness and mercy shall follow me all the days of my life:
And I will dwell in the house of the Lord for ever.

David's Psalms and the Song of Solomon are sublime examples of shepherd poetry and song. To grasp their spirit and to get an idea of what premonarchist Israel's music may have been like, we must turn to the peasant and nomad past of Israel. No pictorial sources and no written music are there to help us in our endeavors to reconstruct the picture of the most ancient Hebrew playing and song; we must rely on comparisons with the culture of the neighboring countries and on the few actual hints contained in the early books of the Bible.

We know little about the musical instruments and the songs of Israel in its earliest history. The Hebrews, who constituted one of the many Semitic tribes which led an unsteady life of migration between the Arabian Peninsula and the northern parts of Asia Minor but who seem to have separated from the other groups during the twentieth century B.C.E., presented a strange mixture of nomads and peasants: they were restless wanderers longing for a secure place of permanent settlement. The country through which they drove their herds of cattle and their flocks of sheep was undeveloped and bare, and no place seemed inviting enough for them to pitch their tents permanently. Highly civilized countries lay to the north and south of their lands: the Sumerians—a non-Semitic people of eastern Asiatic origin—ruled in the fertile plains of Mesopotamia, while in Egypt there flourished the culture of the Old Kingdom. Abraham had come to Canaan from Ur, capital of Sumeria, and his wanderings had led him to Egypt, too; indeed, in his days the first contacts seem to have been made between the two great civilizations after more than seven hundred years of isolation. Musical archaeology actually helps us to examine the cultural relations between Sumeria (and later Babylon) and Egypt, and it also proves that Israel here began—at the earliest stage of its history, and in the days of its oldest patriarch—to play the role it was destined to fill throughout the ages: the role of a mediator between peoples and civilizations.

The ancient Sumerian civilization has provided us with the oldest records of musical systems and musical organization; these records go back to the third millennium B.C.E. For the Sumerian Temple, professional singers and players were trained by an appointed officer; music schools were founded for this purpose in various centers and were later kept up by the Babylonians, successors of the Sumerians as rulers of Mesopotamia. Clappers, cymbals, bells, rattles, and drums are known to have been used in Sumeria; pipes, blowing horns, and trumpets are mentioned occasionally; but it seems that the Sumerians most favored the softer stringed instruments: a large type of lyre, harps, and the lute. It is of special interest for us here that most of the surviving specimens of these musical instruments were found in the royal cemetery of Abraham's native town, Ur.

Sumerian musicians. Vase fragment of the fourth millennium before the Common Era. The two lyres depicted have five and seven strings, respectively. (After Curt Sachs, "Musik der Antike.")

The Old Kingdom of Egypt knew the same instruments as ancient Sumeria, but it appears that there was no contact between the two countries from about 2700 B.C.E. to the time of Abraham (ca. 2000), for the favorite Sumerian instrument of the later third millennium, the lyre, is shown on an Egyptian painting for the first time in that period. Semitic nomads—very probably Hebrews—are there depicted offering presents to the Pharaoh of Egypt, among them a lyre; it has been assumed that the Semites of the picture are none other than Joseph's brethren coming before Pharaoh.

If it seems certain that the Hebrews (from whom in the meantime a new group had detached itself, the Sons of Israel, who on their part were divided into twelve tribes named after the sons of Jacob, or Israel) acted as a link between the highly civilized Sumerians and Egyptians at the time their own history actually opens, the development of a civilization of their own was still hampered by their unsteady nomad life. Organized musical practice, the evolution of tonal systems, and the development of musical instruments—such as those developed by the ancient Hebrews in the neighboring countries—are impossible without the creation of an organized community and of a cultural center, that is, temple or court. The tribes of Israel lived and wandered about in different regions and under different climatic and geographic conditions, and their standard of life depended on the yield of their soil. It was hunger and want that drove some of them—a small fraction, it is true—to the fertile Nile valley, the destination of many Semitic tribes in search of pasture. The cattle drivers and shepherds of Israel eased the boredom of their wanderings by singing and piping their songs or strumming the lyre, giving free rein to their emotions and feelings; they used the instruments and remembered the tunes known all over the Near East—some of them going back to the same central Asiatic cradle from which the Far Eastern civilizations also sprang—but they could not develop a systematized art without first creating a communal and cultural center of their own. And this was not achieved before the times of the Judges and the Kings, a millennium after Abraham had settled in Canaan.

Still, it is certain that the ancient Hebrews loved singing, playing, and dancing as much as did the Sumerians and the Egyptians; the early books of the Pentateuch prove that music was regarded as indispensable by them in joy and in sorrow, at the feast and in the fields. Most ancient peoples attribute the invention of music to a legendary national hero of their own; the writers of Israel's history ascribe the first use of musical instruments to the seventh generation after the creation of the world, when no Hebrews could, of course, be spoken of as yet: Jubal (son of Ada and Lamech, offspring of Methusael, son of Mehujael, son of Irad, son of Enoch, son of Cain, Adam and Eve's first-born) "was the father of all such as handle the lyre and pipe" (Gen. 4:21). And Jubal's half-brother, Tubal, was described as "Tubal-Cain, an instructor of every artificer in brass and iron" (Gen. 4:22).

The myth of Jubal as the inventor of instrumental music inspired various ancient writers and theoreticians to see in the biblical Hebrews the very earliest creators and practitioners of music. One such commentator of the twelfth century C.E., Peter Comestor, first chancellor at Notre-Dame de Paris, author of *Historia Scholastica,* calls Jubal "Tubal," as do some other authors. Comestor describes him as "the inventor of music, that is of consonances, so that pastoral labour might be turned into delights" and refers to Jubal's half-brother Tubal-Cain, as "a hammerer and artificer in every work of brass and iron." Comestor assumed that Jubal listened to the work of his half-brother, and that Jubal "delighted in the sound of metals and devised out of their weights the proportions and consonances which originated in them. This invention has erroneously been attributed by the Greeks to Pythagoras."[1]

Pythagoras, the philosopher and scientist from Samos, of the second half of the sixth century B.C.E., was regarded in ancient Greek tradition as the creator of classical music theory, as documented (in the absence of traces of his own writings) and further developed by Pythagoras's students.

Isidorus of Seville had preceded Comestor by saying in the sixteenth chapter of his *Etymologiarum sive originum libri* XX, Book III (compiled between 622 and 633 C.E.):

> Moses says that the inventor of the art of music was Tubal, who was in the race of Cain, before the flood. The Greeks say that Pythagoras found its beginnings in the sound of hammers and the striking of stretched strings.[2]

Adam von Fulda, composer and historiographer, echoes this in his treatise "De musica" (1490) but concludes that Jubal preceded all "inventors of this art," for "indeed, the Holy Scriptures name him and no other the first inventor."

The names of the biblical "inventor of music" and his family throw an interesting sidelight on the association of thoughts in the minds of the scribes who recorded the history and traditions of the Hebrews in the Scriptures, and also on the parallelisms of myths in the ancient world. The name

---

[1]Judith Cohen, "Jubal in the Middle Ages," in *Yuval: Studies of the Jewish Music Research Centre,* Vol. 3, Jerusalem, 1974, pp. 83–99.

[2]All quotations from Judith Cohen, op.cit.

Jubal, the musician, and Tubal-Cain, the blacksmith, as depicted in *Caedmon Genesis*, early eleventh century.

Jubal is related to the Hebrew *yovel* = ram; the ram's horn, the shofar, was among the first ancient Hebrew instruments, sounded on solemn festive occasions. (The word *jubilee* is derived from the Hebrew *yovel*.) The names Jubal and Tubal, often exchanged in historical writings, are also related; in the Bible Tubal is the inventor of the art of iron, and later writings also associate him with experiments with sounds of brass and iron. Their sister, Na'amah, bears a name related to the Hebrew word *ne'imah*, which means both "melody" and "beauty." Commentators have drawn comparisons between the mythological figures Jubal, Tubal-Cain, and Na'amah and Greek counterparts including Apollo (for music), Hephaistos (the smith), and Aphrodite (the beauty).

That the "invention of music" was attributed by both the Hebrew tradition and Greek historians to artisans and theoreticians of music instru-

Pythagoras, "inventor of music," on a woodcut, Venice, late fifteenth century.

ments—Jubal, Pythagoras—points to their knowledge that singing surely was an older art than the building of instruments for playing music; this is as true in the history of Greek poetry as in that of ancient Hebrew poetry and music.

The common concept of Jubal as the father of musicians and Tubal-Cain as the father of the artificers in brass and iron has recently been challenged. The scholar Hans Seidel (Leipzig) argues that Gen. 4:19–22 should not be interpreted as documenting the origins of music, of arts, of techniques, and of nomad life; it rather describes various professional groups in the communities of land- and city-dwellers as the author and scribe of the Scriptures knew them. The "fathers" of the biblical text are not necessarily personal fathers of inventors but leaders or patrons of professional groupings, the former living in tents and tending cattle and sheep, the latter commanding settled occupations.[3]

The biblical myth of the invention of music has various parallels in the traditions of other civilizations. Arab legend, which goes back to the same treasure of ancient Semitic lore as the biblical stories, also credits Jubal, son of Cain (Qain), with the first song—an elegy on the death of Abel; Lamak (the Hebrew Lamech) is called the inventor of the lute (a European word actually derived from the Arabic *ʿūd*), while his son Tubal is credited with the introduction of drum and tambourine. The same Arab source claims that the tunbur came from the people of Sodom (*Lūt* = Lot); this instrument was in fact the Sumerian lute, the ancestor of most later stringed instruments; the Greek word for it, *pandura*, points to its having been imported from Asia Minor, as in Sumeria the lute was called *Pan-tur*, which means "bow-small" and indicates an origin in the most ancient of stringed instruments, the musical bow.

Another ancient tradition—mentioned in the thirteenth century C.E. by Bar Hebraeus, the Syriac patristic writer of Jewish parentage—has it that the daughters of Cain invented musical instruments; the singing-girl, who played an important part in Arabic music, was called *qaina,* and a similar word describes musicians and singers in the Persian language. This is par-

---

[3]Hans Seidel, "Genesis IV, 19–22 und der Ursprung der Musik?" in *Assaph. Studies in the Arts, Orbis Musicae,* Vol. 10, Tel Aviv, 1990–1991, pp. 28–38.

ticularly interesting with regard to the place ascribed to women in early music. Though women were probably banned from Temple music, they were always found in the spheres of popular musical practice: this, too, is a phenomenon common to all Near Eastern cultures. In ancient Japan women were not permitted to sing or play the religious music of the educated musicians, nor could they join in the music-making of the less educated merchant classes; they were confined to the lowest style of music and forbidden to use the tunes and styles of higher classes even if they had enjoyed a higher education. The student of ancient history can thus find in the women's music of early civilizations the most primitive stages of musical development. Singing and dancing still went largely together in the women's music of the ancient East; simple melodic patterns and rhythmic accompaniment on instruments characterize their songs. In some places in our contemporary world we can still study at first hand the singing and playing that must have been practiced by the women singers of old. Jewish women on the north African Isle of Djerba have been found by a modern scholar, Robert Lachmann, to constitute living relics from eastern civilization of thousands of years ago. Their songs depend on a small store of typical melodic turns; the various songs reproduce these turns—or some of them—time and again. Their tone relations reveal one of the many kinds of practices of vocal music before its subjection to a rational scale system as understood by theory. The women's songs of this island, isolated from the cultural development in the past millennia, belong, says Lachmann, to a species whose forms are essentially dependent not on the requirements of the text but on certain processes of motion.[4] Thus we find here, in place of the free rhythm of cantillation and its very intricate line of melody, a periodical up-and-down movement. This type of song, like the recitation of magic or liturgical texts, goes back to prehistoric times. In the Jewish communities, not only in Sephardic districts, but also, for example, in Yemen, the women accompany their songs on frame drums or cymbals which they beat with their hands. The beats follow at regular intervals; they fall on each period of the melody. They give the length of the unit of line, but

---

[4]Robert Lachmann, *Jewish Cantillation and Song in the Isle of Djerba,* Jerusalem, 1940, publ. before radio and television reached the island.

they do not divide the melody into bars, nor do they bring it within the limits of a systematic rhythmic pattern.

Lachmann's description of ancient women's singing as preserved down to our own days provides us with a fitting picture of how the people sang, played, and danced in ancient Israel; Miriam and her women responding to Moses' hymn of triumph and praise (Exod. 15), Deborah proclaiming victory and joy (Judg. 5), Jephthah's daughter welcoming her father (Judg. 11:34), and the women of Israel coming to greet King Saul after David had slain Goliath (I Sam. 18:6 F.) certainly sang and played in a way not far remote from the style of these living relics, the women of the isolated north African and Yemenite communities.

EARLY SOURCES tell us that singing was always accompanied by instrumental playing, but the instruments actually mentioned in the Pentateuch in connection with Israel's earliest history are very few. The primitive and emotional character of ancient Hebrew music is confirmed by what we know about them—from etymological study, from the sparse descriptions offered by the Bible and by talmudic commentaries, and from comparison with Sumerian and Egyptian types, for no pictorial relics are available for the ancient Hebrew Orient. The six instruments named in Israel's nomadic period are the *'ugab,* probably a shepherd flute of some kind; the *kinnor,* a stringed instrument used for accompanying the singers, a small rounded lyre which may have stemmed from the larger Sumerian prototype; the *tof,* a frame drum; the *pa'amon,* a bell or jingle; the *shofar,* the ram's horn; and the *hazozra,* the loud trumpet.

The flute, the lyre, and the drum—none of them strong in sound—were the instruments of the people and were used to accompany their songs. The ram's horn and trumpet, on the other hand, were the shrill and resounding instruments of Israel's cult: they point to a still-primitive stage in the worship of the Lord. The trumpet, used in pairs in accordance with a most ancient belief in the power of symmetry, fulfills the task ascribed to it in all primitive communities, namely to remind God of his people in worship as well as in war (Num. 10:1–2, 9–10). The bell—"it should be upon Aaron to minister: and his sound shall be heard when he goeth in unto the holy place before the Lord, and when he cometh out, that he die not"

Lyre player, from Egyptian wall painting at Beni Hasan. The lyre depicted is somewhat different from those seen on other paintings of the period; it is probably the biblical kinnor, played with a plectrum.

(Exod. 28:25)—is a relic of magic belief; it protects the priest against evil spirits while he is outside the holy place. The shofar, finally, the only instrument still used in the worship of the Jews on their holiest days, most eloquently indicates the survival of ancient magical associations; not only is the ram's horn—which has purposely remained primitive in form and in tone—blown in times of danger or repentance, but it is covered so that the worshippers may not see it; in many primitive civilizations the sight of sacred objects is denied to the people. The magic power of seven shofarim, blown seven times on the seventh day of the siege of Jericho (the recurring number seven indicates another remnant of ancient sacred belief) makes the wall of the city fall down flat (Josh. 6:20); Gideon the Judge frightens his enemies, the Midianites, by the sound of the Lord's horn blown by three hundred of his men (Judg. 7:16–22); Zechariah believed that "the Lord God shall blow the horn" himself on the day of Israel's salvation (Zech. 9:14); and the belief in the shofar's magic powers still lives on in the people's minds—one need only remember the "Dybbuk" legend.

While the musical instruments used in the service of worship had the shrill or loud sound proper to their purpose, it is doubtful indeed whether

the worshipers themselves were really "crying unto God." Though in primitive belief only the fervent and clamorous prayer will be heard and eventually granted, it seems certain that the Jews were more reserved in the cantillation of their prayers than other Near Eastern religious communities. A
sweet and expressive rather than a strong and loud voice is still favored
today in archaic Jewish-Oriental synagogues, and only at the climax of a
prayer is the singer required to raise his voice. At the nomadic stage of Israel's history there cannot have been a great difference between the tunes
of the shepherd in the fields and those intoned in prayer; they are the flu-
ent, continuous melodies moving within a narrow range of four or, at the
most, six notes and based upon ever-recurring melodic formulas. It is only
with Israel's return from Egypt that definite forms of singing and playing
began to take shape under the influence of a richly developed foreign culture, though the full impact of the Egyptian—and other neighboring—
practices was only felt three centuries after the Exodus, at the time of the
Kings. Biblical narrative, poetry, form, and signs are helpful in drawing a
picture of Israel's music between the time of the Egyptian exile and the
erection of the Temple. But before attempting to describe the state of
music in this second great period of Israel's ancient history, we must cast a
glance at the music of Egypt under the New Kingdom; the Israelites were
slaves and servants in Egypt after a short period of prosperity and wealth, yet
they had full opportunity to become acquainted with the high civilization
and flourishing culture of their oppressors.

The Old Egyptian Empire of the third millennium had had a music
similar to that of Sumeria, and all the musical instruments known in Mesopotamia were in use in Egypt as well. It has already been stated that the contact between the two countries had been interrupted for some seven hundred years and that a new Asiatic influence had made itself felt with the
beginning of the second millennium, the time Abraham came to Egypt.
The character of Egyptian art had greatly changed with the steady influx of
foreign artists in the period of the Middle Kingdom. The kings of the
southwest Asiatic countries subjugated by Egypt had sent singers and players as part of their tribute; the dancing maidens and their instruments, new
and strange to Egyptian eyes and ears, are a prominent feature of Middle
Kingdom paintings. The sweet-sounding vertical flute and the soft dou-

ble-cane reed pipe were replaced by shrill oboe-like instruments; new kinds of harps were introduced, and the ancient small harp was enlarged in size and given more strings; lyres, lutes, and drums appeared in the Egyptian orchestra for the first time. With the new instruments introduced into Egypt, a change occurred not only in the character and sound of orchestral combinations but in melodies and rhythms as well. The quiet and mild music of the Old Kingdom was superseded by a noisy, exciting, and many-colored tonal art, just as the dance scenes depicted in the wall paintings show a sensuous emotion unparalleled in earlier sources. The singing maidens imported from southwestern Asia brought about a change in the social status of music in Egypt, too; Egyptian women also began playing musical instruments and did away with the restriction of professional singing and playing to the upper ranks.

In the eighteenth and seventeenth centuries B.C.E., the civilization of the Middle Kingdom, in which ancient tradition and new trends reigned side by side, was completely destroyed by the Syriac-Semitic Hyksos tribes at the same time as the Kassites conquered the Babylonian Empire. The New Kingdom, whose history opens about 1580 B.C.E., shows a greatly different scene. Though it seems that the dignity of ancient ritual music was preserved in the temples and schools, public life resounded with the new music and the still noisier and more sonorous instruments brought to Egypt from Asia Minor. The traditional music, which had developed some distinct national trends, was regarded as old-fashioned and artificial, while the cosmopolitan character of the newly introduced instruments and their musicians mirrored the widened horizon as well as the refinement, the elegance, and the splendor of life in the New Empire.

The Egyptians had wealthy towns in which, in the course of the centuries, an organized musical life had been developed in the temples and the secular courts alike. The graphic monuments tell us that singing, playing, and dancing were generally practiced simultaneously, and a celebration or feast is usually seen accompanied by entire bands. It is interesting to reflect, in the face of all this splendor and wealth, that of the twenty-six instruments known to have been used in Egypt at the height of its culture, two at the most can be attributed to native origin—the *sistrum* and the *shawm*. The sistrum, for which primitive prototypes can be found, was an

(a) String-instrument player from the sixteenth century B.C.E. Found in Tell-el-ajjul (ancient Gasa) in southern Palestine. (b) Syrian piper, with panpipe-like instrument, an ancestor of the organ (magrepha?). Alexandrian terra cotta from the first century B.C.E. (c) Phoenician ivory plaque, thirteenth century B.C.E., with incised scene depicting musicians. Found at Megiddo, northern Palestine. (d) Seven-stringed Abyssinian kissar with Islamic half-crescent and Jewish shield of David. (e) Figure with drum. Found at Megiddo. (a, b, c, d: Palestine Archeological Museum, Jerusalem. e: After Curt Sachs.)

instrument consisting of a handle and a frame with jingling crossbars. Although in ancient Egypt it was associated with the worship of Hathor and Isis, it entered the Hebrew cult as the *mna'anim* of II Sam. 6:5, where King David and all the house of Israel are said to have played before the Lord "on all manner of instruments made of fir wood, even on lyres and harps, drums, sistra, and cymbals." (Luther's German Bible version rightly translates thus, while the English Authorized Version incomprehensibly has "cornets"; incidentally, the Hebrew word *mna'anim* is derived from the verb *nū'a* = "shook," just as the Greek *seîstron* means "thing shaken.") While the shawms are not mentioned in Jewish sources at all—they may also have lost importance under the New Kingdom of Egypt—all the other instruments first mentioned in Hebrew history after the return from Egypt were as much the common possession of the entire large musical province round the eastern shores of the Mediterranean as were the fundamentals underlying the theory and practice of music. "Mediterranean music"—a term coined for compositions with a southern flavor in the western Europe of the romanticist nineteenth century C.E. and newly created again for one of the young Palestinian composers' schools in the 1940s—once comprised the music of ancient Mesopotamia and Syria, Greece and Phoenicia, Italy, Cyprus and Crete, the land of Israel, Arabia, and Egypt; this unity reigned till classical Greece took over the entire cultural heritage of the East and preserved its highest achievements in new forms. Hellenism then united the eastern Mediterranean region again, and Islam, blending ancient Oriental culture and Hellenistic forces, became in turn the heir of Hellas.

The Jews were destined to play once more the role of mediators between ancient civilizations. In the course of a rapid ascent on the ladder of cultural development, they absorbed from the foreign civilizations about them what seemed best to them and what most fitted their specific character, and they invariably gave their practice a mark of their own. Just as most of their ancient legends and customs, religious or national, were derived from common Near Eastern lore but were molded and interpreted by them in a new spirit, so they created a Temple service and a poetry and art, the origins of which can be traced back to other Oriental sources but which assumed with them a distinctive individual note; just as they originated new moral values and were able to erect the greatest spiritual and cultural center of the ancient world, so they gave music new foundations on which, a thousand years after King Solomon's Temple, western civilization could base its musical style.

Jewish history at the time of its Kings went through the same process of transition that had taken place in Egypt some six hundred years before. Foreign influx and the development of urban life did away with the pastoral calm of their music and introduced the splendor of orchestral sound and of music for dancing; more expressive and powerful instruments replaced the soft-voiced flute and lyre of old. Music became a profession practiced by a religious caste in the Temple and by professional female musicians in the king's or the wealthy nobleman's house, and melodies became subject to systematization and to rational, as well as spiritual, theory.

But in order to be able to draw a dividing line between the two civilizations at the time of Israel's sojourn in Egypt, and again between Egypt under the New Kingdom and King Solomon's empire, we should picture for ourselves an Egyptian orchestra. We might thereby get an idea of the musical theory and practice of the Egyptian musicians, for the abundance in Egypt of pictorial and written evidence must compensate us for the dearth of scriptural sources and the complete lack of pictures that might cast light upon the music history of ancient Israel.

An orchestra characteristic of the Mediterranean civilization at the time of Egypt's New Kingdom is depicted on a bas-relief now at the British Museum. Though it dates from as late as 650 B.C.E., that is to say some seven hundred years after Israel's Exodus from Egypt, and though it is not of Egyptian provenance itself, earlier examples confirm that its typical features were essentially those of the ancient orchestras; moreover, as Israel had in the meantime built its Temple in Jerusalem, it must be surmised that the Temple orchestra cannot have been very much different.

The relief depicts the musicians of the Elamite court coming out to greet King Assurbanipal on his return to Susa from his victorious campaign against Babylon. Eleven musicians open the procession. They are, first, seven harpists (seven was still a holy number) plucking different strings, and players on double reeds and on drums—women among them. The instrumentalists are followed by singers: nine boys and six women. One of the latter compresses her throat with her hand in order to produce a shrill and vibrating tone; this is an old Oriental custom in use to this very day in Syria and Arabia; many ancient pictures show that the singers were wont to produce nasal tones and a high-pitched voice if not necessarily a piercing and loud one.[5] It is interesting to look at the singers on the Assyrian and Egyptian reliefs in the light of a talmudic description with regard to singing in the Second Temple: "When he (the singer) raises his voice in song, he puts his thumb into his mouth and brings his forefinger between the vocal cords, till his brethren the priests get rapidly up behind him" (Ioma—the treatise on the Day of Atonement—38). Were they provoked or irritated by the shrillness of the voice? Returning to the Elamite orchestra, we also note that singing and dancing were still closely allied, for some of the musicians are making actual dance movements, while the singers are clapping their hands.

The Near Eastern orchestra as we know it from Assyrian and Egyptian paintings and reliefs is described in one biblical source which also throws light on the form of orchestral performance in the ancient Orient. This source—Dan. 3:5 ff.—speaks of the musicians of Nebuchadnezzar, King of Babylon, about a generation after Assurbanipal; the book was probably written in the second century C.E.—four hundred years after the events described—and its author may have known the instruments and way of performance from personal experience. The passage tells us that a herald commanded the people to worship the golden image set up by the king as soon as they heard the sound of the *keren,* the *mashrokītha,* the *kathros,* the *sabka,* the *psanterin,* the *sumponiah,* "and all kinds of instruments." We have little difficulty in identifying the four instruments mentioned first: the keren is a horn or trumpet; the mashrokītha was a sort of pipe, as indicated by its derivation from the Hebrew word *sharok* = "to pipe" or "to whistle"; the kathros is a stringed instrument, probably a lyre; the sabka is a kind of harp, which appears in Greek as "sambuca"; the psanterin (= psaltery, mentioned in the Book of Daniel only, 3:5, 10, 15) indicates by its name that it was an instrument used to accompany the psalms, its Greek form being *psaltêrion.* But the most interesting term is the last: *sumponiah.* Some pas-

---

[5]Curt Sachs has pointed to the wrinkles around the noses and mouths of the angels on the Ghent altarpiece as a proof that the nasaling style of the East was still practiced in fifteenth-century Europe (these features cannot, however, be recognized on commercial photographs). See *The Orient and Western Music.*

Musicians of the Elamite court orchestra greet King Assurbanipal on his victorious return to Susa in 661 B.C.E. (From a relief at the British Museum.)

sages in biblical commentaries point to the sumponiah being a musical in-strument (it was once identified with the ancient 'ugab, the shepherd flute, and again described as a composite instrument on the strength of the Greek meaning of the word *symphonia* = "simultaneous sound"); while the mishna (Kelim—on the ritual uncleanness of the objects of daily use—11:6) couples the symphonia with a brass flute in uncleanness. But it has been justly argued that in the Daniel passage "sumponiah" does not mean a sin-gle instrument of music at all but must be quite literally translated as a "combination of sounds" or just "orchestra"; the Authorized Version, in fact, includes the word in "all kinds of music" (in telling the parable of the prodigal son, St. Luke—15:25—also uses the term, and the Authorized Version again translates simply "music"). Though in later times, when many Greek terms were made to change their meanings, a composite musical instrument may well have been described by the fitting name *sumponiah,* it is improbable indeed that the ancient Aramaic text of the book of Daniel should have alluded to a musical instrument by a term that in the original Greek was never used in this sense. Moreover, Curt Sachs has proved that if *sumponiah* is translated as "orchestra" or "band," the entire passage could be understood to describe not the composition of the orchestra but an orchestral performance in the ancient East—and the context makes this entirely plausible. If we accept the Aramaic text word for word, says Sachs, the king's subjects heard the various instruments first singly and then all together—in the way familiar to all students of eastern music. A flourish on the horn or trumpet is designed to attract the attention of the players and the masses alike. The most accomplished musicians of the band then display their virtuoso art in solo passages, improvising upon the melodic patterns of the piece, and only then does the full orchestra combine in playing a "symphony" in the sense of the seventeenth-century Italian *sinfonia;* a short instrumental ritornello. If this interpretation is correct, the additional "all kinds of instruments" may be drums and other instruments of merely rhythmical character, which were not mentioned with the solo performers but which cannot have been missing in the ensemble; it can well be understood that they joined in the music only when the entire band played together. The people were thus advised to wait for the horn signal, followed by solos of the pipe, lyre, harp, and psaltery, after which the full ensemble of these would play together with the percussion instruments.[6]

The orchestral performance described—a kind of concerto grosso without the opening tutti, if we wish to liken it to a form familiar in western European instrumental music—has a parallel in the responsorial singing practiced in the Jewish Temple and in many other Oriental civilizations; it is substantially the same style of performance that is described in the first great piece of poetry in the Pentateuch: Moses' hymn of praise after Israel's deliverance from the Egyptians. On the shores of the Red Sea, Moses

---

[6]See Curt Sachs, *The History of Musical Instruments,* pp. 83–85.

Miriam, sister of Moses, as depicted by an Italian artist. Detail of a fresco at the Sistine Chapel, Rome (by Cosimo Rosselli or Fra Diamanti, fifteenth century).

sang his song unto the Lord and was joined by the children of Israel (Exod. 15:1); then Miriam, the sister of Aaron, followed by all the women, took a timbrel in her hand and responded, taking up the refrain of Moses' song (Exod. 15:20–21).

DURING THE CENTURIES of their sojourn in Egypt the Jews had ample opportunity to admire the splendor of the Egyptian orchestral ensembles, and they took with them a number of the instruments which were in use there as elsewhere in the Mediterranean countries; the practice and style of Egyptian performance left their mark on their own poetry and music—the reason for our having dealt with the music of Egypt at some length. But we have still to consider another important musical heritage that must have greatly contributed to the style of Israel's singing and playing in the post-Egyptian part of their nomadic period and that also helped to shape their music in the subsequent Golden Age of ancient Hebrew life and art—the time of the great Kings. This is the theory and the ethics of Egyptian—and generally Oriental—music as fully developed at the time of the Exodus. The Jews, whose first generations had experienced in Egypt their earliest contact with urban life and civilization and whose subsequent generations were largely brought up in towns, had not known before that music may be more than the immediate expression of emotional sensation or that the shaping of melodies can be subjected to rational and systematic thinking while still keeping its spontaneous character. They learned for the first time the professional aspects of music (Israel's sources in the earliest period never mention professional musicians, though all neighboring countries had music-training schools), and they also experienced the schism between the spiritual music of the highly educated and the popular music of the masses: they must have wondered at the singing maidens, just as the Egyptians had wondered at them some hundred years before when they had been introduced from southwestern Asia.

We need not go into detail here about this professional training, for it becomes relevant only with the erection of the Temple. Regarding the women's music it suffices to say that Jewish women took up singing and dancing immediately, as shown in the Exodus passage quoted above. Palestinian singing- and playing-maidens achieved international fame in later days. The geographer of the time of Jesus, Strabo, advises his readers to present Indian rajahs with musical instruments or pretty singing-maidens from Palestine or Alexandria in order to win their favor. Two hundred years later, the apocryphal Acts of St. Thomas relates that a piper came down to the place where the apostle landed in India, "stood over him and played at his head for a long time: now this piper-girl was by race a Hebrew." But the musical ideas and system of the Egyptians require some discussion for their influence upon Jewish thought and for their significance in the changes apparent in post-Egyptian Hebrew music.

It is in Egypt that composing in certain modes developed into a well-defined system, a practice which the Jews were later to expand and to perfect to serve their own cultural and spiritual needs and which then passed on to the Greeks. The ancient singer or player composed a melody by arranging and combining a limited number of motives. This practice prevails in Oriental civilization down to our own day. In contrast to modern musicians of the western world, who regard each note of a complete melody individually as well as in its relation to other notes, the Oriental thinks in melodic formulas and tonal groups; he is unable to ascribe significance to a single tone out of its context—the step leading up to or away from it. When he sings or plays his melodies he also invariably improvises upon and embellishes them.

The mode is characterized by the way in which certain beginning, middle, and concluding tones are joined and contrasted in the melody sung or played; within the modes chosen the singer or player has every individual freedom of variation and of emotional expression. But the modes not only supplied the purely musical particles of the melodies. They were also associated with spiritual and ethical qualities: the particular modes had their distinct associations with certain holy days or offerings or were characteristic of definite ethical notions.

The Temple music of the Jews must have been based on a modal system at a high stage of perfection; and though their way and style of singing has changed in the course of the three millennia of Israel's subsequent history, the present-day cantillation of the Scriptures and prayers substantially follows the modal theory of the Middle East in the eastern as well as the western Jewish communities. The melodic patterns underlying the modal

melody—the Arabic *māqamāt* and the Hindu *rāgas*—were in the earlier
stage of development composed of motives fitting certain lines of text and
in the later stage of motives for words or short phrases. Folk melodies seem
to have been instrumental in the formation of these melodicles, and they
also provided names for them, as we shall see when discussing the Psalms
and their enigmatic headings. In the East the word *compose* has always been
true to its original Latin meaning—"to put together"; and western music
has by no means ignored the modal technique of motive-combination—
it recurs throughout history from the Gregorian chant to the art of the
German Meistersinger, and from medieval composition to Schoenberg's
twelve-tone system, and the spirit of improvising on short melodic phrases
has been revived in modern jazz.

The systematization of music in Egypt provided the fundamentals for
Hebrew musical theory, in which special modes and motives were assigned
to the reading of the different portions of the Pentateuch, the Prophets, the
Psalms, the Song of Songs, the book of Esther, the Lamentations, and the
prayers. It is characteristic that in Hebrew theory the modes have always
served the religious worship only, while the Greeks, who based their own
musical system on the inheritance of Hebrew as well as of Egyptian music,
ascribed to the various modal motives and scales moral powers and ethical
qualities that implied their use for educational aims.

From Egypt, too, the Jews learned how best to remind the singers and
players of the melodies they had to intone. Hand signs and finger motions
were already employed for this purpose by Egyptian musicians in the
twenty-eighth century B.C.E. and their early use in organized Hebrew
music has been proved. There is little doubt that these hand signs were
largely responsible for the written signs that accompanied the biblical texts
at a time when the oral tradition seemed in danger of being forgotten and
Jewish scholars in Babylon and in ancient Palestine were anxious to preserve
and to hand down to posterity the correct way of vowelizing and chanting
the sacred texts.

We have to imagine the ancient Egyptian chant—and the song of the
Hebrews after the Exodus—performed in complete melodic freedom
within the bounds of the modes. Expression in performance was achieved
by the throat-pressing device described earlier in this chapter. The rhythm

of the melody was largely dependent on the rhythm of the words sung, for the content and the spirit of the words dominated the music as a matter of course; music was not performed to entertain or to elevate a lover of refined art but served the cult as a highly exalted form of speech. Rhythm proved important in nonreligious music only; it was the driving factor in work and dance, as well as in outdoor activities. But the vital impulse given to Egyptian music by the influx of foreign musicians—especially by the singing-maidens and their rhythmical instruments—must have had repercussions in the religious sphere as well.

THROUGHOUT THE HISTORY of Jewish civilization and culture we must attempt to understand the achievements of the Jewish people against the background of those of other nations; for the accomplishments of the Jews are generally due to a thorough absorption and evolution of their cultural inheritance and a characteristic facility for subsequently rejecting qualities foreign to their spirit, for molding forms and styles to suit their own temper, and for raising them onto a highly individual plane. Other people have, of course, done the same in their own particular way, for no historical development takes place in geographical, social, or cultural isolation, but in the case of the Jews the analysis is of special interest because their entire ancient history is one of migration, conquest, and exile, while their modern history down to their return to Palestine unfolds itself within the empires and commonwealths of other nations.

The Hebrews came to Egypt as nomads in search of pasture, and they began their life in their own land again as shepherds and farmers when they returned from Egyptian bondage. But they had acquired a considerable standard of learning and knowledge in many branches of science as well as in the arts. Their leader, Moses, had been taught science and music by Egyptian priests (if we can believe the later testimony of Philo of Alexandria); he even lived on in Islamic tradition as patron of the pipers. The time to apply in full measure the skill and knowledge won did not at once arrive for the generations of Jews who had actually emigrated from Egypt. The decades of wandering in the desert, the struggles for possession of the promised land, and the centuries of wars against her neighbors still denied to Israel the erection of a cultural center and thus the conditions fundamental for the development of an organized art. Musical instruments were not made on ancient Palestinian soil and of local material before the time of the Kings; for we read that King David still ordered instruments of Lebanese cypress and that King Solomon had lyres and harps made of wood from Ophir (the same that he used for the pillars of the Temple and of the royal house); and an ancient legend reports the importation of a thousand musical instruments by Pharaoh's daughter on the occasion of her wedding to Solomon (B. Sabbath 56 b.). (This is a disputed passage which has also been interpreted to mean the importation of a thousand *musical tunes.*) A continuous exchange with Assyria, Arabia, Egypt, and Phoenicia is evident in literary documents, too; but while the Israelites were largely the importers and mere beneficiaries in the period leading up to their eventual rise and prosperity, they succeeded in giving their own high civilization of the Temple era the individual traits that made Jerusalem the spiritual and cultural center of the entire ancient Levant. Music played its own part in the development of Israel's cult and became a dominant feature of the Temple service. If it had not outgrown the inheritance and importations from other civilizations it would never have achieved the towering significance it was to assume in later Oriental and early Occidental history; it could not have supplied in the way it did the foundations for the development of western musical civilization. The music of King Solomon's Temple reverberated through the ages, just as its sounds echoed over the mountains of Judea, and its splendors were told and retold by many a later generation.

CHAPTER TWO

THE HOLY CITY

I N THE POETRY AND ART of the modern world King David has come to be the symbolic figure of the patron of music, and the psalms attributed to the royal poet and musician are sung all over the civilized earth. They formed the backbone of the musical service in the Holy Temple; psalm singing later became popular in all the eastern and western centers of the Christian Church, and a Greek Church Father—St. John Chrysostom, Bishop of Constantinople, called "the golden-mouthed"—voiced general opinion when writing, about 400 C.E.

> If the faithful are keeping vigil in the church, David is first, middle, and last. If at dawn any one wishes to sing hymns, David is first, middle, and last. At funeral processions and burials, David is first, middle, and last. In the holy monasteries, among the ranks of the heavenly warriors, David is first, middle, and last. In the convents of virgins, who are imitators of Mary, David is first, middle, and last.

The psalms have inspired a host of musical compositions throughout the ages; David playing on his lyre is a subject that has attracted the greatest sculptors and painters of the world; and among the masterpieces of contemporary music are an oratorio composed to his praise—Arthur Honeg-

ger's *Le Roi David* and Darius Milhaud's opera *David*. Jewish popular belief and legend ascribed to David not only the organization of the musical
service in the Temple and the creation and singing of the psalms but also
the invention of musical instruments proper: II Chron. 7:6 speaks of "instruments of musick of the Lord, which David the king had made to praise
the Lord"; according to I Chron. 23:5, David himself said to the princes of
Israel, to the priests and Levites, that "four thousand praised the Lord with
the instruments which I made to praise therewith"; and the prophet Amos
castigates the wanton people that "invent themselves instruments of musick, like David" (Amos 6:5). Jewish as well as later Christian belief saw in
King David the musical splendor of the Temple personified, and in medieval and later paintings he is seen to play on a great variety of musical instruments. It seems a pity that the strict commandment not to make a
"graven image, nor any manner of likeness" should have robbed us of
ancient Hebrew representations of David and his kinnor, though we can
surmise with some certainty now that this was a kind of lyre—and *not* a
harp, as it is generally translated and most frequently depicted on the later
paintings. The kinnor is very frequently mentioned in the Scriptures and
metaphorically in the Dead Sea Scrolls; it is usually connected with joyful
occasions and seems not to have been used at times of mourning.

The history of Hebrew music, as well as the history of Israel's higher
civilization in general, begins with King David's reign. It was David, the
second king of Israel, who created a large and united Hebrew kingdom
and made the Urusalim of the Jebusites his capital, Jerusalem. The town
had existed there for more than a thousand years, and the singularity of its
position as well as the striking contrasts witnessed there between desert
and fertile country had made its hills places of nature cult; they were regarded as domiciles of deities associated with ancient pagan worship. Jerusalem lay far removed from the principal trade routes; its strategic position
was well exploited by its kings, vassals of the mighty Pharaoh of Egypt. The
cosmic significance ascribed to the Jewish Temple and to some of its contents and to the garments of the priests shows that relics of the ancient cult
survived in Israel. That much of the music of King David's Temple was
also created under the influence of older practice is attested by the close re-
semblance of the forms, the ideas, and the unrestrained lyricism of the

Saul mit den sinen iagte nach
So daz mennenten alle die
In beiden zieten saben nie
Cus kuniges hof vnd anderswa
Sv warn wunevrowen da
In israhel di singen do
Emen sanc der was also
Saul d kvnich het touset man
Erslagen do er si chom an
Zebentousent sluch dauit
Ditz lobesanc wart schiere wit
Vnd so wiet daz ez gehes cham
Fur den kvnich als erz vernam
Ez waz im leit vnd vngmach
Er zornte in sinem zorn er sprach
Hant si tousent mir bnant
Vnd tvnt daz von dauide erhant

Er sluc zehen tousent man
Den sanc do meinden si dar an
Daz dauit hete in den tagen
Den heidenischen risen erslagen
Vnd si da von den sik erstriten
Waz anders mueste sin vermiten
Da von singen si den pris
Dem hochgborn helde wis
Saul bgan dauiden
Des lobsanges niden
Daz an im was gelett fur in
Von binnen hin bgunde er in
Mit twerhen ougen selen an
So wenne er awitzzen bgan
Vnd in sin vnsin angie
So was mit siner herpfen hie
Vor im der iunge dauit

David (at left, with two followers) plays for Saul (at right, with a servant). His instrument is a lyre; its form resembles a small harp. (From Chronicles of Rudolf von Ems, ca. 1300.) (Photograph: Bavarian State Library, Munich.)

hymns preserved on ancient cuneiform tablets to those of the Hebrew psalms. The heathen origin of Jerusalem was remembered for a long time: "Thy birth and thy nativity is of the land of Canaan; thy father was an Amorite, and thy mother an Hittite" (Ezek. 16:3). It had certainly taken the Israelites long to establish their ethical and religious rule and to make the people forget their local shrines and sites of nature worship. In David they hailed the king who had taken "the strong hold of Zion: the same is the city of David" (II Sam. 5:7) and who built his altar unto the Lord on the site of Araunah the Jebusite's threshing place as he had been commanded by the Lord (II Sam. 24:16 ff.); David and his son and successor Solomon made Jerusalem the national and cultural capital of the kingdom of Israel, the "holy hill of Zion" (Psalm 2:6), "the City of the Great King" (Psalm 48:2), of the Lord "who dwelleth in Zion" (Psalm 11:11).

WITH THE TIME of the kings an end was set to the nomadic period of Israel. The people had taken possession of the country; they were given time to plow its soil and to develop its resources; and they could also shape their own life and thoughts now. The long centuries of unsteady wanderings, of a nomad and warrior existence, gave way to a period of secure farming and to the establishment of an organized cultural life. Jerusalem, at first only the central place of worship and the seat of the national kingdom, soon became a center of pilgrimage as well; and though its cultural level was high above that of the masses, the Temple of the Lord and the king's house were looked to by the entire nation for inspiration and leadership. In a comparatively short time the Israelites achieved such a singularity of life, thought, and creation that they overcame their dependence upon foreign cultural inheritance and created a civilization which, in turn, exerted a far-reaching influence on the smaller neighboring nations.

As the city of Jerusalem grew in the later years of David's reign and in the times of Solomon, his son, the zone of its influence gradually expanded, too; but with the increase in the luxury of its buildings and the splendor of urban life there developed a corresponding widening of the gulf between the clerical and royal nobility on the one hand and the masses in the country on the other. We must not forget that cultural development, in the course of which music assumed its sumptuous role, was now confined to the town. The biblical sources—which are abundant for the period of the Temple in contrast to the spare hints offered by the Pentateuch for the nomadic epoch—tell much of the music in the Holy City, of the musicians serving the Temple and the Royal Court. But the biblical scribes cared as little for the songs of the people as did later the Christian monks of the Middle Ages. We can, however, assume that popular music did not greatly change its aspect: the shepherd continued to sing and to pipe his pastoral song, and the women's music accompanied feast and dance as before. Yet the people's singing, and their instrumental accompaniment as well, must certainly have developed to some degree under the influence of the music in the Holy Temple. This music was heard by those who made pilgrimages to Jerusalem; in addition, the Levites, the bearers of musical culture from King David's days, recruited singers and players among their people in the country. There may even have existed regional preparatory schools in which the prospective Temple musicians received a training that also benefitted other parts of the population.

The same development now took place in Israel that Egypt had experienced many centuries before. Music, which had once been the possession of the broad masses, which had expressed their spirit and served their life, now developed into an art reserved to a chosen few, priests and noblemen. Playing and singing had been a matter of common knowledge and common practice; whenever great happenings or overwhelming spiritual experience shook the hearts of the people, a song was intoned by the leader, and the masses joined him in continuation or response. But the kings introduced professional singers and players; they, in turn, elevated music to an art and subjected it to a system. Popular music largely remained "primitive"; as we have seen the song of women in Jewish communities cut off from the mainstream of civilization for three millennia retained its character throughout the ages. In the civilized town, however, music was given an important function and place in organized life and developed rules and ethics of its own.

KING DAVID chose the Levites to supply musicians for the Holy Temple. Out of the thirty thousand they numbered at his time, the stately number of four thousand were selected for the musical service:

And David spake to the chief of the Levites to appoint their brethren to be the singers with instruments of musick, harps and lyres and cymbals, sounding, by lifting up the voice with joy. So the Levites appointed Heman the son of Joel; and of his brethren, Asaph the son of Berechiah; and of the sons of Merari their brethren, Ethan the son of Kushaiah; and with them their brethren of the second degree, Zechariah, Ben, and Jaaziel, and Shemiramoth, and Jehiel, and Unni, Eliab, and Beniah, and Maaseiah, and Mattithiah, and Eliphelech, and Mikneiah, and Obededom, and Jeiel, the doorkeepers.

So the singers, Heman, Asaph, and Ethan were appointed to sound with cymbals of brass; and Zechariah, and Aziel, and Shemiramoth, and Jehiel, and Unni, and Eliab, and Maaseiah, and Benaiah, with harps on Alamoth, and Mattithiah, and Eliphelech, and Mikneiah, and Obededom, and Jeiel, and Azaziah, with lyres on the Sheminith to lead. And Chenaniah, chief of the Levites, was for singing, he instructed them in song, for he knew it. And Berechiah and Elkanah were doorkeepers for the ark. And Shebaniah, and Jehoshaphat, and Nethaneel, and Amasai, and Zechariah, and Benaiah, and Eliezer, the priests, did blow with the trumpets before the ark of God: and Obededom and Jehiah were door-keepers for the ark (I Chron. 15:16–24).

Of the instruments named here the *nevel* (harp)—mentioned for the first time in I Sam. 10:5—and the *mziltaim* (cymbals) were new to the people of Israel. They played an important role in the music academy, the institution of which is related in the passage quoted above. The nevel (which may have been of Phoenician origin—the Phoenician name was *nabla,* and the Greeks took the term over at a later date) is often mentioned together with the kinnor; it was, however, an instrument of quite different build and character and seems to have been a vertical angular harp: many traits point to its having been larger, louder, and lower in pitch than the kinnor (lyre). Josephus Flavius informs us—two generations before the destruction of the Second Temple—that the nevel had twelve strings, in contrast to the ten of the kinnor; while the latter was played with the hands, the former was plucked with a plectrum. This is confirmed by a passage in the Book of Amos, and Rabbi Jehoshua, who taught around about 200 C.E., adds to our knowledge of the instrument when he says that the strings of the nevel were made of larger animal guts and were rougher than those of the kinnor, which were prepared from the smaller intestines (Mishna Kinnim 3:6). No sure interpretation is possible for the epithets "on

Alamoth" and "on the Sheminith," for the general explanation that they compare the pitch of the two instruments (the former being a "maiden" or high-pitched instrument—from the Hebrew *alma* = "maiden"—and the latter pitched an octave lower—from *shmona*, the Hebrew word for eight) has not been accepted. The notion of an octave was most probably unknown in the ancient world; the harp must actually have been the instrument lower in pitch, and *alamoth* may sooner be connected with the Assyrian word for wood (*halimū*) than with the *alma* or maiden. It is more likely that the epithets refer to the modes or tunes used by the instrumentalists (or in accordance with which they tuned the strings of their instruments?), just as they do in the headings of the Psalms (see p. 70).

The harp and the cymbals were, however, not the only new instruments of the epoch. The name of the *zelzlim* occurs side by side with the mziltaim, and we also find for the first time mention of the *asor*, the *halil*, the *mna'anim*, and the *magrepha*. It would be well to try to identify these instruments before we attempt to reconstruct a picture of Temple music from sources in the Bible and the commentaries.

The *asor* is mentioned in three psalms, twice in connection with the harp (33:2 and 92:3) and once with harp and lyre together (144:9), and all commentators have derived from its etymology (from *assara*, the Hebrew word for "ten") that it must have been a ten-stringed instrument. Curt Sachs has likened it to the Phoenician ten-stringed, rectangular zither—an instrument not found in either the Egyptian or the Assyrian civilization but known from two representations on an ivory pyxis of Phoenician origin and dating from the eighth century B.C.E. and from an illustration contained in a letter attributed to St. Jerome, the Church Father of the fourth century C.E.

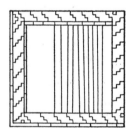

Ten-stringed psalterium (asor?) as depicted in St. Jerome's letter to Dardanus. (After Curt Sachs, *History of Musical Instruments.*)

The halil occurs in the Bible for the first time in connection with the anointment of Solomon (I Sam. 10:5), but though no such instrument is mentioned as having been used in the services of the First Temple, a rabbinical commentator thought that it came from the days of Moses; in the Second Temple two to twelve halilim were used on twelve days of the year—at the first and the second Passover sacrifice, on the first day of Passover, at the Feast of Weeks, and in the eight days of the Feast of Tabernacles. Though in modern Hebrew the halil is a flute, the biblical equivalent has been interpreted as a double reed of the oboe family; no flutes appear on any picture of neighboring civilizations at the time, and the Greek and Latin translators of the Bible were surely right when rendering "halil" by a word describing an oboe. It was probably a double oboe such as we know from many ancient civilizations; an illustration is provided by a talmudic tractate expressly stating that the cadence marking the final verse of a scriptorial passage was marked by the playing of one pipe only—which may mean one cane of double oboe. In later sources, especially in the Aramaic version of the Bible, there appears the new word *abub* (which is "oboe" in modern Hebrew). It is difficult to determine the difference between the ancient halil and abub, but it seems quite probable that the two terms described similar or even identical instruments. Another plausible interpretation is the rendering of *halil* by "woodwind"; in this case the talmudic passage on the cadence being played by one pipe would mean the playing of a soloist out of a group of instruments of the same family. The sound of the halil is thought to have evoked reveling feelings like the *aulos* in ancient Greece; the sources speak of its use at weddings and other feasts, but also on occasions of lamentation.

The percussion instruments introduced in the Temple service and used (as our passage shows) by the singers do not offer particular puzzles: the *mna'anim* must have been sistra (as has been said in the previous chapter); the *zelzlim* were brass cymbals, perhaps a little different in form from the mziltaim; while *shalishim*—if not a triangle-like musical instrument—could indicate a kind of ritual dance based on three steps (*shloshah* in Hebrew = "three").

A peculiar problem is that of the magrepha. It is told that in the Temple the sound of the magrepha gave the Levites the sign to begin their music. The Mishna (completed about 150 years after the destruction of the Second Temple) says that this sound, together with that of the oboes, cymbals, and shofar and of the singing and the proclamations, could be heard as far as Jericho—which is quite possible in the atmospheric conditions of the Jerusalem region. A Mishna passage describes how one of the priests "threw" the instrument between hall and altar after the sacrifice and that it made a very loud sound; yet it is impossible to determine from this whether it sounded while being whirled through the air or only when touching the walls or coming down on the floor. Mishna commentators also use the word in its Hebrew meaning, "shovel"; the instrument can have had this form. Three hundred years after the Mishna commentary it is argued in a talmudic tractate that the magrepha had ten holes and that each of them could produce ten "kinds of song," so that the whole instrument was capable of yielding one hundred "kinds of song." Ten holes capable of producing one hundred sounds each—altogether one thousand "kinds of song"—is the description offered by another, possibly exaggerating, source, which also adds that the measures of the magrepha were one ell (of twenty inches or 50.8 cm) in height and one ell in length (or width?) and that a handle protruded from the instrument. As the holes indicate that the magrepha must have been a kind of wind instrument, it has been concluded that it constituted some sort of organ—an instrument well known in the ancient East. It cannot have been a water organ; various rabbinical sources emphasize that no hydraulis was found in the Temple; Rabbi Shimon ben Gamliel said (about 130 years after the destruction of the Second Temple) that the reason for this was that the hydraulis "disturbs [or spoils] the tune [the sound of the other instruments?]." But the possibility of its having been a primitive pneumatic (wind) organ is not excluded; if this is true, the magrepha was an advanced form of the ancient 'ugab, which has for centuries been translated as "organ" and which is reported in a tractate to have been "one of the two instruments retained from the First Temple, but when it became defective it could not be mended" (Arachin 10, b; Sukkah 50, b). We may perhaps picture the magrepha as a row of ten pipes with the air blown in by the operation of the handle. An instrument similar to this sort of panpipe has been found by Curt Sachs on an Alexandrian terra-cotta figurine from the first century B.C.E. A Syrian piper is depicted on it, singing and playing (see illustration, p.38). He is seen holding a pan pipe about one inch (2.5 cm) under his mouth and seems to sing while operating the instrument. The pipe has long bass canes which are connected with a bag that communicates by a flexible tube with a bellows worked by the man's right foot and compressed by his arm. The Hebrew instrument may have been more primitive in form and use but similar in principle, and there is no reason why its sound should not have been strong and piercing. There remains the nebulous allusion to its having been "thrown" to the altar. Who knows whether this interpretation of a rabbinical scholar was actually correct or whether perhaps the term described different instruments at different times? Or could we believe in a misunderstanding; should we read that the priest *sharak* (piped, blew) not *sarak* (threw) the magrepha? Its derivation from the 'ugab is supported by the fact that it is mentioned in connection with the Second Temple only; that its form must have been primitive seems to follow from the fact that it was used only for signaling purposes—to call the priests and the Levites to their duties—though it remains unexplained why an instrument "capable of yielding one hundred kinds of song" should have served only for signaling.

WHEN KING SOLOMON had finished all work for the Temple and brought in all the things David his father had dedicated, the priests and the congregation of Israel assembled before the ark, and the musical service was begun by the Levites. "The number of them, with their brethren that were instructed in the songs of the Lord, even all that were cunning, was two hundred fourscore and eight," and they were divided into twenty-four classes "under the hands of their fathers" (I Chron. 25:6–31). On the day of consecration

> the Levites which were the singers, all of them of Asaph, of Heman, of Jeduthun, with their sons and their brethren, being arrayed in white linen, having cymbals and harps and lyres, stood at the east end of the altar, and with them an hundred and twenty priests sounding with trumpets; it came even to pass, as the trumpeters and singers were as one, to make one sound to be heard in praising and thanking the Lord; and when they lifted up their voice with the trumpets and cymbals and instruments of musick, and praised the Lord, saying, For he is good; for his mercy endureth for ever: that then the house was filled with a cloud, even the house of the Lord; so

that the priests could not stand to minister by reason of the cloud: for the glory of the Lord had filled the house of God (II Chron. 5:12–14).

When the king and the people had offered their sacrifices, the Levites began to play, "and the priests sounded trumpets before them, and all Israel stood" (II Chron. 7:6).

Though certain forms of singing changed after the Babylonian exile and though some change in the instrumental part of the service seems also to have taken place, the actual musical service in the Second Temple must essentially have been the same as that in King Solomon's Temple; it was most certainly the wish of the Jews rebuilding their country and the House of the Lord to do this in keeping with their knowledge of Jerusalem's glory of old. The description contained in a talmudic tractate (Tamid 7:3–4) of Temple music in the beginning of the Common Era may thus well be applied to the earlier forms of service as well. The Talmud passage describes how the priests on duty followed up the sacrifices with benedictions and prayers and then read the Ten Commandments and some additional passages from the Scriptures. After the sacrifices the magrepha was sounded, which was the signal for the other priests to enter the Temple to prostrate themselves, and for the Levites to begin their musical performance. The high priest entered the Temple last and was solemnly received; he gave the blessing and burned the offerings on the altar. The description goes on to say:

> They gave him the wine for the drink-offering, and the Prefect stood by each horn of the altar with a towel in his hand, and two priests stood at the table of the fat pieces with two silver trumpets in their hands. They blew a prolonged, a quavering, and a prolonged blast. Then they came and stood by Ben Arza, the one on his right and the other on his left. When he stooped and poured out the drink-offering the Prefect waved the towel and Ben Arza clashed the cymbals and the Levites broke forth into singing. When they reached a break in the singing they blew upon the trumpets and the people prostrated themselves; at every break there was a blowing of the trumpet and at every blowing of the trumpet a prostration. This was the rite of the Daily Whole-Offering in the service of the House of our God. May it be His will that it shall be built up again, speedily, in our days. Amen.

The same source informs us that the Levites sang a different psalm on each of the six days of the week and on the Sabbath, and other tractates treat of the relation between choir and orchestra, of the forms of singing, of the training demanded of singers and instrumentalists, and of the style of the actual performance.

The chorus, placed on the estrade, had to consist of a minimum of twelve adult singers but could be enlarged at will. (It will be noted that the number twelve recurs everywhere: the twelve tribes of Israel, twenty-four, or twice twelve, training classes for singers and instrumentalists, twelve leading musicians, one hundred and twenty trumpets at the consecration of the Temple, and twelve strings for the harp. Five and seven had been numbers holy to the ancient Orient and the earlier Jewish civilization alike: the lyre had ten strings and the trumpets were seven.) The singers had passed through five years of training and usually performed their Temple service between the ages of thirty and fifty. Boys of the Levites often joined the choir "to add sweetness to the sound," but they were placed outside the estrade. The orchestra, on the other hand, consisted of two to six harps, nine or more lyres, two to twelve oboes (employed only on the special days mentioned above), and one pair of cymbals. This means that the number of musicians in the orchestra equaled that of the singers; the minimum comprised twelve vocalists and twelve instrumentalists, and on the days on which an "innumerable quantity" of instruments were used (to quote the actual words of a tractate) the number of singers was enlarged accordingly. After the Babylonian exile, however, a decline in the appreciation of instrumental music set in. A larger number of singers was opposed to a smaller number of instrumental musicians, and the priests evidenced their depreciation of instrumental music by permitting non-Levites to take up playing while singing in the Temple remained the privilege of the Levites.

The orchestra here described was used to accompany the singing of the trained choir—with the possible exception of the cymbals, which marked the intervals. The trumpets are missing in the description of the service, which shows that they did not form a part of the accompanying orchestra but were used separately only, in the way outlined in the passage quoted earlier. Drums were also absent from the Temple; rhythm and movement thus seem to have been of no importance in the shaping of music used for the religious service. The drums were in fact the instruments of the women, as they were in other Oriental civilizations, and the participation of women singers or players in the Temple is nowhere mentioned.

Only in secular, especially court, music were women the leaders: singing and playing servants are often mentioned in the Bible. When Barzillai the Gileadite had conducted David over the Jordan but refused to accompany him to Jerusalem, "he said unto the King: How long have I to live that I should go up with the king unto Jerusalem? I am this day fourscore years old: and can I discern between good and evil? Can thy servant taste what I eat or what I drink? Can I hear any more the voice of singing men and singing women?" (II Sam. 19:34f.). The 200 singing men and singing women singled out from 7337 servants and maids returning from Babylon (Ezra 2:65; Neh. 7:67 counted 245) belonged to the wealthy families. Women musicians are also mentioned in connection with the tribute demanded from King Hiskia by Sennacherib, King of Assyria, with the mourning and funeral ceremonies, and with feasts and celebrations.

The exclusion of women from the Temple service is further indicated by the fact that ritual dances are reported to have been executed by men, the most famous passage telling how "David danced before the Lord with all his might" (II Sam. 6:14); he continued dancing as the procession moved through the city with the holy ark, and it is interesting to reflect why Michal the daughter of Saul who "looked through a window and saw King David leaping and dancing before the Lord" (II Sam. 6:16) should have despised the royal dancer in her heart. This kind of ritual dance was surely well established; it had come from Egypt but seemed to have fallen into disuse at a later time, for it is rarely mentioned in connection with Temple practice. Processional dancing must, however, have lived on, as it is still practiced in the synagogue in our own days.

The dance confronts us with yet another of the many peculiar problems offered by the ancient biblical texts. This concerns the word *machol*, used in the meaning of "dance" in modern Hebrew and in the common translation of many biblical passages, but also often interpreted as a term for a musical instrument. It first occurs in the Pentateuch, when Miriam and her women are said to have followed Moses' song of praise with singing and playing *B'tupim uw'imm'choloth* (Exod. 15:20). The Authorized Version translates this as "with timbrels and with dances," and so do most European Bibles. But a rabbinical scholar ("Pirkei d'Rabbi Eliezer," second century C.E., XL, 2) comments upon this passage as follows: "And where did they

King David dances in front of the Ark of the Covenant and plays on a six-stringed arm-viol; Michal looks down from the window, disdained. (Guilio Clovio, 1546. Städel Gallery, Frankfurt/Main. Photo by Ursula Edelmann.)

get *tupim* and *mecholoth* in the desert? . . . At the time of their exodus from
Egypt they made tupim and mecholoth," and thus shows that *machol*
meant a musical instrument in the Hebrew tradition of his time. The same
interpretation is met with as late as the fourteenth century in the commentaries of Gersonides, while Menachem b. Saruk also used it in his explanations written about 975. Psalm 150, which mentions eight different kinds
of instruments and, like the Exodus passage, links the machol with the
drum, makes little sense when we read "Praise him with the timbrel and
dance" (v. 4), and the same is true of the preceding Psalm (v. 3). The Syrian translators of the Bible also interpreted *machol* as an instrument, and no
passage could possibly be found in the Bible where this interpretation does
not fit. As machol is mostly mentioned together with the drum, Ibn Ezra
(eleventh century) may be right in supposing that it was a kind of pipe (*machol* and *halil* have similar etymological roots), perhaps one that was popularly used for the accompaniment of dances. We would then have to add
the machol to the list of instruments discussed in the preceding and the
present chapter.

THE SOURCES provide us with quite a clear picture of the musical service in
the Temple, but they have not preserved for us the actual melodies sung
and played; yet the forms of singing described in the Bible, in the talmudic
literature, and in comparisons with archaic liturgies permit us at least to
form an idea of how the singing and musical performance may have actually sounded. What we know in this field concerns, however, almost exclusively the post-Babylonian practice; the Levites—many of whom are said to
have remained in Palestine, especially in the suburbs of Jerusalem, during
the forty-eight years of the Babylonian exile (486–538 C.E.)—reconstructed the Temple service in accordance with the ancient tradition. But it
seems that the antiphonal singing that became characteristic for the later
Jewish liturgy as well as for Christian church music was developed only in
the stricter and more systematic service of the Second Temple.

Down to our own days the Passover Hallel and many other hymns and
songs are performed, especially by Near Eastern Jews, in the form commonly known as antiphony—that is to say, with the choruses alternating
and responding to each other. The first examples in the Bible of such re-

sponsive singing are the song of Moses and Miriam after the passage through the Red Sea (Exod. 15:1 and 20–21), the triumph of David's victory over the Philistines ("the women sang one to another in their play. . . ." I Sam. 18:7), and the return from Babylon (Nehemiah "appointed two great companies that gave thanks and went in procession: on the right hand half of the princes of Judah and certain of the priests' sons with trumpets, and Judah, Hanani, with the musical instruments of David; and the other company of them that gave thanks went to meet them. . . ." Neh. 12:31 f. and 38). A talmudic tractate commenting upon the passage over the Jordan (Josh. 4) depicts antiphonal singing as it was certainly still practiced—though, of course, on a smaller scale—in the talmudic epoch:

> When Israel crossed the Jordan and came unto Mount Gerizim and unto Mount Ebal in Samaria . . . six tribes went up to the top of Mount Gerizim and six tribes went up to the top of Mount Ebal. And the priests and the Levites stood below in the midst; and the priests surrounded the Ark and the Levites surrounded the priests, and all Israel were on this side and on that . . . and began with the blessing . . . and both these and these answered, Amen! (Sotah 7:5)

Antiphonal singing was a common practice in the ancient East. It can still be heard in Abyssinia (Ethiopia), in upper Egypt, and in Middle Eastern Christian communities, and the western church has modeled most of its psalm singing on it. The use of a recurring refrain in Assyrian hymns points to their having been sung in responsive style by the priests and the choir or by two opposing choirs in alternation; their poetry as well as their music proved a great influence on Hebrew song.

The best way of getting an idea of the different ways of performing music is an analysis of the poetical forms. The most primitive style of singing was the recitation of the prayer or psalm by a soloist and the response of the congregation with "Amen" or "Hallelujah"; at a later stage the short refrains were replaced by complete phrases such as "for his mercy endureth forever" (Psalm 118, Psalm 136). This primitive antiphony has parallels in other Oriental civilizations. An Assyrian hymn, for instance, begins:

> O Lord, who is like thee,
>> Who can be compared to thee?
> Mighty one, who is like thee,
>> Who can be compared to thee?

and Psalm 27 opens:

> The Lord is my light and my salvation;
>> Whom shall I fear?
> The Lord is the strength of my life;
>> Of whom shall I be afraid?

In the Temple service the leader and soloist usually began by singing a half-verse, and the choir repeated it; the leader then continued in half-verses, and the choir or congregation interpolated the refrain after each of them, as is particularly obvious from Deut. 27:15 ff.:

> Cursed be the man that maketh any graven or molten image, an abomination unto the Lord, the work of the hands of the craftsman, and putteth it in a secret place.
>> And all the people shall answer and say, Amen.
> Cursed be he that setteth light by his father or his mother.
>> And all the people shall say, Amen.
> Cursed be he that removeth his neighbor's landmark.
>> And all the people shall say, Amen.

In this form the "Hallel" is sung by many Jewish communities to this very day, and many popular hymns have refrains of the same kind.

The next step in the development of antiphony was the singing by the leader and the choir in alternating half-verses, with the choir sometimes varying the words of the first half-line:

> Praise ye the Lord.
>> Praise the Lord, O my soul.
> While I live will I praise the Lord:
>> I will sing praises unto my God while I have any being.
>>>> (Psalm 146)

In this form the children used to be instructed at school in talmudic times.

The most developed—and truly responsive—form was the real alternation in verses; it was the form in which the Sh'ma Yisrael prayer was recited:

> Hearken, O Israel:
>> The Lord our God is one Lord.
> And thou shalt love the Lord thy God with all thine heart,
>> And with all thy soul, and with all thy might.
>>>> (Deut. 6:4 f.)

This developed form of responsive singing still characterizes the practice of Babylonian Jews, especially their singing of the Hallel for Passover. A talmudic tractate (Sukkah 38:2) informs us that all three forms—the answering in refrains, the repetition of half-verses, and true responsive antiphony—were in use in the later Jewish liturgical service. They have all been preserved both in the Jewish liturgy and in the Catholic Church (which took them over from the Temple service) and contributed much to the evolution of western art music. Their origins point back to universal Oriental custom and ancient Jewish practice; their systematic cultivation must be ascribed to the Levites serving the Second Temple.

How were the melodies formed and sung, and how did the Temple music actually sound? We have already considered the modal system of the East and the influence that the Egyptian practice of singing in modes must have had on the Jews. It was in the Temple service that the use of the different modes was systematized and that they assumed definite characteristics. Early instrumental music and popular singing seem to have been pentatonic—based on scales or chords of five tones—and strict in rhythm; but the vocal music that dominated the liturgy was rhythmically free and followed the irregular rhythms of the words, setting the text to music by the use of carefully chosen modal motifs. The scales in which the modal motifs moved were not pentatonic but apparently diatonic-tetrachordal; though the melodies themselves, as they were preserved by the secluded communities of the Yemen, of Babylonia, and of Persia, rarely have a range exceeding that of the fifth or sixth interval. The ancient singers did not ornament their melodies with virtuoso coloraturas, as do the cantors of modern synagogues; the coloratura embellishment, often improvised, developed with the rise of the professional precentor in the Christian Era. Nevertheless, the necessity of adapting modal motifs to words or lines of different length obviously called for melismatic treatment. The singer's melismas were born of an inner urge and not of a wish to exhibit virtuosity.

The development of Hebrew language, thought, and ideas offers distinct clues to the student of ancient Hebrew music. Comparing the earliest examples of biblical poetry with the poetical lyricism of the Psalms and the Song of Songs, or the language of the Pentateuch in general with that of the Prophets, we notice an evolution from the expression in simple verse of a driving urgency and sweeping passion to a highly developed emphatic and eloquent language in freely shaped rhythm. The characteristic traits of the Hebrew language—its abundance of hard consonants and gutturals, of explosive sounds, and of doubled letters—were exploited to the full, and there are in the Bible many instances of actual tone-painting by means of words.

Though in its lyricism ancient Hebrew poetry has, as we have seen, parallels in Oriental literature in general, it was unequaled in the fervent force of its expression. The very language of ancient Israel was musical in the highest degree, and various biblical passages say that music actually inspired the songs and the visions of the leaders and prophets: "And it came to pass, when the minstrel played, that the hand of the Lord came upon him," says the chronicler of II Kings 3:15 of the prophet Elisha, and the spirit of the Lord came upon Samuel when he met a company of prophets descending from a hill accompanied by players sounding their musical instruments (I Sam. 10:5 ff.). The highly emotional character of ancient Hebrew music is thus attested by the poetry and prose of the Bible; but just as the prophets subordinated expression and form to the moral and ethical demands of their speech, so did the musical expression emphasize a higher ethical value.

The character of Hebrew verse did not allow metrical rhythmization; Hebrew poetry was rather poetical prose, free from rhythmical accentuation and dynamic in its expression, and the musical motifs closely followed the word accents. When Jewish scholars early in the Christian Era added their interpretative symbols to the written biblical texts, they intended both to hand down to posterity the correct vowelization and accentuation of the words and to remind the reciters which appropriate motifs to use for the chanting of the passage. These accents indicate the existence of a theory and system in ancient Hebrew music; but not all details of the system have been sufficiently explored and explained by later generations and by modern scholars. The theory concerned itself especially with the intervals characterizing the melodic patterns, each of which started from or moved around a basic note in a characteristic way.

In trying to reconstruct the melodic elements (or to analyze them from the remnants that have come down to us by way of the archaic Jewish liturgies and the early Christian chant), we must be careful to note that "high" and "low"—and accordingly "up" and "down" (used often in interpreting the accents)—meant in ancient Semitic usage, as later in Greek musical theory, the opposite of what they stand for in music today. *O* and *U* were called "high" vowels by Jewish grammarians, and in Hebrew script they are indeed depicted by a dot *above* the consonant after which they are sounded; while the vowel *I* is regarded as "low" in sound and indicated by a dot *below* the consonant. (Compare this with the dot above the *I* in modern Occidental languages, in which the *I* is regarded as a high sound and the *O* and *U* as low or dark sounds.) Here again, language and music go hand in hand in the ancient Orient; it was not the actual sound that was described by the notions of "high" and "low," but the way the sound was produced: a "high" or "tall" pipe or string produced a low or dark sound, while the "short" or "low" instrument gave out a sound we call "high" today. Thus when in Oriental music a melody is said to "jump up," it means that its melody sank, while a step "downward" must be rendered by a melodic ascent.[1]

The ancient Temple liturgy ascribed special melodies to each portion of the Holy Scriptures that figured in the service, and each melody was composed of either two modal motifs or of three or four motifs sung in alternation. The motifs were flexible enough to permit their use for texts (words, half-lines, or verses) of different syllabic lengths; and most of them seem to have been given descriptive names in order to enable the singers and players to intone the right mode at once if the name was indicated. It must be surmised that all or most of the motifs and melodies used in the Temple were folk songs (some of them may even have been of foreign origin) and the Levite music leaders only modified them and sanctified their use; this was the practice followed by clerical authorities throughout the ages, down to the Lutheran Protestant Reform. And—likewise in accordance with historical experience in most civilizations—the Temple melodies exerted their influence on the people in turn, the *An'she Ma' amad* (persons of high standing), who represented in turns the districts and settlements of the country at the offerings and prayers of the Temple, brought the knowledge of Temple music back home with them after their two weeks' service.

---

[1]Compare Curt Sachs, *The Rise of Music in the Ancient World*, pp. 69–70.

With our knowledge of the origin of Temple music comes some enlightenment about the hitherto enigmatic headings of the psalms; they were erroneously translated by most biblical scholars and almost invariably associated with the names of musical instruments. It did not strike the commentators that none of the instruments known—and occurring frequently in the psalms themselves—are mentioned in these headings. Most probably the headings—such as *al mût lab'ben* (on the death of the son), *ayelet ha'-schachar* (aurora), *schoschanim* (roses)—indicate the folk songs used for the modal melodies, in the way we might write a community song to be performed to the melody of a current hit. The descriptions preceding the psalms have parallels in Arabian māqamāt and Hindu rāgas, where not only actual tunes (like the above) but also numbers (like *haschminith* = the eighth in the psalms), geographical places (the Hebrew *gittit* may mean "wine press" or "from the town of Gat"), and even combinations of two modes are named in the headings. Curt Sachs had the logical idea of testing this interpretation by the comparison of moods of psalms that have similar headings.[2] The investigation indeed shows that six *n'ginoth* psalms (4, 54, 55, 61, 67, 74) are all prayers for escape, based on confidence in God and his power and magnificence; that three *gittit* poems (8, 81, 84) are gay and mirthful in character; and that three *jeduthun* psalms (39, 62, 77) show a common mood of resignation. In Psalm 39, "A Psalm of David," the heading is "To the Chief Musician, even to Jeduthun," and Psalms 62 and 77 are similarly labeled. The word *selah,* so frequently used in the psalms and not satisfactorily explained to this day, must have something to do with the musical rendering as well; but we do not know whether it marked a pause or cadence, or whether this too pointed to a definite melodic mode or to a change or modulation.

WE HAVE ATTEMPTED to draw the picture of Temple music from the available sources and have found it to be many-colored indeed. The urge and

---

[2] *The History of Musical Instruments,* pp. 124–127. While Dr. Sachs's general theses are enlightening and fully acceptable in the light of more recent research, there are some errors in the transcriptions and translations from Hebrew. For an extensive and thorough more recent investigation, see Batya Bayer, "The Titles of the Psalms," in *Juval,* Vol. 4, Jerusalem, 1982, pp. 29–123.

passion of its vocal expression, together with the impressive orchestral coloring of the accompaniment and the far-sounding flourishes on the trumpets during the intervals in the singing, can well be imagined from what we know of the musical service in the ancient Holy City. But it was not only the splendor and dynamic impressiveness of Temple music that made the ancient civilizations admire the achievements of Jerusalem; its inner force and its ethical elevation proved their powerful impact in many centuries to come. Other Oriental civilizations had poetry and music as emphatic and lyrical as that of Israel, but Israel turned from primitive sensualism to religious pathos, from an unrestrained reign of emotion to the fanatical search for truth of expression—a characteristic trait of many a later Jewish composer of art music. In this light we can appreciate why Clement of Alexandria, the Church Father at the threshold of the third century C.E., admonished the Christians to abandon "chromatic" harmonies and modulations and turbulent melodies and to return to the temperate modal art of the psalms of David.

In the Jerusalem of the first millennium—the Holy City of Israel's kings and the spiritual and cultural center of the post-Babylonian Jews—music had the functions it fulfilled in seventeenth-century Europe, and it was most probably felt by contemporaries and by posterity to be as magnificently "baroque" as seventeenth-century music has been considered by contemporary and later generations. Music served three different spheres—the Temple, the Court, and the country—and it accordingly developed three different styles. The organized Temple liturgy, the music at the feast and celebration in the nobleman's house, and the pastoral music of the people differed in their function, their form, their executants, their instruments, and their very character; yet a permanent mutual influence can only have been natural. But while instrumental music completely disappeared in time and only some of the primitive forms of popular music have been preserved, the liturgical song has retained its essential character throughout the two millennia of Jewish dispersion. The musical tradition was preserved in southern Arabia, where the Yemenite Jews lived in seclusion for more than thirteen hundred years; in Babylonia, where the Jewish community has never ceased to exist since the days of the exile; in Persia, the Jewish community of which is as old as the Babylonian center; in Syria; in North Africa;

on the Italian peninsula. It also lived on with the Sephardim—descendants of the Jews expelled from Spain in 1492—and in some of the oldest eastern and central European Jewish centers.

The ancient Hebrew melodies and modes were not preserved *as music* by the various communities. They were passed on in the same way that the religious and ethical heritage was kept alive. When the Jews lost their own statehood, they replaced their national life with a life in God; the perpetuation of their belief and their laws helped them to endure the difficult and the miserable years of dispersion and oppression. In the short Babylonian exile they had already begun to interpret their once rural and national festivals as religious holy days when they could not celebrate them on the land. In the many hundreds of years of the Diaspora following the second, fatal, destruction of the Temple, the interpretation and meaning of the Jewish ritual was subjected to a far-reaching change; music changed its function with it. Instrumental music, little favored even in the last centuries of the Second Temple, was no longer cultivated; pastoral poetry and folk songs were imbued with new, religious, significance for use in the houses of worship.

The concentration of all thought and speculation upon the Kingdom of God and the resurrection of the Holy City and its glorious Temple gave the Jews of two millennia a purpose in life; it provided them with the moral power to resist assimilation and cultural surrender and preserved the character of the Jewish people. The ancient Orient yielded its power to Greece and Rome, and the mighty conquerors built their states and their civilizations on the remainders of its erstwhile glory. Greece and Rome in their turn disappeared from the platform of power, and vacated their places to newly rising nations; their own cultural heritage now helped to form new civilizations. The Jews saved their legacy as other nations crumbled and fell. They lost their nationhood and their country but perpetuated their law and ethics. The people of Israel's strong sense of tradition not only preserved Judaism as such, but handed down to countless generations a poetry and music regarded by all civilized nations of the ancient and the medieval world as heights of achievement. This estimate was not altered, in fact, till the evolution of completely differing ideals denied to the Occident a thorough appreciation of Oriental culture, much as it has haunted the minds of people throughout history. The legendary splendor of the Holy Temple and its music continued to attract the imaginations of poets, artists, and musicians. They may have known less than we do of the shape and real character of Temple music, but indirectly it became responsible for many creations of later music. It is thus that histories of music invariably open with a chapter devoted to the music of the ancient Hebrews and that King David, the founder of the Temple and the organizer of its music, is regarded as the patron of music wherever the art of singing and playing is practiced.

THE FOLLOWING music examples depict some ancient Oriental song types: women's songs (examples 1 and 2); Jewish and Arab songs (3 and 4); and Oriental scale technique (5).

Example 1. Song of Yemenite women (Jewish), transcribed by E. Gerson-Kiwi. The song is sung by two women who accompany their singing with frame drum and cymbal. A small, pentachordic motif is repeated many times. The rhythmical period in four-part time is clear. The drum figure is more or less independent of the rhythm of the melody.

Example 2. Song of Algerian women (Arabic), transcribed by R. Lachmann. This melody is melodically similar to the Jewish women's song of Example 1. There is, however, no instrumental accompaniment; the women clap their hands in regular rhythms instead.

Example 3. Hymn of Moroccan Jews, transcribed by E. Gerson-Kiwi.

Example 4. Ramadan song of Palestinian Arabs, transcribed by E. Gerson-Kiwi.
A comparison of the two hymns shows that the melodies are quite similar in scale
composition and melodic turns. But their purpose is quite divergent, and so is their
rhythmical texture. The Moroccan hymn, which is purely vocal, proceeds in different
meters; the Ramadan Palestinian song, which is for soloists, chorus, and orchestra,
has a strict rhythmical frame.

Example 5. Hymn of Moroccan Jews, transcribed by E. Gerson-Kiwi, which is a typical example of Near Eastern scale technique (fundamentally the same as the modern twelve-tone technique): the first phrase contains the exposition of the whole series; the variations and modifications of the theme bring an intensification and contraction of the original series.

(Examples 1–5 by courtesy of Dr. E. Gerson-Kiwi, from her book *Music of the Orient—Ancient and Modern*, Tel Aviv, 1949.)

CHAPTER THREE

HELLAS AND ROME

URING THE TWO CENTURIES of Persian rule in Asia Minor the Jewish state was allowed to develop its national and religious existence in peace and prosperity; the historical and sacred writings got their final redaction, religious canon and civil law were unified, and Israel became a community united both by belief and by the form and rules of life. But in the second half of the fourth century B.C.E. the Oriental world was shaken by an event of far-reaching sway: the first collision between Orient and Occident. Hellas was first in establishing Occidental rule over the eastern Mediterranean countries, and Rome wrung the reign from it later; but not for a long time was the West able to crush the Oriental world and establish cultural centers that could vie with those of the ancient Orient.

Hellas conquered the Middle East in the third decade of the fourth century B.C.E. Alexander the Great was about to materialize his dream of a vast empire that would comprise Europe, Africa, and Asia and be subjected to Greek political and cultural domination. His troops crushed Persian rule in the Orient and then turned south to Egypt; Judea they conquered on their way. The Jews did not at once realize the significance of the change in supremacy; it did not matter much to them that they had once again come under the rule of another power. But the importance of the new development was brought home to them when Alexander's successors divided the empire, for the partition entailed a complete separation of the southern, Egyptian, Diaspora from Judea. Alexandria, Alexander the Great's own foundation (331 B.C.E.), became the cultural center of the Hellenistic world, and the Jews there were subjected to the influence of Greek life, morals, and culture, just as were the Egyptians among whom they lived. Judea, on the other hand, was able to preserve its cultural independence for quite a long period.

For the history of Hebrew music the Hellenistic epoch is of little importance during the time that the Temple still stood in Jerusalem. There were few points of inner contact between Greek and Jewish culture and thought. The Jews saw the ideal state in a Kingdom of God; the Greeks, with their many deities modeled on human types and imbued with human character, did not search for the harmonious unity between creed and life as the Jews did, but attempted an ideal worldly life regulated by human reason and dominated by the harmony of physical training, language, movement, and form. The spiritual achievement of the Jews had been the creation of monotheism—the abstraction of religion—by doing away with the myths of nature and magic. But they had remained Orientals by refusing the last step in rationalization: life remained for them within the compass of their belief, and they fervently rejected rational science as well as art, which is the visualization of things irrational. The Greeks, however, were Occidentals in the mode of life; reason and logic shaped their life and creed, and their music mirrors their spiritual ideas as much as do their philosophy and their art.

Though a few Greek melodies have been discovered and deciphered, our knowledge of them is limited. We hardly need their confirmation, however, to prove that the music of Greece and that of the ancient Orient were direct opposites in their very theory. In Hebrew Temple music a spiritual character was ascribed to the modes, and to each portion of the Holy Scriptures was assigned an appropriate tune; the Greek modes, on the other hand, were associated with ethics and morals and were given their place in the general system of rational physical and spiritual education. In Greece music became a worldly power and served worldly ends. While Hebrew theory was guided by the search for eternal truth, the Greeks searched for the good and the beautiful in life.

There can be no doubt that mutual influence modified the life and culture of the two great civilizations, though in the Hebrew sphere—particularly in Palestine—this influence made itself felt on a larger scale only with the decline of Jewish national power and with the destruction of statehood and the Temple. The influence of Oriental thought as well as its poetic and musical expression is evident in Hellenistic art. A number of musical instruments—and surely the kind of music associated with them—were brought to Greece from the Oriental countries: Greek poets and historians often alluded to the foreign origin of Greek music, which rose to its highest level of perfection only after its encounter with the Orient. Hebrew music, on the other hand, hardly changed its character, though a certain influx of Greek tunes is proved by the fact that some later-day rabbis demanded that they be excluded from the Jewish house and synagogue. Greek influence became especially strong in the last two centuries before the Common Era, at the time when the Greeks intensified the Hellenization of the East and when the Greek language replaced Aramaic as the main tongue of Asia Minor.

While religious cult and spiritual music retained its traditional character, the influence of the emotionalism, the many-coloredness, and the beauty of Greek life made itself felt in daily life, particularly in that of the wealthier classes. It seems almost sure that Hebrew secular music witnessed a great development under the impact of Greek musical art, but—naturally—neither direct literary evidence nor actual music has confirmed this to posterity. But before we examine the sources regarding the religious practice and the secular music of the period, we must complete our historical survey down to the times in which the Jews had to replace their central Temple by places of learning scattered throughout their world and erect the edifice of their law perpetuating the biblical tradition.

The Hellenistic epoch came to an end politically with the Maccabean victory and the rededication of the Holy Temple in 165 B.C.E. Direct contact between Hellas and Judea now ceased, while the Egyptian Jewish center remained under Greek supremacy and influence. But about a hundred

years after Judea's victorious repulse of Hellas, the Orient had to surrender
to the mighty thrust of another Occidental power. In 63 B.C.E. the Romans entered Jerusalem under Pompey and subjected the Jews to their
rule. Judea did not gain independence again after this fatal defeat: the civil
war between the successors of the Hasmonean kings was exploited by the
Romans, with the result that Judea was made a Roman province, and the
dispute about Jesus the Nazarene and his teachings, the opposition to him,
and his persecution and eventual crucifixion (ca. 29 C.E.) proved of para-
mount significance in the history of the Jewish people. In 70 C.E. Jerusalem and her proud Temple were destroyed by Titus, and the Jews set out
on their wanderings through the world.

While the remnants of the Jewish people, the survivors of almost a century of civil strife and of war against Rome, were forced to look for new
abodes in the Oriental and Occidental world, there were two groups of
Jews whose fate proved decisive for Jewish as well as for general history.
Both of them had left Jerusalem before the Romans captured and destroyed
the erstwhile capital. One was composed of the disciples and followers of
Jesus, who renounced Judaism and went out to propagate a new religion in
the world; the other founded a new center of Jewish worship and learning
at Yavneh in southern Palestine and there perpetuated its tradition. It was
the academy of Yavneh which laid the foundations for the scholastic system
and for the doctrines and comments later collected in the Mishna and the
Talmud. Centers like these became characteristic of Jewish history throughout the ages of the Diaspora, and as they had no political or governmental
power they could change their place whenever this was necessitated by the
flow of events. Neither the suppression of Bar-Cochba's heroic revolt nor
the Christian attempts at extermination, neither Inquisition nor pogroms
have been able to destroy the spiritual power of Judaism, for the Jews preserved their law and mode of life in clandestine spiritual centers if they had
to fear oppression in the open.

AN OUTLINE of Israel's political and spiritual history is necessary for an appreciation of its musical history. Music was regarded as part of the ancient
Hebrew cultural heritage, yet it retained only a fraction of its former role in
the religious service and in communal life—an evocation of its erstwhile

glory. As, however, the mishnaic and talmudic sources abound in references to singing and musical instruments, it seems that music was still considered an indispensable branch of learning. The Jewish communities continued to cultivate their ancient forms of worship and singing in their Palestinian, Babylonian, and Egyptian centers and rejected all outside influences. Though Hellenistic civilization and art had temporarily had a strong hold over Hebrew thought and music, Roman culture held no attraction for the Jews, for Rome had no mature and elevated art of its own; pagan Roman music was of a purely showy virtuoso character, while the beginnings of Christian Roman music were based—many centuries after Rome's conquest of Jerusalem—on the foundations of Hebrew Temple music.

The centuries in which the spiritual heritage of Judaism was gathered, put down, and annotated by the Tannaim and Amoraim, who organized the Mishna and Talmud, also saw the development of the synagogue, the service of which was modeled after ancient Temple practice. The synagogues served small communities only, and an imitation of the scope and magnificence of the Temple sacrifices and ceremonies could not very well be attempted. Though the musical service thus lost most of its *raison d'être,* music did not lose its importance in any way; the scholars' detailed discussion of ancient Temple music and their remarks about singing in the places of worship as well as in their home demonstrate their great interest in the musical side of the Jewish cult.

The role of music in the synagogue service was severely curtailed in comparison with the importance it had in the Temple of Jerusalem. There, the Levites, who were the music teachers and leaders of divine music, had been professionally trained performers who probably did not disclose the secrets of their art to any outsiders. In the synagogue the traditional Levitical provision of music for the ritual of the Sanctuary, the choral singing and all instrumental music—apart from the blowing of the shofar on solemn occasions—disappeared completely, and the inheritors and successors of the Levites were honorary lay precentors.

The precentor was called *hazan* and is known by this term in the synagogue to this very day. In ancient sources the hazan was referred to as a servant of the priests, *hazanim* (the Hebrew plural) are sometimes also

Levites, who were considered servants of God. But sources also describe the
hazan as a general overseer of services—the Hebrew word *hazan* derives
from the verb *hazoh* = to look, to see—and this may have been the function
of this synagogue officer in the earliest times. Not only after the destruction
of the Second Temple were synagogues instituted as houses of worship;
their history goes back to pre-Israelite times when there were houses of assembly; both the Hebrew term *be'it ha-knesset* and the Greek word *syna-
goga* mean just that—for worship, for study, and for jurisdiction. Throughout the Scriptures and post-biblical literature such assembly houses are
mentioned. For example, in I Chron. 16:39, Zadok the priest (in King
David's time) and his brethren the priests prayed "before the tabernacle of
the Lord in the high place that was at Gibeon. . . ." Four hundred years
later, about 600 B.C.E. in Jer. 39:8 "the Chaldeans burned the king's house,
and the house of the people." *Be'it ha'am* (= the people's house) is wrongly
translated "the houses of the people" in the Holy Bible of the British and
Foreign Bible Society edition.

The first real synagogue-like temple seems to have been in use after
the destruction of Jerusalem by Nabukadnezar's men in 587 B.C.E.—"the
house of the Lord" at Mizpah is mentioned in the tragic story about
Gedalyah (Jer.41:5). Psalm 74, the prayer after the desolation of the sanctuary, says in v. 8, "they have burned up all the houses of God in the land."
The existence of synagogues is also indicated by two later inscriptions,
found in Upper and Lower Egypt, dated from the third quarter of the third
century B.C.E. There were synagogues in Galilee in the early first century
C.E.; synagogues seem to have been numerous at the time of the preaching
of Jesus. The style of synagogue prayer and worship assemblies seems to
have attracted early Christians who sometimes attended synagogue services
and patterned their own services after these models.[1]

There are also parallels in terms for synagogue and church officers.
When the hazan became reader of the Holy Scriptures and precentor, he
was often compared to "an angel of the Lord." Similarly, the deacon of

---

[1]For summaries and analyses of the extant ancient sources, see especially Samuel
Krauss, "Synagogale Altertümer," Berlin/Vienna, 1922, and J. A. Smith, "The
Ancient Synagogue, the Early Church and Singing," in *Music and Letters*, London,
1984.

the early church is named "angel of the church" in "The Revelation of St. John" (1:20, 2:1, 3:1). The word *deacon* is from the Greek *diakonos* (= servant), similar to the early meaning of the Hebrew *hazan*.

Ancient accounts of the form and style of religious services in the early synagogue and of the office of the hazan paint a picture of the function of music in places of worship. The earliest sources describe the service held in Jerusalem after the return of the captives from Babylon. This took place in the open air, not in a house or tabernacle of worship; the synagogue services were surely held in a similar way:

> And all the people gathered themselves together as one man into the street that was before the water gate; and they spake to Ezra the scribe to bring the book of the law of Moses, which the Lord had commanded to Israel. And Ezra the priest brought the law before the congregation . . . and he read therein . . . from the morning until midday, before the men and women . . . and Ezra stood upon a pulpit of wood . . . and opened the book in the sight of all the people . . . and when he opened it, all the people stood up; and Ezra blessed the Lord, the great God. And all the people answered, Amen, Amen, with lifting up their hands; and they bowed their heads, and worshipped the Lord with their faces to the ground . . . (Neh. 8:1–8).

This account, ascribed to Nehemia, governor of Judah (fifth century B.C.E.), also mentions the Levites as teachers of the people and in Neh. 8:16 speaks of the "courts of the houses of God," which certainly means synagogues. That the reading of The Law was chanted psalmodically is testified by various sources, which is also appropriate in view of the structure of Hebrew poetry with its half-verse parallels. The tradition of the recitation was transmitted from generation to generation, as neither texts nor melodies were noted down till rather late in the Common Era. Just as in the description in Nehemia's book, the synagogue services centered around the recitation of the sacred texts, with its portions regulated by the liturgical order of the year and the main Holy Days; the reciters had to know the texts and their appropriate ways of chanting them by heart, and the congregation knew to respond at the proper places. Already in the earliest times the rule must have applied that to read the Torah without chant is tantamount to "the laws that I gave them were not good" (see below; Babylonian Talmud, tractate Megillah, Chapter IV, fol. 32 a, quoting Ezek. 20:25.)

As synagogues were spread probably all over Palestine and a number of synagogues were proved to have existed also outside Palestine, the style and forms of worship and services held in them as well as of religious services held in open places—even on the Temple Mount of Jerusalem when the Holy Temple did not stand there—and in homes, at meals, and in the frame of domestic festivities, took on a character shaped by way of mutual influence among the various communities. The forms of traditional singing in the Hebrew service—antiphony of all kinds—were retained in principle though the practice declined where there was an insufficient number of choristers. Antiphonal forms were also cultivated by the Greeks and were taken over by the Christians for the church service. However, two important changes took place in the development of Hebrew music in the first centuries of the Christian Era: the style of singing assumed a different character, and a sharp dividing line was protectively drawn by the rabbinical teachers between the music of the religious service and secular music.

For primitive peoples and for the Oriental civilizations, singing serves no artistic ends: man raises his voice in song because of his fear that ordinary speech cannot be heard by the supernatural powers shaping his life and deciding his fate. Even in the highly developed musical system of the Hebrew Temple, music was always dominated by the nature of the service: instrumental music only accompanied the ceremonies, and the singing closely followed the words of the texts. The choice of mode was dictated by the occasion or by the portion of the Scriptures to be chanted; the actual "composition" subordinated the melody to the rhythm and content of the words. But the possession of a fine voice and an artful chant became the most desirable features of a precentor in the synagogue (the Greek notions of beauty and artistry had taken hold in the world) and the melodies were embellished and were impressively performed. The chanted recitation of the scriptural texts—which was taken over from the Temple into Christian music, too—is characteristically termed "psalmody" in the western languages, as psalm-singing especially became an important part of the Christian church service.

That the study of the Mishna was also accompanied by a chanting of its chapters is evident from the famous remark of Rabbi Jochanan recorded in the Babylonian Talmud: "He who reads the Scriptures without melody and

the Mishna without song, of him it can be said as is written: the laws I gave
them were not good." The linking of study and singing served as valuable
means of memorizing as well as of interpreting the law. The Mishna texts
were noted down with the signs and accents used for the biblical books,
and the mode of recitation was thus indicated to the student. It has not
been possible yet to establish the exact age of the accents. Till the Dead Sea
Scrolls were discovered scholars inclined to believe that the accents were
added to the texts in the period between the completion of the Talmud
(ca. 500 C.E.) and the time of the first Ge'onim, the intellectual leaders of
the Babylonian Jewish community (at the academies of Sura and Pum-
pedita) between the sixth and eleventh centuries. However, when scholars
started exploring the ancient manuscripts found at Quirbet Qumran near
Jericho from the late 1940s onward, they discovered in the scrolls possibly
dating from late in the first century B.C.E. to the middle of the first Christian century signs that can well be interpreted as early examples of hints as
to the way texts should be read; they may also only serve to underline certain important passages in the texts. Eric Werner has pointed to obvious
parallels between these signs and paleo-Byzantine neumes found in ancient
Byzantine-Slavonic sources as in the Kontakia-type of Byzantine hymns of
the fifth to the seventh centuries where an influence from old-Syriac and
Hebrew poetry is noticeable. If it can be proved that the marginal signs in
the Dead Sea Scrolls are of authentic ancient origin and were not later-day
additions, this would mean that the accents and neumes are of much older
derivation than noted in most current accounts of musical history.[2]

The interesting testimony of a rabbinical scholar proves that in the talmudic epoch the accents still had a cheironomical (hand-sign-indicating)
character in addition to their mnemotechnical (memory-assisting) and musical functions. Rabbi Nahman bar-Yizhaq says that the right hand used to
indicate the signs (Berahot fol. 62 a), and Rashi commented that the hand
was moved in accordance with the musical accents. We also know that the
interpolation of the "cadenza" between the separate parts of the daily song
was developed into a great art and that this was one of the secrets with

---

[2]See Eric Werner, "Musical Aspects of the Dead Sea Scrolls," in *The Musical Quarterly*, January 1957.

which the Levites were not willing to part. The end of a biblical passage was also marked by certain closing cadences in the melody (Megilla fol. 3 a).

THE WAYS of singing and of performing music in both Temple and Synagogue became a decisive factor in the development of Occidental music; the earliest Christian precentors were brought up in the Jewish houses of worship and only adapted ancient Hebrew custom to a new purpose when converted to Christianity. To the purely musical evidence documentary proof is added: the discovery of two fifth-century Roman epitaphs praising the art of Christian cantors who had been born Jews. One is found on the tombstone of a cantor whose Latin name, Deusdedit, is a translation of the Hebrew for Jonathan:

> *Hic levitarum primus in ordine vivens*
> *Davitici cantor carminis iste fuit*

The singer of David's psalms is herewith alluded to. Another tombstone, of the "lector" Redemptus, reads:

> *Prophetum celebrans placido modulamine senem*

The "prophet" meant here was surely David, as his psalms were treasured by the Christian Church. Both cantors are known to have come to Rome at the time of Damasus I (Pope from 366 to 384), who once had been Bishop of Jerusalem.

The German scholar A. Stuiber challenges the common view that the term *levitarum primus in ordine* hints at a Levitical descendant of Deusdedit; he argues that *levita* was the official title of a Roman deacon and *primus in ordine* was an archdeacon.[3] However, we can refer here to the early office of the hazan as servant, beadle, corresponding with the old Greek/Christian concept of *Diakonos* = Deacon; at times the hazan-beadle was a Levite.[4]

The Christian Church took over from the Hebrew services the responsive singing, the modal melody, and many other eastern features. The

---

[3]See Eric Werner, *The Sacred Bridge,* Vol. 2, New York, 1984, p. 198.

[4]See above, p. 80, *f.,* and S. Krauss, *Synagogale Altertümer,* 1922, p. 126.

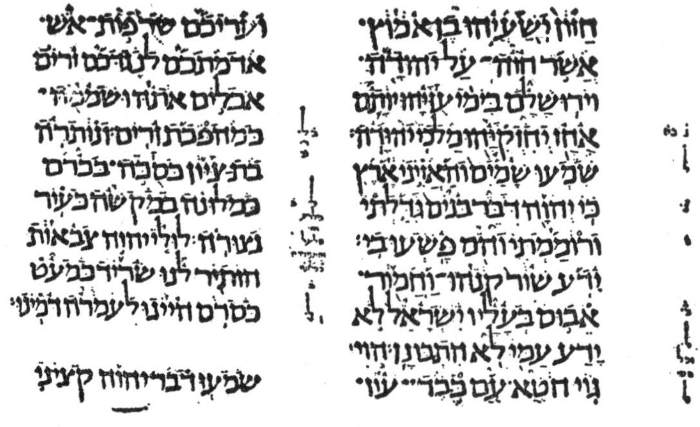

a

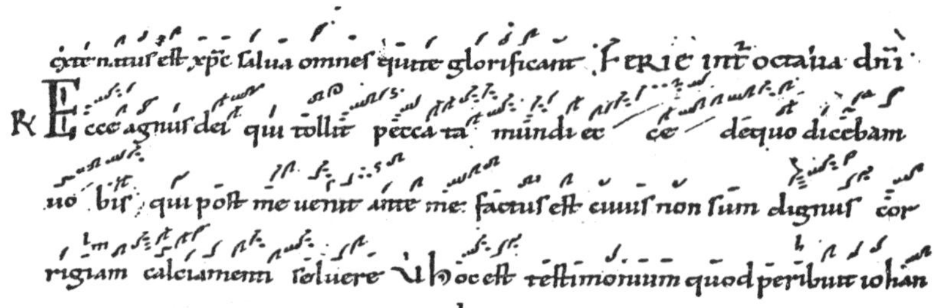

חזון ישעיהו בן אמוץ
אשר חזה על יהודה
וירושלם בימי עזיהו
אחז יחזקיהו מלכי יהודה
שמעו שמים והאזיני ארץ
כי יהוה דבר בנים גדלתי
ורוממתי והם פשעו בי
ידע שור קנהו וחמור
אבוס בעליו ישראל לא
ידע עמי לא התבונן הוי
גוי חטא עם כבד עון

ורעים בנים משחיתים אש
עזבו את יהוה נאצו את
קדוש ישראל נזרו אחור
כה מה תכו עוד תוסיפה
סרה כל ראש לחלי וכל
לבב דוי מכף רגל ועד ראש
אין בו מתם פצע וחבורה
ומכה טריה לא זרו ולא
חבשו ולא רככה בשמן
ארצכם שממה עריכם שרפות אש

שלש עשרה דברי חזון קדש

b

R Ecce agnus dei qui tollit peccata mundi ec   ce dequo dicebam

uo bis qui post me uenit ante me factus est cuius non sum dignus cor

rigiam calciamenti soluere Hoc est testimonium quod peribuit iohan

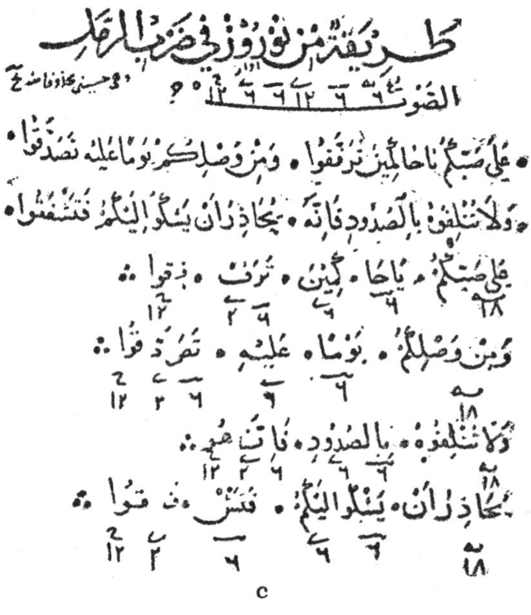

c

(Left) The development of early musical notation: (a) Hebrew Bible accents, from a
tenth-century manuscript; (b) early Christian neumes, eleventh century; (c)
Medieval Arabic notation, fourteenth century.

hand signs (cheironomy) and the accents were also adopted, and from these
signs—called by the Church *neuma,* a Greek word meaning "note" or
"sign" and closely related etymologically to the Hebrew word *ne'ima* =
"song, melody"—there developed in the beginning of the second millennium of the Common Era the first musical notation that indicated the exact
pitches and durations prescribed by the composer. But in early western
music, just as in the Temple and in the synagogues of the first Christian centuries, the signs added to the liturgical texts indicated not a single note but
the modal formula—a series of related notes—the rhythms of which had to
be created in accordance with the word rhythms; the vague character of
the signs was the reason for their being differently interpreted in the various Christian communities just as the ancient biblical cantillation signs
were differently interpreted in the various centers of the Jewish Diaspora.
The earliest known Christian neumes date from the same period in which
the final organization of the Hebrew system must have taken place. Where
the neumes developed into a more complex and definite notation, the Hebrew accents did not depart from their ninth-century character.

By far the earliest known notation of Hebrew chants dates from the
twelfth century. It was not till four hundred years later that synagogal
chants and biblical cantillations were transcribed in musical notation by
Christian humanist scholars, followed another one hundred years later by
Jewish musicians. Between the years 1102 and 1150 it is surmised that the
Norman nobleman Jean Drocos (or Dreux) from Oppido in Apulia, born
between 1050 and 1075, who converted to Judaism in 1102 and thereafter
called himself "Obadya ha-Gēr" (Obadya the Proselyte), then setting out
to the Near East (Babylon, Syria, Palestine, Egypt), wrote down chants in
biblical Hebrew in neumatic notation, fragments of which have been preserved, as has his autobiography. Their style seems to reflect the practice of
eastern Mediterranean hymnody, as well as the influence of early Gregorian
chant; cantillation similar to that apparent in Obadya's chants may still be
heard in Mediterranean Jewish communities. Since the discovery of a *piyut*

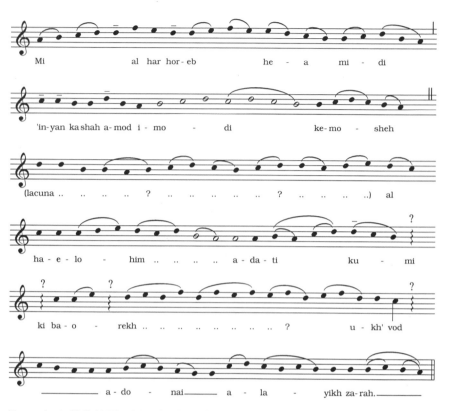

Example 6. "Mi Al Har Horeb," by Obadya. (Transcribed from the ancient neumes by Hanoch Avenary; original fragment from the Genisa Collection of E. N. Adler, Jewish Theological Seminary, New York.)

(liturgical poem) in neumatic notation in the Elkan Nathan Adler collection of Hebrew manuscripts in 1918 and its description by various scholars, as well as additional findings from the Cairo Genizah, the Obadya Scroll has become the subject of numerous scholarly investigations and modern transcriptions. Early views were summarized by Eric Werner in "The Oldest Sources of Synagogal Chant," in *Proceedings of the American Academy for Jewish Research*, Vol. 16, 1947. The most extensive report and analysis are contained in Israel Adler's paper, "The Notated Synagogue Chants of the 12th Century of Obadya, the Norman Proselyte," (French in *Journal de Musicologie*, 1967; English in *Contributions to a Historical Study of Jewish Music*, edited by Eric Werner, 1976, pp. 166–199) and in the same author's "Melodies Notated in the 12th Century," with modern transcriptions of the chants (Israeli Music Publications, Tel Aviv, 1969).

A similarity exists between Hebrew and Christian liturgical music in the use of specific cadences to mark the different parts of the recitation. External features were also retained by the Church—among them the placing of the singers on the steps leading to the altar: this practice most probably led to certain psalms being called "Schir-ha-ma'aloth" (Song of Degrees) in Hebrew and "graduale" (from *gradus* = "step") in Latin liturgy. The Hebrew practice is confirmed by Nehemiah, who says (9:4), "Then stood up upon the stairs, of the Levites, Jeshua, and Bani, Kadmiel, Shebaniah, Bunni, Sherebiah, Bani, and Chenani, and cried with a loud voice unto the Lord their God," and the Mishna Sukkah (5:4) tells that on the Feast of Libation the playing Levites stood with their instruments on the fifteen steps that led from Israel's Temple to the women's section—against the fifteen Songs of Degrees in the Book of Psalms.

At the time the precentors of the early Christian communities took over melodies of the ancient Hebrew service and developed them in their own way—lending new meaning with the new, Latin, texts—some new trends can also be found in the way the talmudic scholars discuss music. It has already been noted that it was probably the Greek influence that made the Jewish rabbis discover that singing had not only purely functional sides but could also be beautiful. They soon began to choose for precentors men endowed with a particularly fine voice, and a passage in the Proverbs of Solomon (3:9), " Honour thy Lord with thy substance," was interpreted to mean that every possessor of a beautiful voice was obliged to lead in prayer; the Mishna goes so far as to say that the word *hon,* "substance" or "wealth," should read *garon* "throat" (which in Hebrew script is a change of one consonant only). A story from the time of the last Mishna scholars (late second century) relates how a certain Chija bar-Ada, nephew of bar-Cappara, was found to have a good voice and was at once compelled by his uncle to officiate as precentor.

It was only natural for the office of precentor to be gradually transferred from the priests to those chosen on account of their voice and musical abilities; theirs became an honorary post, which could, however, be filled only by men of high moral reputation. A description of the ideal precentor is

given in the second century by Rabbi Judah ben-Illai (B. Taanith fol. 16 a):
he should be a learned man who has music in himself and is endowed with
an agreeable voice, who is humble, has a pleasant appearance, is recognized
by and popular with the community, is conversant with the Scriptures, able
to preach a sermon, and well-versed in law and folklore, and who knows all
the prayers by heart. He should also be poor and needy, for then his prayer
will come out of his heart. At a later stage the precentor was given two assistants, called *tom'chim* or *mesayim* (supporters); they had also to remind
him of the prayers and their tunes, as the writing down of prayers was not
permitted till the seventh century. The two assistants have been retained in
the synagogue service down to our own days. They stand by the precentor
in many communities, especially on the Day of Atonement.

IN THE DECADES following the completion of the Talmud the Jews suffered under Christian oppression in Palestine and from the fanatic Magi
caste in Babylonia. Many of their cultural centers were destroyed, and for
a time the schools had to close their doors. The hardship of the times
brought about great difficulties in the organization of worship and learning,
and as it proved impossible to find honorary precentors, the institution of
a professional *shaliach tzibur* (envoy of the community) as hazan became
necessary; after the destruction of the Second Temple the term simply
meant a beadle. As the beadle was always present at the synagogue service,
it had been logical to introduce him to the office of precentor. With the
times he acquired professional knowledge and skill; names of outstanding
hazanim have come down to us from the earliest centuries of the post-tal-
mudic period. The obstacles of the times are mirrored in the ruling of some
eighth- and ninth-century scholars that youths of seventeen or eighteen,
and in case of emergency even boys of thirteen, were eligible for the office
of hazan.

The service was generally divided between two precentors, one sitting
with the congregation and the other standing before the pulpit facing in the
direction of Jerusalem. The first precentor used to recite the "Hearken Israel" (Sh'ma Yisrael) and the benedictions, while the second followed him
with the prayer proper; on the Sabbath and the holy days the morning
prayer was recited by the first and the additional prayer by the second pre-

centor—a custom that has survived down to our own days. As the second precentor recited the more elaborate portions of the service and those reserved for the festival prayers, his office was considered superior to that of the first. The musical elaboration and embellishment of the synagogue chant is due to the efforts of these hazanim.

The mutual influence characterizing the development of synagogue and church in the early Christian centuries is shown by the foundation of Christian music schools modeled on those of the Temple and the synagogue and by the institution in the church of a lector (reader) and cantor (singer) alternating in prayer and chant. The forms of responsorial antiphony and the liturgical chant retained their character for many centuries, but the difference between the worlds of the Orient and the Occident was soon apparent. The Occident had no understanding of the word-born, emotional, and flexible melody of Oriental singers. The early Christians disdained sensuality and ecstasy, as they saw in the earthly life nothing but a preliminary existence and a preparation for Heaven; they thus had as little use for the worldly ethics of art preached by the Greek philosophers as for the notions of the beautiful that had crept into synagogue music. The Church Fathers feared, on the contrary, that a fine voice and artful elaboration of the liturgical chant might divert the worshipers' attention from the content and purpose of the prayers.

The fundamental problems of all religious music, as well as the gulf dividing Occidental from Oriental thought, are evident from a passage contained in the *Confessions* of St. Augustine, written about 400 C.E.

> So often as I call to mind the tears I shed at the hearing of Thy church songs, in the beginning of my recovered faith, yea, and at this very time, whenas I am moved not with the singing, but with the things sung (when namely they are set off with a clear voice and suitable modulation), I then acknowledge the great good use of this institution. Thus float I between peril and pleasure, and an approved profitable custom: inclined the more (though herein I pronounce no irrevocable opinion) to allow of the old usage of singing in the Church; that so by the delight taken in at the ears, the weaker minds be roused up into some feeling of devotion. And yet again, so oft as it befalls me to be moved with the voice rather than with the ditty, I confess myself to have grievously offended: at which time I wish rather not to have heard the music.

The early Christian Church tended to cut down the part of music in the service to a minimum, as it was a constant reminder of pagan customs and of the ancient faith. But it was impossible to dispense with music altogether, for its sacred associations were declared not only by the ancient Bible—holy to the Christians—but also by the New Testament Scriptures. Instrumental music and the use of popular tunes became, of course, intolerable in the eyes of the Christian Fathers; but their very antagonism toward them suggests the extent to which folk music and instrumental playing must actually have flourished. The belief in the magical power of prayer and incantation, which the Jews had apparently overcome to a great extent, still haunted people's minds in the early Christian centuries; the widely used exclamation *Kyrie eleison* ("Lord, have mercy") has come down from pagan sun rites via the Jewish Temple to Christian liturgy and still begins the Mass as well as its musical settings. Some of the church ceremonies were accompanied by musical instruments down to the sixth century, and some eastern churches—the Copts of Ethiopia, for instance—use them to this very day. The organ, the principal musical instrument found in the western church today, gained a permanent place in the church only at the beginning of the second millennium; the Jews, who had most probably had a similar instrument in the Second Temple, then argued that it was a "Christian instrument" and thus inadmissible in Jewish service.

THE ROMAN CHURCH based its liturgy and its music on two direct sources: on the music of the Temple perpetuated by Christianized Jewish cantors and on Byzantine music. Byzantine music, too, had the closest affinities with ancient Temple music; the Byzantine authors themselves said that their psalms and their musical system and modes as well as their forms of singing were derived from the art of King David and King Solomon. In stark contrast to Rome, which had developed no culture of its own, Byzantium had reached a very high stage of cultural evolution—in which ancient Hebrew and later Hellenistic influences were the foremost shaping forces. The Byzantine influence on the western Church proved strong till the final separation of Byzantium from Rome in 1050; but then the western world had already begun to develop decisive traits of its own.

Eastern art and music became a dominant factor in the cultural development of the East of Europe, while the history of western music proper begins with the diffusion of the liturgical chant named after Pope Gregory the Great (who was pontiff from 590 to 604). The Oriental influences began to recede gradually; the new features shaping church song seem characteristically Occidental. The embellishment of certain syllables or words, necessitated by the adaptation of the modes to various texts and then exploited by the professional precentors for virtuosic ends, seemed excessively emotional to the Church Fathers: this can be noted especially in the development of the singing of the "Hallelujah." The ending syllable "jah" may have been adorned with melismas by Jewish precentors, but probably by short cadenzas only—scholars have found no references in Jewish literature to a possible extension of Hallelujah melodies. In the Catholic Church the Jubilus was sung to a single vowel as a vocalise, but the widely extended Christian Alleluia, as practiced in the eastern and the western churches, seems, in contradiction to earlier views, not to have had a Hebrew precedent or parallel.[5]

The first famous mention of the "Hallelujah" in Christian literature is found in the liturgical treatise *De ecclesiasticis officiis* (I,13) of Archbishop Isodorus of Seville, written ca. 600 C.E. *Laudes, hoc est Alleluia canere, canticum est Hebraeorum.* Early scholars, including Peter Wagner and Egon Wellesz, interpreted this statement as Isodorus' acknowledgment that the singing of the "Hallelujah," that is of the Laudations, was of Hebrew origin. An unprejudiced reading of the words, argues the Israeli musicologist Hanoch Avenary, does not, however, disclose more than "Singing the lauds, i.e., Alleluia, is an utterance of joy with the Hebrews" because the Hebrew origin of the word *Alleluia* is *Hallelu-Jah,* or "praise the Lord."[6]

---

[5]See J. A. Smith, op. cit.; Eric Werner, "The Doxology in Synagogue and Church, A Liturgico-Musical Study," *Hebrew Union College Annual,* 1945–1946, and *The Sacred Bridge: the Interdependence of Liturgy and Music in Synagogue and Church During the First Millenium,* Vols. 1, 2 (1968, 1984); Hanoch Avenary, "Reflections on the Origins of the Alleluia-Jubilus," in *Assaph, Studies in Art: Orbis Musicae,* ed. Judith Cohen, No. 6., Tel Aviv, 1978, pp. 34–42, with extensive bibliography and acknowledgments to earlier studies of Eric Werner, Edith Gerson-Kiwi, Walter Wiora, and Egon Wellesz.

[6]Hanoch Avenary, "Reflections . . ." op. cit.

The practice of closing the Alleluia with a melismatic extension of the syllable "ah" probably originated in the very earliest Christian congregations. Its reason has been sought in the religious, almost mystic exaltation, "the speaking with tongues" (*loqui linguis*), mentioned in the New Testament, particularly in Acts and Epistles: from these sources and from apocryphal literature derives the notion of incantations in a mystical, angelic, visionary vocal style. Avenary (op. cit.) points to peculiarities in eastern Alleluia tunes underlying this notion: melismas were not sung to a single vowel as in Plain Chant, but changing syllables of nonsensical, even absurd, meanings were put to the melody. Avenary finds that "irrational rendering in sound of deepest religious experiences was finally formalized . . . and sung to syllables from beyond every earthly language"; proof is found in a saying of Augustinus in his "Ennaratio in Psalmum" 99: "Whoever jubliates, does not utter words; it is rather a certain ringing out of joy without words. . . . The exuberant joy of man bursts forth with unspeakable and unintelligible words, a nonverbal language of exaltation."[7]

Strange as these theories on the melismatic extension of the Alleluia may sound, scholars through the centuries have found the ancient practice surviving in Syrian, Russian, and Coptic communities. In 1924 the scholar Dom J. Jeannin reported "strange syllables" in Syrian and Chaldean singing of the Alleluia. In 1899 Dom J. Parisot reproduced music in which nonmusical texts were sung to a melisma during the Epiphany in Syrian and Jacobite services in his "Report sur une mission scientifique en Turquie d'Asie." Egon Wellesz found senseless Alleluia melismas in Byzantine manuscripts. G. A. Villoteau, who accompanied Napoleon on his Egyptian campaign, heard an Alleluia-song by Copts with fancy syllables of various kinds.[8] Mystic exaltation seems to have been spread in the most ancient Christian communities, connected surely with the Christian belief in a "Kingdom in Heaven," a notion foreign to Jewish thinking. Jewish mysticism was of a kind different from Christian mystical thinking and belief; it

---

[7]Augustinus, "Ennaratio in Psalmum," No. 99, quoted in Avenary, "Reflections . . ." op. cit.

[8]See his "Description de l'Egypte" of 1799 and the later "De l'état actuel de l'art musical en Egypte," Paris, 1826.

seems that even in the most ancient times it combined rational thinking with religious interpretations and visions of the Divine presence. "Songs of Praise" of an exalted character—as ancient texts prove—never end in unintelligible words in a language denoting that it is "unearthly," but on the contrary contain an especially noble and rich poetic "word music." The development of the Jubilus melismas, says Avenary, is in full accordance with Christian thinking and belief.

The basic Hallelujah melodies of Hebrew origin, sung to new Latin texts, became the basis of western church singing; the Christian cantors of Jewish parentage extended the melismas on the last syllable "jah" and with the progress of time separated the Alleluia from the main text, singing newly composed words to the notes of its cadence. The texts written especially to fit the melismas constitute the first original sacred poetry of the Occident; a much later step became the independent setting to music of the new texts and thus their final and complete detachment from the Oriental origin. When in the early Middle Ages the practice of many-voiced singing and—still later—of harmonization was applied to liturgical melodies, western music finally achieved musical independence. The Oriental origin of the liturgical chant—which can be demonstrated by a comparison of the basic melodies with those of the ancient Jewish communities—was still to be divined; nevertheless, medieval history drew a clear dividing line between synagogue music, which became static and archaic, and church music, which developed forms of art that were to prepare the ground for the great art music of the western world.

Church Fathers—such as St. John Chrysostom ca. 400 C.E.—were conscious of the transmission of customs and liturgical practice and music from the Hebrew cult to the Christians; and the most prominent music historians of later ages have examined the interrelation between ancient synagogal music and the musical services at the Temple of Jerusalem and early Gregorian chant. In the eighteenth and nineteenth centuries, however, some scholars who heard the assimilated singing in western synagogues of their times could not believe that this music could have had roots similar to those of Christian liturgical chant; further, their research and judgment were colored by a general antagonism toward Jewry. Thus wrote Johann Nikolaus Forkel, known as Johann Sebastian Bach's first biographer, very blatantly in his *Allgemeine Geschichte der Musik* (Leipzig 1788 and 1801), quoting a French author: "even under immediate instruction by divinity [Christ] the culture of that nation [the Jews] remained so backward, that it is not to be counted among the number of cultured nations."[9]

The Austrian Raphael Georg Kiesewetter argues in his *Geschichte der abendländisch-europäischen Musik* (Leipzig 1834): that "Grecian, or, as some authors have supposed, Hebrew melodies should have found their way into the assemblies of Christians, seems altogether impossible. . . . The Christians evinced an equal anxiety also to separate themselves from the Jews; and their object was, in fact, more especially to found a peculiar art of song distinct from that of any other religion."

Giovanni Andrea Bontempi wrote in Perugia (1695) in his "Historia musica . . . seconda la dottrina de' Greci, in quali enventata prima da Iubal avanti il Diluvio . . ." that he denies an influence of Hebrew chant on Christian liturgy, and the Swiss scholar Jacques Handschin wrote that "If St. Paul often recommends to the faithful the singing of psalms, hymns and spiritual hymns, we must not assume that he meant to impose upon them (in Antioch) some tunes which might have been as strange to them as missionary chorales to Africans."

Eric Werner adds to this passage in Handschin's "Geschichte der Musik" (Zürich, 1948) that "the new songs" the Swiss historian believes were composed for the Christians were in fact the "Psalms, Hymns and Spiritual Hymns" which St. Paul knew from the Old Testament canticles and it is to them that he referred. Humanist scholars and theologians (Werner especially names Michael Praetorius and Wolfgang Caspar Printz) did connect early Christian music with Hebrew models. An early eighteenth-century British writer, Arthur Bedford, states in "Temple Musick, or an Essay concerning the Method of singing the Psalms of David in the Temple" (London 1706) that Plain Chant "was the method used by the Primitive Christians in the most Early Ages of the Gospel, and this they bor-

---

[9]This quotation and the following quotations from Kiesewetter, Bontempi, Handschin, are taken from Eric Werner "Musical Tradition and Its Transmitters between Synagogue and Church," in *Yuval*, Vol. 2, Jerusalem 1971, pp. 163–180, as are some of Werner's conclusions. See also Werner, *The Sacred Bridge*, Vol. 2, 1984, last chapter.

rowed from the Jews . . . the Saints in Heaven . . . sang the song of Moses, the Servant of God and of the Lamb. . . ."

The debates for and against the Hebrew origin of sacred Christian music have a long and varied history throughout the ages and find a place the general musical history books and in a host of specialist studies, including the ground-breaking studies of Abraham Zvi Idelsohn and Peter Wagner (Idelsohn's *Thesaurus of Hebrew Oriental Melodies* of 1912–1932 and Wagner's *Gregorianische Melodien* of 1911 and 1921–23). It was not until the twelve-year-interlude of the Nazi Third Reich, declared to be destined to last for a thousand years, that the Jewish heritage in Christian music was denied by official decree. In October 1934, at the convention of the Union of National Socialist German philologists and school teachers at Trier, Dr. Joseph Schmidt-Görg, then lecturer at Bonn University, after the fall of the Nazi Reich esteemed director of the Bonn Beethoven Archive, tried to "save Gregorian music from the black mark of a possible Jewish style" by putting forward a diagnosis of "Frankish, i.e. Germanic" elements in Gregorian chant. The German musicologist Hans Engel of Koenigsberg University wrote in 1944 that "the scientific character, the orderly system inherited from the ancient Greek spirit have provided early Christian music with its educational value. It was thus that there was shown the strength with which the Germanic and later the German nation understood to assimilate foreign cultural elements. . . . Already in the sphere of Gregorian chant did the creative potency of the inborn Germanic gifts permeate. . . ."[10]

WHILE THE ROOTS of early Christian music surely must be sought in the entire ancient eastern world, it clearly originated in the liturgical singing of Levitical and lay cantors who had come to Rome from Jerusalem. Some other links between the ancient East and early western practice were provided in the antagonism toward secular and instrumental music shared by the Christian Church Fathers and the spiritual leaders in the eastern countries, even though the reasoning differs in the different religious communities and their religious laws. The Church frankly admitted that music, if

---

[10]Translated from the German quotation in Fred Prieberg's in *Musik im NS Staat,* Frankfurt/Main 1982, p. 362.

cultivated as an art, distracted from the religious service, and the Islamic authorities (followed by some of the later rabbinical writers) expressed similar opinions. The talmudic scholars prohibited the use of secular and instrumental music as unfit for a people that had lost its Temple and with it its religious and national center. They admonished their fellow-Jews to sing religious hymns at the festivals; Greek tunes were described by them as harmful to the mind, and the use of secular melodies for the reading of the Holy Scriptures was said to be against the spirit of the law, as Moses himself had heard the traditional sacred tunes on Mount Sinai and imparted them to the people of Israel. The preference of the Hebrews for vocal music, in contrast to the instrumental-minded Greeks, seems to be proved by the fact that the Hebrew language abounds in terms for melody, vocal forms, vocal range, and sound, while Greek has a larger vocabulary for instrumental music and the instruments proper.[11] The rabbis of the Hellenistic period went so far in their condemnation of instrumental music that they even scorned the use of those instruments actually used in the Jerusalem Temple of old: "They (the faithful) do not pour blood of sacrifices upon the altar; no tympanon is sounded, nor cymbals, nor the aulos with its many holes, instruments full of frenzied tones, not the whistling of a pan's pipe is heard, imitating the serpent, nor the trumpet calling to war in wild tones," says a famous Hellenistic-Judaic source.[12] It is important to know that the instruments mentioned were largely associated with Greek pagan worship and also partly with the secular orgies so abhorred by the Jewish authorities.

The cultivation of the traditional vocal music was thus considered of foremost importance, and singers with fine voices who declined to serve the synagogue were severely castigated and punished. Drastic measures were also taken, or at least contemplated, against indulgence in secular music: a rabbi of the third century demands that ears listening to such music should be cut off, and a little later a house in which music is cultivated is said to be marked for destruction. One third-century Babylonian

---

[11]Eric Werner, "The Conflict Between Hellenism and Judaism in the Music of the Early Christian Church," *Hebrew Union College Annual*, Vol. 20, 1947.

[12]Oracula Sibyllina 8, 113. See Eric Werner, "The Conflict," pp. 415–416.

rabbi prohibited all secular music in his community. Thereupon all festivities and social affairs were suspended, for nobody cared for social life without music; this led to a complete standstill in social intercourse and commercial life and brought about such a crisis in the market that another rabbinical authority had to relax his colleague's ruling. The prohibition of instruments on weekdays as well as on the Sabbath and at festivals soon became general, and exceptions were made only for weddings and mourning ceremonies. The authorities did all in their power to stop the people's natural merrymaking associated with light and popular music; the breaking of a dish in front of a bride and groom at their wedding seems to have come from the wish to remind them in the midst of their merriment of the destruction of Jerusalem. It is also related that when the gaiety at a wedding was becoming extravagant, some prominent sages would suddenly break the most costly dishes of the house in order to shock the guests and thus tone down the joy, so that they would not start irreverently singing serious religious music.

The fact that the depreciation of secular and instrumental music on the part of the religious authorities was common to all the centers of the eastern and western Mediterranean at approximately the same time makes a priority difficult to determine; it can be guessed, however, that the exuberance and lasciviousness of life under Roman influence were the common ground on which there grew an aversion to all matters secular. The Jewish rabbis gave vent to their indignation by reminding Israel of its national sorrow, the Church Fathers exhorted the Christians to imitate neither pagan worship nor the obscene theater, and the Islamic theologians followed suit in their condemnation of all those listening to profane music. Psychological and national considerations were additional reasons underlying the sharp words of the clerical authorities against the use of instruments and the singing of popular songs. It must be surmised that the music performed at Jewish weddings and other festivities was not of Hebrew origin, for a real musical tradition had so far been cultivated only in the religious field. Popular songs and instrumental music had largely been influenced by Greek music or had actually been taken over from Hellenistic sources, and the rabbis must have had every cause to keep these influences away from their flock. A similar motive may be assumed in the case of the Islamic authorities, for Arabic secular music had also been subjected to foreign influences to a large degree. The case is somewhat different in the Christian Church: in its own sphere secular music meant the music at the luxurious ceremonies of the Roman Emperor's court and at the extravagant circus or theater. The theologians of the three great religious communities were thus one in their condemnation of foreign influence endangering—so it seemed to them—the preservation of their religious tradition, and in their concentration upon the essential values of music in divine service.

The continuous exhortations of Church Fathers, Islamic theologians, and rabbinical scholars make it sufficiently clear that their campaigns against secular music did not meet with the success desired. The Jewish sources confirm that no weddings or feasts were celebrated without singing and playing, and the rabbis were forced to cancel some of their prohibitions. One scholar even dared to argue that the Greek language was best fitted for songs. The working songs of the boatmen and plowmen were expressly permitted, but those of the weavers were prohibited as obscene; the professional wailing-women continued to sing their threnodies accompanied by pipes (two at the least), and music retained its dominant role at processions and celebrations, at which even aged rabbis could often be seen rising from an opulent meal, clapping their hands, and joining in a dance to the strains of merry music.

Even the sparse evidence we could quote here for the first centuries of Jewish history after the destruction of the Temple amply proves that music did not cease to fulfill important functions both in the cult and in the daily life of the Jewish communities. Throughout the insecure period of wanderings and oppression characterizing the early Christian centuries, tradition and law were steadfastly adhered to; the remembrance of Temple music and the wish to perpetuate its essential features went a long way toward shaping the synagogue song of two hundred centuries of dispersion, while at the same time it provided the fundamentals for western art music. The secular music of Israel, on the other hand, could begin developing a characteristic style of its own only when the Jews were given another period of rest and prosperity; not until they lived free from suppression and fear could they truly cultivate poetry and art. And such an era dawned when they followed the Islamic conquerors to southwestern Europe, where the

Jews were destined to enjoy a golden age of their own in the cultural centers of medieval Spain.

EXAMPLES 7–12 show a mode used by different Jewish communities and by the early Church. (After E. Werner, "The Doxology in Synagogue and Church, A Liturgical-Musical Story," *Hebrew Union College Annual*, Vol. 19, 1946, pp. 333–35, where all sources for transcriptions used are also given.)

Example 7. The model framework of the Tropos Spondeiakos, which is a modification of the Dorian scale. Clement of Alexandria (*Paedagogus* II, Ch. 4) says that the Greek drinking songs were sung in this mode "after the manner of Hebrew psalms."

Example 8. Gloria of the Mass in Festis Simplicibus (*Liber usualis*, p. 55).

Example 9. Psalmody of the Moroccan Jews (after Idelsohn).

Example 10. Chant of the Babylonian Jews on the high holy days (after Idelsohn).

Example 11. Syrian psalmody (after Parisot).

Example 12. Byzantine hymm of the eleventh to twelfth centuries (after Tillyard).

Examples 13–18 show a melodic style common to Greek, Roman Christian, Spanish Hebrew, and early European secular song.

Example 13. The Skolion of Seikilos, of Tralles in Asian Minor (first to second centuries C.E.).

Example 14. Roman antiphon Hosanna filio David of the Roman Church (after Gastoué, *Les Origines du chant romain*, Paris, 1907, p. 40).

Example 15. Spanish Hebrew folk song "Rachelina" (sung by the Sephardic Jews of Salonika, quoted after Lazare Saminsky, *Music of the Ghetto and the Bible*, New York, 1934, p. 151).

Example 16. Thirteenth-century troubador song (after Angles; see Davidson and Apel's *Historical Anthology of Music*, Cambridge, Massachusetts, 1947, p. 15, No. 18 c).

Example 17. Hebrew hymm, composed to a text by the eleventh-century poet Ahi Gaon (Sh'ma koli) and probably introduced from Spain into the various countries in which the Jews took refuge after their expulsion (after D. A. de Sola-Aguilar, *The Ancient Melodies of the Liturgy of the Spanish and Portugese Jews*, London, 1857).

Example 18. A Spanish cantiga of the Villancico type, thirteenth century (quoted after Ribera from Davidson and Apel's *Historical Anthology of Music*, Cambridge, Massachusetts, 1947, p. 20, No. 22 c).

CHAPTER FOUR

THE SETTLEMENT

OF THE WEST

T HE TALMUD, an echo of Israel's splendor and greatness of old, was the last spiritual creation of the Jews on the soil of the ancient East. The centuries following its completion mark a large-scale migration to the West, whose political and cultural hegemony became firmly established. The Jews began to settle throughout the countries bordering the Mediterranean as well as in central, western, and eastern Europe and to play their own part in the erection of the great edifice of civilization and culture rising on European soil. They were instrumental in the laying of the foundations, then receded into the background for some centuries when they neither derived great benefit from the younger civilizations nor contributed to their development. Finally in modern times they again took an active part in the cultural activities of nations which had meanwhile soared high above the Jews but whose achievements were soon turned to good account by their Jewish citizens. Some Jews distinguished themselves and rose to fame as inventors, craftsmen, thinkers, or artists of great individuality. Many of these renounced their link with the people from which they had originally sprung, and the products of their minds belong to the culture of the people among whom they lived.

The Jewish migration which set in soon after the destruction of the First Temple led to the foundation of the Babylonian community, of the Egyptian Diaspora (which later became the center of the Jewish-Hellenistic culture), and of various settlements in the Mediterranean world; after the Romans' fatal blow against Jerusalem the Jews settled throughout the Roman Empire. But the large-scale migration to the countries of the West and the rise of the first western Jewish communal and cultural centers date from the period in which the youngest Oriental power, Islam, pushed forward into the West and established a strong foothold in Spain.

Islam had originally been the creation of certain Semitic tribes, among whom there also lived a great number of Arabic Jews; but after the death of its prophet, Mohammed, it became a powerful national-religious movement. Islam set out to wring Syria, Palestine, Egypt, and the North African coast from the Byzantine and Roman Empire and on its way also brought most of the Jewish Diaspora under Arab supremacy. The conquests were soon extended to Europe, and everywhere Jewish communities became part of the realm. As trade and commerce flourished in the new Islamic centers, Jewish merchants also followed the routes of the conquerors; Jews prospered in southern Italy and in Spain and also moved northward into Franconia, eastern Europe, and the central European countries. By dint of their connections with the Oriental world they became important agents in the trade between West and East and established their centers in the cities of Europe. After a long period of stagnation the Jewish world had been set moving again; it played its part in the attempt of Islam to subdue the Occident after the century-long supremacy of Hellas and Rome over the Orient. Islam succeeded in maintaining its rule and influence over Spain for seven centuries, and the Jews flourished in its commercial and cultural centers. A lively spiritual exchange between Jews and Arabs on the one hand and between the eastern and western civilizations on the other characterizes cultural development in the course of these centuries; the Jews again played their role as mediators. History shows that their talent for assimilating what was best in the ways of both Orient and Occident enabled them to remain in Europe and play their part in its cultural life when Islam was forced to give up the positions it had held for so long and returned to the countries of the Orient.

The reasons for the victorious advance of Islam in Europe were not only its fanatical desire for power and conquest and the driving force of its armies but also the inner dynamics and spirit of its achievements. Islam had united the heritage of the ancient Oriental civilizations in a grandiose synthesis. As a cultural force it was greatly superior to the cultures of the West, which were still in the formative stage. Islam's emphatic belief in the beauty of the earthly world, the magnificence of its buildings, the many-coloredness of its stories, and the vivid rhythm of its life proved irresistibly attractive to the countries ruled by the dogma of a church that denounced earthly pleasure and kept a wary eye on art; Islamic culture radiated its light from Spain throughout the Occidental world. While in the sphere of church life and art the Oriental heritage was disclaimed in an ever-increasing degree, the impact of Oriental culture was instrumental in creating western secular art. The young poetry of southwestern Europe, the rise of the troubadour song, and the cultivation of instrumental playing—on instruments mostly imported from the Near East—owed their origin in large measure to the eastern poets, singers, and musicians at the courts of Islamic Spain. The great inner power of the culture of Islam can well be imagined if we compare the towering influence of the eastern forces on medieval Europe with the negligible impression made by the western crusaders on the eastern world.

The Arabs had conquered Spain in the year 711; in 750 this most western outpost of the Arab Empire became an independent political and cultural province. There had been Jewish settlements in the country before, but the Jews had been hated and oppressed by the Spanish Christians. The Arabs did away with the restrictions under which the Jews had had to suffer and let them participate in their economic and cultural life, for they found their character and modes of life more congenial with and related to their own Near Eastern ways than those of the Spaniards, who ware hostile toward the Islamic conquerors and represented a creed and life foreign to them. The Jewish communities thus began to thrive and attracted new settlers from other parts of the world, and the Spanish Diaspora soon prospered to such a degree that it took over the place of Babylon as the cultural center of Israel.

DURING THE EXISTENCE of the Jewish commonwealth and until the destruction of the Temple, music had been recognized only in its liturgical functions, and in the Diaspora under Greek and Roman rule the will for self-preservation had expressed itself in rigid laws on the use of music. Now the Jews entered upon a new phase. Hebrew music and Jewish musicians had hitherto found their place within their own community only, and their work had been prescribed by liturgical needs; Jewish popular music had largely been shaped by foreign influences and had not been permitted to develop freely. In Islamic Spain the Jews found themselves for the first time in modern history partaking in a flourishing civilization and enjoying its privileges as free citizens. They lived and traded unhindered by restrictions; they held important positions in various branches of the political, economic, and cultural life; and their own development derived great benefit from the impact of a civilization which in its origins was not remote from their own and whose language they had adopted in the Oriental world as well as in the new European settlements. With the establishment of the Arab rule in Spain there ended for the Jews the period of mere colonization; they could turn to organization and creation in all spheres of life. As so often in history, at this point we can once more witness the characteristic trend in Jewish culture: again the Jews based the foundations of their life and art on those of another civilization but adapted and remolded old forms in a spirit of their own.

The worldly spirit of the Arab philosophy of life was mirrored in an ever-growing emphasis on the emotional in Jewish thought. The laws of the Talmud were found to be too rigid, too much the product of cold reasoning, and devoid of an understanding of the demands of heart and soul; it is significant that the most popular religious book of the eleventh century should have been called *Duties of the Heart*. Life and cult without beauty no longer satisfied the community, and the traditional synagogue service was embellished by products of sensitive minds and hearts—by poetry. The creation of liturgical poetry (*piyut*) was due to a good many factors at once: the popularity of church hymns throughout the western world, the secular poetry of the Arabs, and the wish on the part of the precentors to find vehicles for their artistry. In the Christian church the hymns were created in a desire to add purely Christian poetry to the traditional liturgical texts of eastern origin; the Jewish hazanim based their religious hymns on free elaborations of scriptural texts.[1]

An early example of a Jewish poet and singer may be found toward the end of the fifth century: a converted Jew born in Syria and active in Constantinople wrote hymns modeled on eastern patterns for the Greek Church. This poet, who called himself Romanos, was regarded in his own time as the greatest Byzantine hymn-writer and was called *Melodos* ("Maker of Songs") by his contemporaries; about a thousand poems—mainly based on biblical passages—and their melodies were attributed to him. The work of Romanos became of importance to eastern Christendom and seems to have influenced later Hebrew poets as well; but it was only under the influence of the Arab lyrical poems that there developed a Jewish religious poetry of characteristic imprint. The earliest Hebrew poems known are based on Arabic meters, and this implies that they were most probably sung to Arabic melodies. That Arabic tunes were still popular with the Jews in the golden age of Hebrew poetry and song is shown by the fact that eleventh-century scholars and poets—among them Hai (Chiya) b. Sherira ha-Gaon, Isaac Alfasi, and Yehuda of Barcelona—found it necessary to express their opposition to the excessive use of poetry and Arabic tunes in the synagogue. Maimonides permitted the introduction of poetry into the service under certain conditions only and demanded that it should not interrupt the prayers and benedictions; he stressed the inadmissibility of popular and instrumental music. Yehuda Hadassi argued that the worshipers paid better attention when a hazan endowed with a beautiful voice intoned a fine melody and that his song could purify and ennoble their minds. An admirable definition of the purpose of singing is contained in the *Book of the Pious* of Yehuda he-Hassid (died 1217): "If you cannot concentrate in prayer, search for melodies, and if you pray choose a tune you like. Then your heart will feel what your tongue speaks; for it is the song that makes your heart respond." The same rabbi forbade the Jews both to teach He-

---

[1]A most elaborate historical account of the ancestry and development of the *piyut*, its poets, and its singers is contained in Eric Werner, *A Voice Still Heard: The Sacred Songs of the Ashkenazic Jews,* University Park and London, 1976.

Eleventh-century musicians of probably Near Eastern origins. From the chapter "De Musica" in the encyclopedia *De Universo Libri XXII* by Hrabanus Maurus. (The manuscript is preserved in a library at Montecassino, Abbazia, Italy.) The name of the author (or editor) points, of course, to his Arabic origin.

brew melodies to the Christians, and to learn tunes from them. Religious songs, he also taught, should never be used for secular purposes, not even for lulling a baby to sleep.

The general attitude of the religious authorities toward music is well summarized in the writings of Maimonides, who saw in all activities of man a means of creating and maintaining "a perfect condition of the instrument of the soul," and in the argument of a twelfth-century Arab writer (Al-Gazālī) that there can be opposition to music only if one listens to it "for its own sake and not for recreation." The necessity of adorning religious as well as secular life was admitted in this golden age of poetry and art, and the debates fought by the thinkers of the period only symbolize that greater dispute of the time on the preponderance of reason or heart in the regulation of life and worship—a dispute characterizing the entire spiritual development of Judaism in European civilization and forming the dual basis of many Jewish minds, with Spinoza's philosophy as the towering example.

The medieval debates on the place of poetry and music in the synagogue have furnished posterity with a wealth of information regarding the musical practice and the philosophy and aesthetics of music in the Spanish period. We learn that the theory and science of music formed part of the curriculum in higher studies from the beginning of the tenth century; this branch of learning was generally described as "science of music" or " science of composition," while the practical side of instruction was simply called "singing" (*zimrah*). Just as in the Arabic schools, the study of music in Hebrew science was divided into two separate branches: theoretical and practical. Yizhaq ibn Sulaiman (Isaac Israeli), the first prominent Jewish philosopher of the Middle Ages (ca 842–932), saw in music the last but the best of the disciplines that had to be studied; and the leading thinkers of the following centuries testified to the fact that mastery in the theory of music was counted among the accomplishments regarded by Jewish scholars as highly desirable.

Yet in spite of the abundance of testimony regarding the teaching of music and its part in Jewish cult and education, it is difficult to separate Jewish original thought from Greek and Arabic aesthetics and from a philosophy common to the entire Orient. It has been established that the basic philosophy and aesthetics of music originated in Asia Minor and Mesopotamia, certainly earlier that 1500 B.C.E. Greek philosophers transformed and systematized the ancient Oriental ideas and carried them back to Asia Minor, where they were absorbed by early Christianity and Hellenistic Judaism. Syrians and Jews were the mediators between Hellenistic philosophy and Islamic thought, and the medieval world drew its science from the Latin writers, who based their ideas on those of the ancient Greeks, and from the Spanish cultural centers.

This long line of development explains the fact that many old Oriental trends are still found in medieval philosophy. The magical origins of customs and prayers still haunted the mind; the belief in the magic power of music—predominant in medieval writings—was justified by a reference to the famous healing of Saul's mind by the music of David: "and it came to pass, when the evil spirit from God was upon Saul, that David took a lyre, and played with his hand: so Saul was refreshed, and was well, and the evil spirit departed from him" (I Sam. 16:23). Isaiah had castigated the magicians of Babylonia (47:9 ff.) in scornful language, yet Jewish belief in magic was in no way less strong than that of the other Oriental peoples; it has already been noted that the shofar symbolizes magic spells to this very day. In the medieval sources—both Arab and Jewish—it is often related how musicians were called to relieve the pains of the sick in the hospital, and an ancient Hebrew manuscript contains a picture in which a lutenist is seen sitting in a physician's anteroom, probably called upon to cleanse the mind of the possessed or to perform his part in the healing of the sick.[2]

But side by side with the ancient eastern ideas of magic and incantation, the influence of classical Greece and its ethics is not denied in medieval musical aesthetics and science. The ethos of certain melodic scales, of defined rhythms, and of the different musical instruments, as well as their influence on the soul and character of man, recurs in the medieval writings; and the idea of a harmony of spheres took firm root in the minds of both the Greeks and the later Jewish philosophers, who could quote in support a passage in the Book of Job (38:7): "the morning stars sang together, and all the sons of God shouted for joy."[3] Greek and Arab authors said that only Pythagoras had been able to hear the celestial harmonies, but a Jewish source (Philo Judaeus 2:299) ascribed the same capacity to Moses—who was regarded as the patron of musicians in the Islamic Orient.

Astrological considerations fill a prominent place in both the Arabic and the Hebrew writings of the Middle Ages (they are a most ancient heritage from the Chaldeans and Babylonians), and the relations of the strings and tones to the planets and seasons and the influence of sounds, melodies,

---

[2]The manuscript is described in H. G. Farmer, *Sa'adyah Gaon on the Influence of Music*, London, 1943, p. 6. An extensive treatise on Sa'adyah was published by Hanoch Avenary in the *Hebrew College Annual*, 1968, pp. 145–162, and reprinted in *Contributions to a Historical Study of Jewish Music*, ed. Eric Werner, New York, 1976, pp. 37–54.

[3]See Eric Werner and Isaiah Sonne, "The Philosophy and Theory of Music in Judeo-Arabic Literature," *Hebrew Union College Annual*, 1941.

and rhythms on the humors of the body are discussed at length by the scholars of the period.[4]

NEW TRENDS in Hebrew music are indirectly attested in the writings of the first Jewish scholar who devoted to music a complete chapter of his philosophical system—Sa'adyah Ha-Gaon, who was born in Fayyum, Egypt, in 892 and died in Sura, Mesopotamia, in 942. The tenth chapter of his *Book of Doctrines and Beliefs* (933), a book famous among both Jews and Arabs, contains an important paragraph on music; and as Sa'adyah's teachings exerted a great influence on all centers of Jewish learning, it must be surmised that his musical aesthetics was as widely discussed as his religious philosophy. An interesting feature is the absence in Sa'adyah's writings of a discussion of the problem that very much occupied the minds of scholars in Spain—the admissibility of music in the cult; it has been deduced that in contrast to other Jewish centers, the Babylonian Jewish community, by far the oldest community in the Jewish Diaspora, had raised no objection to music. Sa'adyah's paragraph on music deals with the influence of music on the mind and is part of a general discussion of the effects of sensual impressions—seeing, hearing, smelling—on the human soul. In the sphere of seeing and smelling Sa'adyah expresses the opinion (in the footsteps of Al-Kindi, the great Arab philosopher before him) that single colors or aromas cannot produce a beneficial effect on the soul, whereas a combination of colors or perfumes pleases the senses and stimulates the soul. The same argument is applied with regard to music, where also only the mixture of colors can exert a beneficial influence on soul and character.

Sa'adyah's paragraph on music has long puzzled scholars, as it has come down to us in a number of divergent copies and translations. But a thorough investigation of the different versions has led Dr. Farmer (op. cit., see footnote 2) to demonstrate that Sa'adyah's interest centers round the rhyth-

---

[4]For a survey of theories and practices in early western chant and an attempt to reassess the scope of eastern influence on the western musical history, see Shai Burstyn, "The Arabian Influence Thesis Revisited," *Current Musicology* 45/47, Festschrift for Ernst Sanders, New York, 1990, pp. 119–146. See also *Basler Jahrbuch für historische Musikpraxis,* Vol. 1, ed. Wulf Arlt, 1977, with treatises by different scholars. Burstyn's study includes an extensive bibliography.

mic and not the melodic modes, as was hitherto thought. and that he spoke, therefore, in favor of a mixture of "rhythmic colors." This is most important for the history of musical theory, as in ancient Oriental music the rhythmical—like the melodic—practice had not been theoretically systematized. The prominence of rhythmical questions is due to the rise of poetry built on metrical verses—a concept foreign to ancient Hebrew poetry—and it is only natural that the philosophy of music as well as the theory of rhythm should have been taken over by the Jews from the Arabs, whose poetry had actually inspired their own hymns and songs. Not only Sa'adyah, who is much indebted to Al-Kindi, but all the scholars who then flourished in the Spanish centers based their theory on Arab writings and actually recommended Greek and Arab texts to their disciples and readers for study—and theory, of course, is but a mirror of factual practice. Yussuf ibn 'Aknin (died 1226) copied for his teachings on music almost half of the theoretical writings of the greatest Arab theoretician, Al-Farabi, and the echoes of Arabic theory resound in all textbooks of the Jewish world. But with the continuous increase in the circulation of Hebrew writings, the Spanish Jews preferred to base their speculations on Jewish authors—even if those had originally derived their knowledge from Arab sources; among the best-known writers on music, apart form those already mentioned, were Abraham bar-Chiyah (died ca. 1136), Yehuda ben Shmuel ibn 'Abbas, and Shem Tow ben Yosef ben Palakera (both thirteenth century), Immanuel ben Shlomoh, the Italian-Jewish poet of the fourteenth century, and the cabalist Abraham ben Yizhaq of Granada (fourteenth century). The Hebrew theory of music remained dependent on Arab models much longer than other branches of science, in which original traits can be found at a comparatively earlier time; the Greek influence is also strong and can be explained both by direct contact and by the Greek elements in Arab philosophy.

In addition to the musico-theoretical writings in Arabic or Hebrew, there was one important Jewish contribution to musical theory which was written in Latin; this is the *De numeris harmonicis* (1343) of Magister Leo Hebraeus or Gersonides, whose real name was Levi ben Gershon (died 1344). The treatise was written at the suggestion of Philip de Vitry, one of the most outstanding European poets, composers, and theoreticians of the time, the pioneer of the *ars nova* movement in France. It is significant that rhythmic changes should be among the dominating elements of the new music superseding the "old art."[5] The last contribution of medieval Jewish scholars to musical theory dates from the end of the fourteenth or the beginning of the fifteenth century. It is contained in a fragment found at Genizah near Cairo, written in Hebrew characters but in Arabic language; it most probably constitutes a copy from an Arab compendium of science and the arts. The story of musical theory shows the Jews in the Middle Ages as active in the fields of science and philosophy as they were destined to become in more modern times; while enjoying the blessings of a flourishing civilization in medieval Spain, they slowly prepared the ground for independent thinking. In the degree to which they developed their thought and philosophy, they must surely also have shown traits of their own in the field of living music proper; but here again—just as in the most ancient history of Israel—no actual notation and description have come down to us, and we must rely on comparisons and speculation if we want to get an idea of the music sung and played by the Jewish musicians at the Spanish courts and by the singers and instrumentalists interpreting the poems of the time.

IN ORDER to appreciate the changes brought about in Hebrew music by the impact of the Islamic world, we have only to look at the development in the precentor's position. Not only had the hazan meanwhile gained the status of an accomplished master of his craft whose name was handed down to posterity and whose achievements were marveled at both by his own community and by people in remote places, but he had also assumed other than purely liturgical functions. The hazan of the Middle Ages was poet, singer, and composer, and in the course of the centuries he was also given the task of entertaining the community on the Sabbath when no work was being done. The many-sidedness of his office and his cultivation of many talents put him in the same rank with the Arab singer (*shu'ar*), the French troubadour, and the later German minnesinger; the art of all these poet-singer-player-composers was indeed nursed by one common source—the (Arab, Greek, and Jewish) Near East. When in our own days we can note an astounding similarity in melodies sung in eastern communities, in certain

---

[5]See Eric Werner and Isaiah Sonne, op. cit., 2nd part, 1942–1943.

Balkan regions, and in districts of southern France, as well as those noted down in medieval troubadour manuscripts, we can imagine how great was the effect of the eastern Mediterranean lyric song on the western world; moreover, we can divine the character of the melodies composed by the medieval Jewish *paytanim* (the creators of Jewish religious poetry).

There is evidence that Jewish singers based their songs on melodies borrowed or adapted from foreign sources; it is expressly stated in some Judeo-Spanish prayers that they are to be sung "to an Arabic tune," and in other cases Spanish popular songs are indicated as tunes for synagogal hymns. But the paytanim also composed melodies of their own, many of which have remained in favor down to our own day; we are not quite sure, however, whether the tunes that have come down to us were entirely their own creation, and it is also difficult to determine to what extent these were adapted and changed by later generations. An important figure among the early precentors and hazanim is Rabbi Yehuda Ga'on, who lived in the eighth century and who seems to have codified Jewish musical tradition as well as introduced new hymns into the synagogue service;[6] the introduction of the Kol Nidre prayer for the Day of Atonement is ascribed to this sage; the tune familiarized through the arrangements by nineteenth-century composers is a compilation—containing only a few archaic elements—of a much later, Ashkenazic origin, while in Sephardic synagogues an ancient (perhaps medieval) version is still employed. Famous examples of later piyutim are *Ata Hu Eloheinu* and *Ein Kamocha,* by Meshulam ben Kalonymos (ca. 1100), *Adon Olam,* by Salomon ibn Gabirol (eleventh century), *Yigdal,* by Daniel ben Yuda (thirteenth century). The *Selichot* (prayers of penitence) were also created by paytanim; they go back to the sixth century, but no names of their poets and composers have come down to us.

The art of the paytanim, among whom was included the genius Yehuda Ha-Levi, flourished down to the fifteenth century, though the conditions of life had in the meantime changed for the Jews once again. They created Sabbath songs (*Zemirot*), the songs for the Seder service on the eve of Passover (with the exception of the ancient and traditional *Hallel*), and

---

[6]See Eric Werner, "The Doxology in Synagogue and Church, A Liturgico-Musical Study," *Hebrew Union College Annual,* 1945–1946.

later songs for the Hanukka and Purim feasts, and for the ceremonies of circumcision and wedding—most of them still in use today. The last poet-singers whose melodies were popular and well known throughout the Jewish world were three Palestinians of the sixteenth century: Solomon Alkabetz, author of the popular Sabbath hymn "L'cha dodi"; Isaac Luria, who wrote cabalist songs—in the Aramaic language—which achieved great popularity in the Hassidic movement; and Israel Najara, who published in 1587, in Safed, the first songbook ever printed in the Orient (*Zemirot Yisrael*). Najara's song collection—reprinted later in Venice—is arranged after the pattern of an Arabic *Divan*: the songs are grouped according to the tunes used for them. The origin of many of his melodies is Arabic, Greek, Turkish, and Spanish; but the collection of foreign tunes—to which Najara added many of his own creations—shows the Jewish spirit at work, for even the songs most popular in character were adapted to suit the style of synagogal hymns. Israel Najara was the last poet, hazan, and composer in the direct succession of the paytanim, who created their religious-lyrical songs in Hebrew for use in the houses of worship and introduced poetry, beauty, and lively rhythm into a service that had become stilted and was lacking in creative force.[7]

In the golden age of Jewish poetry and music in the Spanish centers, we also find a number of Jewish musicians at the Islamic and Christian courts, where they seem to have undergone the same process of emancipation that became typical for western European Jewry in the nineteenth century. The eminent Spanish scholar and the most prominent expert on music in the Iberian world, the late Msgr. Iginio Anglès, wrote in 1968 that "the circumstance that Jewish communities existed in Spain for so many centuries . . . until 1492 should be regarded as a boon to the development of music in the Iberian peninsula."[8] A large number of Jews settled on the Mediterranean coast of Spain and on the Balearic Islands; Taragona, Toledo, and Il-

---

[7]See A. Z. Idelsohn, *Thesaurus of Hebrew Oriental Melodies,* Vol. 4.

[8]Msgr. Anglès, who died in 1969 at the age of almost 82 years, contributed the article, "Jewish Music in Medieval Spain," to *Yuval: Studies of the Jewish Music Research Centre,* Vol. 1, Jerusalem, 1968. It is published (in English) in *Contributions to a Historical Study of Jewish Music,* ed. Eric Werner, New York, 1976, pp. 207–227. Our following summary is based mainly on this scholar's studies.

liberis (Elvira) near Granada had especially sizable Jewish populations. The Council of Elvira (300–303) placed a ban on the intermarriage of Jews and Christians—which shows that such marriages were taking place—but until the sixth century Jews are known to have participated in Christian religious ceremonies and liturgical rites, and there seem to have been exchanges of music between the Christians and the Jews prior to the Arab invasion. During the period of the Arab domination of Spain, the Jews made "signal contributions" (Anglès) to the development of Moslem culture; in their own poetry, on the other hand, they imitated the technique and forms of Arabic literature. The Jews rejoiced when the Arabs invaded Spain; the pre-Moslem rulers, the Visigoth monarchs, had cruelly persecuted them. The Jews sided with the Moslem rulers and became very influential advisers, scientists, and artists at the Andalusian courts of Granada and Cordova. At the same time, the Christian kings of Castile and Aragon respected their Jewish citizens; the scientific and artistic talents of the Jews were held in high esteem by the Christian kings. The period between 900 and 1400 was marked by singular creative productivity in the field of Hebrew religious poetry of hymnodic character and neo-Platonic philosophy. The highest points of development were reached during the Cordova Caliphate in the days of Abd er-Rahman III (912–961) and Al-Chakam II (961–972) and the centuries following them, while in music the groundwork for a flourishing new art had been laid a century before them by the cooperation of a prominent Moslem musician, Ziryāb, and his Jewish friend Al-Mansūr.

Musical settings for the liturgical and secular chants of the Jews of that time seem not to have survived, but theoretically we know what they must have been like. The liturgy of the synagogue took over rhythmic-metrical elements from Hebrew and Arabic rhythmical and metrical poetry. Proof of this development is found in the writings of Hai Ga'on, Isaac Alfasi, and Judah of Barcelona (early eleventh century) and of Maimonides (a century later), who protested against the "new trend" of a chanting of poetry in the synagogue to Arabic tunes.

The relationship among Christians, Jews, and Arabs is explicitly described in a document entitled "Chronica Aldefonsi Imperatoris," written after the triumphal entry of Alphonso VII, King of Castile and Leon, into the city of Toledo in 1147:

All the princes among the Christians, the Saracens, and the Jews, and the entire population of the state went out of the city a long distance to meet him, with timbrels and lyres and psalteries and all kinds of musicians, each according to his language, praising and glorifying God because He had granted prosperity to all the Acts of the Emperor.[9]

The Church tolerated at that time sacred Jewish and Arabic music in divine service, even at Mass. In 1458 six Jewish rabbis intoned funeral chants in a public place before the catafalque of Alphonso V, King of Aragon and Naples, and dirges especially written for the occasion were sung by Jewish wailing women—the memorial service of the Christian mourners had taken place before in the Church of Cervera in Catalonia. But at the same time, while Arabic and Jewish sacred music entered the Church, the Church authorities abhorred the secular music of "the Jews and Saracens . . . these real infidels, who make much noise with their voices and with Heaven knows what instruments."[10] The organ was the sole musical instrument permitted in the Christian liturgy of medieval Spain.

The names of many prominent Jewish musicians, composers, and music theoreticians have survived from as early as the year 822 C.E., but no actual noted music has been preserved—or, at least, it has not been found so far. The earliest known Jewish musician at a Spanish court is Al-Mansūr al-Yahudi, court musician of Sultan Al-Chakam I (796–822) and of his successor Sultan Abd ar-Rahman II (822–852), son of Al-Chakam. Both rulers were generous patrons of science and the arts and did much to foster the cultivation of music in Arabic Spain.

One of the most famous and esteemed Arab musicians was Ziryāb, who came to Cordova from Bagdad in 822. Ziryāb and his family are regarded as founders of a distinct Hispano-Arabic school of music, and it can be taken for certain that he closely cooperated with his Jewish friend Al-Mansūr.[11] Al-Mansūr al-Yahudi was chosen by the Sultan to prepare a fes-

[9]E. Florex, *España Sagnada*, Vol. 21, Madrid, 1766, p. 379, quoted in Anglès, "Jewish Music in Medieval Spain," in *Contributions,* op. cit.; see footnote 8, above.

[10]The Council of Vallodolid, 1322, quoted by Anglès in *Contributions,* p. 212.

[11]On Ziryāb see E. Lévi-Provencal, *La Civilisation arabe en Espagne,* Paris, 1961, pp. 69–74; H. G. Farmer, *Encyclopédie de l'Islam,* supplément, 1938, pp. 285–286; Gilbert Chase, *The Music of Spain,* New York, 1959, pp. 25–26; Simon Jargy, "La musique arabe," *Que sais-je?,* No. 1436, Paris, 1971, pp. 46 ff.

tive reception for Ziryāb at Algeciras. It is even believed that Al-Mansūr had been responsible for asking the Sultan to invite Ziryāb to his court. Ziryāb's real name was Abu 'l-Hasan Ali abn Nafi, and he was nicknamed "Ziryāb" because of his very bronzed complexion—Arabic ichab = brownish. He was born in Mesopotamia in 789 and had to leave Bagdad hurriedly for surpassing his famed teacher Ishak al-Mawsili at the court of Harun ar-Rashīd; he feared for his life because of the teacher's jealousy. After a short stay in Cairo, he accepted the invitation of the Andalusian court. Ziryāb's excellent musical training and outstanding talents and his friendship with the prominent and influential Jewish musician, whom the Arabs called Abu 'n-Nasr Mansur, went a long way toward establishing an exchange of ideas, of musical knowledge, and of music proper between the Islamic and Jewish musical world.

Ziryāb, on whom the Sultan showered invaluable presents and who became legendarily rich, opened a music school in Cordova where he taught the foundations of Oriental theory and vocal and instrumental music. He also introduced new instruments (such as the five-string lute, to replace the earlier three-string lute, also of Near Eastern origin), new melodies, and new styles that were of a lasting influence in Spain. It is said that he also taught the people of Cordova how to dress, how to cook, and how to live an elegant life. He even opened a beauty salon. He had eight sons and two daughters, all of whom became musicians and further developed his musical style and techniques. Ziryāb, who was called in his time "the singing nightingale," died in Cordova in 857. His songs were collected by one of his sons-in-law, Aslam ibn Al-'Aziz; his vocal training techniques are described in books of Arab historians between the eleventh and seventeenth centuries.

A later Jewish musician whose name has come down to us was the virtuoso Yizhak ibn Sim'an, who was well known in Cordova in the eleventh century. At the end of the eleventh century a Jew named Dani is reported to have conducted an orchestra and to have held his audience spellbound at a festival in Toledo. At approximately the same time Ibrahim ibn al-Fahâr, a Jew, was court musician, envoy, and confidant of the king, in Toledo during the reign of the Christian King Alfonso VI. A Jew known by the name of Ismael was a musician and "juggler" at the court of King San-cho IV of Castile, who reigned in the years 1293–94; Ismael was known for his performances with his wife, fifteen Moors, and thirteen Christians. The juggler, *juglar* in Spanish (*jongleur* in French), was the main propagator of secular music in the Middle Ages. The male juggler was interpreter only and not necessarily a composer,[12] while the female musician, the *juglaresa* or *juglara*, sang, played, and danced, not only for the kings and nobles, but also for the amusement of the people. Women as well as men are depicted on medieval miniatures, with their instruments, especially in the *Cantigas de Santa Maria* attributed to but possibly not written by King Alphonso X of Castile and León (1221–1284) "el Sabio" (the Wise), and in the Portuguese early fourteenth century "Cancioneiro da Ajuda." Among the jugglers were a considerable number of Jewish men, Jewish (and Arab) female singers, and Christians. Their repertory included pieces on Jewish themes; in the *Cantigas* can be found, according to Anglès, "historical and legendary data centering around Jewish figures . . ." (for instance *Cantiga* 107, which recalls the tale of the renowned Jewess Marisaldos, "the heroine of Segovia").[13] Alphonso employed Jews at the academies of Toledo, Sevilla, and Murcia, and wanted—as the *Cantigas* show—Jews to take part, along with Arab and Christian musicians, in performing the hymns to Maria, "the Blessed Virgin." Yet Anglès has found no traces of Near Eastern melodies of Arab or Jewish origin as sung all over the Spanish-Portuguese peninsula; some six hundred foreign jugglers, cantors, and organists must have been active in Aragon and Catalonia during the fourteenth century, and must have contributed to the colorful musical scene of the Iberian world. The music of this region constituted a major influence in the western world of liturgy and musical poetry, with a marked Jewish contribution constituting at least one important part.

When the Jews were expelled from Spain in 1492, their singers and musicians from synagogue and secular feasts took with them melodies and instruments that had been shaped in the Arabic-Hebrew-Christian-Iberian centuries of outstanding multicultural, scientific, and artistic achievements of this multicolored world. A clearly discernible substratum of Iberian

---

[12]See Gilbert Chase, op. cit., see footnote 11, above, pp. 33–36.

[13]See Anglès, *Jewish Music in Medieval Spain*, pp. 218–219.

music has been faithfully preserved in the *Romancero* and the songs of the Sephardim, the religious chants and the Spanish metrical romances.

A universally known remnant of ancient Iberian musical tradition is the *cante jondo* (or *cante hondo*), literally translated as "deep song." To this day this form inspires Spanish and non-Spanish composers in their musical works and singers and instrumentalists to create their colorful variations. It is most probably the oldest—and remains the most characteristic—type of Andalusian folk song and clearly shows Near Eastern melodic traits, such as the distinct use of microtone intervals, frequent sliding from one note to another in singing, and the insistent repetition of tones, usually accompanied by appoggiaturas from above and below. This repetition produces the effect of an incantation, as in the earliest known ritual dances and songs.[14] Msgr. Anglès is skeptical regarding a theory put forward by the Spanish scholar Máximo José Kahn (Medina Azara)—who for some time served as Spanish ambassador to Greece—that the *cante jondo* was once a solemn chant of the Jews, for it shows obvious similarities to early synagogal chant. Other scholars speak of Byzantine–Near Eastern roots. Máximo José Kahn claims that the term *cante jondo* is a Spanish bowdlerization of the Hebrew *yom-tov* = Holy Day. Kahn supposes that flamenco songs were originally sung by Spanish Jews who had to hide their Jewish identity at the time of the Inquisition. He suggests that they called these songs flamenco to give the impression their singers were Flemish (*flamenco* means Flame or Flemish in Castilian Spanish; Flanders is "Flandes"). The ornate melodic embellishments reflect emotional eagerness to express the religious exuberance elicited by the words of the prayer. These embellishments point to a Near Eastern origin—possibly but not proven to be Hebrew.[15]

---

[14]Gilbert Chase, op. cit., devotes an illuminating chapter to the *cante jondo*, pp. 224–226.

[15]Máximo José Kahn, "Chant populaire Andalou et Musique Synagogale," in *Cahiers d'Art*, Nos. 5–10, Paris, 1939; published earlier in *Rivista de Occidente*, 8, 1930.

Manuel de Falla, various publications, the very first printed anonymously: "El Noticiero Granadino," February 1922; "El Defensor," Granada, April 2, 1932; three essays published in Sevilla in April, March 1932 in *ABC*, *El Liberal*, and *El Noticiero*.

The poet and literary scholar Federico García Lorca and his music teacher Falla collaborated on lectures and publications tracing the history and the charac-

IN MUSLIM SPAIN musicians in a king's or sultan's service and some of the well-educated Jews of their courts could travel freely in the Spanish realm and abroad. Thus even before the fifteenth-century reconquest and the expulsion of Jews and Arabs, the highly developed Hispanic-Islamic-Hebrew culture spread to many European countries. Here a lyrical poetry sprang into being under the impact of Near Eastern poems and songs. Already then—and to an ever-increasing degree after 1492—the Jews once again became trade agents and mediators of civilization, carrying the Spanish–Near Eastern culture to remote places on their missions. The knightly singers and musicians derived inspiration from the flowery language and the lyrical-metrical music of their Oriental prototypes; just as the metrical verses of the Arab hymns had helped the Jewish paytanim to enliven the service in the houses of worship and to introduce new elements into the traditional cult, thus there now rose in the Christian countries of Europe a new popular art that was to exert a far-reaching influence on liturgical practice. The "new art," supported by the treatise of Gersonides, the Jewish theoretician, received its main impulse from the popular rhythmical song; only as a consequence of its reforms did European art begin its soaring flight to sublime heights. It achieved the supreme synthesis between the spiritual and the purely artistic and popular—the synthesis denied to the Jews, who soon had to suffer the destruction of yet another center of their cultural activities.

IN ORDER to follow the succession of paytanim down to their last representatives in the medieval world, we have far transgressed the boundaries of place and time set for this chapter. For in the fifteenth century great changes again occurred in the political power spheres of the East as well as of the West, and the Jews—victims of other nations' political fate from the destruction of the Temple till modern times—were greatly affected by them. In the East Constantinople fell to the Turks in 1453, and in the West the Arabs were finally driven from Spain in 1492—the year Columbus discov-

---

teristics of the Andalusian song. Lorca added an essay on the *cante jondo* to his "Poema del Canto Jondo," 1931. For a German translation entitled "Dichtung vom tiefinnern Sang," the translator and editor, Enrique Beck, wrote a Postscript and explanatory notes; there he also quoted and commented upon the theories of Máximo José Kahn (Insel-Verlag, Zweigstelle Wiesbaden, 1956).

ered the New World. The Turkish conquest put an end to the eastern Roman or Byzantine Empire once and for all and thus expelled western influence from the lands of the Orient; the expulsion of the Arabs from Spain dispossessed the Orient of its powerful stronghold in the West. The Jews were driven from Spain—together with their Arab brethren—and sought havens in the countries of western, central, and southern Europe; their prospering cultural centers were destroyed, and once again they could save only their spiritual possessions. The Sephardim—descendants of the Spanish Jews who were able to escape the massacres of Spain—established their communities and continued to cultivate their old traditions in new European centers; large numbers also followed the Arabs back to the East and settled in the countries from which their forefathers had once set out with Islam to conquer Europe. In the Turkish empire Jewish tradition was continued by the Oriental as well as the newly migrated Sephardic communities—a mixture that was to produce characteristic features of its own.

A subject that still awaits more extensive scholarly investigation is the musical practice of the Marranos—the Jews who pretended to have been converted to Christianity but had never really embraced it. It has often been stated that the Marranos had no liturgy of their own before the Jewish expulsion from Spain, but a number of manuscripts have come to light to show that the secret Spanish Jews had actually developed their own liturgical practice. Eric Werner has made accessible one such manuscript out of a dozen which are known to exist but which have not been published so far;[16] this is a three-part motet for cantus, tenor, and contratenor written about 1450 in northern Spanish notation. The text of this motet contains words in different languages—Hebrew, Spanish, Arabic, and a number of unidentified, probably corrupted words—and this has been taken to show that the text is written in a semisecret code of the Marrano Jews, to camouflage Hebrew liturgical texts before the dreaded Inquisition. The music is composed of three different tunes; the cantus sings the ancient Ashkenazic tune of the preamble of the Kedusha for the high holy days; the tenor

---

[16]See Eric Werner, "The Oldest Sources of Synagogal Chant," *Proceedings of the American Academy for Jewish Research*, Vol. 16, 1947, pp. 228 ff. See also illustration on p. 124.

Dr. Eric Werner's transcription of a Spanish-Jewish
manuscript of the thirteenth century, a three-part Kedusha
motet.

seems to imitate the shofar signals; the contratenor has the tune of the Gregorian hymn "Alma redemptoris mater." The skill of the composer in combining this material is remarkable; if the remaining manuscripts are of a similar character we could well presume a high standard of composition among the Spanish Jewish musicians. Whether or not the piece was actually written in northern Spain—which might have meant death for the scribe—or belongs to a slightly later period in a north Italian center (a theory advanced by Rabbi D. A. Jessurun Cardozo[17]), this curious piece represents an early example of an art later developed by the Mantua school of Jewish musicians headed by Leone da Modena and Salomone Rossi; the Marranos undoubtedly carried with them the tradition of their liturgical practice.

----

[17]See Werner, "The Oldest Sources," op. cit.

ONE BLOW set an end to a magnificent chapter in Jewish civilization—a chapter that never found a real continuation. The history of the Jewish people and of their culture, art, and music characteristically never continues in one place for more than a certain period of time; but while one flourishing center is cut off and destroyed, another has already risen into importance and developed interesting traits. The history of the music of Israel continues in another Mediterranean country about a century after the expulsion of the Jews from Spain; it is there that Jewish composers created the first art music that became of importance for their own—spiritual—sphere as well as for the general development of musical art. But before turning to the music of the Renaissance period in Italy, we shall have to survey the state of music in the Jewish settlements of medieval Europe.

CHAPTER FIVE

JEWS IN MEDIEVAL EUROPE

I N THE SPANISH CENTER under Islamic rule, conditions were most favorable for a prospering Jewish community and culture, as the Jews could take part in the economic and cultural life of the ruling nation. In the central European countries, however, they were completely cut off from such participation. This was a matter of seclusion rather than suppression: the Jews enjoyed freedom of movement and trade—especially in southern France and in Germany—with only temporary violations of their peace through persecution of individuals or communities. Even the Crusades, which resulted periodically in horrible oppression and massacre of the Jews, were over by the end of the thirteenth century, and the Jews were again able to enjoy a life of comparative peace. But the Catholic Church, which had completed the first phase of its cultural development toward the end of the first millennium, was the spiritual center of all Europe in the Middle Ages. As a result the Jews were excluded from all phases of life that centered in the church. They lived together within the sphere of their own community and took no part in the life of the Christians and in their economic, social, political, cultural, and artistic activities, which were all directed by the omnipotent Church of Rome.

The conditions of Jewish life in the central European countries offered no foundations for cultural development or for the creation of poetry and music such as the Jews were able to contribute in the Spanish sphere. At the same time European musical art reached its first great synthesis. In the eleventh and twelfth centuries France was the great musical center, and the masters of Notre Dame de Paris created musical forms equaling the Gothic architectural design and style in purpose and character. The liturgical chant was enriched by the addition of a second, a third, and a fourth polyphonic voice—invented and constructed with much care by a composer and not improvised on the spur of the moment; the liturgical melodies thus lost their real inner connection with the ancient Hebrew chant. In the fourteenth century there arose a "new music," full of individualistic traits and taking over the emphasis of rhythm from popular art and Near Eastern dance songs; with this "new music" art emancipated itself from the realm of the Church, but since it became the art of the higher strata of society, it was as inaccessible to the Jews as was the clerical art. In the fifteenth century the musical hegemony passed from Paris to Burgundy and to the Netherlands, where grandiose religious musical works were created by masters who are among the greatest in musical history. Secular music—though cultivated in an always increasing measure by the composers who now stepped out of anonymity and were widely acclaimed—did not as yet achieve complete independence from clerical forms; the final emancipation was reserved to Renaissance Italy. Almost the only representatives of profane singing and playing throughout the history of medieval music remained the (mostly anonymous) successors of the wandering minstrel, troubadour, and minnesinger, whose kinship with the Oriental musicians has been found to be uncontestable.

As long as great music could grow only in the realm of the Church or was cultivated by composers who were men of the cloth, the Jews had no place in the development of this art; it seems that the only Jewish personality who stepped into the sphere of nobility met with eventual failure. Characteristically it was a minnesinger who achieved temporary fame outside his own community; his picture can be found in the illuminated manuscript prepared about 1300 and kept in the Heidelberg Library as a most important source for the German minnesong. The picture shows a Jew with a long beard and a broad-brimmed hat, standing beside a nobleman and a clergyman; his name is given as "Süsskind, the Jew of Trimberg." Of the twelve poems attributed to him, six have been proved to be genuine; of his life very little is known, and his poems—and this must also be true of his melodies, none of which have come down to us—seem at first sight to differ very little from the songs of other poets of the time. A more thorough study of the poems shows, however, that many of the verses derive from phrases or lines of the Bible or Talmud and that some passages were even taken from Jewish prayers; and this minnesinger sings in praise of the perfect wife, whereas the German poet would have sung of a noble lady or of the Virgin Mary.[1]

This minnesinger seems to have been a solitary exception in the medieval world. But the existence of Jewish wandering minstrels (*Spielleute*) is documented by various extant works, such as an epic entitled *Gudrun,* written in Hebrew characters, and an "Abraham" epic, which contains performance directions for reading "in the tone of the book of Samuel" (*beniggun Shmuel-buch; Shmuelbuch* is of course, Yiddish).[2] This book is a Judeo-German paraphrase of the biblical books of Samuel and Kings published in Augsburg, Germany, in 1544. It is written in the meter and stanza of the German *Nibelungenlied* and was probably melodically recited to popularly known tunes. This practice must have become popular at the time, judging from the response of Rabbi Jacob ha-levi ben Moshe Mollin, called Maharil, rabbi in Mayence (Mainz), Germany (1358–1427), who demanded the faithful preservation of the tunes of pure Jewish tradition and prohibited the singing of religious texts in Judeo-German jargon. The first collection of popular Yiddish songs was published by Eisik (Isaac) Wal(l)ich in Worms, Germany, 1595–1605. Most tunes were of German origin, but they were printed with the texts in Hebrew letters; others were traditionally

---

[1] The Jewish identity of Süsskind has been challenged by some scholars on various grounds.

[2] See Eric Werner, *A Voice Still Heard: The Sacred Songs of the Ashkenazic Jews,* University Park and London, 1976, pp. 21–22; Peter Gradenwitz "Zu Herkunft, Charakter und Verbreitung der Jiddischen Volkslieder," in *Zeitschrift für Deutsche Philologie,* 100. Band, 1981, pp. 232–253; Peter Gradenwitz, "Die schönsten jiddischen Liebeslieder," Dreieich, 1988, in the foreword, pp. 9–22.

"Susskind, the Jew of Trimberg," and a page of his songs. (From the Manessian manuscript of the thirteenth century, preserved at Heidelberg, Germany.)

Jewish or were Yiddish transformations of German models. The first collection of German polyphonic secular songs was at least partly written by a probably Jewish scribe, Wölflin von Lochheim; this important source for German musical history, compiled ca. 1450, bears the scribe's dedication to his wife Barbara, written in Hebrew characters.[3]

AS THE JEWS were given no chance to partake actively in the literature, art, and music of Medieval Europe, they concentrated on developing their own religious and home life. Though not always enclosed by the walls of a ghetto, they lived a life of seclusion within their own communities and disdained all foreign influence on their mode of living and their customs. Especially in periods of persecution, they always escaped into their own domain: the study of Bible and Talmud, which recalled in their minds the echo of Israel's magnificent past and inspired them with hope for a brighter future. The dilemma between reason and heart—which figured so prominently in the theological discussions on Spanish soil—was before the Jews here as everywhere: it was decided in favor of the heart when in the thirteenth century the *cabbalah* was created in southern France and in Germany out of a desire to give free rein to emotional religious experience without the reasoning control of the talmudic laws. Oriental mysticism and an unbridled emotional expression characterized the world of the cabbalah, which later became instrumental in forming the thoughts and emotions of the Hassidim and found expression in prayers, in literature, and in music alike.

The spiritual centers of Jewry during the period just discussed were the settlements in southern France and in southern Germany—provinces where Jewish communities are known to have been in existence in the earliest centuries of the Common Era. In the Provence and in the Rhenish cities the Jewish settlements prospered, and with the expulsion of the Jews from England (1290), Spain (1492), and Portugal (1497), a new influx swelled the French and German communities. It is thus that the Ashkenazim (as the western, especially German, Jews had been called since the early Middle

---

[3]On the "Locham Song-Book" see Walter Salmen, *Das Lochheimer Liederbuch,* Leipzig, 1951.

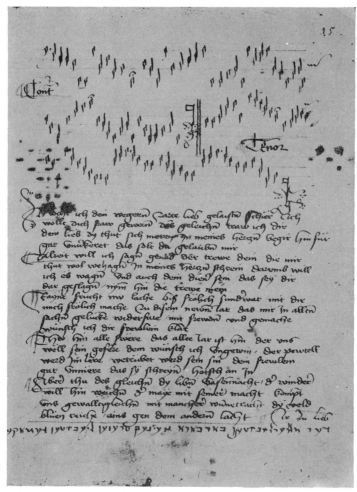

A page from the Lochheim Songbook, written by Wölflin von Lochheim, ca. 1450, with the dedication in Hebrew characters in the last line.

Ages—with reference to a passage in Gen. 10:3: "Ashkenaz, son of Gomer") rose to a prominent position with the destruction of the Sephardic center; with the later migration eastward and the resettlement in central Europe, Ashkenazic Jewry amounted to more than 90 per cent of the total number of Jews, and its language—derived from middle high German and spiced with words and phrases from Hebrew—became the universal language of the Diaspora Jews. It is comprehensible that customs and manners as well as the forms of worship, the regulation of life, and the singing of the Ashkenazic Jews in the synagogue and in the home should have become universal in the medieval Jewish world.

Life in the Jewish communities at that time must have been many-colored, for it seemed greatly attractive to the Gentiles. The fact that from the earliest centuries of Jewish settlement in the European countries kings and bishops vied with each other in forbidding the Christians to celebrate the Sabbath together with Jews, to adopt Jewish songs, and to waste time in studying the Hebrew language and writings, certainly suggests that this was exactly what the Christians liked to do. The Jews, on the other hand, prohibited the use of Christian music, which, owing to the highly developed and distinctive forms and styles, threatened to overwhelm synagogal chant. The Jewish authorities in medieval Europe were confronted with the same situation as that which had characterized the Hellenistic period; they had to isolate Jewish communal life in order to preserve the fundamental character of Judaism and thus were forced to prohibit the influx of foreign tunes which could pollute the traditional chant. But the authorities could arrest the course of events as little as their forefathers had been able to do at the time of Greek political and cultural supremacy; the songs of worship and prayer of medieval Europe exerted their influence on Jewish musical custom, and the Jews could not escape the impact of popular song which they heard everywhere in the streets. Many folk songs of Provence and of German origin crept into the synagogue, but there they gradually lost their popular character and were adapted and transformed to suit the spirit of the occasions.

But the influx of folk music into the synagogue song—paralleled by an increasing influence of popular song on the church service—is only one aspect of music in the Ashkenazic sphere; the Ashkenazic song developed other traits that gave it a specific character of its own and distinguished it from music in the Sephardic and Oriental spheres. European music had in the meantime departed from the practice of absolute polyphony based on the ancient ecclesiastic scales, drawing nearer to the modern conception of harmony. The changes in the character of European music were mirrored, of course, in the development of the synagogue chant; the traditional chant preserved by the Jews from Oriental times gradually adapted its melodic lines under the impact of European song and, much later, also introduced polyphony and harmony. Another peculiarity of the Ashkenazic song was the custom of rabbis and hazanim to choose for each holy day in the Jewish year specific tunes believed to be especially suited to the occasion in mood and character; thus one and the same prayer was sung to different melodies in accordance with the day on which it was chanted. This custom has been preserved to this very day, though the tunes chosen are different in the various Ashkenazic communities.

The influence of Christian church music on Jewish singing was felt in the house as much as in the synagogue, all the more since no basic difference existed between synagogue and popular song. The synagogue was both house of worship and community center; and just as popular tunes were adapted for the synagogue service, so the most popular hymns were sung in the Jewish homes and on the occasion of feasts and celebrations. It seems plausible that the German folk song entered the Jewish sphere by way of the home and only from there found its way into the synagogue.

The more the Jews had to suffer under oppression and restriction, the more they were wont to cultivate their own spiritual possessions and the less they could be expected to have inspiration for creative efforts. Not even the hazan, whose importance in office could have led him to raise the standard of singing and composing, was given leisure to develop creative talents; for the dwindling of a community here and the rise of another there, the expulsion of Jews from one place and the establishment of new centers elsewhere made the hazan lead an unsettled life. He often changed his place of employment, and in order to be able to compete with singers who wanted to serve the more prosperous communities he concentrated on the artistic, virtuoso qualities of his singing rather than on the musical and creative side. Brilliant coloratura and great emphasis on the emotional attributes of prayer were his main concern, and the traditional chant suffered no little from his exhibitory and sometimes even ill-suited performance; his mannerisms became worse still with the triumphant rise of Italian opera in the seventeenth century.

The music of the Ashkenazic communities was adopted by the Jewry of the greater part of Europe when persecution of the Jews in Germany necessitated a new migration. The Ashkenazic Jews found in the countries of eastern Europe a Jewish community that differed greatly from their own in many respects. The early settlements of the East had considerably grown in the medieval epoch, when the Turkish Empire had received large numbers of Jews expelled from southern European countries; the Osmanic rule permitted them to prosper in Asia Minor as well as in eastern Europe. In the latter province the communities were largely made up of Near Eastern Jews; these communities grew to such an extent that as early as the thirteenth century the Poles granted them privilege and independent administrative facilities. Eastern Jewry was so strictly organized that it had very little contact with the outside world, and the influence of eastern European life on the Jews was therefore negligible. The influx of the Ashkenazic Jews which set in during the fourteenth century brought about considerable changes in the life of the eastern communities, which suddenly met with a Europeanized Jewish culture superior to theirs; the Slavonic dialects spoken by the eastern Jews gave way to the German-Jewish language, and the Oriental character of the synagogue service and of the melodies used for its prayers was greatly modified under the impact of Ashkenazic custom and song.

But the meeting of western and eastern Jewry by no means produced a one-sided picture. The Ashkenazic rite and song changed, too, and the art of the hazan especially was influenced by Oriental custom. The freely improvised melodic elaboration of the liturgical chant and a highly emotional style of singing characterized the Oriental as well as the Ashkenazic practice, but the eastern communities had retained the modal style and free recitation to a larger extent than the Ashkenazic precentors, whose song had taken over so much from German popular music. The eastern hazan had also preserved the many-sidedness of his office since the earliest times of the hazanuth and particularly since the period of the paytanim; he was the main bearer of the musical tradition and enriched the spiritual life of his congregation by his own hymns, poems, and musical settings. The mutual influence exerted by the western and eastern hazanim and their music led to extensive debates in rabbinical literature; the biblical passages on music and the talmudic comments were subjected to a new interpretation in the light of contemporary practice, and the merits of important or famous poets and hazanim were discussed in great detail. Where the art of the Ashkenazic hazanim had developed great virtuosity for its own sake, the character of eastern synagogue music had retained one important and fundamental feature of ancient Hebrew music: the shaping of the music and its performance in agreement with the content of the words sung. In order to give vent to their emotions, the eastern rabbis and hazanim revived a good many poems and hymns from the golden age of Hebrew poetry and song—many of which were unknown in the western sphere—while most German singers had been particularly concerned with variety in the brilliant musical interpretation of a popular hymn they especially favored. The synagogue of later times shows a synthesis of the diverging elements which was arrived at before the remigration of large numbers of Ashkenazic Jews into the western European countries.

WE CLOSE OUR SURVEY of Jewish music in medieval Europe with a short account of popular music in the ghetto, in which Jewish life was concentrated down to the age of assimilation in the eighteenth century. The Purim feast and the wedding were, just as they had been since time immemorial, the main occasions for general rejoicing and for extensive musical performances and folk plays. The Purim plays centered around the biblical figure of Esther. One is reported to have been performed in the ghetto of Venice in 1531, while the earliest preserved text of an "Esther" play was written by Lazaro Gratiano and Solomon Usque in Spain in 1567 (or possibly as early as 1559). In Frankfurt-Main, Germany, an *Ahasveros Spiel* (a play about Queen Esther's husband, King Ahasuerus) was published in 1708. Its music contained a serious tune that became very popular, later returning to accompany a lamentation on the conflagration of the Frankfurt Jewish Quarter (1771), written by David Saugers of Prague. A great many Purim plays are also recorded from later times.

In some districts the rabbis enforced in the medieval ghetto the talmudic prohibition of instrumental playing with such rigor that Christian musicians had to be employed to provide the music at the Jewish festivals. On the Sabbath, too, non-Jews came to play in the ghetto, but it was forbidden to invite them expressly to perform. Many centuries passed before the Jews began to take up instrumental playing themselves: in the sixteenth and seventeenth centuries Jewish music guilds were founded as documented in Frankfurt on the Main and in Prague.

The Jewish musicians were originally called "lezim" or "lezanim," a term found in the Talmud with reference to secular music ("the fiddle played by the lezim"): later they were also described as "badchanim," and this word is still used by eastern European Jews in the same sense. The repertoire of these popular musicians consisted of Judeo-Spanish, Judeo-Provençal, and Judeo-German melodies; their character as wandering minstrels—and the very word used to describe them (meaning jesters)—reminds us of the singing instrumentalists, the minstrels and jugglers of the earlier Middle Ages in Europe. The rabbis had no friendly word for them, but it cannot be denied that they played their own modest part in the preservation of Jewish tradition and created a typical Jewish folklore.

Though originally Jewish popular music had been derived from the folklore of the people among whom the Jews had been living, it was nevertheless considered strangely different by the Gentiles; this proves that the Jewish musicians changed the original melodies considerably in order to make them suit Jewish taste. As the lezim or badchanim played their music not only at the Jewish festivals but also at popular celebrations outside the ghetto, we find notices about it in different sources; in addition there have come down to us the descriptions and actual melodies of "Jews' Dances," in which non-Jews tried to imitate the manners and forms of Jewish dancing or to caricature the Jewish melodies that sounded so strange to Gentile ears. The "Jews' Dances," preserved in manuscripts in France, Germany, and elsewhere, are the first examples in a long series of musical parodies by non-Jews, such as are later found in an Augsburg song book of the eighteenth century, in the piece "Samuel Goldenberg and Schmuyle" contained in Mussorgsky's *Pictures at an Exhibition,* in Richard Strauss's opera *Salome,* and in other great musical works.

One traditional style of Jewish instrumental music performance has come down to modern times, even enjoying a veritable renaissance in Europe, in the Americas, and even in Israel—the art of the klezmer. The word *klezmer* is derived from the Hebrew *kle'i-zemer,* literally meaning instruments of song, and is used for musicians of the wandering minstrel, or juggler description of medieval centuries. Klezmerím (the plural of klezmer) appear in medieval Jewish and non-Jewish legends and stories, and in anti-Jewish anecdotes. In Austria "der Jud mit a geign" was a contemptuous figure, while in the Rhine-Main region of Germany and in some eastern cities, such as Breslau, Prague, and Budapest, the klezmerím were respected as professional musicians; they played not only at Jewish weddings, social events, and even in the synagogue, performing instrumental preludes and interludes in the service, but were asked by Gentile neighbors to provide music at their own festive gatherings. (In some places they were forbidden by the Church authorities to play at Christian festivities and even at Jewish weddings inside the ghetto; in Prague in 1741 their rights of performance were restored by the ruling archbishop.) In the sixteenth century some Jewish lutenists and harpists from northern Italy were applauded in Prague and Vienna. In addition to the lute and the harp, the klezmer's main instruments were the violin, flute, organ, and percussion, while in the eighteenth and nineteenth centuries the klezmerím excelled especially as players of the clarinet and the trumpet. The most famous klezmer known by name was Josef Guzikow (1806–1837), a Polish flautist and virtuoso on the dulcimer and xylophone.

In modern times the klezmer has been immortalized by Marc Chagall's paintings; his "Fiddler on the Roof" became the leading figure of the internationally performed and filmed American musical. In the late-twentieth-century hassidic, klezmer and soul music converged in the art of the world-renowned Israeli clarinetist Giora Feidman. A klezmer fiddler has been poetically depicted in the poem *Oif Mayn Chas'neh* (At My Wedding) by Yankev Yitzchok Segal. As he played an old tune, primitive and sad, "people were raised out of their seats . . . the fiddle kissed, tore, and bit, and went too far, and cut the taut heart-strings till they bled"; the klezmer spends his nights and days in small villages and plays at all-night Gentile drinking parties. He hardly sleeps, he hardly eats, he can barely read a line of Hebrew, but his playing is a miracle. Leonard Bernstein set the moving poem to music as No. 6 of his song cycle "Arias and Barcarolles" (1988), with the piano accompaniment imitating the fiddler's music.

Music emanating from the ghetto also included songs for folk plays, especially the Purim plays as well as those for the story of Joseph. The number of Jewish klezmer musicians grew greatly in the eighteenth and nineteenth centuries; even women were among them. Some five hundred Jewish instrumentalists and singers are said to have been in Constantinople then; in the European countries, klezmerím were seen to travel from one place to the other. In Prague there was established an entire guild of klezmerím, whose emblem was a violin. One important place of activities for various klezmer bands was the Leipzig Fair (famous since the end of the fifteenth century). Different groups played there while it lasted. It is a provoking thought to imagine Johann Sebastian Bach hearing their music: the Thomaskirche and Thomasschule, where he lived, played, taught, and composed, bordered on the marketplace where the Fair was held. The choirs of the Jews in his St. John Passion (Johannespassion) give an impression of sounding somewhat different from other choral passages in this work, in the St. Matthew Passion and the Mass in b-minor: could there be some influence here from "Jewish music" on the marketplace?[4]

OUR SURVEY of early Jewish music in the countries of western and eastern Europe outlines a development of many centuries and brings our story down to the seventeenth and eighteenth centuries—the period in which the "Jewish Middle Ages" came to an end, more than two hundred years after the European peoples had overcome medieval life and thought. The beginning of a new time for Europe was marked in the fifteenth century by liberation from the rigid rule of clerical authority—the foundation for a free development of science and art—while the discovery of new continents enlarged the outlook of trade and intercourse with the world; in that period the Jews had nothing but their spiritual mission and their religious life to seek refuge in while being chased from one domicile to another. Only in the course of the eighteenth century did conditions in Europe favor emancipation of the Jews and development of their spiritual and artistic qualities; but then it appeared that a specific Jewish culture could not grow without a national or spiritual center to guide them, as the creations of great Jews became possessions of the entire civilized world.

---

[4]The above is a personal view of the author. For literature on the klezmer see especially "Klezmer," in *The New Grove Dictionary of Music and Musicians*, Vol. 10 (Shlomoh Hofmann); A. Z. Idelsohn, *Jewish Music in Its Historical Development*, New York, 1929, pp. 433 ff., 455 ff.; Walter Salmen, "Das Bild vom Klezmer in Liedern und Erzählungen," in *"Dona Folcloristica," Festgabe für Lutz Röhrich*, Frankfurt/M., 1990, pp. 201–212; Walter Salmen, . . . *denn die Fiedel macht das Fest. Jüdische Musikanten und Tänzer vom 13–20 Jahrhundert*. Innsbruck, 1991.

The Hassidic movement, taking its spiritual roots from the mystic and sensuous world of the cabbalah, is the last creation of the Jewish Middle Ages; many of the "Zadikkím," the successors of its original founder, Israel Baal-Shem-Tov, granted singing and music a prominent place at their "courts." The depth of emotion and the pronounced sentimentality characterizing the Hassidic world are mirrored in the song of the Hassidim; not only the folk song but also the hazan's prayer tunes were greatly influenced by these elements, and their seemingly exotic coloring inspired many a Jewish and non-Jewish composer to serious musical works.

The Hassidim prospered at a time when western Jewry had just begun to seek entrance into the general culture of the period and to put an end to the secluded life the Jews had for so long been forced to lead. The period of enlightenment and reason that dawned upon the western world favored Jewish emancipation to a degree the Jews had not before experienced—or had experienced only for a short stretch of time in seventeenth-century Italy, a period that forms an important chapter in the history of general music as well as in that of the music of Israel.

CHAPTER SIX

JEWISH MUSICIANS IN RENAISSANCE

ITALY AND TUDOR ENGLAND

THE CONDITIONS of Jewish life in the Middle Ages sufficiently explain why the Jews had not been able to take part in the cultural activities of the people with whom they lived, and why they do not figure in the general history of medieval music. The music of medieval Europe was firmly rooted in the religious sphere, in the creed and belief uniting all Christian people and nations. The purpose, language, and style of the great religious music—composed on Latin liturgical and non-liturgical texts by all the masters—spread beyond the boundaries of states and nations, and it was understood by the entire Christian world.

While the great church music of the Middle Ages rose to the sublimest heights of perfection in the works of the Flemish masters—followed, in the Renaissance, by the Latin and Germanic nations—secular music only slowly developed a style of its own. The art of the troubadour, of the minstrels, and of the minnesingers—whose popular style owed many traits to Oriental models—served as a basis for the different forms of song and dance that gained prominence toward the end of the Middle Ages. The people began to demand their due, and with a general rise in the standard of education and knowledge they took possession of the art forms as well. Highly skilled performers—"composers" in the original sense of the word—were able to elaborate dance tunes in the style of church polyphony and to accompany a melodious song.

Music became popular both with the nobility and with the masses: minstrels performed merry music at all festivities, and the feasts resounded with their playing. Foreign visitors to a town were greeted at the gates and accompanied into the town by musicians, and tournaments and chases as well as performances of plays were other occasions for the sounding of instrumental music. Instruction in music and dancing gradually became part of the general education of a nobleman, and the music cultivated in earlier days by roaming minstrels only was raised to a higher level. The musical instruments—most of which had been introduced by musicians from the East—were perfected, and new instruments were designed to fill the needs of the players. The secular art lagged behind church music in passing the stage of mere improvisation and molding its forms and style of performance, and till well into the baroque era there was no distinction between vocal and instrumental music; all pieces could be sung or played, or sung *and* played by a variety of (unspecified) instruments at will.

The slow rise of secular music can be witnessed almost simultaneously in various countries, but the first creation of truly independent instrumental forms and original types of secular songs must be ascribed to Renaissance Italy. Italy had not taken part in the great development of polyphonic music that had flourished in France and the Netherlands; it had only enjoyed its last fruits and supreme synthesis in the works of Palestrina. The Roman Church had not favored the musical embellishment of the service to the same extent as the northwestern European centers; on the other hand, there had developed in Italy much earlier than in other countries a highly colored social life: the country's position in trade and commerce had led to a great economic and social prosperity of the towns, and it is urban life that leads to the organization of musical activities and the growth of specific forms of musical expression. Italy was the country of a nature-loving society enjoying common singing, playing, and dancing; many Italian paintings represent musical scenes, and the stories of the Renaissance—particularly its most characteristic book, Boccaccio's *Decamerone*—as well as its poems prove how greatly Italian society craved music and the dance. Secular choral singing reached its greatest heights in the madrigals of the sixteenth and seventeenth centuries—songs for mixed voices composed on lyrical poems and in colorful polyphony—while the perfection of the stringed instruments and of the keyboard instruments for *continuo* purposes stimulated (about 1600) the development of a new type of social instrumental music: chamber music.

Italian society was first in diminishing the domination of the Church, for it enjoyed art as such and acknowledged no spiritual or stylistic bonds with the clerical sphere. Singing and chamber music were cultivated for the sake of social and artistic pleasure only, and no view of a higher spiritual purpose guided their forms. The Church soon could not afford to deny the worshippers the pleasures they so greatly looked for at the court, the theater, and social festivities; without magnificent choral singing and instrumental music the churches would soon have become empty. So in the church, too, music gradually ceased to be a servant to a higher purpose only but took on an aspect of artistic embellishment and attraction; it was no longer the privileged possession of pious communities but became an art practiced by skilled individual musicians for the sake of society. Individual expression and magnificent coloring had come to characterize music as much as the paintings of the Italian masters. The strict polyphonic style—symbolizing the spirit of community and unity of purpose—gave way to a style in which one individual melody dominated the vocal or instrumental voices of an entire piece; and the performing virtuoso wanted to attract the attention and gain the applause of society as much as the original creator of the music—composer and performer being in most cases united in one person in the sphere of instrumental music. With this development the clear distinction between clerical and secular art—the revolutionary innovation of this period—was established once and for all.

The historical and sociological development of music in Italy enabled the Jews to contribute for the first time to European musical art; though several Jewish communities in Italy were in ghettos where living conditions were dreadful, the spiritual position of the Jews was raised by the fact that they represented a valuable heritage of the ancient world which the Renaissance tried so hard to revive in all spheres of philosophy and art. Italy had had much contact with the Orient throughout the centuries; Emperor

Frederick II (1194–1252), who had crowned himself emperor in Jerusalem, drew to his pompous court of Palermo a great number of Arabic and Jewish scholars and attempted in Italy an imitation of Oriental court life and art. Oriental studies were pursued at the Italian academies throughout the Middle Ages, and the growing commerce of the Italian cities greatly favored relations with the Near Eastern world. The Oriental and classical spirit gave Renaissance style its specific stamp, and the Jewish world—particularly that of the mystic cabbalah—proved an especially attractive part of the Orient. Life in fifteenth-century Italy, with its emphasis on the social instead of on the spiritual elements, stimulated the Jews, too; and in the works of Leone Ebreo, son of Don Isaac ben Yuda (Abravanel) of Portugal, a Jew succeeded in blending Oriental-Jewish thought and Renaissance spirit.

Jewish history in medieval and Renaissance Italy is as much a story of the rise and fall of communities and of tolerance and persecution in turn as that of other European centers; but the spirit of the times favored in Italy—in stark contrast to central Europe—the cultural development of the Jews. With the migration to Italy of Sephardim expelled from Spain and Portugal and of Ashkenazic Jews from northern European countries and with the steady influx of Oriental Jewish traders, the Jewish communities in Italy soon became the most universal of all Jewish centers. This made itself felt in music as much as in other spheres: it is known that just as singers from all civilized countries came to Italy to perfect their technique and instrumentalists sought the instruction of the great Italian virtuosos, so hazanim were sent to Italy to study the art of song in the synagogues. Prominent singing teachers in their times were Abraham Sagi and the hazan Jacob ben Isaac Finzi ha-Levi (early seventeenth century). Both were singers and probably also composers serving the Ashkenazic community at Casale Monferrato in the Po region (Piedmont).

The first field in which Jews excelled outside their own community and partook in the cultural activities of the Renaissance period was the dance, and it seems that in this sphere the Jews could boast of a long tradition. (The name has been preserved of one famous Jewish dancing master active in Spain in the fourteenth century, Rabbi Hacén ben Salomo, who was called to teach Christians a dance in a Spanish church in the year 1313.) In Renaissance Italy Jews were noted for their art of dancing, and in 1575 a special license was granted by the Pope to two Jews from Ancona for the teaching of dancing and singing. At the same time the Jews Ambrosio and Guglielmo Ebreo—said by contemporaries to have danced "above all human measure"—taught dancing at the court of Urbino, and Guglielmo's disciple Giuseppe continued in his master's tradition. It is interesting to note that the Jewish dancing masters were instrumental in gaining an honored place in society for professional dancing in general; dancers had stood in low regard in the Middle Ages, but in Renaissance Italy they could become confidants of dukes and princes. On the other hand, the high perfection reached by the Jews in the art of the dance—and at the same time in music—also improved their own position with the secular and clerical authorities.

In the fifteenth century Jewish schools of music and dance are known to have existed in Venice, Pesaro, and Parma. Two Jewish scholars wrote in the same century on the importance of music in general education and social life: Jacob ben Haim Farissol and Yohanan ben Isaac Alemanno.[1]

Jewish musical activities in schools and houses as well as in the synagogues of Italian cities are documented in many writings of the sixteenth century. Florence, Venice, Mantua, and Ferrara were then especially mentioned as centers of Jewish learning and music making. One of the most important treatises on music of that time is contained in the selection of sermons Rabbi Yehuda ben Joseph Moscato collected under the title "Nefuzot Yehuda" ("The Disperse of Yuda"). It was first published in Venice 1588–89, one year before the rabbi's death in Mantua in 1590. The opening sermon, *higayón be-chinnór* ("the tune of the lyre"), synthesizes traditional Greek, biblical, talmudic, theological, and cabbalistic opinions and contemporary Italian music theory. Moscato envisions every being, including man, as created to musical proportions—God himself is the master of perfect music—and he discards the theory that Pythagoras discovered music, in

---

[1] cf. Israel Adler, "The Rise of Art Music in the Italian Ghetto. The Influence of Segregation on Jewish Musical Praxis," in *Jewish Medieval and Renaissance Studies*, ed. Alexander Altmann, Cambridge, Mass., 1967, pp. 321–364, and the same author's entries on the scholars and musicians named here in "Hebrew Writings Concerning Music" in *Repertoire International des Sources Musicales*, Munich, 1975. Also see A. Z. Idelsohn, "Jewish Music," op. cit.

favor of Jubal and Tubal-Cain.[2] Other important sixteenth-century writers followed: Samuel ben Elhanan Archivolti's treatise, "A Bed of Spices" ("Arugát ha-Bossem") on Hebrew grammar and prosody, was published in Venice in 1602; Abraham ben David Portaleone, a physician, speculates in his "Shiltei ha-Gibborim" (Mantua 1611–12) on the nature of music and musical instruments in biblical times; and Rabbi Yehuda ben Moses Saltaro da Fano, who brings us to the most prominent Jewish musical figures of Renaissance Italy—Rabbi Leon(Yehuda Arie) Modena of Venice and the violinist and composer Salomone Rossi of Mantua. Saltaro da Fano added an approval to Modena's responsum in favor of the choral chant in the synagogue (Ferrara 1605); Fano's writing appeared in the 1622–23 edition of Salomone Rossi's "Shir ha-Shirim asher Li-Schlomoh" (see pp. 149–150).

In the second half of the sixteenth century a considerable number of Jewish musicians distinguished themselves at the Italian courts, the Papal Court included. Venice and Mantua, however, were the places of their outstanding activities—the former the state with the most developed Oriental connections and thus dependent in some degree on Jewish good will, the latter ruled by dukes who did not have much love for their Jews in general but who were great patrons of all artistic activities.

The court of the Gonzagas at Mantua was served by many especially privileged Jewish musicians. There have come down to us the names of the harpists Abramo dall' Arpa Ebreo and his nephew (or grandson?) Abramino, of the composers Davit da Civita and Allegro Porto (whose name "Allegro" is said to have been the translation of his Hebrew name *Simcha* = "gaiety"), and the lutenist, singer, dancer, and ballet-master Isacchino Massarano. These musicians belonged to the court band, which was organized and led by one of the greatest violinists and composers of early instrumental history, Salomone Rossi.[3] It is possible that the entire band consisted of Jewish musicians, as a letter written to the court and preserved in the archives contained a request that "Solomon the Hebrew be sent together with his party" to entertain at the festivities of another court.

---

[2]Moscato's treatise is analyzed in Herzl Shmuëli, "Higayón be-chinnór," Philos. Dissertation, University Zürich, published Tel Aviv, 1953.

[3]Rossi dedicated one of his ballets for orchestra to Massarano.

A parallel is offered by the dramatic society led by the Jew Leone de Sommi Portaleone, who himself was a playwright and also wrote the *Dialoghi sull' Arte Rappresentativa*—the first extant work on the art of the stage. Rossi's own sister was a stage singer famous in the world of early opera; she was commonly called "Madama Europa" and is known to have taken part in the first performance—staged at Mantua in 1608—of the opera *Arianna,* the work of the first great master of opera, Claudio Monteverdi. Monteverdi himself was attached to the Mantuan court from 1590 to 1612 and must have been in constant contact with Salomone Rossi and his musicians; his *Arianna* was actually performed on the occasion of the wedding festivities at the court in which Rossi was also represented by a composition: one of the intermezzi for the drama *L'Idropica* was from his pen.

Salomone Rossi, who always added "Ebreo" to his name, stemmed from an illustrious family which claimed to have come to Rome with the earliest settlers after the destruction of Jerusalem as captives of Emperor Titus. The name of Asarja dei Rossi (died in Mantua in 1578) had become famous through his religious philosophy, which united elements of Jewish-Hellenistic thought and talmudic-rabbinical tradition. But Salomone Rossi, his descendant, who was probably born in the early 1570s, became as well known as the learned and much-disputed rabbi; his instruction in violin playing and the services of his orchestra were much sought after, his printed works bear dedications to some of the most prominent noblemen of the time, and the various editions of his madrigals and instrumental music reached the courts of many European countries (where down to our days they may be found in the libraries). The King of Portugal's library, which was unfortunately burned in 1755, contained the entire works of the composer, as is confirmed by the extant catalog.

We know little of Rossi's life, but his activities at the Mantuan court from about 1589 to 1628 are established by the works published in this period. He was highly esteemed by the Gonzagas and by the court nobility, and in 1606 he was absolved from having to wear the yellow badge prescribed for the Jews—an exception only rarely made from the rule established by the Lateran Council in 1215 (originally the yellow badge had been introduced by a Moslem ruler for "unbelievers" of all creeds), but which Rossi shared with the actor and dramatist Leone de Sommi.

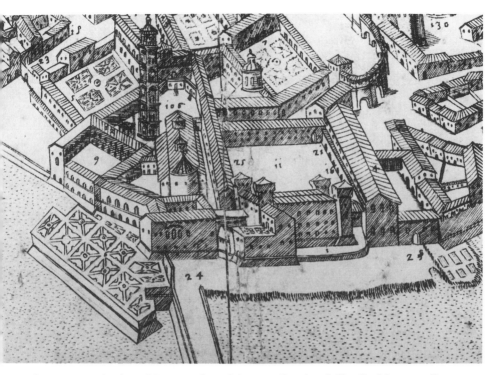

The Gonzaga Castle at Mantua, where Salomone Rossi and Claudio Monteverdi served the duke. (From a contemporary design, photographed by Giovetti Fotografia, Mantua.)

In general music history Rossi has his place as a composer who was among the first to apply to instrumental music the principles of monodic song (in which one dominant melody is accompanied by secondary, accompanying parts—in contrast to the polyphonic style, in which all melodic parts are equal in importance); the monodic style had so far been cultivated mainly in opera. Just as in opera the monodic aria served virtuoso singers as a vehicle for an exhibition of their vocal brilliancy (Monteverdi was then almost alone in endowing the aria with a profoundly emotional content), so in instrumental music there developed a virtuoso art for entertaining the society present at court or in the theater. The novel monodic and virtuoso instrumental music of the late sixteenth and early seventeenth centuries marked the first steps in the evolution of musical forms designed to attract an audience; only in the second half of the eighteenth century—that is, with the rise of the public concert and the symphonic form created for its sake—did the seventeenth-century reforms attain their goal. In Mantua there also rose, under Salomone Rossi's leadership, the first great school of violinists; this marked the beginning of a magnificent line of instrumentalists who spread Italy's fame throughout the seventeenth-and eighteenth-century world.

In his madrigals and in his instrumental chamber music Rossi shows a specific melodic talent, characteristic of many Jewish composers. Harmony, the typical Occidental musical feature, held no attraction for him; this makes his music strikingly different from that of his great contemporaries, who made dramatic use of bold and colorful harmonic combinations. Rossi is among the very first composers to develop the form and technique of variation; he wrote variations on Italian popular melodies, many of which were later sung in the synagogues, and he seems also to have used for his variations tunes that were already popular in the synagogue or the ghetto.

In the field of the synagogue Rossi was the first composer to attempt complete reforms in the style of traditional liturgical music. His collection of religious songs which appeared in Venice in 1622, printed by Pietro and Lorenzo Bragadini, under the title *Ha-Shirim Asher Li'Shlomo* (in allusion to the Biblical Song of Solomon), contains thirty-three musical versions of the ancient liturgical texts; the music is conceived in the style of the madrigal period. Rossi had undertaken the composition of the psalms and prayers "to glorify and embellish the songs of King David according to the rules of musical art" (as stated in his Hebrew dedication), and they were set for three, four, five, six, seven, and eight voices, for chorus and solos. The music was printed—the parts only—in the customary way; but the texts were added below in the Hebrew characters running from right to left in complete lines (not as Hebrew songs are printed today: with one Hebrew syllable printed below the note to which it is to be sung). Rossi's synagogal songs contain veritable gems of choral music, but they preserved little of the traditional character of synagogue music; the Italian composer's reform thus meant the first step in the process of assimilation which Hebrew religious music underwent in the European countries; Sulzer, Lewandowski, Naumbourg, and others completed this musical assimilation in the nineteenth century.

Frontispiece from Salomone Rossi's song collection *Ha-Shirim Asher Li'Schlomo*, Venice, 1622.

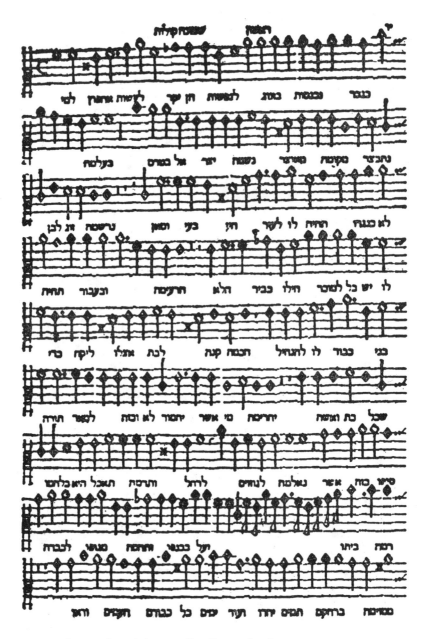

A page of music from Salomone Rossi's songbook.

Although none of the earlier renowned scholars in the Jewish field had hitherto found traces of synagogal chant in Rossi's music, a recent reappraisal of his sacred music suggests just that. Joshua Jacobson, an American scholar, has pointed to two divergent influences on the music of Salomone Rossi: stylistic traits characteristic of the motets of Rossi's Christian contemporaries Lodovico Viadana and even Orlando di Lasso; and leanings toward synagogal chant, as shown in at least one of his four-part motets (Psalm 80, v. 4.: "Elohīm hashivēnu"). Here Jacobson sees

> the most old-fashioned motet, in the sense of pre-baroque melismatic polyphony. It is also the only motet wherein a melodic theme reappears three times, each time in a different setting. This would seem to suggest that Rossi had employed a pre-compositional melodic idea, one which he repeated in several variations, to insure that it would be recognized by his listeners.[4]

There was a strong opposition on the part of the rabbis to musical reforms, which could endanger the preservation of the ancient tradition, and Rossi had a difficult stand against the rabbinical authorities. His compositions were regarded as a precedent, but though they were indeed the first to appear in print, he had had a forerunner in this attempts to introduce new elements into the synagogue service. In 1605 one of the most versatile Jewish scholars of the Italian Renaissance, Yehuda Arieh (called Leone) da Modena, a skilled musician and singer himself, had conducted a choir of six to eight voices in the Ferrara synagogue and led them "according to the relation of voices to each other, based on that science," which means in the harmonic style of the period. The innovation had met with strong opposition but was upheld after the rabbinical assembly had expressed its approval. This progressive scholar and musician, the outstanding figure in Renaissance Judaism, now stepped to the defense of Salomone Rossi against the antagonistic authorities and introduced the printed edition of the composer's songs with a lengthy foreword. This is a most characteristic document: it is spiced with quotations from the Bible (especially from the Psalms and the books of the Prophets) and the Talmud and abounds in skilled and

---

[4]Joshua R. Jacobson, "The Choral Music of Salomone Rossi," *The American Choral Review,* 30:4, 1988, and "A Possible Influence of Traditional Chant on a Synagogue Motet of Salomone Rossi," *Musica Judaica,* Vol. 3, pp. 52–58.

learned puns, and the admonitions addressed to the opponents of reform in synagogue song throw a most interesting light on the debates of the time. As no absolutely accurate modern translation of this foreword is available, we here present a new version—with only minor omissions of passages that have no direct bearing on our subject:[5]

> Yehuda Arieh of Modena, the eldest son of Rabbi Isaac, addressing all ears that can understand the truth.
>
> "The lip of truth shall be established for ever"[6]—the poet is right when he lets music speak to the non-Jews:[7] "Indeed I was stolen away out of the land of the Hebrews."[8] For the scholars have grown like grass and have spread all sciences of Israel and have mounted up to great heights like eagles with wings, and all peoples have admired and feared them. Like other sciences, music was also adopted from the Hebrews by other people. Who could forget King David, who taught music to the sons of Asaph, Heiman, and Yeduthun—as is told in the Chronicles—and made them understand singing and the playing of instruments, and who sang and played as long as the House of the Lord stood in its place, the first and second [Temple], and preserved its tradition ever after. But our dwelling in foreign lands, our dispersion all over the world, and our troubles and persecution have made them [the people of Israel] forget all knowledge and lose all understanding. The wrath of God was kindled against the people, and he fenced them and gathered them out and cast them into a pit empty of all knowing.[9] And when they lived in lands that did not belong to them, the

---

[5]The French version contained in Naumbourg's modern edition of Rossi's music (Paris, 1877) and the German translation given by Paul Nettl in *Alte Jüdische Spielleute und Musiker* (Prague, 1923) and reproduced several times later are highly inaccurate; our interpretation is based on the thorough study made of the original by Mr. Ephraim Trochae-Dror and contained in the Hebrew book on the *Music of Israel* published by this author in 1945 (pp. 79–86). The text abounds in biblical quotations and allusions, and the author makes frequent use of Hebrew word-plays and puns; we have used biblical phrases in most cases in which the original did so, but it is not always possible to reproduce the original style, especially where the author plays with Hebrew words and their different meanings. We have annotated only such passages as demand an explanation; interpretative additions of our own are marked in the text by brackets.

[6]Proverbs 12:19.

[7]The poet Emanuel ha-Romi Manuello, an Italian-Hebrew poet and friend of Dante.

[8]Genesis 40:15.

[9]Passages from Isaiah 5:2 and Genesis 37:24.

wisdom of their wise men perished, and they had later to borrow what had been left of it with their neighbors. Let us praise the name of the Lord, for Solomon alone is excellent[10] in this science in our days and wiser than any man, not only of our own people: for they liken and equal him to many famous men of the earth, because of which he was taken into the service of the Dukes of Mantua, having served the late Duke and now being with the present Duke. May he rise and prosper in his majesty, Amen. May his music printed in foreign language[11] meet with just appreciation, as it was liked by non-Jews—and they hanged their lyres upon the willows in the midst thereof and said: The Lord openeth the eyes of the blind.[12]

His power is unto his God, and he actively served the profane and the sacred to honor the Lord with all his talent. He tried to perfect the work that had made him famous in spite of the opposition of his brethren and constantly added psalms, prayers, hymns, and songs of praise till he could collect them in one volume. And as the people sang them and were pleased by their excellence and the listeners shone—and whosesoever ear was delighted by them desired to hear more—he was urged by the nobles of the community, and first among them that generous and noble rabbi Moses Sullam (May God guard him from above!), to have them printed, so as to give him a name lasting longer than children (for he begins and will not be surpassed, and such music has not existed in Israel) and for the good of his friends, so that they may sing it and that the rabbis may embellish the service and feasts. I, who have been one of his admirers from the beginning, have also very greatly urged and requested him, till at last, thanks to the Almighty, he came to bring forth and agreed to the printing as he had promised. . . . And he asked me to watch that nothing untoward should happen to his composition, to prepare it for printing, and to read the proofs carefully. And though my lyre has turned to mourning and I am sad about the heart of the fallen—my beloved son Zebulun, aged twenty-one, musically gifted, endowed with a sweet voice and a comely countenance, was murdered six months ago . . . —I did not want to refrain from fulfilling the demand, and I thought the Lord would reward me by having

---

[10]This is an adaptation of verse 13 from Psalm 148, in which the word *shmo* = "his name" has been changed to *shlomo* = Solomon; the wisdom of the composer is, of course, likened to that of his biblical namesake, King Solomon.

[11]This can mean the Italian songs—set in a language foreign to the Jews—or the Hebrew synagogal songs proper—composed in a language foreign to the Duke, Rossi's patron.

[12]The scholar may have intended a pun here, as the Hebrew word for "the blind," *iw'rim*, has the same pronunciation—though a different Hebrew spelling—as the word for "the Hebrews."

mercy in his soul and it would be brightness and joy to all Jews. And so I stand here to watch the work done and say that it is not easy as it has never been done before—and so I must be forgiven for errors. The reader will see that the author preferred that the words be read backward [This means that the Hebrew words follow each other from right to left.] contrary to our Hebrew custom . . . to changing the music notation.[13] He also omitted the writing of the vowel signs, for our expert singers know the texts by heart and read correctly without the signs—which is to their great honor.

And now, my brethren, you are blessed, because we were able to start, the great man [the composer] having taken his pen and the songs of praise having been written and engraved. Praise the Lord with these songs in His house of worship on the holy days! Teach them to your children to instruct them in the science of music, and the teacher to the pupil—as is said of the Levites—for I am sure that from the day of their publication the students of music in Israel will grow in number to praise our Lord with these and similar songs.

There will certainly be found among us some people who fight against all that is new and against all knowledge—which is beyond their understanding—and will unreasonably ban them; and so I have thought fit to refer to the answer I wrote with regard to this question eighteen years ago, when I was rabbi of the community at Ferrara, in order to silence a confused antagonist, and all great contemporary scholars of Venice agreed with me.[14] . . . Many who have so far shunned the science [of music], even though they desired to sing and play, should learn and perform it—till the Lord has mercy on us and builds again His holy House and commands the Levites and their families and classes to perform their music at their times, and all singing in the House of the Lord and in all Israel will be happy and joyous again—not like today, when each of us sings with a heavy heart and in anguish of spirit and heavy bondage for the pain of our dispersion, and while he sings his heart is sick: for then there will be no song in Israel without joy; they will have their silver and gold with them, their fields and vineyards, and their God shall be their everlasting light, and they will lift up their voices together: for they shall see eye to eye when the Lord shall bring Zion again quickly. Amen.

Leone da Modena's preface to the printed edition of Rossi's songs is followed by his reprint of the answer given in the rabbinical dispute at Fer-

---

[13]Hebrew script is read from right to left, but in setting Hebrew words to music, the syllables are usually printed below the note (or notes) to which they belong, and thus run from left to right with the music.

[14]The response is actually added to the Preface of Leone da Modena—see below.

rara and alluded to in the foreword. The learned scholar seeks to prove in this "judgment" (as he himself calls it) that both the Bible and the Talmud permit singing and the use of musical instruments in the house of worship *provided it is in accordance with the custom of the times*. Five Venetian authorities signed his declaration.

Salomone Rossi dedicated his sacred songs to Moses Sullam, a member of one of the most esteemed Jewish families in Renaissance Italy and a prominent and wealthy citizen of Mantua; his parents had already supported Rossi in his youth, and he himself was an ardent patron of the arts; his daughter-in law, who lived in Venice, was the poetess Sarah Copia-Sullam, who is said also to have been musically gifted. It is of interest to quote some passages from Rossi's dedication to Sullam; it is written in the same style as Leone da Modena's preface and similarly abounds in quotations from biblical and talmudic passages and allusions to traditional phrases:

> For a long time now the Lord has endowed me with a talent for music and for the science of singing . . . and this inspired me to praise the Lord with my song as best as I could. And God helped me and put new songs in my mouth, which I had composed according to the laws of art for the occasions of joy and the holy days. . . . I always attempted to glorify and embellish the psalms of David King of Israel according to the rules of musical art so that they might be more pleasant to the ear. And after the Lord had permitted me to finish my work, I saw that it would be worth letting the people enjoy it by printing a selection of my songs; and I did this not for my own sake but in honor of my Father in Heaven Who has given me this life and Whom I shall always praise. . . . And as I thought in my heart: to which noble man could I dedicate this token of thanks? I saw I could offer it to no better than to you, esteemed and great man in Israel; for the entire community knows your merits and virtues. . . . And thus I felt it my duty to dedicate my songs to you. And more: for you have often supported me and I have endeavored to create my songs and to return to you what you have given to me. . . .[15]

The Dedication is dated:

Mantua, Rosh-Hodesh Heshwan 5383 [Winter, 1622]

And signed:

---

[15]The passages left out by us are either further praise of the Lord or an enumeration of all the virtues of the dedicatee.

Shlomo Mi-ha-Adumin the Young(er) [Rossi, like other members of his family, used to translate his Italian name into Hebrew].[16]

But with Rossi's dedicatory preface we do not reach the end of the forewords preceding the music of the songs; the printed edition contains yet another document of great historical interest: a notice signed by four rabbis, Leone da Modena among them, in which the reprint or sale of an "unauthorized version" of Rossi's music is prohibited in the strongest possible terms; this is of particular importance because an *author's* right in his creations is commonly supposed to have been recognized for the first time in the Statute of Anne (Queen of England) in 1710, though copyright provisions for *printers* had been confirmed in Venice in 1491. The notice contained in Rossi's collection of songs—though a quite indisputable interpretation seems impossible—doubtless concerned the rights of the author, and they are reserved in forcible language indeed:[17]

> We are [herewith] complying with the justified request of the Right Honorable Salomone Rossi of Mantua, may God bless him, who has labored much and was the first ever to print Hebrew music.[18] He has [however] issued a deficient[19] edition, and he ought not to come to harm by anybody's [? re-] printing them [i.e. copies of this edition] or by their being purchased from any [other?] person. Therefore, having been granted permission from the distinguished Court authorities, we, the signatories to this document, herewith issue a strict prohibition, by the decree of the watch-

---

[16]"The Young(er)": this could allude to an elder (the father?) of the composer, somebody well-known in his time, or could be simply a customary formula. The only known Rossis who may have been relatives of our composer were Matteo Rossi, who appears in a pay list of the Mantua Court in 1621 as a bassist; Anselmo Rossi, a composer who printed a three-part motet in Mantua in 1618; and the writer Bastiano de Rossi. Some Italian composers and musicians by the name of Rossi were non-Jews.

[17]This translation and its interpretation are also based on the studies of Mr. Ephraim Trochae-Dror, contained on pp. 91, 92 of the above-mentioned book. Additions and explanations are again added in brackets.

[18]This is the first instance known of the term "Hebrew music" being used in a Hebrew document.

[19]The meaning of the Hebrew word used here (*bilti-m'suderet*) is dubious. Literally it means "not in order." This may be interpreted as "containing errors" (on the part of the composer or the printer), as "incorrect," or as "not arranged" with regard to the printer's or author's rights.

ers and the word of the Holy Ones, and by the bite of the serpent,[20] that no Jew, wherever he may be, may print under any circumstances within fifteen years from this day the above-mentioned work, the music, or part thereof, without the consent of its author or his heirs, nor may any Jew, according to this decree, buy from any person, whether Jewish or not, copies of any of these compositions, without the composer's having authorized their sale by a special mark on them. And every son of Israel shall hear [the words of this edict] and take care not to be entangled in the net of this curse—and the obedient shall dwell in peace and abide under the shadow of the Almighty.[21]

With the blessing of Amen,
    Izhaq Gershon
    Moses Cohen Port
    Yehuda Arieh of Modena
    Simha Luzzato
    Venice, Heshwan 5383 [Winter, 1622].

The edition of *Ha-Shirim Asher Li'Shlomo* has come down to us in a small number of the printed parts only, and no variants have been discovered so far in the copies extant. It seems that the "deficient" version has not been preserved in manuscript or print, to the satisfaction of the signatories and the composer in whose favor the rabbis issued their decree, but to the utter dissatisfaction of the modern scholar, who would certainly be glad to know what kind of "deficiency" was deplored by one of the foremost masters of the early Italian baroque and by one of the outstanding Jewish composers of all time.[22]

In the 1620s an epidemic of plague raged in Mantua; thousands of people died, and the Jewish population was also decimated. In 1627 the last of the Gonzagas died, and three years later, the town was stormed by Austrian troops. The rest of the Jewish population, which since 1610 had been

---

[20]The words here used for the ban or curse are condensed from passages from Daniel 4:17: "By the decrees of the watchers, and the demand by the word of the Holy Ones" (according to rabbinical interpretation, "watchers"—literally "angels" or "guardians"—and "Holy Ones" stand for "Jewish scholars") and from Ecclesiastes 10:8: "And whoso breaketh an hedge, a serpent shall bite him." The condensed phrase became the official formula for decrees of this kind.

[21]The concluding formula is taken from Psalm 91:1.

[22]See Gradenwitz, "An Early Instance of Copyright," *Music and Letters*, Vol. 27, 1946.

enclosed in a ghetto, were called upon with all other citizens to man the for-
tifications and to build new walls; not even on the Sabbath were they permitted to rest. The Jewish inhabitants fought in the actual battle, but the
city could not withstand the armed hordes and fell after a seven months'
siege. The ghetto was ravaged, and some 1,800 Jews fled the town; Emperor Ferdinand, approached by a Jewish delegation at Regensburg, ordered the Governor of Mantua to permit the resettlement of the banished
Jews and to return to them their homes and possessions; but migration
and death had greatly reduced their number, and only a few came back to
the devastated city. No trace is found of Salomone Rossi and his musicians
after that catastrophe, and a short but magnificent intermezzo in the story
of the music of Israel thus came to a sudden and tragic end. It is surmised
that Rossi left Mantua at the time of the plague[23] or in 1628, when his last-
known publication was printed, and that he settled in Venice where Leone
da Modena was *maestro di capella* at the Accademia musicale del ghetto
veneziano. In 1648, the year in which Modena died, he mentioned Rossi
in one of his poems; a Hebrew source of the year 1645 lets us believe that
Rossi was still alive then. He must be presumed to have died between 1630
and the late 1640s.

ROSSI'S MUSIC was destined to temporary oblivion. As an instrumental
composer he suffered the fate of many pioneers: the splendid works of a
long line of ingenious successors made him seem a mere forerunner of
greater masters to come. His first *Sonata a Tre,* with its variations on a popular dance tune, was one of the earliest trio sonatas, if not actually the very
first, and the sonata called by Rossi himself *La moderna* (published 1613)
offers the earliest example of the four-movement type of sonata which was
four decades later called *sonata da chiesa,* church sonata, in contrast to the
sonata da camera. This four-movement sonata consisted of a slow movement in polyphonic style and in quadruple time, a quick fugal movement in
triple time, a slow and homophonic-melodic movement in quadruple time,

---

[23]The authorities of Mantua kept death roll lists; they are preserved in the Gonzaga
archives. As Jews were buried in special sections of the cemetery, their names were
marked in these lists with special strokes of the pen: in examining the records of the
1620s we have found no Rossi family name recorded among the dead and buried.

and a quick homophonic finale in triple rhythm. Masters like Legrenzi, Vitali, Bassani, and Corelli perfected the form created by this early master of instrumental chamber music; and the great later virtuosos that made Italy famous throughout the world caused their contemporaries to forget the founder of the splendid Mantua school. Rossi's secular vocal compositions—from his canzonets of 1589 down to the last known publication from his pen, twenty-five *madrigaletti* for two sopranos or two tenors, Opus 13, published 1628—were charming contributions to popular "utility music" but could not hold their own beside the great creations of Luca Marenzio and Claudio Monteverdi. A pioneer in instrumental music, Rossi seems to have been a composer of a delightful yet common brand of songs.

The fate of Rossi's synagogal music was sealed by historic events. The segregation of the Jews from non-Jewish society as a result of the anti-Jewish Catholic "Counterreformation" was further enforced, the Austrian conquest was badly felt, and a virtual disappearance of Jewish musicians from non-Jewish gatherings ensued. These were also times for reforms in Jewish life and the synagogue. The rabbinical authorities watched the keeping of tradition with increased zeal. It is doubtful indeed whether seventeenth-century Jews knew of Rossi's novel music, let alone heard or sang his songs. More than one hundred years after the endeavors of Leone da Modena to introduce new music into the synagogue service of Ferrara, a citizen of that town, Nehemia Cohen, was excommunicated by the rabbinate when he dared to introduce a new musical version of the priestly benediction.

However, the enforced segregation turned the Jewish communities to the development of cultural and artistic activities within their own walls. The harder they felt the strictures of being cut off from the society surrounding them, the more the Jews endeavored to create cultural values of their own, musical values among them. Before the advent of Leone da Modena and Salomone Rossi, during their time, and later, many treatises on music and musical works were written and printed; some sixteenth- and seventeenth- century examples of more than common interest have been preserved.[24]

Since the middle of the seventeenth century, special ceremonies for the

---

[24]See Israel Adler, "The Rise of Art Music," op. cit.

dedication of synagogues became popular in Italy, and music played an important part in them. The first known—and partly preserved—were held in Venice in 1661–62, 1729, and 1810; in Livorno in 1742; in Torino, 1784; Siena, 1786; Florence, 1793; Padua, Verona, Reggio, and others followed in 1828, 1854, and 1883.[25] In Holland, England, and Germany, cantatas for the inauguration of synagogues were also written in an ever-increasing number—Jewish and Gentile composers wrote music for the synagogue cantatas with their traditional Hebrew texts. Among the exceptional examples is the commission offered to Ludwig van Beethoven by the Jewish community of Vienna to write a cantata for the consecration of their new synagogue in the Seitenstettergasse "Wiener Stadttempel" on April 9, 1826. Community dignitaries approached Beethoven in January or February 1825, and Beethoven seriously contemplated writing the cantata, even studying "Hebrew music" for the purpose. In the end, he did not write the work. The cantata was composed by another non-Jewish composer, Joseph Drechsler of St. Stephans' in Vienna.[26] In Holland cantatas written for the Sephardic synagogue have been preserved. Their composers were from various countries.[27] From Amsterdam we also know of a musical farce, printed in 1793 and entitled "Shir Shevach" (Song of Praise). It appears in a collection of "old hymns and prayers" published by three poets who in a foreword admonish the performers to attend to correct diction and good attunement of words and music. Twenty-seven tunes are named in the collection but are not noted down; most of them seem to have been traditional, but some are described as "lachan chadásh" (= new tune). [28]

[25]The Haifa, Israel, music historian and collector Moshe Gorali lists sixteen cantatas in Italy between 1661 and 1912; twenty-seven in Holland from 1685 to 1924; twenty-nine in England from late eighteenth century to 1959; twenty-one in Germany from 1797 (Breslau) to 1934. His studies appeared in various issues of *Tazlil* (The Chord), a forum for music research and bibliography of the Haifa Music Museum and Amli Library, published periodically, edited by Gorali, 1960–80.

[26]See Peter Gradenwitz, "Ludwig van Beethoven und die hebräische Liturgie," in *Menora, Jahrbuch für deutschjüdische Geschichte*, Munich, 1991, pp. 215–244.

[27]See Israel Adler, "La Pratique musicale dans quelques communautés juives en Europe aux XVIIe et XVIIIe siécles," Paris-Hague 1966, and the same author's editions of some of the cantatas in the series *Early Hebrew Art Music*, Israeli Music Publications, Tel Aviv, 1965 ff.

[28]See M. Gorali, *Tazlil*, op cit., 1963, pp. 165–169.

Example 19. Music for the Vienna Synagogue, which Beethoven did not write: a psalm composition by Joseph Drechsler, as published in Sulzer's *Schir Zion*.

Of special interest in this field is the "Cantata Celebrating with Joy the Consecration of the House" ("Ssimchat Mitzvah al Chanoch ha-Bayit"), the text published in 1793, for the inauguration of the Italian Synagogue of Florence. The words of the cantata are by Daniel Terni, and the music was composed by Michael Bulafi, both noteworthy personalities of their time. Daniel ben Moshe David Terni from Ancona was rabbi in Florence and published various works between 1791 and 1803. Donati Terni, probably his relative, was also born in Ancona, and wrote the music for an oratorio, *Noam,* performed by Yeshiva students in Pesaro in 1770. Five years later he composed *Moshe in Sinai.* Research has established that music, mainly singing, was taught in the Italian yeshiva. The composer Michael Bulafi, who also conducted the performance of his cantata at the Italian Synagogue, seems to have been the descendant of the Spanish family Aboulafia. His name is recorded in the archives of the Cherubini Conservatoire of Florence as the composer of another cantata, "Il mese armonico" for voice, guitar, and piano, and of *Canzonette.*[29] Michael Bulafi probably remained famous beyond his times (he died in 1846 at the age of 77), for his music was included in a later nineteenth-century manuscript volume of synagogal compositions, extant in the Library of the Rubin Academy of Music in Jerusalem. This volume contains works by other composers from Italy: David Garzia, (Elia) Nunes Franco, and one named only Penso.[30] All four are thought to have been active in Livorno, another flourishing Jewish cultural center; Bulafi—spelled Bolaffi in this manuscript—went from Livorno to Florence, while Garzia later lived in Alexandria, Egypt.

JEWISH MUSICIANS from Italy seem to have journeyed to many western European countries as early as the fifteenth century. They left Italian ghettos when life became dangerous for the Jews; battles constantly raged in northern Italy, and Papal decrees and Spanish influence threatened the Jews and their activities. They found little encouragement for music in their own communities while the non-Jewish world was closed to them. In the western countries they could count on the great interest in music and musicians from Italy. It Italy music had undergone decisive changes since the period in which composers and musicians from the northern countries— foremost the Flemish masters such as Willaert, Josquin, Dufay, Isaac—had

---

[29]See M. Gorali, *Tazlil,* 1961, pp. 85–92, where the (Hebrew) text of the "Consecration" cantata is also printed.

[30]The manuscript volume is described and its contents are completely listed, with a thematic catalogue and information on the texts, by Claude Abravanel—with English and Hebrew information—in *Tazlil,* ed. M. Gorali, Haifa 1979, pp. 129–137.

dominated the Italian musical scene and greatly influenced the composers of Italy. Italian music had developed trends of its own, with theater performances containing choral and solo vocals, prototypes of opera. Then came opera itself, and Italian writers published treatises on the art of singing, as well as on instrumental music. Vocal and instrumental groups started touring in western Europe, and some outstanding Italian musicians were offered permanent positions at churches and courts. To what extent Jewish singers and players were among them has not yet been sufficiently studied. It is known that Italian Jews (and Portuguese and Spanish Jews who had emigrated to Italy and left their Italian domicile) had been conspicuously numerous at the Tudor court since the reign of King Henry VIII (1509–1547), and that his daughter Queen Elizabeth I (1558–1603) also employed Jewish musicians. Some musical families, veritable dynasties that handed down their musical knowledge and art from one generation to the next, dominated the King's Musick and the Queen's Musick until the Civil Wars of the 1640s and even beyond.[31]

The Jewish musicians who left Italy must have been especially attracted to England, where the particular character of the Reformation was anti-Papal as well as anti-Lutheran—both the Papal establishment and the German brand of the Reformation were anti-Jewish. In England they were not prosecuted, were appreciated as masters of their art, and could lead a free and probably carefree life. It was known to the court that they were Jews; there was no prejudice against them, and they were loyal to the Crown— at the cost, of course, that they could not live as practicing Jews.

King Henry VIII had shown respect to the Jews in turning to Jewish scholars in Venice in 1531 for advice about the legality of his marriage to Catherine of Aragon (his first wife). (The Pope's unwillingness to dissolve the marriage had led to the English Reformation.) The King was also known as a patron of music and a champion of contemporary innovations; on his search for good "modern" musicians he turned to Italy, especially to Venice, the city that had the best commercial ties with England and har-

---

[31]See Roger Prior, "Jewish Musicians at the Tudor Court," *Musical Quarterly*, New York, Spring 1983, pp. 253–265, on whose research our survey is mostly based.

bored a host of progressive musicians, both Christians and Jews. It fact, the Jewish players brought from Italy to the Royal Household outnumbered their Gentile colleagues. The King's Musick had at least nineteen Jewish members in the 1540s; they had arrived, as records show, in the 1520s and 1530s, many of them with their families. The names of the musicians have made their identification as Jews rather easy.[32]

There were not only instrumentalists but also instrument makers in the Bassano family, which settled in London in 1539 after a preliminary visit of four Bassano brothers eight years earlier, when they already played with the King's musicians. The family originally came form the north Italian town Bassano—Jewish family names were in most European countries often derived from towns—but it is thought that their ancestors originally were Ashkenazic Jews from southern Germany. No connection has been established between the Jewish Bassanos and some well-known Gentile composers—Bassano, Bassani—from Padua and Venice. In 1540 there were five Bassano brothers in the Royal wind band; four additional wind players were also Jewish: Peregrine and Anthony Simon from Padua, Anthonius Moyses from Castello, and Anthony Cuson or Cossin (possibly originally Gerson, Gershon) from Torino and Venice. The Royal consort of viols was founded by six Jewish musicians who came to England from the duchy of Milan but were of Spanish or Portuguese descent, Sephardim, possibly *Marranos,* fugitives from the Inquisition. They were involved in a complaint on the part of the Spanish king that "secret Jews" were among "some Portuguese nationals" living in London, were arrested, set free, sent back to Italy, and called back to London again; they then brought with them another Jewish musician, Francis Kellim—his name is derived from the Hebrew *kelìm* = instruments.

It seems certain that the large contingent of Jewish musicians from Italy introduced to England the practice of playing instruments in consort, in the style and manner that had developed in Italy. The Bassano family has additionally been credited with providing the royal band with musical instruments of their own making which were recorded as being "so beautiful

---

[32]Roger Prior, op. cit., provides convincing proof for the Jewish origin of the musicians cited.

and good they are suited for dignitaries and potentates."[33] The Bassanos had their own workshop. A chest containing forty-five of their instruments was sent to the house of the Bavarian banker Hans Jakob Fugger "the Rich," banker to emperors and popes, thus traveling back to a region noted as a German center of wind-instrument manufacturing and from where the ancestors of the Bassano family from Bassano and Venice had probably originated. Between 1540 and 1640 there also were at the court eight members of the consort of viols by the typically Jewish name of Lupo; one of them, Thomas Lupo, son of the violist Joseph was not only violist but also lutenist, singer, and composer. That the Jewish musicians at the Tudor court contributed to the modernization of English music making and the manufacture of musical instruments fits well into the innovative roles Jewish thinkers, poets, artists, and musicians have filled in the general history of world culture—first-line motivators of novel thinking and innovators of artistic trends. It seems, however, not recorded—and it is not very likely— that the Jewish players attended synagogue services in London or contributed in any way to the music of the English Jews; some of them seem to have taken on the religion of their English hosts. Only in the eighteenth century did the Jewish community in England begin to show interest in the creation of new music for the synagogue.

IN CONTRAST, the Gentile society in Italy knew very little, if anything, of the music in the Jewish ghetto, and the ghetto musicians did not appear at Gentile sacred or secular observances. It may thus be regarded as a certain irony of history that a hundred years after a Jew—Salomone Rossi—had provided the Hebrew psalms and prayers with new music with little concern for the traditional synagogue chant, a Gentile composer was attracted by ancient Hebrew traditional melodies and based a fine collection of psalm settings on Sephardic and Ashkenazic melodies that he had heard in the synagogue of Venice. He was Benedetto Marcello (1686–1739), and his psalm settings were published in Venice in 1724–1726. The eight-volume

---

[33]Roger Prior citing old sources, op. cit., pp. 264–265. For a recent, more detailed study, see *The Bassanos: Venetian Musicians and Instrument Makers in England, 1531–1665* by David Lasocki with Roger Prior. Aldershot, Hampshire, 1995.

work contains fifty settings in arrangements for one to four voices with occasional solos for violin and violoncello and with figured bass added, under
the title *Estro poetico-armonico,* "a pompous, truly baroque title,"[34] probably a collection of pieces written over several years. He introduced each
volume with extensive prefaces giving his views on the music of the Greeks
and the Hebrews. Regarding the settings of the original Jewish melodies
Marcello heard in the synagogue, some of Sephardic and others of Ashkenazic provenance, he wrote that he "introduced recitatives, in order to afford the listeners . . . a suitable pleasure . . . also in order to approximate to
a certain extent the practice, as one finds in a sacred scripture, especially
with reference to precentors, characteristic of the Jewish people." In another passage Marcello explained his use of choral polyphony in the settings
of original melodies: "In order to adjust to our [i.e. Italian] verses and meters, their [time] value had to be lengthened, and the tunes had to be repeated several times. Yet nowhere and never was the original intonation
altered in any way, although certain mannerisms are employed in Jewish
chant, such as *portamento di voce* and others." Marcello also points to the
"surely typical differences recognizable between the chants of the Spanish
and the German Jews." This confirms that in the Venetian synagogue both
Sephardic and Ashkenazic melodies were sung to the liturgical texts; these
were, as historic and melodic analysis reveals, of sacred and folkloristic, of
truly Jewish and non-Jewish—even German—origin.

The rich variety of melodic material noted by Marcello in the synagogue of Venice testifies to the cultivation of music by a succession of gifted
and active composers and performers. Venetian Jewry had a rich musical
tradition, and its chain had not been broken so cruelly as that of Mantua.
At the time the Jewish musicians flourished in Mantua there must have existed a magnificent musical practice in Venice. Names of outstanding composers or performers have not come down to us, it is true, but it is known
that the Jewish music teachers enjoyed such a reputation that many Christian noblemen asked them to instruct their children—a custom against

---

[34]See Eric Werner on Benedetto Marcello in *A Voice Still Heard,* University Park
and London, 1976, p. 127, which also includes the excerpts from the Prefaces.
Tunes in Marcello's work are analyzed in Werner's book, pp. 119–121.

Musicians in Purim procession, woodcut, Amsterdam, 1723.

which the clerical authorities issued a decree. But musical performances in the ghetto of Venice went on, and many Christians came to listen to them there. It may be remembered here that Venice had actually been the first city to relegate Jews to a ghetto and that the very word "ghetto" is of Venetian origin: in 1516 the Jews were given a domicile in a district in which since 1306 there had existed a "ghetto"—a cannon foundry.

The Jewish actress and singer Rachel achieved great fame with the Venetian nobility and was often invited to appear at court (in the first decade of the seventeenth century), and the poetess Sarah Copia-Sullam—whom we mentioned in connection with the dedication of Rossi's psalm book—was also famous in Venice. When in the ghetto a musical comedy was performed in 1607 with the participation of the entire Jewish community, a large audience enjoyed the show, and many Christians made it a rule to attend the festivals of the Jews. Instrumental music was permitted in

E S T R O
POETICO-ARMONICO.
P A R A F R A S I
SOPRA LI PRIMI
VENTICINQUE SALMI.
POESIA
D I

GIROLAMO ASCANIO GIUSTINIANI,
M U S I C A
D I

B E N E D E T T O   M A R C E L L O
P A T R I Z J   V E N E T I.

T O M O   P R I M O.

V E N E Z I A   MDCCCIII.

PRESSO SEBASTIANO VALLE.

Title page from Benedetto Marcello's collection of psalm settings, *Estro-poetico-armonico.*

"O sing unto the Lord a new song, sing unto the Lord, all the earth"—from Benedetto Marcello's *Paraphrases on the First Twenty-five Psalms*, Vol. 1, Venice, 1724.

the Venetian synagogue; a complete orchestra officiated in the Sephardic synagogue, while in another house of worship orchestral playing was replaced by an "imitation of the movements of musicians." When, on the occasion of the Rejoicing of the Law (*Simhat-Torah*), an organ was brought to the Sephardic synagogue to augment the orchestra, there came such a crowd of both Christian and Jewish listeners that the police had to be called to prevent disorder at the doors. The organ was then removed, and the experiment was never repeated; but the orchestra was permitted to remain. In 1629 an academy of music was founded in the Venetian ghetto, and twice a week concerts were arranged there by the Jewish musicians: it is most probable that this academy was a foundation of musicians that had fled from Mantua (who knows whether Rossi himself had been among them?). Leone da Modena became the leader and conductor of the society, which adopted the name *B'sochrenu et Zion* ("Remembering Zion") in quotation of Psalm 137, which also formed part of Salomone Rossi's liturgical work.

The activities of the musical society in the ghetto were greatly hindered and undoubtedly curtailed by an epidemic of plague in 1630; we know no more about the academy than that it existed for about ten years. But we may be sure that the tradition was fostered in the Venetian ghetto throughout the seventeenth century—for how else could the musical life of the Jews have so greatly prospered a hundred years later! Marcello was not the only musician to testify to the high standard of Jewish music in Venice, but he has erected a lasting monument to his fellow-musicians of the Jewish ghetto.

Marcello achieved universal fame by this very work, the fifty psalms; he was ever after regarded as a "prince of music" in Rome and Bologna, and the songs themselves were widely performed in Italy as well as in Germany, France, and England, where they were translated into the vernacular. For the purely Jewish sphere Marcello's music has as little importance as Rossi's synagogal songs: only indirectly did both prove their influence when new attempts at a reform of synagogal music in the contemporary style were made in nineteenth-century Germany. But Marcello's book stimulated new interest in Hebrew music, which had in former periods so much occupied both the Jewish and non-Jewish scholars. The great humanist Reuchlin had published his treatise on the Hebrew accents in 1518 and was followed in his investigations by other scholars of his century: among them Yehuda Moscato, who devoted his first sermon to music; Abraham Portaleone, the learned author of *Shiltei ha-Gibborim*, who wrote some chapters on Temple music, which he pictured in a true Renaissance spirit; and Yehuda ben Yizhaq, whose fragment of Hebrew musical theory was based on the work of the fourteenth-century Italian author Marchettus of Padua.[35]

WITH THE DECLINE of the Jewish communities in the Italian cities the Jews again disappeared from the annals of musical history. They took no further active part in the cultural life of the nations with whom they lived till there dawned a new cosmopolitan era—the period of enlightenment and reason of the eighteenth century, which did away with the barriers that had so long separated the Jews from the society of Gentiles. It is only then that Jewish participation in general culture again produced distinctive works of art, but then the desire for emancipation became so strong that the creators and artists left Judaism far behind them and felt no obligation to serve their own people.

Leone da Modena and Salomone Rossi—two ingenious men, progressive and daring in spirit and creative will—turned against tradition in their own way; but their reform aimed at an enrichment of their own, the Jewish, sphere. Rossi remained the "Ebreo," the Hebrew, in title as well as

---

[35]Eric Werner and Isaiah Sonne, "The Philosophy and Theory of Music in Judeo-Arabic Literature," *Hebrew Union College Annual*, 1941.

in feeling and purpose throughout his life, even though the majority of Jews did not recognize his artistic reforms in his lifetime and posterity was quick to forget them. Thus he belongs in Jewish musical history to a much greater degree—in spite of his creations being Italian music of late Renaissance and early baroque character—than some of the emancipated Jewish composers of nineteenth-century Europe.

CHAPTER SEVEN

FROM MENDELSSOHN TO MAHLER—

A CENTURY OF EMANCIPATION

T
HOUGH THE STORY of musical activity in the synagogue and the Jewish home goes on without a break through the centuries of Jewish settlement in Europe, there is a conspicuous hiatus in the field of art music between the period of the first great Jewish master of European music, Salomone Rossi Ebreo, and the composer who opens the next chapter in our historical survey of the *Music of Israel*, Felix Mendelssohn-Bartholdy. Considering the fact that Jewish artists have so often played important roles in periods of transition, it is somewhat puzzling that they had no part at all in the great stylistic changes that occurred in eighteenth-century music, when creative artists broke loose from the bonds of patronage and began to serve a middle-class public rather than a prince of the church or the court.

The history of the place of the Jews in seventeenth- and eighteenth-century European society is responsible for the absence of Jewish musicians in the history of music after that short and magnificent intermezzo at the court of Mantua; only nineteenth-century liberalism opened the doors for Jewish participation in the cultural activities pursued in the European countries. For the "Middle Ages" of Jewish history in Europe ended with the victory of the slogan of the French Revolution: Liberty, Equality, Fraternity. The call to forget national barriers and to recognize the universality of mankind and of philosophy, science, and the arts was addressed to all civilized men, Jews included. And who could indeed so eagerly grasp the idea as the Jews, whose life had been made miserable by the very lack of tolerance and liberal thought? For centuries they had been stamped as foreigners and had been forbidden to practice any but the lowest trades; with the French Revolution various western European countries allowed them to become citizens. As such they could take part in the political and economic life of the countries to which they belonged, and it was only natural that they should always side with the liberal and progressive forces in all spheres of political, social, and cultural life.

But the Jew's progress in nineteenth-century society occasioned tragic conflicts: on the one hand, he was not always accepted by society as enthusiastically as he himself plunged into it for sheer joy over the doors being opened to him; on the other hand, he placed himself in opposition to his own tradition-bound community, which watched the process of emancipation with suspicion and foreboding. Since time immemorial it had been the strength as well as the weakness of Judaism that its laws combined the religious code with the foundations of ethics, morals, politics, and science; though this had impeded the development of independent thinking and scientific progress, it had given the spiritual achievements of the Jews a singular unity. With participation in liberal politics and their occupation in all branches of progressive science, the Jews left the world of the ghetto and the synagogue far behind them. The enlightened Jews who continued to keep the traditional laws and observe the prayers and holy days did so to placate their conscience; they also held some sentimental affection for the ancient ceremonies and perpetuated in them the memory of their parents and ancestors. But liberal science and religious tradition were irreconcilable in Judaism, and with his emancipation the nineteenth-century Jew entered a historical phase that opened the gates of the world to him but also put him in a spiritual vacuum—for Gentile society continued to think of him as a member of his own community, to which he no longer wholeheartedly belonged.

With the emancipation there began an epoch that witnessed great achievements by Jews in all branches of science and art, but most of them have little or nothing to do with the Jewishness of their authors. The Jew was quick to learn what had been denied to him for many centuries, and the development of European culture away from the ecclesiastical and feudal order to a middle-class rule favored his entrance into European society. Moreover, as the Jews had always been excluded from agriculture and thus been forced to turn to urban occupations, they were able to play a conspicuous role with the rapid rise of the towns in the nineteenth century and with their ever-increasing commercial and social life. It is thus that Jews quickly appeared in all urban free professions: their thorough training in the legal subtleties of talmudic literature made them eager students of the law, a century-long interest in medicine had created a unique medical tradition, their preoccupation with the world's most ancient Book of Books had developed their literary and philosophical talents, and their traditional affection for music now also found new outlets. Faculties that had before been subdued in the desperate fight for existence could now be devoted to creative activity and applied to an almost unlimited range of subjects.

The period of assimilation and emancipation brought about a complete estrangement between the Jewish centers in eastern and western Europe. The West had hitherto drawn much of its cultural strength from the East, but when the western Jews plunged deep into a civilization remote from the ideals of Judaism and renounced many of their own spiritual possessions, there ensued a sharp separation. The liberation from Jewish seclusion was a comparatively slight step for the western communities, in which the tradition had become somewhat cramped and had little bearing on everyday life; but in the East the living contact with the tradition and the moral forces of Judaism had just been rekindled by the Hassidic movement. The eastern Jews continued to live their Judaism with all their emotional and spiritual might and condemned all occupation with the liberal arts and sciences—as practiced by their western brethren—as heretical; they preserved the religious and social code of Jewry, and the East could thus become the birthplace of the Jewish national renaissance at a time when the Jews of the West had lost almost all their contact with Jewish life and ideas.

AGAINST THE SPIRITUAL BACKGROUND of Jewish emancipation was written another chapter in Jewish musical history, yet this is no longer the story of Jewish music but the story of music by Jewish masters. Synagogue music began to drift away from its most ancient heritage and to lean more and more toward western musical styles, becoming less typically Jewish with the times. Most Jewish composers of secular music liberated themselves from Jewish bondage yet remained Jews in the eyes of the writers and musicians around them. Just as in politics and economy, in philosophy and science, the Jews could play their own part in the development of the arts; Jewish musicians and composers abound in the history of European music. Some of them were active in the Jewish as well as the general sphere, but none of the greater Jewish nineteenth-century composers created works that had a decisive bearing on the history of Hebrew music—as did Salomone Rossi in seventeenth-century Italy.

The approximately one hundred and fifty years of Jewish emancipation in European music are bounded by two ingenious composers, both conspicuous figures in general music history: the period opened with Felix Mendelssohn-Bartholdy, a musician who stemmed from a family famous in the Jewish world but who gradually abandoned all bonds with Jewish tradition till his interest centered solely in Christian ideas and German music; it closed with the spiritual development of Arnold Schoenberg, who came from completely assimilated circles but was irresistibly drawn toward the values of Judaism and was inspired to a number of important works by the greatest creation of the Hebrew spirit—the Bible.

THE SUDDEN BREAKING of the Jews into western culture and music was not the immediate consequence of the impact of the French Revolution only. Music itself had undergone a far-reaching evolution, the very foundation of which enabled the Jews to play a part in its cultivation. The stylistic transition of the mid-eighteenth century was based on the same ideas as the movement that led to the French Revolution: it also marked the change from the feudal order to the rule of middle-class society. In feudal Europe the Church had been the center of musical science and practice, and the Jews had for this reason been denied an active participation in European musical art; in seventeenth- and eighteenth-century Europe another center of music making had been created—that is, the aristocratic court—but this, too, was inaccessible to the central European Jews. Individualistic traits began to show in the musical works and their performance, but there still reigned in them the community spirit, expressed in the polyphonic style, which gave all singers and players an equally important share in the performance of music. The creative as well as the performing artist—generally united in one person—was in the service of a clerical or worldly lord; only at the Italian courts had Jews temporarily been able to penetrate beyond the feudal barrier.

Johann Sebastian Bach was the last great master of this epoch, and his compositions are the final examples of an art created almost exclusively in fulfillment of the demands of service and loyalty. But already in his lifetime there began to develop the public concert, an institution which enabled the middle classes for the first time to enjoy the luxuries hitherto reserved to nobility and to purchase the pleasure of a musical evening like any other commodity. In Bach's time were found the first signs of the stylistic transition which was to lead to the symphonies and the chamber music of masters like Haydn and Mozart and which was—sociologically as well as musically—crowned by the symphonic work of Ludwig van Beethoven. Haydn was still the servant of a noble prince and derived his income from service,but his music breathed the spirit of the new times and conquered the young concert halls of the world; Mozart's tragedy was the social descent from pet child prodigy to struggling and unappreciated master which paralleled his development from an obliging composer and performer of entertainment music into an individual artist whose works of sublimest perfection were created in complete indifference to the tastes of superficial society; Beethoven, finally, was able to establish the demands of genius and liberated the artist from the bonds of service once and forever.

While the Jews can often be found in the first row of innovators or pioneers—Salomone Rossi serves as an early example, and in modern times there are many instances of this fact—they took no early part in the period of transition and the creation of the symphonic style in the eighteenth century. It is interesting to inquire into the cause of their late appearance in the general history of music: the creation of the public concert (in England at the end of the seventeenth century, and in France early in the eighteenth century) was the work of a privileged middle class at a time when the Jews had not yet been admitted into non-Jewish society; and the first musicians searching for new ways of expression and eventually paving the ground for forms and style suiting the new public came from Italy, Austria, southern Germany, and Bohemia—Catholic countries in which the Jesuits educated the youth in their schools, colleges, and universities. The social background of the public concert and the spiritual education given to its first composers were thus unfavorable to Jewish participation in the early history of classical music, and only with the eventual victory of the middle-class order do Jews appear in the annals of musical history.

Among Mozart's friends and supporters we find a number of prominent Jewish personalities. Members of the wealthy financial circles of Vienna were among the subscribers to his printed compositions, and the Jewish Baron Wetzlar was his temporary landlord and the godfather of one of his children; Mozart's association with the Italian poet of Jewish parentage, Lorenzo da Ponte, was responsible for his greatest operatic works. Beethoven's connections with Jewry came principally through his making the acquaintance, at the Bohemian resort of Teplitz, of Rahel Varnhagen, the Berlin Jewess whose salon was the meeting place of the spiritual elite. In 1825 he was requested by Viennese Jewish dignitaries to compose a cantata for the dedication of a new synagogue. This task, like many others proposed, he did not carry out, but he seems to have seriously contemplated its execution for some time (see above, pp. 160–161).

SHORTLY BEFORE BEETHOVEN'S DEATH a seventeen-year-old Jewish musician surprised the world with two enchanting compositions—an octet for strings, which was a perfect romantic work in a medium that had never been used before, and a truly fairy-land overture to Shakespeare's *Midsummer Night's Dream* fantasy. He was Felix Mendelssohn-Bartholdy, grandson of Moses Mendelssohn, the profound Jewish scholar and one of the great figures in the period of the enlightenment in Germany. Moses Mendelssohn (died 1786) had come from a narrow ghetto milieu, where his father kept a Hebrew day school, and had risen to be one of the best-known thinkers of his age. His life's work was mediation between the Jews and their surroundings: he wanted the Gentiles to understand the Jews and to accept them in their society, while he desired the Jews to study the language and the cultural achievements of the Germans. An encyclopedic

Lorenzo da Ponte, Mozart's Italian-Jewish librettist.

knowledge and a lofty character secured Moses Mendelssohn a prominent place in the high society of Berlin, where his second son, Abraham, was born in 1776. Abraham Mendelssohn took to banking and greatly succeeded in business; he made many friends by the straightforwardness of his character and by his wide sympathies and high cultural standard. In 1804 he married Leah Salomon, a wealthy banker's daughter and a remarkable woman of many talents, especially for languages, drawing, and music—talents all four children inherited from their mother. Abraham Mendelssohn had lost contact with the Jewish world after the death of his father, though his wife came from a religious Jewish family too; when his children were born he decided to follow the trend of the times and educate them as

Protestants. In order to distinguish their family from the branch that did not renounce Judaism, the Christian Mendelssohns added to their original name that of Bartholdy—the name taken on by Abraham's brother-in-law after he had become a Christian.

The house of the Mendelssohn-Bartholdys was a model home, and the education of the children was exemplary in its many-sidedness. Abraham himself was a connoisseur of the arts and exerted great influence on the spiritual development and artistic views of his children. Young Felix (born 1809), the second of Abraham and Leah's four children (Fanny was born four years before him) grew up in an artistic atmosphere: among his parents' friends were some of the brightest luminaries of the time, and the parties and Sunday morning concerts at their house were famous throughout Berlin. The prominent visitors included the politician and philosopher Wilhelm von Humboldt, the diplomat and writer Varnhagen von Ense and his wife Rahel, Goethe's music friend Carl Friedrich Zelter, who was director and conductor of the Berlin Singakademie, Adolf Bernhard Marx, the Jewish theoretician and editor of an important music journal, and the composer and piano virtuoso Ignaz Moscheles. After 1822, when the musicales were instituted for Felix's sake, the house was crammed full on Sunday mornings.

At the age of seven the talented boy had already been to Paris and had taken piano lessons there after initial instruction from his mother; when he was thirteen he went to Switzerland, and at eighteen to Paris again. He could then boast of having met and played to the best-known musicians of the time—among them Weber, Spohr, Hiller, Moscheles, Cherubini, Meyerbeer, Rossini, and Halévy—and having delighted the aged poet Goethe by playing to him the music of Haydn, Mozart, Beethoven, and Johann Sebastian Bach. He had enjoyed a thorough general education and musical training, and in 1829—in his twentieth year—embarked on extensive travels which led him to England, Wales, and Scotland, to Italy (where he met Berlioz), to Switzerland, and to France (where he met Liszt and Chopin). He played the piano, conducted, sketched landscapes, and composed, and he never knew repose. "The habit of constant occupation instilled by his mother made rest intolerable to him," said his friend Eduard Devrient. "To spend any time in mere talk caused him to look frequently at his watch, by which he often gave offence; his impatience was only pacified when something was being done, such as music, reading, chess, etc." His must have been a singularly attractive personality: "You had only to be in his presence for a few moments to feel how completely his appearance and manner represented the genius he possessed . . . ," wrote John C. Horsley, one of Mendelssohn's English friends, in a letter to Sir George Grove when the latter prepared his *Dictionary of Music and Musicians*, "he had a lithe figure, was very active and had a great deal of what may be termed sinuous movement in his action, and which was inimitably in harmony with his feeling of the moment. . . . It would need a pencil of fire to catch the brightness of Mendelssohn's countenance and wonderful animation of manner."[1]

The restlessness and continuous activities soon told on Mendelssohn's health, and in 1837 he confided to his friend Hiller that "two months of constant conducting takes more out of me than two years of composing all day long. . . . I often think I should like to retire completely, never conduct any more, and only write; but then again there is a certain charm in a musical organization, and in having the direction of it. . . ."[2]

Felix Mendelssohn found haven and happiness in the exemplary family life of his parents' home and always followed the advice of his father—to the extent of giving up the composing of small forms and turning to the composition of large-scale religious works. His father's death in 1835 was a severe blow for him, and only his marriage a year and a half later could bring happiness into his life again. He had meanwhile met Schumann and Wagner, become conductor of the Leipzig Gewandhaus concerts (in 1843 he opened the conservatory in that city), and had made history by conducting, at the age of twenty, the first revival of J. S. Bach's *St. Matthew Pas-*

---

[1]The quotations are taken from Jack Werner's article on Felix and Fanny Mendelssohn in *Music and Letters,* Vol. 28, 1947, pp. 303–337. The decisive book on the composer is Eric Werner's *Mendelssohn: A New Image of the Composer and His Age,* New York, 1963.

[2]Compare Mendelssohn's disclosure with Leonard Bernstein's: "I will not compose a note while my heart is engaged in a conducting season; nor will I give up writing as much as a popular song, while it is there to be expressed, in order to conduct Beethoven's Ninth. There is a particular order involved in this [which] must be adhered to most strictly" (see Gradenwitz, *Leonard Bernstein,* Zürich/Mainz, 1995). Leonard Bernstein is a modern counterpart of Mendelssohn also in the description "lithe figure, . . . sinuous movements, . . . animation of manner."

Felix Mendelssohn-Bartholdy (1809–47).

sion at the Berlin Singakademie. As a conductor he was much sought after, and the list of his compositions began to swell. In 1834 he published the first of his eight volumes of *Songs Without Words*, the most popular piano pieces ever composed and a definite departure from the piano music current at the time. And though his restless traveling and creating also necessarily produced works of minor inspiration, Mendelssohn's immortality is firmly based on his "Italian" and "Scottish" Symphonies, the violin concerto, the delicate chamber works, the fine lyrical songs, the psalms and oratorios, and the *Midsummer Night's Dream* music. Mendelssohn's death at the age of thirty-eight was mourned by musicians great and small the world over, and even though uninspired imitations of his music have brought some

The Gewandhaus concert hall in Leipzig in Felix Mendelssohn's time (1845).
(Courtesy of Leipzig City Museum.)

undeserved discredit to his own compositions, his creative genius never
needed assertion or vindication.

Felix Mendelssohn believed in the values of Christianity but never forgot his Jewish roots: he also suffered from anti-Semitic attacks. The defama-
tion of his character and the ban on his music in Nazi Germany interrupted
its popularity for the barbarous twelve years only. He wrote Christian cantatas and biblical psalms, the oratorio *Paulus* on the New Testament figure
of the converted Saulus-Paulus and *Elias* on the Hebrew prophet. He had
felt an affinity for sacred music from his earliest youth. His teacher in composition, Carl Friedrich Zelter, Johann Wolfgang von Goethe's musical
friend and director of the Berlin Singakademie, took the gifted young boy
on as an alto singer for the Academy in 1819 and had his music for the
nineteenth Psalm performed there the very same year. Two years later he
traveled with him to Weimar and let him play for Goethe.

Felix Mendelssohn's first concert at the new Gewandhaus concert hall, Leipzig, 4 October 1835.

The search for Jewish features in Mendelssohn's work has revealed a single instant of obvious Jewish identity. It occurs in the great dramatic scene near the end of the oratorio *Elias*. This is the climax of the work, believed to have been planned by the composer before he started writing the score. At the words "Behold, God the Lord passed by" the music takes up

Statue of Felix Mendelssohn-Bartholdy in front of the Gewandhaus concert hall in Leipzig; erected about 1900, it was dismantled in 1936 by the Nazis. It was replaced by a new statue of a different character in 1947. (Courtesy of Leipzig City Museum.)

an ancient Hebrew intonation "Adona'i, Adona'i, El rachamím ve-hanun," traditionally sung in all German synagogues since the fifteenth century on the highest Holy Days only. The melody must have come to Mendelssohn in connection with the "appearance of the Lord."[3] There may be other remembrances of Jewish melodic material in Felix Mendelssohn's works, perhaps in the opening theme of the e-minor Violin Concerto.

Friedrich Nietzsche called Felix Mendelssohn "the beautiful incident of German music," but it did not take long for anti-Jewish circles to start agitating against the unreserved acceptance of a "Jewish composer." Mendelssohn himself, though endowed with many Jewish traits and apparently Jewish in appearance, is known to have alluded to his descent only once in his life—on the occasion of his conducting Bach's *St. Matthew Passion*. "To think," Mendelssohn is reported to have said to his friend Eduard Devrient, the singer and actor, in a triumphant voice, "that it should be an actor and a Jew that give back to the people the greatest of Christian works." Zelter, Goethe's musical friend, had still described the composer as "son of a Jew but no Jew," but during the barbarous intermezzo in German history a century later Mendelssohn was labeled "a Jew who falsified the sacred treasures of German culture" and "whose true intentions are obvious in the oratorios, the heroes of which are a Hebrew prophet (Elias) and Paul the apostle who implanted Jewish thinking into young Christianity."

Though such libelous criticism—springing from a general anti-Semitic attitude and not from factual analysis—cannot really be considered seriously, it remains an astonishing fact that no Jewish genius—not even the one who believed himself most remote from Judaism and most perfectly assimilated—ever found unreserved acceptance in Gentile society: if he himself had completely forgotten his descent, there was always the other side there to remember, maybe to remind him as well. Few were the occasions in the era of emancipation when Jewish writers and artists actually encountered outspoken anti-Semitism, but a large number of critics—both Jewish and non-Jewish—have attempted to prove Jewish traits in the poetry

---

[3]Erich Werner, in *Mendelssohn*, op. cit., reproduces and analyzes this musical sequence.

of Heine as well as in the music of Mendelssohn, Meyerbeer, Offenbach, Mahler, Schoenberg, and others; and whenever personal dislike, bitterness, or competition entered the relations of Christian and Jew, the latter was reminded of his foreignness. A notorious example of a composer campaigning against Jewish musicians in a period of physical and mental exasperation is Richard Wagner's scurrilous pamphlet, *Judaism in Music* (1850).

The question has often been asked whether there do exist any common traits linking Jewish musicians together in the same way that the great masters of Bohemian music or the composers of France can be identified by certain common national characteristics throughout the ages. The search for Jewish traits uniting works as far apart in time and spirit as, say, Mendelssohn's *Midsummer Night's Dream* music and Offenbach's naughty satirical operettas or as Rossi's Italian madrigals and Schoenberg's string quartets seems ridiculous and farfetched at the outset. It is difficult enough to explain in the unbroken chain of a national history such phenomena as the completely different styles of "Russianism" in Mussorgsky's and Prokofiev's music or the fact that the Austrian spirit could produce in one period such widely diverging musical characters as Anton Bruckner and Johann Strauss; nevertheless the existence of some typical national traits cannot be denied in the case of the great musical nations. The works of Jewish composers living in their midst might be expected to be more characteristic of the musical tradition of the people who gave them their background and education than of the Jewish culture which they had left behind them. But even the most complete assimilation into another culture has seldom destroyed all traces of the emotional and spiritual heritage of the Jews. It might be expected, then, that such emotional and spiritual traits would find expression in their creative work.

"The older the culture of a people, the more does intellect predominate over instinct," says the great Jewish sociologist Arthur Ruppin. Indeed, the conditions of living had forced the Jews to concentrate on the intellectual professions; their meticulous study and interpretation of Bible and Talmud pursued through the centuries had sharpened their wit, and their role as economic and cultural mediators between countries and continents had broadened their outlook. As they had been excluded from the land and become early town dwellers, they had developed the white-collar professions in an ever-increasing degree: in 1933 a quarter of the Jewry of the entire world was concentrated in nine capital cities—New York, Budapest, Buenos Aires, Kiev, London, Moscow, Paris, Vienna, and Warsaw—and a large percentage was active in the intellectual world. The exigencies of life had always demanded from the Jew intellectual agility and a knack for quick decision and action, and this again had developed in him a singular talent for adaptation and adjustment. Considering the Jewish composers of the different periods, we can in fact discern the prevalence of intellect over impulse; this is particularly striking in the romantic era, where music served artists as a vehicle for an unrestrained effusion of emotion and feeling. The Jews, intellectually awake on the one hand and warned to restrain their instincts on the other, did not bring forth a composer as demoniacally profound as Mozart or as spiritually transcendental as Beethoven; nor have they produced musical masters as free in lyricism and romantic sensitiveness as Schubert and Schumann, and the sublime synthesis of classical form and romantic spirit achieved by Johannes Brahms had been denied to Mendelssohn. The Jewish composers are characterized by a highly developed sense of formal design, by a skillful utilization of musical and technical means, and by their universality.

This should not be understood to mean that the Jews are incapable of experiencing or of giving artistic expression to their inner life. But in Jewish art there seems to be a deeper gulf between art and nature than is commonly found elsewhere. "Genius learns from nature—from his own nature—while talents learn from art," Arnold Schoenberg once said, and this remark may serve to explain the opinion—frequently, and not quite unjustly, expressed—that the Jews can boast of a great number of talents but individuals of real musical genius are rare. Living among other people whose hostility they had always to fear, Jews were compelled to mask their feelings and restrain their natural impulses; their nature seemed distorted and their inner life buried under the demands of their intellect. They suppressed their nature and checked their emotion, but easily mastered the rules of art found in the sublime creations of other composers. It is thus that in the works of many Jewish musicians mastery of craftsmanship is met side by side with lack of emotional depth and playful artistry often replaces meditation. Where the great romanticists are passionate and expansive, exalta-

tion and contemplation characterize the compositions of the masters of
Jewish descent, many of whom seem possessed by a vehement yearning for
another being and a different world—Gustav Mahler providing the most
extraordinary case in point.

In Mendelssohn's music we can feel an ardent longing for the serenity
of classical antiquity and for the past splendors of German music, and there
is in it a characteristic cosmopolitanism and universality of talent and style;
his supreme command of form is shown particularly in his pianistically perfect *Songs Without Words*, in which he adapted vocal forms to instrumental
purposes in an original way. Meyerbeer was a virtuoso master of the opera
technique of three countries—Germany, Italy, and France—without being
able to penetrate to a grasp of real life and drama. Mahler's dilemma was his
ardent desire to mediate between his Jewish-spiritual heritage and the Catholic spirit, and between the mysticism of his belief and artistic being and the
simplicity of the German folk song. Each of these three great figures in
nineteenth-century musical history was a split personality in his own way
and a foreign element in all spheres of activity. In the works of Offenbach,
the ingenious critic of French society, there appeared still another trait characteristically Jewish: sarcasm, satire, and irony, which the Jews had developed as weapons of the weak and helpless against the powers of oppression.
We can often find Jews as masters of caricature and satire—in literature,
painting, and music—and the *grotesque* has always attracted them.

It is of little avail to search for suggestions of synagogal or popular Jewish melodies in the works of the assimilated composers of Jewish descent.
Reminiscences or affinities of the kind can be proved in a good many cases,
but they are inconclusive; for not a conscious or unconscious use of certain
melodic phrases but only the composer's personality and the spiritual background of his creative activity can give us clues to the understanding of his
works and his art.

Though it is interesting to inquire into the characteristics that distinguish Jewish composers from their Gentile fellow-artists, we should avoid
the danger of ascribing all personal traits in their work to their Jewishness.
We must remember that romanticism, the mainstream in nineteenth-century music, generally fostered the development of a highly individualized
personality, and that the isolation of the artist from his surroundings and

from the reality of life had created a deep gulf between artist and public as between a privileged and an ordinary person. An analysis of the individual achievements of great Jewish composers can thus never intend to claim their works for Jewish musical history, though the Jewishness of these masters does offer an explanation for *some* characteristics of their life, their artistic growth, and their aesthetics.

WHEN WE DESCRIBE Felix Mendelssohn as the first of the long line of Jewish composers who rose to extraordinary fame and created immortal works of music, we are apt to forget that a long tradition had developed the Jewish talent for music, though it had been able to express itself only in the synagogue and the popular, and not the purely artistic, sphere. The Mendelssohn family itself had cultivated music for many generations. Felix's grandfather, the philosopher, is known to have been greatly interested in music; it was not only mathematical interest that led him to the study of piano tuning and equal temperament, a science about which he actually published a treatise. Moses Mendelssohn counted among his friends in Berlin a number of outstanding theoreticians and musicians and himself took piano lessons; he also wrote on the aesthetics of music. His son Abraham, Felix's father, was musically gifted and interested, too, and his tastes and opinions exercised a decisive influence on his son. From his mother Felix had also inherited musical talent, and his sister Fanny, who married the painter Wilhelm Hensel in 1829, was a fine pianist and composer in her own right. The composer's bonds with her were so strong that her premature death in 1847 accelerated his own physical decline: he died six months after his beloved sister.

The youth and spiritual background of Jacob Meyerbeer—by eighteen years Mendelssohn's senior but acknowledged as a composer much later in life than he—were similar to those of the early romanticist. He, too, grew up in a well-to-do banker's house in Berlin and showed musical talent at an early age: he was an accomplished pianist at the age of eight. His father's house, like that of the Mendelssohns, was a social center visited by Prussian courtiers, by nobility, and by spiritual luminaries, and the young musician was denied no means in his general and musical education. He added Meyer, a name of his grandfather on his mother's side, to his family name,

Beer, and thereafter became known in the musical world as Meyerbeer.
His name Jacob he later Italianized into Giacomo.

Jacob Liebmann (Lippmann) Beer (Giacomo Meyerbeer) was born in
a covered wagon (his mother was probably on her way to her ancestors'
house in Frankfurt on the Oder) in a small village near Berlin in 1791 and
died in Paris in 1864. His father, Jacob (Juda) Herz Beer, was a wealthy in-
dustrialist who had business connections with Italy and with Salomon
Heine, Heinrich Heine's uncle. His wife, Amalia, was the eldest daughter
of Uri Lippmann Mayer (also Liebmann Meyer) Wulff, whose family had
originally come from a little town in Bohemia, settled in Vienna, and
reached Berlin in 1670 when the Jews were driven out of Austria. He was
respected as a businessman and entrepreneur in the Berlin financial world,
was appointed by the Prussian king as head of the mail coach service, and
became general leaseholder of the Prussian lottery. For the upbringing and
education of his grandson Jacob, it was a decisive factor that Lippmann
Wulff had his own synagogue in his house; both he and Jacob's parents
provided a thorough Jewish education. Unlike Mendelssohn, Meyerbeer
never embraced Christianity. He had a private teacher in Hebrew, Bendix
Schottländer, and a general tutor, Aron Wolfssohn. When Schottländer
wrote a Hebrew cantata (*Kol Simrah* = Voice of the Song) for the fifty-
fourth birthday of Meyerbeer's grandfather on September 4, 1799, eight-
year old Jacob probably sang in the choir or played the keyboard; he was already an accomplished pianist.[4] Schottländer, teacher and friend of the
family, had come to Berlin from Danzig (he was born there in 1763) via
Poland and Silesia. When Jacob was ten years old, he left the Wulff family
to become tutor, later director with the title of Hofrath, at a school at
Seesen, where he died in 1846. He had shortened his name to Schott, and
while he remained a Jew all his life, he had all of his ten sons christened. The
name Schott is, of course, well-known in the world of music. The Mayence
House of Schott (publishers of music) was founded in 1770 by Bernard
Schott, of an earlier generation than Bendix Schottländer.

Meyerbeer never forgot the religious atmosphere in the house of his

---

[4]See A. M. Habermann, "A Cantata in Honor of G. Meyerbeer's Grandfather," in
Tazlil, ed. M. Gorali, Haifa, 1966, pp. 21 ff (in Hebrew).

Giacomo Meyerbeer (1791–1864).

parents and grandparents, and the many anti-Semitic attacks which he suffered affected him deeply. From his grandfather and his parents he had inherited a commitment to charitable causes. He especially supported writers, artists, and musicians with financial donations, recommendations, or personal efforts. A beneficiary of his magnanimity was Heinrich Heine, who wrote of him in 1842 that "around his name turns the entire history of music for the past ten years" and "judging a musician nowadays one unintentionally comes upon the question in which relationship he is placed regarding Meyerbeer. . . ." The musician most generously supported by Meyerbeer was Richard Wagner, who maintained, in 1839 at the age of 26, that "Meyerbeer wrote universal history, a history of the hearts and feelings, he destroyed the barriers of national prejudices, overthrew the constraining frontiers of language-idioms, he wrote deeds of music. . . ." This was written eleven years before a generally disillusioned, self-assertive, combatant Wagner defamed Meyerbeer, together with Mendelssohn and Jews in general, in his unsavory pamphlet "Judaism in Music" which was to usher in a period of widespread contempt for Jewish musicians. Wagner's pamphlet became a hallowed guide for Fascist/National Socialist ideology, but it failed to impede Jewish lovers of musical drama and music in general from admiring Richard Wagner's inimitably great art.

Meyerbeer's star rose more slowly on the musical firmament than that of Felix Mendelssohn. He completed his first large-scale work at the age of twenty, in 1811; this was an oratorio, *Gott und die Natur*. It was followed two years later by his first opera, *The Vow of Jephtha*. His first compositions were taken from the religious sphere; with his second operatic work, a comic opera, *Abimelek, or The Two Caliphs* (1813), he turned to the Oriental world. Though Meyerbeer never completed a large-scale religious or biblical work again, he once considered writing a "Judith" opera and also composed some psalms and a biblical romance, *Rahel to Naphtali*. Between the first operas and his next attempts in this form there is an interval of five years in which Meyerbeer traveled extensively till he found himself in Italy, where he had immediate success with some skillful works in the style of the time. For ten years he failed to produce anything but occasional works till his visit to Paris in 1826 proved to be the experience decisive for his future life; he made Paris his second home and wrote most of his future compositions for the Paris Opera. The death of his father and the loss of the two children born in the early years of his marriage kept the composer away from public activity for a considerable period, but he devoted much time to a thorough study of the principles and theatrical possibilities of opera. When in 1831 his first operatic drama in French—*Robert le Diable*—was produced in Paris, it met with instantaneous success; this opera ushered in his greatly successful French stage works. The combination in his music of Italian songfulness, French pathos, and German romantic spirit created a unique and novel species of opera; his sense of dramatic stage action added to the effectiveness of his works. With his *Huguenots* (Paris, 1836) he made a spectacular impression and overshadowed even the success of Jacques

Fromental Elias Halévy's *La Juive*—the French Jewish composer's best-known work, which had been produced in Paris a year before.

Halévy, who was born in Paris in 1799 and died in Nice in 1862, has been underrated as the versatile musician he was and as a teacher; among his students were Georges Bizet, who married his daughter, and Charles Gounod. He was the son of a cantor, teacher, and Hebrew poet who had come to Paris from the Bavarian town of Fürth, and was active in the Jewish community. He convinced the community to invite to Paris the Strasbourg composer and cantor Samuel Naumbourg, who introduced far-reaching musical reforms into the synagogue and published an edition of Salomone Rossi's "Shir ha-Shirim asher liShlomoh." In the Jewish field Halévy composed a setting of Psalm 130 in Hebrew, and pieces for the synagogue. In addition to *La Juive* (1835), he wrote the operas *Le Juif errand* (1852), *Le Nabab* (1853), *Les Plagues du Nil* (1859), and also issued a textbook for singers. An opera found unfinished after his death, *Noé*, was completed by Bizet. In the *Encyclopedia Judaica*, edited by Cecil Roth and Geoffrey Wigoder, Jerusalem 1971 ff., Halévy's activities as a Jewish composer are entirely disrespected, as is unfortunately the case in the generally sadly deficient entries on music and musicians.

Meyerbeer was a true genius of the theater and a master of musical effect, and all operatic composers after him have studied his scores—and the dramatic librettos of Scribe—with profit. This is particularly true of the young Richard Wagner, whom Meyerbeer had supported in his early attempts to gain the stage but who later criticized and abused the older master. Meyerbeer's merits remained remarkable even in comparison with the mighty musical dramas of Wagner; the great German conductor Hans von Bülow was certainly right in maintaining: "Good old Meyerbeer is by no means a vanquished dragon, and the young dilettantes had rather put their noses in his scores than turn them up at him." Meyerbeer's operas are distinguished by rich musical invention, a splendidly colored orchestration, and exciting changes of mood within the dramatic scenes; lack of depth is made up for by musical effects that are at times genuinely stirring. And though many scorn some of the musical content of his scores nowadays, his works can still serve as perfect models for sound operatic theater, while his adaptability and intellectual skill may well be marveled at even in the light of the greater achievements of profounder masters. Meyerbeer died in 1864 at the age of seventy-three, having witnessed in his lifetime the rise of the star of Richard Wagner, who was to perfect many of his own theatrical innovations and who overshadowed all his predecessors.

MENDELSSOHN AND MEYERBEER conquered the great world of music and decisively influenced the development of musical history, each in his own way. A distinguished part in the history of German romanticism was also played by Jewish musicians and composers who were minor masters in comparison with the ingenious romanticists and who have therefore been unable to hold the interest of posterity to the same degree as the men of greater genius. But some had been greatly successful in their own day, and a number of their works are still widely played.

An outstanding figure in romantic Vienna was Carl Goldmark (1830–1915), a composer of Hungarian-Jewish descent who made his home in Vienna and there produced some successful operas, among them *The Queen of Sheba* (1875) and *A Winter's Tale* (1905); in the orchestral field his Orientally colored *Sakuntala* overture and his symphonic suite *The Rustic Wedding* have become famous, violinists still perform one of his two violin concertos, and among his vocal works there is a fine setting of Psalm 93. Goldmark endowed his music with a subtle romantic coloring, and rich and warm melodic invention distinguishes his symphonic and chamber music; in opera the composer was much influenced by the works of Meyerbeer and, later, by the early music of Wagner. Slow and contemplative creation and continuous rewriting and polishing of an almost finished composition characterized Goldmark's work, and though lacking the last touch of genius his music is a remarkable contribution to the treasures of romanticism.

Less successful than Goldmark but an attractive romantic composer in his own right was Friedrich Gernsheim (1839–1916), who was active as a conductor and teacher at Cologne, Rotterdam, and Berlin. His most felicitous medium of expression was chamber music, but he also composed some choral works and four symphonies, the third of which is entitled *Miriam*.

Of Moravian extraction was Ignaz Brüll (1846–1907), who passed most of his life in Vienna and there produced in 1875 his best-known work,

The Golden Cross, an opera which was widely performed in his time and which remained in the operatic repertoire for a considerable period. Brüll composed nine other operas, a number of symphonic and chamber works, and some Jewish songs. He was a noted teacher and traveled widely as a piano virtuoso, no less successful than other nineteenth-century Jewish virtuosos. Among the latter the prominent figures were Ignaz Moscheles (the friend of Beethoven, Mendelssohn, and Meyerbeer), Sigismond Thalberg, and Henri Herz.

A singular position in nineteenth-century musical history is held by Joseph Joachim (1831–1907), a Jewish violinist of Hungarian extraction. This outstanding musician was the first to perform widely the violin concerto and the chamber music of Beethoven—especially the quartets, which he played with his famous Joachim Quartet—and his friendship with Schumann and Brahms led these great masters to write concertos specially for him. Joachim also composed a few musical works himself, among them a *Hungarian Concerto*; of his chamber music the "Hebrew Melodies" for viola and piano have become popular. Joachim instructed an imposing line of pupils, many of whom were among the best-known violinists of the twentieth century; the most famous was Bronislaw Hubermann. Nor was the violin the only instrument favored by Jewish artists; a long succession of piano virtuosos opened to the Jews the salons and concert halls of the world.

TWO INTERESTING JEWISH MUSICIANS were active in nineteenth-century England. One was Isaac Nathan (1791–1864), son of a Canterbury cantor, who enjoyed a great vogue as a singer and composer; the other was John Braham (1777–1856), a famous operatic tenor who took part in the first performance of Weber's operas in London and also made a name as a composer. Both men have a noted role in the history of Lord Byron's beautiful "Hebrew Melodies."

Isaac Nathan had in 1813 set to music Byron's *Bride of Abydos—A Turkish Tale* and sent a printed copy of his music to the poet a year later. Shortly after this he wrote a second letter, dated 30 June 1814, with the following request:

> I have with great trouble selected a considerable number of very beautiful Hebrew melodies of undoubted antiquity, some of which are proved to

have been sung by the Hebrews before the destruction of the Temple of Jerusalem, having been honoured with the immediate Patronage of her Royal Highness the Princess Charlotte of Wales, the Duchess of York and most of the Names of the Royal Family together with those of a great number of distinguished personages. I am most anxious the Poetry for them should be written by the first Poet of the present age and though I feel and know I am taking a great liberty with your Lordship in even hinting that two songs written by you would give the work great celebrity, yet, I trust your Lordship will pardon and attribute it to what is really the case, the sincere admiration I feel for your extraordinary talents. It would have been my most sanguine wish from the first to have applied to your Lordship had I not been prevented by a knowledge that you wrote only for amusement and the Fame you so justly acquired. I therefore wrote to Walter Scott offering him a share in the publication if he would undertake to write for me, which he declined, not thinking himself adequate to the task, the distance likewise being too great between us, I could not wait on him owing to my professional engagements in London.

I have since been persuaded by several Ladies of literary fame and known genius, to apply to your Lordship, even at the risk of seeming impertinence on my part, rather than lose the smallest shadow of success from your Lordship acceding to my humble entreaties. If your Lordship would permit me to wait on you with the Melodies and allow me to play them over to you, I feel certain from their great beauty, you would become interested in them, indeed, I am convinced no one but my Lord Byron could do them justice. . . .

Byron accepted the suggestion of Isaac Nathan—who, by the way, seems to have tried his own hand at Hebrew melodies before—and assigned to the composer the copyright of his poems. Poet and composer became close friends, and Nathan annotated and commented upon the poems of Lord Byron. A curious episode in their relationship is Nathan's sending of Passover cakes (*matzot*) to the poet when the latter embarked on a voyage.

When the printed edition of the songs was offered for subscription, John Braham showed great interest in the "Hebrew Melodies" and not only subscribed for two copies but offered to perform them in public and to assist Nathan in the arrangement of the music on condition of his being given an equal share in the publication. "To this I readily consented," reported Nathan himself, "under the impression that I should but be paying a just tribute to the first poet of the age by having his verses sung by the greatest vocalist of the day, and I accordingly paid Mr. Braham his moiety arising from the sale of the first edition." The collection was dedicated to Princess Charlotte of Wales, who was Nathan's singing pupil, and signed by Braham as well as Nathan. It is difficult to determine the share of Braham in the actual composition and arrangement, but it cannot have been extensive, as his name was later withdrawn from the publication. Braham—whose original name was Abraham—was probably a blood relation of Nathan's, and the latter called his first-born son after him. "A beast of a man but an angel of a singer"—thus Sir Walter Scott called the celebrated singer who, after the decline of his voice, sank into obscurity. Nathan, after some involved legal and financial affairs, settled in Australia and there died at the age of seventy-three after a street accident.

A FIGURE of peculiar interest in nineteenth-century music is Jacques Offenbach (1819–80), son of the hazan Isaac Juda Eberst or Ebersht, who had left his native town of Offenbach to marry and settle in Cologne. The father had published a synagogue songbook and a Passover Haggadah with some new melodies, and had composed songs and piano music. The son's musical talent was soon detected, and he began learning to play the violoncello. In 1833 the fourteen-year-old boy was sent to Paris, where he studied at the Conservatoire for four years and earned some money by playing in the orchestra of the Opéra-Comique. He then took to conducting, and in 1849 became conductor at the Théâtre Français. Offenbach had not then discovered his own particular talent for theater music, for he made his first attempt at a work for the stage as late as 1853—at the age of thirty-four—when he produced his first operetta, *Pepito*. It was only when he took over the Théâtre Comte, which he renamed "Bouffes Parisiens," under his own management in 1855 that there began the long line of delightful stage pieces which Offenbach then turned out in quick succession to create a repertoire for his theater. In the course of twenty-five years he composed no fewer than ninety operettas. He gave up the management of his "Bouffes Parisiens" in 1861; but he felt unhappy without a stage of his own, and in 1873 he took over the Théâtre de la Gaîté, which he managed till 1875. In the following years he went to America, but finding that France was the only proper soil for his works, he returned to Paris. There he was occupied

Jacques Offenbach (1819–80).

for many years with the composition of his masterpiece, the lyrical romantic opera *Les Contes d'Hoffmann*; fate did not permit him, however, to complete this crowning achievement of his life: after his death in 1880 the opera
was revised and its orchestration completed by Ernest Guiraud.

Offenbach was the sharp and witty critic of the Second Empire and its
superficial and decadent society, but though itself mercilessly ridiculed in
the operatic satires, the public was delighted by the charm of Offenbach's
melodic invention, the sparkling fire of his cancans, the delicate sentimentality of his airs, and the fine orchestral coloring of his scores. Even today
the freshness of his enchanting music has not worn off, and Offenbach's operettas are popular in many countries. In his only serious opera, *Les Contes*

d'Hoffmann, he left parody and satire behind and wrote a work full of yearning for an alter ego—a fantastic opera of deep spiritual content.

Among the long lists of musical works of Jacques Offenbach—stage works, orchestral and chamber music, songs, piano pieces, dance music, and some writings—a very few have Jewish subjects. As an eighteen-year-old he wrote a suite for piano entitled "Rebecca," a number of waltzes on Hebraic motives from the fifteenth century (1837). In 1854 he composed a ten-movement suite for piano, of dances in various national dance rhythms and styles, "Le Décameron dramatique." The first of the ten pieces is "Rachel—Grand Waltz," and the suite is "dedicated to the artists of the Comédie française." The dance pieces all have female names, of such actresses as, for example, the universally famous Rachel; portraits of each actress and short verses from illustrious poets of the time accompanied the publications.

Among Offenbach's satirical works is a skit on Richard Wagner's claim to represent "The Musician of the Future"; he had published his *Das Kunstwerk der Zukunft* in 1849. When Wagner was in Paris, Offenbach wrote for "Le Carnaval des revues," performed in the 1860 carnival season at the Bouffes Parisiens, a sketch entitled "Le musicien de l'avenir" with a "Symphonie de l'avenir" as climax—parodying lines from *Tristan und Isolde* and *Tannhäuser.* The scene is set in Elysium, where Carl Maria von Weber, Modeste Grétry, Christoph Willibald Gluck, and Wolfgang Amadeus Mozart wait for a concert to begin. A gentleman enters, declaring he is The Composer of the Future. He denounces the musical past and proclaims revolution.[5] No more notes, he says; no more harmony, no more pitch, scales, sharps, flats, naturals! No *fortes*! No *pianos*! So Gluck asks, "No more music, then?" The Composer replies, "Yes, but a strange, unknown, vague, indescribable music." The Great Masters wish to hear a sample of such music, and the "tone-poem," "Symphonie de l'avenir," is then played until Mozart and his fellow composers haunt the "revolutionary" off the stage.

---

[5]We follow the description of the unpublished work in the excellent Offenbach biography of Alexander Faris, London, 1980, pp. 73–77, where a page from *Symphonie de l'Avenir* is also reproduced.

Wagner was infuriated by Offenbach's satire, the success of which added to the disastrous rejection of his own music by the Parisian public and press and his failure to secure financial help to cover his debts. For all this he blamed "Jewish corruptibility" and the manipulations of Jewish bankers and a "Jewish-infected press." He attacked Offenbach in an article printed in Paris, saying that he "possesses the warmth lacking in Auber, but it is the warmth of the dunghill; all Europe is wallowing in it." Ten years later he wrote a singularly infantile mockery, "Eine Kapitulation," vituperating Offenbach and the Parisians, and reissued his pamphlet, "Judaism in Music," adding more vicious malice to its erstwhile text. There was one more "reason" for Wagner to despise the successful French Jew Offenbach: When *Tristan und Isolde* was scheduled to be performed at the Vienna Opera in 1863, it was officially withdrawn because the leading tenor, Alois Ander, had fallen ill and was also "eventually considered inadequate for the part of Tristan" and actually died the year after—he had been a famous "Lohengrin" in his time. For the next premiere at the Opera, a work for which Offenbach was especially commissioned was chosen, probably on a recommendation by Eduard Hanslick: Offenbach's *Die Rheinnixen* (February 1864). Wagner, however, felt snubbed, yet he could change his opinions from one day to another. He enthusiastically praised the music of Halévy, especially his opera *La Juive* (1842), regarded Meyerbeer as a great composer in his beginnings, took from Heinrich Heine the subjects of his *Fliegender Holländer* and *Tannhäuser*, and set to music his ballad "Die beiden Grenadiere," regarded Felix Mendelssohn as a genius in music, and vilified all of them in his pamphlet. Thus Wagner wrote of Offenbach a year before his own death, in a letter to the conductor Felix Mottl, "Look at Offenbach. He writes like the divine Mozart . . . the truth leaps to the eyes: Offenbach could have been like Mozart."

OFFENBACH'S WORKS, with their biting satire on a decadent world, are typical of the general crisis and decline of romanticism, for even in his own contribution to romantic opera he symbolically shows the dual aspects of the romantic and the fantastic. His turbulent cancans swept away sentimental meditation and dreamy romance just as, at the same time, the polkas and Viennese waltzes of Johann Strauss brought a fresh spirit into a declining world. But the decline of the romantic era, which expressed itself in one way in the rise of the masters of satire and the dance and later in quite another form in impressionism and in the revival of classical ideals, also had serious sociological aspects. A reaction had set in against the liberal and cosmopolitan tendencies of the classical and romantic ages and late romanticism developed distinctly national trends. Nationalism had already been a latent force in early German romanticism. Carl Maria von Weber's "Lyre and Sword," on poems by Theodor Koerner, was its earliest example in music. With Richard Wagner's revival of ancient German legend and lore in his great music dramas, national consciousness had deeply penetrated into the sphere of art. At the same time there arose national schools of composers in northern and eastern Europe whose works put a number of countries on the musical map that had not played a part in the history of the art of music up to that time. They, too, revived their national legends and folklore and thus also attempted to oppose literary and musical values of their own to the ever-growing influence of German romantic art.

The cosmopolitanism and the tolerance of society in the eighteenth and early nineteenth centuries had enabled the Jews to vie with the luminaries of the nations with whom they lived in all branches of science, literature, and the arts. The national trends in late nineteenth-century romanticism shattered the dream of equality and fraternity and the feeling of security harbored by the Jewish Europeans, and some storm signals disquieted them. But the reaction set in very slowly and was at first heeded only by a few far-sighted men. The actual catastrophe occurred—as far as western and central Europe were concerned—only in the first half of the twentieth century. Only then were the processes of emancipation reversed and the assimilated Jews of Europe taught that their actual place was within their own community.

CHAPTER EIGHT

THE GREAT CALL—

GUSTAV MAHLER AND

ARNOLD SCHOENBERG

IT IS A CHARACTERISTIC SIGN of the times that in the years 1894–95, two momentous and stirring works were completed, created in the same city by two men of exactly the same age but of diametrically opposed ideas: Theodor Herzl's bold "fantasy" of a "Jewish State" and Gustav Mahler's Second Symphony, the symphony of the life, death, and resurrection of all that is earthly. Mahler's mighty symphonic work is crowned by a finale originally styled "The Great Call," which contains the composer's own credo: "Prepare to live . . . for you will rise again, my heart." This musical genius, of Bohemian-Jewish descent, was possessed by the mysticism of the Catholic world, and in his symphony pictures the call to Judgment Day, on which the beggars and the rich, the people and the kings will be equal before the Creator; Herzl's visionary "Great Call"—originating from the alarming implications of the Dreyfus Affair, which brought home to him the failure of Jewish emancipation—was addressed to the Jews in dispersion in order to stir them up from their lethargic indifference and to gather them in the upbuilding of a new and independent community. Mahler's mystic creed, part of an unhappy and dual personality tortured by his struggle for artistic truth, stamps the style of his musical works, which in tendency as well as in content and expression mark the end of the romantic period; Herzl's vision points toward a realistic future. The tragedy of the epoch in which the Jews believed that they could be completely absorbed in European society is profoundly mirrored in Mahler's music, which—though we can hardly call it Jewish—had always proved singularly attractive to the Jews, while the German musicians showed a hostile attitude toward his symphonic works under varying pretexts, even before racial discrimination had poisoned their minds.

Gustav Mahler (1860–1911) is an important figure in musical history as one of the last symphonists of the romantic era and as an outstanding precursor of the Vienna modernist school. The Jewish aspects of his personality can be detected in the mental and spiritual background of his creative work. In his symphonies, in which—according to his own words—he built himself a world with all the means of musical technique at his disposal, there is mirrored a probing mind deprived of its roots; intellect and spiritual uproar shape his emotion; his ecstasy is that of the biblical prophets. Mahler loved the German folk songs and employed his own folk-song settings for large-scale symphonic works. In his music resound the martial rhythms of the regiments whose march he watched in his small native Bohemian town—but strange melancholy strains transform these melodies and march rhythms to such a degree that they almost resemble the plaintive Jewish songs of eastern Europe. In his final masterpiece, *The Song of the Earth*, his inspiration is guided by Far Eastern poetry: this exotically colored symphonic song cycle—the style of which imprinted itself on Mahler's last symphony as well as on the works of many a later composer— is a moving portrayal of an artist and a man who lived in a spiritual world of his own and longed for fulfillment in remote, inaccessible spheres.

The tragedy of Gustav Mahler is that of nineteenth-century western Jewry. It represents the failure of the emancipation movement at a moment when the Jews began to realize that the European countries would one day set the clock back and close the doors that an enlightened period had opened wide to Jewish citizens. A few far-seeing Jews were early in their recognition that the century of liberty and equality was drawing to an end, and they took the consequences in various ways: some tried to fight against anti-Semitism and to defend the Jewish position, while others

Gustav Mahler (1860–1911).

looked out for the restoration of an independent Jewish religious or national community. But Herzl's prophetic appeal and the activities of a few
ardent followers of his "Jewish State" idea made slow headway, and only in
mid-twentieth century did the growing Zionist movement of central and
western Europe find contact with the national renaissance that had already
gained momentum in the eastern European countries.

The Jewish way of Arnold Schoenberg (1874–1951), who succeeded
to the musical and ethical heritage of Gustav Mahler, is in many respects
typical of the development in the western European sphere. It began in
the paths of late romanticism, in the assimilated circles of Vienna, but the
First World War brought home to Schoenberg the absurdity of Jewish as-

similation, and he tried to give his searching ideas literary form. In a pro-phetic drama of the early 1920s, the composition of which he once con-sidered but never actually began, he attempted to make it clear that the Jews could not entrust their fate to other people and would soon learn this on a large scale. In this drama, *The Biblical Road,* Schoenberg points to the possibility of an independent Jewish state on the models of biblical times; but even before the ideas leading to *The Biblical Road* had taken shape he had sketched the text of another work connected with ancient Hebrew lore. This was an oratorio, *Die Jakobsleiter (Jacob's Ladder),* in which Schoenberg gave allegorical expression to his own personal philos-ophy: the rationalists, the cowards, the skeptics, the cynics, the cunning ones, the journalists, and the unclean ones are all lined up on Jacob's lad-der in order to ascend to Heaven; before them and nearest to the goal are the demons, geniuses, stars, gods, and angels. The angel Gabriel opens the work with words that have often been quoted as typical of Schoenberg's own aesthetic creed:

> Whether right or left, whether forward or backward—one must always go on without asking what lies before or behind one. That should be hidden; you ought to—nay, *must*—forget it, in order to fulfill your task.

Schoenberg stated that life in Austria during World War I opened his eyes to the failure of Jewish assimilation. It was then that he began to study the ancient teachings and the history of Judaism. He also became inter-ested in more recent Jewish history, though Herzl and Zionism seem to have been unknown to him even when he wrote *The Biblical Road.* Schoen-berg knew the implications of the Jewish question. The religious-spiritual as well as the political aspects of Judaism never ceased to occupy his mind once he had started studying them. Mahler never denied being of Jewish birth; but his entire life inclined toward escaping the world of his origin, his environment, his family. A Christian heaven and its angels, nature and its sounds, "Brother Death" ("Freund Hein"), and the horror of demons per-vade his symphonic creations. Schoenberg explored the beliefs, the histor-ical background, and spiritual heritage of his own people even when he thought the Church was the appropriate mentor of his soul-searchings. When Schoenberg professed his return to Judaism at a Paris synagogue in

1933, after leaving Nazi Germany, he really closed a chapter of history that had opened with the conversion to Christianity of the Mendelssohn family four generations before, and his own at the age of eighteen.

"I AM THRICE HOMELESS," Gustav Mahler is reported having once pronounced; "as a native of Bohemia in Austria, as an Austrian among Germans, and as a Jew throughout the world. Everywhere an intruder, never welcome." He was born in a small town of southern Bohemia; his father was a man of all trades with cultural ambitions and a ruthless character; his mother a delicate, frail woman whom the domineering husband compelled to bear twelve children, five of whom died very young. Poverty and tragedy accompanied his early childhood. Mahler grew up in suffering and never-ceasing tension. When Mahler consulted Sigmund Freud on the occasion of the psychoanalyst's visit to Holland in the summer of 1910 (about a year before Mahler's death), he confirmed the deep influence the unhappy early life had on his entire life and work—the gloomy home, the cruelty of the father, the suffering of the mother, the hostility of the environment. He was not a particularly good scholar and passed his final examinations only with difficulty; his best marks were in philosophical propaedeutics and in religion. His father must be credited with doing everything in his power to send the boy to Vienna once his musical talents (as a pianist, to begin with) had been discovered.

In the intellectual-artistic atmosphere of the musical city Mahler quickly developed these talents; but it may be surmised that even in cosmopolitan Vienna he was made to feel his Jewish descent: Joseph Hellmesberger, principal of the famed Conservatoire, was a stout guardian of musical tradition, and no friend of the Jews; as he disliked the fiery temperament of pupils like Hugo Wolf (who was expelled from the Conservatoire), it is probable that he also had little love for the Jewish boy from Bohemia (who once was very near to being expelled). In Vienna, Mahler also fell under the spell of Richard Wagner; he joined the Wagner Society and—following a demand made by Wagner at this particular time—became both an abstainer and a vegetarian. Mahler seems to have disregarded the fact that the same Wagner at the very same time taught that the only solution of "the Jewish problem" lay in the disappearance of Judaism, the effect of which would in Wagner's opinion contribute as much to the "regeneration of mankind" as the abolition of meat-eating ("the cause of the decline of the Christian religion and its influence")[1].

A Viennese composer whom Mahler admired very much was Anton Bruckner; Mahler joined a circle of young musicians who looked to Bruckner for guidance, criticism, and advice. The friendly master talked of the Jewish musicians among them as *die Herren Israeliten*. He felt special affection and had great understanding for the quickly developing and maturing Mahler. The composer Ernst Křenek said that the common center of interest in Bruckner's friendship for Mahler was both men's enthusiasm for Wagner, while "the mutual attraction between Jewish intellectuality and endemic *naïveté* is also a peculiar Austrian phenomenon."[2] Křenek wondered "with what feelings the elder musician . . . looked upon the nervous, talkative Jewish boy from Bohemia." The address "*Herren Israeliten*" might hardly have had a friendly ring when pronounced by people other than Bruckner. There must have been much pressure upon Mahler to embrace Christianity in order to further his career. Neither Mahler nor his advisers foresaw at that time that the formal step of conversion would not solve any problem except providing the *Entreebillett* to the Directorship of the Vienna Opera.

Mahler and Schoenberg were seen as contemptible Jewish composers by some German critics long before racial thinking permeated all criticism in Nazi-Germany. Anti-Jewish feeling already played an important part in the condemning review of Mahler's Second Symphony by the Preussische Kreuz-Zeitung in the late 1890s. In 1909, Rudolf Louis wrote in *Die deutsche Musik der Gegenwart* (published in Munich):

> If Mahler's music would speak Yiddish it would be perhaps unintelligible to me. But it is repulsive to me because it *acts* Jewish ["Aber sie ist mir widerlich, weil sie *jüdelt*"]. This is to say that it speaks musical German, but with an accent, with an inflection, and above all, with the gestures of an eastern, all too eastern Jew. So, even to those whom it does not offend di-

---

[1]Richard Wagner, "Religion und Kunst," *Bayreuther Blätter*, October 1830.

[2]Ernst Křenek, "Gustav Mahler," a biographical essay in the American edition (New York, 1941) of Bruno Walter's, *Gustav Mahler*, trans. James Galston, London, 1937, pp. 162–163.

rectly, it cannot possibly communicate anything. One does not have to be repelled by Mahler's artistic personality in order to realize the complete emptiness and vacuity of an art in which the spasm of an impotent mock-Titanism reduces itself to a frank gratification of common seamstress-like sentimentality. (This English translation by Nicolas Slonimsky appears in *Dictionary of Musical Invective*, New York, 1953, page 121.)

Similar criticism was voiced by many German critics in the 1920s, among them Hans-Joachim Moser in his three-volume *Geschichte der deutschen Musik (1920–1924)*. There is little difference between the verdicts of these earlier writers and the remarks on Schoenberg in the Nazi publication *Lexikon der Juden in der Musik* (Berlin, 1941) by T. Stengel and H. Gerigk. This reference book relies on Riemanns *Musiklexikon* of 1929, which had branded Schoenberg's tendency to negate all that was before him, and adds:

> These are the old tested Jewish tactics which are always put into practice, at an opportune moment, to destroy the cultural values of the host peoples in order to set up their own as the only valid ones.

It is tempting to quote the concluding passage of this article's appraisal of Schoenberg:

> It may be stated that Schoenberg after his emigration from Germany soon fell into oblivion—a swift but just verdict of History.

The Nazis of 1941 were certainly rash in their conclusions; more prophetic was Schoenberg himself when he told his student and friend Josef Rufer in the early 1920s that he had "discovered something which will assure the supremacy of German music for the next hundred years"—meaning, of course, the discovery of a method to deliver music from the straightjacket of strict major-minor tonality and to compose works based on rows of twelve different tones related entirely to one another.

It would, however, be wrong to disregard the effect of the hostile criticism. Not only was it elaborated in many ways (as when the German musicologist Blessinger "analyzed" what he styled Gustav Mahler's "rabbinical mind"[3], but it had a decisive impact on musicians and music-lovers, also on many who condemned the anti-Semitic connotations but had not come

---

[3]Karl Blessinger, *Mendelssohn, Meyerbeer, Mahler*, Berlin, 1939.

to terms with "modern" music. They felt no longer a need to make any further effort; this music seemed to be so different from everything they knew and revered that they would probably never grasp it with all its foreignness and strange content. In the appreciation of art, layman and connoisseur usually tend to accept the way of least resistance rather than to overcome prejudice and mental laziness; this is why totalitarian states of fascist as well as communist character, and even enlightened countries where ministers seek public support, invariably foster the conventional, the easy-to-comprehend, the mediocre at the expense of the novel, the demanding, the high-soaring work of art. In Nazi Germany independent thinkers and artists were condemned and banned as Jews—where applicable—or else as *Kulturbolschewisten*; Stalinist Soviet Russia described her "degenerate artists" as "formalists", "bourgeois," or "cosmopolitans."

But objective critics, too, discovered the Jewish element in Mahler and Schoenberg long before the Jewish world became conscious of the problems involved. Gustav Mahler found sympathetic listeners as well as performers among Jews at an early date and cultured Jews claimed him—who became a fervent Roman Catholic (though never denying his Jewish descent)—as a Jew in line with Mendelssohn, Meyerbeer, Heine, and Offenbach, while Schoenberg enjoyed very little early recognition in the Jewish world although he had written on Jewish questions and dramatized biblical themes ever since the days of World War I. Many friends and pupils of Mahler were Jews, while most of the disciples and friends of Schoenberg were Gentiles. The mystic, erring, disquieted as well as disquietening mind, the ahasveric nature of the professing Christian Gustav Mahler, seems to have come closer to most Jewish hearts and minds than the clear, well-organized, expressionist, daring romantic and idealist, who was a pronounced Jew, Arnold Schoenberg.

We can certainly ascribe the inner tension, the deep searchings, the escapist trends in Mahler's music to the environment and mental attitude surrounding the composer in his formative years. Max Brod may have gone too far when he believed to have discovered Jewish strains in Mahler's minor-major "popular" melodies coming up at various unexpected points in the symphonies. Romanticists, artists as well as composers, have often felt an urge to incorporate in works of art some seemingly naïve folklorist motive—this is true of poetry, painting and music in the romantic era; Weber, Dvořák, Brahms, and Liszt come to mind. Mahler is a case in point rather than an exception to the rule. In his interview of 1910 he reported to Freud that when as a young boy he rushed away from his parents' house during an especially painful scene between father and mother, he heard a hurdy-gurdy in the street grinding out the popular Viennese air *Ach, du lieber Augustin.* The ensuing conjunction of high tragedy and light amusement seems to have had a never-to-be-forgotten impact upon Mahler's inner mind so that the interplay of the lofty and the mundane, the depth of emotion and the triviality of superficial play became an all-important characteristic of his creative work. The importance of the childhood incident seems to be underlined by Gustav Mahler's remark to his wife during their New York stay that the "lovely barrel organ" playing in the street below their hotel window took him straight back to childhood. It is true that some of Mahler's folk melodies show affinities with certain Hassidic tunes (as noted by Max Brod) but then we must not forget that the Hassidic songs were as much indebted to Slav melodies as the popular music and the march tunes young Mahler heard in his native town. When comparing such melodic strains in the symphonies of Antonin Dvořák and Gustav Mahler, we are inclined to doubt "Hassidic influence."

However, Mahler himself once confirmed that he remembered ancient synagogue songs. Before the turn of the century, a young singer in his early twenties was engaged by Angelo Neumann, director of the Prague German Opera House (himself a singer), as bass soloist. Neumann let him sing the important parts on the opera's repertoire and the solo in Beethoven's Ninth Symphony. For a Prague Festival performance of the Ninth, Mahler came to Prague as guest conductor and was apparently so much impressed by the young man's performance that he invited him to join him for a cup of coffee at a coffee house he knew from his youth. He was very moved when he heard that the singer came from a traditional Jewish family and had studied the art of a synagogue cantor. Mahler requested him to come with him to a music room and asked the singer to sing Hebrew tunes for him and to explain their modal foundations. Mahler argued that the tunes had little interesting musical content, but when he heard the singer improvise on some prayer texts he whispered with a dry voice: "Yes, this is religious. That's how I heard them as a child. From the old precentor in the small village temple." There were no more words, remembered the singer—"And suddenly Mahler sits down at the piano. He plays. He improvises. Phrase after phrase as I improvised them, and he added to the melodies wonderfully blossoming harmonies. It was as if he had to overcome violent inner emotions. Nothing was spoken any more. Mahler left and said cordially, 'I shall remember you'."[4]

Mahler enjoyed nature, the singing of the birds and the rustle of the trees, whenever he was able to flee from the exigencies of city life. He loved a rural atmosphere and picturesque scenery, and soon became a "summer composer," not attempting to create music during his busy activity as conductor in the winter season. His music breathes much of carefree summer feeling; dramatized inner tension provides tragic contrast. Another important factor is Mahler's interest in the German folk-song collection *Des Knaben Wunderhorn*. This collection consists partly of folk poetry noted from authentic sources and partly of poetry written in the vein of traditional folk-songs; Mahler, probably unaware of the difference, invariably chose his texts from the latter kind, which may have had greater appeal to his sophisticated mind.

The complex setting to music of the less genuine folk poetry as well as the ahasveric nature of Mahler's searchings may be the origin of the rather instinctive rejection of his works on the part of the Germans, while probably for the same reasons his music struck sympathetic chords in many a Jewish intellectual and artist. A restless Jew, in continuous conflicts of loyalty, his conscience perturbed by the not-to-be-questioned wisdom of the boundless and inconceivable God, Mahler was haunted by eternal questions on the sense of earthly life and on the ultimate destiny of man. His music is not as devout, as humble, as pious as is Anton Bruckner's—in

---

[4]This hardly known, illuminating episode was told by Magnus Davidsohn from the town of Beuthen in Silesia, who in later years became chief cantor in the Synagogue Berlin Fasanenstrasse. He had sung the bass solo in Beethoven's Ninth under Gustav Mahler in Prague in 1899 and told the story in the German-Jewish *C.V. Zeitung* (of the liberal Berlin Jews) of 1 January 1935. Bernd Sponheuer includes the story in his essay "Musik im Jüdischen Kulturbund" in *Musik in der Emigration,* ed. Horst Weber, Stuttgart, 1994, pp. 108–135. It is here translated from German by the author.

whose symphonies the romantic spirit found true Christian expression. The deeper the Jewish composer delved into the mystical, the religious, the philosophical, the more pronounced became the impact of his spiritual heritage and the reverberations of the tragedy of the composer's own life in his so strongly autobiographical music.

During Mahler's own life and for some time after his death, his music was hotly debated in musical circles, yet the attempt was hardly made to probe deeper into the riddles of his searching soul; both friends and foes had little real understanding of his musical cosmos. Eighty years after Mahler's death the problematic side of his music—his wrestling with folk-styles, with religious thoughts, with poetic ideas, and last but not least with symphonic form—seems of small importance in comparison with the musical and ethical heritage he left to his disciples and through them to the music of the twentieth century: the example of a creative mind completely unconcerned with the wants and demands of the music consumer but only with the search for depth and truth of expression. Mahler was an artist who had the "courage to follow only his own leaning" and therefore was doomed to suffer, take upon himself "this horrible martyrdom" of hostile rejection and lack of understanding. The music of the 1920s posed new problems, indebted though it is to Mahler's works and Mahler's spirit, and the music of the 1950s opened up completely new worlds. Arnold Schoenberg, in whose progress Mahler took special interest ("What shall become of Schoenberg when I am no more?" was one of his last concerns), can in many respects be regarded as an heir to Mahler even if his break with the romantic tradition occurred during the elder master's lifetime. Mahler followed the younger composer's development with ever-growing interest, and we cannot dismiss the notion that Schoenberg exerted some influence on Mahler's musical thinking in his last creative epoch.

Schoenberg, on many occasions, acknowledged Mahler as his mentor and teacher. He often wrote and talked about his contribution to music and to musical ethics. But not only did Schoenberg's musical development lead on to novel ideas and the discovery of new possibilities, new rules, and even new sounds, his thinking, philosophy, and religion became diametrically opposed to those of Gustav Mahler. Long before the cruel lesson of Nazism

Arnold Schoenberg (1874–1951), self-portrait.

taught the world that emancipation had not solved the problem of Jewry, it had become clear to Schoenberg that the Jews were in dire need of spiritual rejuvenation and national renascence; they seemed to have forgotten their Holy Bible and their Holy Land and could not but fail in their attempts to imitate the customs and ways of life of the nations with whom they were permitted to live. Schoenberg's writings on Jewish problems range from analytical essays to political programs and from religious philosophy to biblical drama. Among the latter are the (musically incomplete) oratorio *Die Jakobsleiter*, the drama (without music) *Der biblische Weg*, the music drama *Moses und Aron*, and various vocal compositions—all with words by Schoenberg himself; the former include articles and essays like "Aufsätze zur Judenfrage," "Die jüdische Regierung im Exil," "Der Geld-jude" (1923), "Stellung zum Zionismus" (1924), "Notizen zur jüdischen Politik" (1933), "Forward to a Jewish Party" (1933), "Address on Jewish Situation" (1934), "We Young Jewish Artists" (1935), "Two Fragments on Jewish Affairs" (1937), "Notes on Kol Nidre" (1938), "A Four-point Program for Jewry" (1938). Schoenberg's letters also abound with remarks on Jewish questions and prove his almost continuous preoccupation with the problems of spiritual as well as political Judaism.

Schoenberg's inner religious development seems to have been dictated independently of his formal confession. He had grown up in Vienna in an assimilated Jewish home. As a youth of eighteen he embraced Protestantism but soon studied the Bible and occupied himself with basic questions of Judaism and Jewish life in a Christian environment. He was forty when for the first time he gave literary form to his religious thought and wrote the words for two oratorios of religious-philosophical content: *Totentanz der Prinzipien* and *Die Jakobsleiter*, both of which he intended to set to music—but only part of *Jacob's Ladder* was completed in score. It is in this work that Schoenberg's philosophical attitude and artistic creed found their first formulated expression.

His idea of fulfilment and selfless dedication to the highest task occupied Schoenberg's mind from his early days to the very last words he wrote just before his death. In a poetical *Credo*, set to music as his Op. 27, No. 2, for unaccompanied chorus, Schoenberg expressed the very same idea in the following words:

> You shall not, you must!
> You shall not make unto you any image!
> For an image confines within limits, seizes
> What should remain boundless and inconceivable.
> You must believe in the spirit!
> Directly, without emotion,
> and selfless.
> You must, God's elect, must, if you wish to remain it![5]

---

[5]Free translation by P. Gradenwitz from German original.

Totentanz der Prinzipien and *Die Jakobsleiter* were written in 1915; the chorus was composed in 1926. In 1933 he called his chorus his first published *Credo*, while shortly before his death he acknowledged that the beginnings of his preoccupation with religious problems date back to the period when he wrote his first oratorio texts: "I am of the opinion that we should try to revive our ancient religion again," Schoenberg wrote in April 1951. "It seems to me that the time of dull belief in science has finally passed—for me it was over more than forty years ago," Schoenberg wrote three months before his death to his friend and physician Dr. Georg Wolf-sohn, Jerusalem.

IT IS CHARACTERISTIC that the oratorio texts should have been conceived and written during World War I, during which Schoenberg became acutely aware that Jewish emancipation and assimilation had not been as success-ful as it seemed to be if looked at from the outside; even where anti-Semi-tism was not openly admitted it often influenced official decisions and artis-tic evaluations, and in many fields a line appeared to be drawn between Gentile and Jew. The direct outcome of Schoenberg's reflections on the Jewish question was a drama, of which it is not known whether Schoenberg ever intended to set it to music; he called it *Der biblische Weg*. This work—published only in 1994—was begun in 1922, at about the same time Schoenberg was forced to leave the resort where he was on holiday (Mattsee near Salzburg, Austria), as it was hinted to him that Jewish guests were not desired there. Shortly after, the painter Wassily Kandinsky, who had been a close friend of Schoenberg's for many years, invited the com-poser to cooperate in the establishment of a cultural center at the *Bauhaus* at Weimar. But it had come to Schoenberg's knowledge that some of the *Bauhaus* leaders had made anti-Semitic pronouncements, and he declined the invitation in a letter to Kandinsky, writing *inter alia*:

> What I was forced to learn during the past year, I have now at last under-stood and shall never forget it again. Namely, that I am no German, no European, maybe not even a human being [*ein Mensch*]—at any rate the Europeans prefer the worst of their own race to me—but that I am a Jew. I am satisfied with this state of affairs. Today I do not wish to be treated any longer as an exception. (Letter of April 20th, 1923, cf. *Briefe*, ed. by Erwin Stein, No. 63, p. 90.)

When Kandinsky replied, pointing to the difference between a Schoenberg and the "rest of his race," Schoenberg became more outspoken and even prophetic:

> Where shall anti-Semitism lead to if not to atrocities? Is it too difficult to imagine this? For you it may suffice to deprive the Jews of their rights. Then Einstein, Mahler, myself and many others will have no right of existence any more. But one thing is sure: those much tougher elements, whose power of resistance has, without protection and against all mankind, perpetuated Judaism for two thousand years, they will not be able to wipe out. For they are apparently organized in such a manner that they can fulfil the task God had given them: to preserve themselves in exile, pure and unbroken, till the hour of redemption will come! (Letter of May 4th, 1923, *ditto*, No. 64, pp. 91 ff.)

The last sentence in this strongly worded letter reveals the central idea underlying Schoenberg's *The Biblical Road* and also his later music drama *Moses und Aron*: Jewish fulfillment of the mission as outlined in the Bible and the road to redemption. That *The Biblical Road* and *Moses und Aron* are closely linked in subject and content is obvious from a study of the two works and is also documented by Schoenberg in a letter in which he says that *Moses und Aron* started to occupy his imagination in 1928 but was first conceived at least five years before that: *Der biblische Weg*, begun in 1922, was given final form in 1926–27. Schoenberg himself regarded his first drama as proof that he had become a conscious Jew again. It is true that he formally returned to the faith of his fathers and forefathers only after his forced emigration from Nazi Germany, at a Paris synagogue in 1933, but in fact "my return to the Jewish religion has taken place long before."

In *The Biblical Road* Schoenberg shows the return of the "Chosen People" to the ideals, forms of life, ethics, and constitution of biblical times. The nation shall gather again, build a new theocratic state, and fulfil the prophecies of the holy books. The hero of the drama is called Max Aruns; he aspires to the leadership of his people. Like the spiritual leaders of the biblical epoch, Max Aruns must set out to fight against material, ideological, human prejudices in his own circle of friends and followers as well as in the surrounding world. But he does not abandon his mission and tries by all possible means to convince his adversaries and to inspire friends and foes in order to realize his vision. But only frustration awaits him. He does not

possess the sublime power, the decisive courage needed for a lone and ob-
stinate fight. Human passions obscure his way; the Biblical Road remains
closed to him and he dies before his vision materializes. Only his successor
in the leadership of the people, young Guido, finds the redeeming formula:

> We want to perfect our spirit, want to dream our dream of God—as all
> the ancient peoples who have risen above all earthly matter.

Among the interesting detail of Schoenberg's conception it must be
noted that Max Aruns did not plan to bring Israel back to Zion directly.
The Bible had taught him that God did not lead Israel out of Egypt straight
to the Promised Land: they had to pass through a period of purification and
of welding-into-a-people in a land that was not their own, in the barren
desert where there was ample time for contemplation, meditation, and spiritual maturing. Max Aruns follows the Biblical Road and wants the in-
gathering exiles to pass a similar period of maturing in a land called As-
mongäa; a later generation will be ready to resettle in the ancient holy Land
of Israel, which will be returned to its historical occupants in peaceful conquest, though the use of force, including an all-destructive "rocket"
(prophetically described by Schoenberg), may become necessary both for
compelling the world's nations to let their Jews go and for the occupation
of the land.[6]

Der biblische Weg discusses a wide range of problems—belief and religion, orthodox teachings and liberal interpretation, socialism, political
Zionism, the historical precedents, success and failure of Jewish emancipation, religious and political leadership. A socialist Jewish state is envisaged
by those who plan it; but, says Schoenberg: The Jews are

> a nation consisting of scholars, artists, merchants, and bankers; a nation
> without laborers and farmers! How perturbing for the socialists, as they
> have first to create the social differences before they can think of obliterat-
> ing them!

---

[6]Schoenberg was reported saying in a conversation in the early 1930s that the
drama was inspired by his sensing the world's mounting enmity against the Jews
but that back in Vienna he had known little of Theodor Herzl's work and of Zionist literature. When friends later acquainted him with Zionism, he showed special
interest in the theories of the more militant Vladimir Jabotinsky.

The followers of Max Aruns, the leader, demand that "New Palestine will become the *State of the Future*." His answer is classic: "First the State, then its future!" At a great festive assembly (climax of Act One), Max Aruns addresses the gathering in a programmatic speech summarizing Schoenberg's own belief in the mission of Jewry:[7]

> People of Israel!
> What does this celebration mean?
> Is it a sports festival? A parade? A party assembly? A gathering of the people?
> Is not this day a day like all other days?
> No, it is not. But it is a day that will go down in the history of Jewry as a memorial day, to be remembered for all times.
> Just as the day on which the youngest asks:
> *Why do we all sit learning today?*
> But here and now he will ask in a different way:
> *Why do we all stand erect today?*
> *Why did we rise and get up? Why did we not remain sitting, cowering on the ground, humble, like all days before now?*
> We have risen, we stand erect, we are tall and great such as nobody ever thought we could be.
> We have again straightened the rounded backs, bowed as they had to be, ready to receive every slap deserved by others. We stand upright again like the old, tough, obstinate people of the Bible: but today we are obstinate no longer against our God as were our forefathers, but for Him who has chosen us as His own people.
>
> We are an ancient nation.
> We do not need miracles: persecution and contempt have made us strong, have multiplied our toughness and endurance, have created and strengthened organs to stiffen our power of resistance.
> We are an ancient nation.
> Not everyone among us can as yet conceive our notion of God completely; resign himself to the idea that everything depends on a highest Being whose laws we feel and acknowledge but are denied the right to question their meaning.

---

[7]The excerpts from *Der biblische Weg* were translated by the author from the original German manuscript by special permission from Arnold Schoenberg's widow, Mrs. Gertrude Schoenberg, and first published in the author's essay "Gustav Mahler and Arnold Schoenberg" in·*Year Book V* of the Leo Baeck Institute, London, 1960, pp. 262–84. Reprint permitted by Lawrence A. Schoenberg, 1996.

But as soon as everyone can do this up to the last consequence:
Then the Messiah will have come.
The Messiah of innermost equilibrium!

. . . for our youth we aspire everything.
To them belongs the future; they will enjoy the fruits of our work, when
no Jew will have to care any more for respect or contempt on the part of
people of other races . . .
You young people, you shall be pioneers in the new land; you shall cultivate the soil, lay the foundations on which the proud new state will be
built.
And this is the deeper meaning of this celebration . . .
Today you sacrifice to your people here all your erstwhile aspirations for a
spiritual life that served the diaspora. And today, here, you document with
your own might that you wish to serve a higher knowledge than is the wisdom of man;
That you want to enable your people to live its idea of God, to dream it to
the end!

Max Aruns is seen to fail in his effort to unite the diverging parties and
reach the goal. His ideals are pure and his aims are high, but he is not able
to set fulfillment of the mission above all earthly matters. A dramatic dialogue between Asseino, who symbolizes traditional Jewry, and Aruns lays
open the basic clash of ideas as seen by Schoenberg (Act Three):

ASSEINO: God has blessed your work up to now and He will bless it further if you are faithful to His word and trust only the spiritual power.
ARUNS: . . . After having once understood that the Bible shows the road
to liberation, I thought everything else would develop naturally. It would
be taken for granted that we could not accept our independence through
the generosity of other nations; that we would have to fight for it with our
own power; that we would have to use means of struggle appropriate to
our own times . . .
ASSEINO: Max Aruns, you want to be Moses and Aaron in one person!
Moses, to whom God gave the idea but denied the gift of speech; and
Aaron, who could not grasp the idea but could formulate it and move the
masses. Max Aruns, you who could interpret the word of God in so modern a manner, did you not understand why God did not unite both gifts in
one person?
ARUNS: . . . Moses and Aaron signify two activities of one single person, in
my opinion: of one *statesman*. His two souls do not know of each other;
the purity of his idea will not be polluted by his public actions . . .

Again, Schoenberg's vision assumes a rather prophetic ring when he lets Max Aruns reply to Asseino's condemnation of what the orthodox spokesman calls his materialistic approach:

> ARUNS: A nation of this day cannot blow out its furnaces and close its electric power stations every Friday.
> ASSEINO: God has given you the idea, to live only for HIM, to trust only Him and not earthly matter . . .
> You have not trusted the spirit. You have not talked to the rock but have "struck the rock twice with the stick."
> Upon the might of earthly matter, the power of a machine, have you founded the renascence of the Jewish people.
> ARUNS: . . . The lower things, the earthly matter, must needs remain eternally unable to hold their own in the struggle against the higher, the spirit.

In the machine Aruns sees only the auxiliary means, comparable to the trumpets of Jericho:

> Had I unconsciously sinned, like Moses, I would not set foot, like him, on the Promised Land . . . but then a Joshua would come and lead the people on . . .

Asseino was right when he foretold the eventual failure of Aruns, who wanted to be Moses and Aaron in one and could not persevere in his search for eternal truth. Dissatisfied insurgents attack Aruns and beat him to death.

> ARUNS (dying): So Asseino was right when he said that I reached too high wanting to be Moses as well as Aaron.
> I die, but I feel that Thou (God) will permit the idea to live.
> ASSEINO (at the bier): The idea, conceived in lust, born in pains, raised in poverty and want, does—like God—not permit us to create an image, attempt material realization. He who lives for the idea must either renounce any attempt of realization, or has to be satisfied with a reality that he does not want to live to see. This is why all those devoted to an idea become its martyrs; this is why invariably others will reap the fruits of their work; this is why he will never himself step upon the soil of the Promised Land.

Guido, destined to become the people's new leader, then concludes the drama, pronouncing:

> We now have a new aim: we want to feel secure as a nation. We want to know for certain that nobody can force us any longer to do something against our will, nobody can hinder us from doing what we want to do. But we do not wish to exert any influence whatsoever on other nations . . .

We want to perfect our spirit, want to dream our dream of God—as all the ancient peoples who have risen above all earthly matter."

The Biblical Road was completed in July 1927. At the same time Schoenberg was already occupied with the text for the biblical opera, *Moses und Aron*, the first two acts of which were completed in score five years later. From the perspective of this work, probably Schoenberg's greatest, we can still better understand Max Aruns, the hero of the earlier drama, as a personality in whom the opposing characters of Moses and Aaron seem to be united but struggling against each other in his own breast. Even the very name Max Aruns points to the unredeemed innermost split. The hero dies—like the biblical Moses—before the ultimate goal has been reached. In *Moses und Aron*, according to Schoenberg, it is Aaron, the persuasive leader of the people, who fails. Moses, who at the end of the second act (where Schoenberg's score is completed) still believes that he has also failed

Opening scene of Arnold Schoenberg's opera, *Moses und Aron*, Salzburg 1987. Stage design and direction, Jean-Pierre Ponnelle. (Photograph: Christa Cowrie.)

in his mission, comprehends at last—in what seems to be the final version of Schoenberg's text to the third act—how the task may be fulfilled; but not how he shall fulfil it. Schoenberg has said that his literary texts get their final shape only at the time when the music is composed; the third act of *Moses und Aron* underwent many changes before the final scene now printed in the libretto and vocal score was written. Whatever changes Schoenberg might have introduced had he ever composed the scene (for which only few thematic sketches are extant), the published text probably contains his last thoughts on the subject. Here Moses says to the people:

> Whensoever you go forth amongst the people and employ those gifts—which you were chosen to possess so that you could fight for the divine idea—
> Whensoever you employ those gifts for false and negative ends, that you might rival and share the lowly pleasures of strange peoples,
> And whensoever you abandon the wasteland's renunciation and your gifts have led you to the highest summits,
> Then, as a result of that misuse, you will always be hurled back into the wasteland."

And Moses concludes:

> But in the wasteland you shall be invincible and achieve your goal: Unity with God.
> (Translation based on Allen Forte's English version published by B. Schott's Söhne, Mainz, with minor corrections, where Forte in his translation changed the tenses used by Schoenberg in the original German.)

Schoenberg regards it as the tragedy of Moses that he did not find words to make the message from Mount Sinai comprehensible to all. In the opera, at the end of the second act, Moses' despair is expressed in the final outcry: "Oh Word, thou Word, that I lack!" It is impossible to give complete visible and audible expression to the "inconceivable" and "inexpressible." This is what Schoenberg himself must have felt when setting out to compose Act Three. The score of Act Two was completed in 1932. In 1933, Schoenberg left Berlin and reached the United States via Paris. It took him some time to settle down to composing again, and a number of vocal and instrumental works were written. But the third act of *Moses und Aron* made no progress. In 1944, he wrote to Dr. Wolfsohn in Jerusalem that the completion of the opera was part of a "five-year-plan" he had made for himself on the occasion of his seventieth birthday; he prayed God would let him live long enough to finish *Moses und Aron* and *Jacob's Ladder*. Five years later he announced he had already conceived "to a great extent the music for the third act, and I believe I should be able to write it in only a few months." Another year and he thought he could complete the single scene of the third act within a year, while shortly before his death he said he would agree to a dramatic performance of the third act, without music, in case he should not be able to complete the composition. This is what was actually attempted in the 1959 Berlin performance of the work. The Zürich stage première of 1957 had been limited to the musically complete two acts. In Berlin, the conductor Hermann Scherchen used some music from the first act as "background" to the third. A curious misinterpretation of the final scene occurred when Moses was understood to address not only the Jewish people but the entire audience—mankind in general—in proclaiming the mission of the chosen people: "In the wasteland you shall be invincible and achieve your goal: unity with God."

One of the most unusual aspects of the *Moses und Aron* score seems its projection of Schoenberg's philosophical ideas by purely musical means. Moses, the man of the spirit who is not able to give voice to his thoughts, never sings but only speaks. Aaron, quick-voiced leader of the people, is a lyric tenor, whose expression ranges from declamatory singing through recitative to pure operatic brilliance. The choral sections are also partly declamatory and partly melodic, and the opposing forces clash in startling dramatic juxtaposition. In his "orchestration" for voices, Schoenberg found a completely new style and handled it with a virtuosity that grips the listener from the opening of the work. *Moses und Aron* silenced those critics who used to speak of the composer as of one "who replaced inspired composing by constructive engineering" and paved the way toward a better understanding of his unique and singular art. The force of his biblical argument deeply impressed listeners, Gentile and Jewish, though Jewish orthodox as well as certain Christian circles fervently opposed Schoenberg's interpretation of biblical history.

The composition of the two large-scale religious works—*Jacob's Ladder* and *Moses und Aron*—had to be laid aside during the composer's hectic early American years. Schoenberg could return to them only much later, and even then he was unable to complete the scores. But the religious and social problems that had originally led to Schoenberg's preoccupation with biblical matter and Jewish themes continued troubling his mind. Some of the essays, articles, and papers quoted above originated during the early 1930s. After his "formal return to Judaism" in Paris in 1933 he sent a letter to a number of friends, proposing to them the foundation of a new "Jewish movement" which he would be ready to lead himself:

> I have decided to start myself in the meantime, as there is no better man available at the moment. After all it is known that I have run my head against walls and it was not *I* that has been destroyed. One could follow me until somebody better is found.

In a postscript to this letter Schoenberg says: "We have only to do what is useful for ourselves: Nothing against anybody. All for the Jews."

This is the ideology of *Der biblische Weg* all over again. Similar thoughts occur in some of the essays written over the next few years. Nothing came out of the projected "new movement" and Schoenberg himself turned his attention now to purely religious rather than political subjects.

In 1938 Schoenberg completed the composition of a *Kol Nidre* for speaker (rabbi), chorus, and orchestra, commissioned by an American temple. In preparation of this work, which is based on the traditional Ashkenazi version of the liturgical chant, Schoenberg studied the meaning and significance of the Day of Atonement in Jewish tradition, the musical characteristics of the liturgy, and previous compositions of the prayer; his thoughts on the subject are laid down in a series of essays.

For the composition Schoenberg wrote an introductory text based on ancient rabbinical lore which is recited before the chorus intones the prayer melody; Schoenberg says that the idea of the introduction was originally suggested by Rabbi Dr. Jakob Sonderling, who had commissioned his work.

Schoenberg's following work in the religious sphere was the "Genesis" Prelude written in 1945 for a suite commissioned by Nathaniel Shilkret from six composers, the others being Darius Milhaud, Mario Castelnuovo-Tedesco, Alexandre Tansman, Ernst Toch, and Igor Stravinsky (the latter the only non-Jew among these composers), with Shilkret himself also contributing one piece. Schoenberg's contribution characterizes the creation out of chaos, with a chorus—symbolizing the appearance of man—toward the end of the orchestral fantasy. In 1947 the dramatic cantata *A Survivor from Warsaw* was written to commemorate the victims of the Nazi holocaust; its thematic material is based on the concluding section of the work, the "Sh'ma Yisrael" prayer. Here Schoenberg uses original Hebrew words for the first time; *Kol Nidre* had been set to an English adaptation of the text. His last completed compositions are the unaccompanied chorus on Dagobert Runes' poem *Three Times a Thousand Years* and the six-part a cappella psalm *Mi-Ma'amakim* set to the original Hebrew words of Psalm 130. Before this, Schoenberg had started composing a short poem, inspired apparently by the foundation of the State of Israel; the final form of the text dates from June 1949, but only the beginning of the poem (the three opening lines) was completed in score—planned for mixed chorus and orchestra. The poem again summarizes Schoenberg's conception of Israel's eternal mission:

> Israel exists again.
> It has always existed,
> though invisibly.
> And since the beginning of time,
> since the creation of the world
> we have always seen the Lord
> and have never ceased to see him.
> Adam saw him.
> Noah saw him.
> Abraham saw him.
> Jacob saw him.
> But Moses
> saw He was *our* God
> and we *His* elected people:
> elected to testify
> that there is only one eternal God.
> Israel has returned and will see the Lord again.

A year after writing this poem Schoenberg completed his psalm *Mi-Ma'amakim*. The story of his studies for this work gives a revealing insight into his preoccupation with liturgy and religious content in the last years of his creative life. The choral conductor Chemjo Vinaver had asked Schoenberg to contribute a composition to his *Anthology of Jewish Music*: Schoen-

berg agreed to write such a work based on a biblical text. Vinaver then sent
Schoenberg a collection of traditional Hebrew prayer tunes and pointed
to the characteristics of Hebrew prosody and cantillation. It seems that
Schoenberg studied this material with great interest and thoroughness, but
he then told the conductor that to use any existing material was against his
principles and contrary to his own style. He would compose the psalm independently. Although Schoenberg generally followed the demands of Hebrew prosody in his composition of the text, there are passages where his
melodic accents are different from those of the Hebrew words; this cannot
be ascribed only to Schoenberg's unfamiliarity with the language. The same
holds true with regard to his compositions of German and English texts.
The composer laid down his opinion on the relation between words and
music in an essay as early as 1912, arguing:

> . . . the outward correspondence between music and text, as exhibited in
> declamation, *tempo* and dynamics, has but little to do with the inward cor-
> respondence, and belongs to the same stage of primitive imitation of na-
> ture as the copying of a model. Apparent superficial divergencies can be
> necessary because of parallelism on a higher level. ("Das Verhältnis zum
> Text," in English as "The Relationship to the Text," in *Style and Idea*,
> New York, 1950.)

In his psalm *Mi-Ma'amakim* Schoenberg employs all kinds and styles of
vocal expression, from spoken recitation to exalted singing, and achieves a
sublime synthesis, the roots of which may be found in *Moses und Aron*.
H. H. Stuckenschmidt has called the work "a compendium of vocal art, a
last composition as has never before been written." When Serge Koussevitzky contacted Schoenberg in 1950, while work on this composition was
in progress, and asked him to contribute a psalm for his projected "King
David Festival" in Jerusalem to celebrate the three thousandth anniversary
of the city becoming the capital of Israel, Schoenberg proposed this opus as
his most fitting contribution. He dedicated the work to the young State of
Israel.

Two-and-a-half months after completing his composition of *Mi Ma'a-
makim*, Schoenberg sketched the first of a series of philosophical meditations which were posthumously published as *Modern Psalms*. The first
manuscript bears the date of 29 September 1950; its original title, in

Schoenberg's own handwriting, was "Der 131. Psalm"—this is interesting, for Schoenberg, who had earlier written his composition of the 130th Psalm, apparently forgot for a moment that the number of biblical psalms is 150. However, the figure "3" was later changed into a "5" in his own hand; finally, he crossed out the entire title and wrote instead (in English) "A Psalm." The following manuscript, dated 25 December 1950, is entitled "A Modern Psalm—No. 2"; two additional manuscripts of the same date are headed, respectively, "*Ein anderer moderner Psalm—No. 3*" (the title in German, "No." in the English spelling), "*Ein moderner Psalm* No. 4," "*Moderner Psalm* No. 5" followed on 29 December, "*Moderner Psalm* No. 6" and "*Moderner Psalm* No. 7" on 31 December. Two more "Modern Psalms" follow in January 1951; No. 10 was written on 9th February, 1951.

Schoenberg regarded the ten "psalms" as a first group, and it seems that they were given final and definitive literary form. For when he sent a typescript to Dr. Wolfsohn in Jerusalem on 20 April 1951, three months before his death, only the above ten were included, although Schoenberg had already written additional texts in March and April. The copy was destined to reach Dr. Wolfsohn on 30 April 1951 for his own birthday and it is Schoenberg's accompanying letter in which Schoenberg expressed his opinion "that we should try to revive our ancient religion again" and continued:

> . . . I believe that the forms of the ancient biblical language are no longer convincing in our present use of the language. One has to talk to the people of our time in our own style and of our own problems.
>   Thus I have started writing *Psalms, Prayers and other Conversations with (and about) God.* I am sending you—and you are the very first to get this—a small selection of those that are almost ready [Schoenberg says "eine kleine Auswahl solcher, die halbwegs (eben nur *halb*wegs) fertig sind . . ."] and I hope that you will accept this idea in a friendly spirit.

On the typescript we find the same title as given by Schoenberg in the accompanying letter: "Psalms, Prayers and Other Conversations with (and about) God. 1950–51." But Schoenberg added, in his own hand: "The title *Modern Psalms* has to be deleted everywhere. The one given here is also not final." Indeed, none of the six additional poems written between 23 March and 3 July 1951 (ten days before Schoenberg's death) is any longer entitled "Modern Psalm"; Schoenberg just headed them "Psalm No.–", with the actual number left open.

The subjects of these interesting texts are varied: it seems that "Meditations" would be the most appropriate description for them. The first series of ten is concerned with the hopefulness of prayer, the justification of punishment, the martyrdom and pride of the Chosen People, mystery and superstition, God's miracles ("God's planning is like that of a chess-player foreseeing unto eternity"), the Ten Commandments as the foundation of all morals and ethics ("The time will come when all people will believe in the Eternal One, Almighty, Inconceivable, as do today the best among us Jews"), the position of Christ in Jewish history, and holiness of love. The six additional poems take up the ideas of some earlier ones—on love, on faith and religion, and on the mission of the Chosen People. The texts cannot be said to be of the highest literary caliber, but they are moving as the spontaneous confessions of a passionate heart and mind. A good deal of mysticism also enters into Schoenberg's thinking now and there is much wisdom to be found in these lines noted down in days of agonizing physical suffering.

Ever since the creation of the State of Israel Schoenberg took a lively interest in the development of the new experiment, in which he must have seen partial fulfilment of much that he had foreseen. In a letter, written on 26 April 1951, announcing to the Israel Academy of Music in Jerusalem his acceptance of the official invitation to visit Israel and become President of the Academy, Schoenberg said:

> For more than four decades it has been a most cherished wish of mine to see erected an independent Israeli state. And more than that: to become a citizen residing in this state,

and in a letter to Dr. Wolfsohn, sent a few days earlier, he commented:

> You do not realize, how much I envy you your courage to move to Jerusalem where I would so much like to live myself.

In the same letter to Dr. Wolfsohn he also told his friend of long standing that he had received the invitation from the Israeli Academy and was drafting his letter of acceptance: "This letter shall become a real document," he said. It turned out to be not only a "real document" of deepest significance but also a most moving credo as to the mission of the artist in general and of an artist in Israel in particular. Unfortunately it has been printed in an incomplete version.

Close analysis reveals that not only has Schoenberg's preoccupation with liturgy left its mark on his religious compositions, but it has also influenced works that are not connected at all with religious texts or contents. A distinct relationship between the ancient Oriental systems and modern western serial composition can be proved as well as many cross-relations between Near Eastern musical conception (as preserved to some degree in traditional Hebrew chant) and Schoenberg's musical thinking. Many parallels are of interest to the historian as well as to the musician and composer; but while many younger composers today may be conscious of their implications, Schoenberg himself took little interest in analysis of this kind and all links, resemblances, and parallels must probably be regarded as subconscious. We should not, however, dismiss them as solely accidental; for we know now how keenly and profoundly Schoenberg studied every subject which interested him and how much the Hebraic spirit and heritage meant to him during at least forty years of his life. His religious works occupy a prominent place in the relatively small but the more significant catalogue of his compositions. His final works—words and music—show all the insight, wisdom and religious contemplation characterizing the last creations of most great masters of the arts: his earlier works point to the same ideas of Judaism as a religious as well as a political force as his last writings and compositions. *Der biblische Weg, Moses und Aron,* and the smaller works belong in the context of our times; but we must remember they were written in an era when such ideas were new and uncommon. A direct line leads from the words the Archangel Gabriel pronounces in *Jacob's Ladder*:

> . . . one must always go on without asking what lies before or behind one. That should be hidden; you ought to—nay, you *must* forget it, in order to fulfill your task. (1915)

to what Schoenberg called his first published *Credo*:

> You shall not, you must!
> . . . .
> You must believe in the spirit!

> Directly, without emotion,
> and selfless.
> You must, God's elect, must, if you wish to remain it! (1926)

And from there to *Moses und Aron*:

> . . . in the wasteland you shall be invincible and achieve your goal: Unity
> with God. (1932)

In the last lines Schoenberg set to music, words of "Psalm No. 1," he was concerned with the sense and meaning of prayer. Three months earlier he had composed "Psalm No. 130": "Out of the depths have I cried unto Thee, O Lord. Lord, hear my voice: let Thine ears be attentive to the voice of my supplications." His last, unfinished, composition is set to the words:

> O, thou my Lord, all people praise Thee and assure Thee of their faithful-
> ness.
> But what can it mean to Thee whether or not I do the same?
> Who am I that I should believe my prayer to be of necessity?
> And yet I pray to Thee, as everyone living prays, and yet I request mercy
> and miracles: fulfilment.
> And yet I pray to Thee. . . .

The text continues in Schoenberg's manuscript. The music breaks off with the affirmation of faith.

In historical as well as in Jewish perspective, Arnold Schoenberg seems to have found the answer to many a question that Gustav Mahler had asked and was unable to solve. Mahler lived in an era that appeared secure on the outside. Signs of approaching storms were certainly to be felt, and Mahler was not insensitive to them. He had embraced Christianity as his position demanded it. He had longed for a deeper understanding of German and Austrian poetic lore and later turned to the poetry of the Far East—but he knew all these from second-hand transcription only. He had delved with his soul and his mind deep into the mysticism of Catholic teachings—but could not gain innermost peace. Mahler pursued the search for truth and eternity during a lifetime of work and creation and remained a martyr of his cause, a martyr of his own tortured soul. Schoenberg, though also experiencing the martyrdom of the creative artist who possesses "the courage to follow only his own leanings," gained peace within himself—in an epoch that was so much stormier, so much fuller of tragedy than Mahler's. The world around could remain hostile—he need not mind. He had found strength in the knowledge that a new era had dawned, that "Israel has returned and will see the Lord again."

THREE DISTINCT TRENDS characterized early-twentieth-century music: one following the paths of national renaissance, another reviving the polyphony of the baroque era, and the third concentrating on the purely melodic values which had been drowned in the luxurious harmony of the late romantic works. All these trends attempted to give music a new stimulus and to reestablish active listening in place of the musical revelry of the late nineteenth century. National music stressed the rhythmic forces and the directness and naturalness of musical expression: the early Stravinsky started from an almost barbaric emphasis on the rhythmical impetus; Béla Bartók, the Hungarian master, provides the greatest representative of contemporary music which grows on national soil but can still soar to sublime artistic heights. The revival of the polyphonic style symbolizes the composers' desire to make music again the possession of a community united in ideals and purpose; Paul Hindemith is the leading spirit of a movement that was originated, and largely promoted, by musicians siding with progressive youth.

It cannot be incidental that the regeneration of melody was the achievement of a Jewish composer, who on his way smashed the edifice of romantic harmony that was so typical a product of the western tradition in German music. Schoenberg put melody high above all other musical elements and based the structure of his music on a unifying melodic idea, which not only produces in his works all the other ideas but also regulates their accompaniments and the chords, the harmonies. He thus disregards the limitations exercised by the seven-tone major or minor scale and returns to the most ancient principles of composition. He finds his ideal in twelve-tone-scale themes that serve as basic scale as well as melodic foundation for an entire musical work. The twelve-tone scale, making use of all the half-tones included in the octave of the equal-tempered scale, cannot but remind us of the ancient Oriental technique, in which mode is basic scale and motive in one.

Arnold Schoenberg's art is expressionist, predominantly lyrical—as purely melodic music must necessarily be. The exquisite lyricism of his early compositions has finally led to universal recognition of his genius, though the first listeners to these works—in the beginnings of the twentieth century—were utterly bewildered by what seemed to them a complex and incomprehensible style. It later appeared to his critics that the composer had abandoned the lyricism and romanticism of his early works and turned to a "purely mathematical way of composition" and "replaced inspired composing by constructive engineering." The reason for this verdict was the unprecedented degree of concentrated elaboration and emotional content in the later compositions and their renunciation of romantic harmony. The critics overlooked the fact that an almost unequaled wealth of inventive ideas characterizes both the early and the later Schoenberg works and that even when dressed in a cloak of romantic harmonies, as in the first compositions, the richness of variation and elaboration had been beyond the powers of appreciation of many listeners. In fact, as Cecil Gray observed as long ago as in 1924, the early works occasioned only that "negative and obviously insincere admiration of the see-what-he-can-do-when-he-likes order which is always so profusely lavished upon the immature productions of a master by those who most detest and abominate his later works, simply because they sound more like the music to which they are accustomed."

Schoenberg shares this fate with Mozart as well as with Beethoven, Wagner, Mahler, and Richard Strauss; it took him decades of unwavering steadiness to achieve the recognition due to his genius. That a great affinity exists between the principles of his musical style and the characteristic eastern way of composing cannot be denied; that only "decadent Jewish minds" can create and appreciate music of this kind (as not only the outspokenly anti-Semitic writers have asserted) is clearly refuted by the fact that there is hardly a single twentieth-century composer who has not passed through a stage of joining issue with Schoenberg and his music—no matter whether to the effect of acceptance or rejection—and that an ever-growing number of composers, the majority of whom are non-Jews, have been developing his aesthetics and theories of musical composition since the formation of his new style.

THE YEARS after the First World War witnessed a particularly high activity of Jewish musicians in the countries of the West, and they held a conspicuous place in the universal search for new ideals and new ways of expression in a shattered world. Research conducted in 1933 threw interesting light on Jewish participation in American music. The percentage of Jewish players in symphony orchestras was found to be 34 percent in the string section, and 23.9 percent in the percussion section, but only a little more than 9 percent in the woodwinds and brass—with an individually higher figure for trumpet and oboe. The total percentage of Jewish musicians in the major orchestras was 25.7 percent, while the figure for conductors was 45.9 percent, for violin virtuosos 47.5 percent, for piano soloists 35.4 percent, for cellists 14.3 percent, for composer-artists 23.8 percent, and for (American) composers 14.5 percent. Research into the musicality of Jewish children aged 10–11 years showed no basic difference in comparison with non-Jewish children of the same age (Keith Sward, "Jewish Musicality in America," *Journal of Applied Psychology*, Ohio University, Athens, Ohio, Vol. 17, pp. 675–712, 1933).

Vienna, Berlin, and Paris were the prominent centers of the activities of Jewish musicians before 1933, and they also took an active part in the newly founded International Society for Contemporary Music and in the international musical research of the time. At the same time the spectacular rise of music in the New World exerted its attraction on Jewish musicians, and they figure largely in the recent music history of the most liberal of countries.

The central figure among French musicians after the First World War was Darius Milhaud (1892–1974), descendant of an ancient Jewish family that claimed to have been among the very first settlers in southern France after the destruction of Jerusalem. Milhaud was a most prolific composer, writing music for every combination and in all fields of composition; traditional prayers of southern French Jewish communities inspired him to some of his finest religious songs, and ancient legend is the background to his Purim opera *Esther de Carpentras.* Jewish folk songs and Hebrew poems figure in the long list of his lyrical songs, and in America during the Second World War Milhaud composed a symphonic work for a ballet on the story of Cain and Abel. Milhaud belonged to a group of composers ("Les Six") who strove to get away from romanticism and to fight for clarity of expression and form. His main interest, like Schoenberg's, lay in the melodic element; while typical French playfulness and easy charm also give his music a

Darius Milhaud (1892–1974) discusses one of his piano compositions with Menahem Pressler.

characteristic imprint. Milhaud's own contribution to modern musical language is "polytonality"—the simultaneous sounding of melodies in different tonalities—created in the desire to increase the melodic content of a composition.

The most significant among the considerable number of Milhaud's works inspired by biblical and Jewish themes is his large-scale opera *David* for which he collaborated—as earlier for *Esther de Carpentras*—with his

life-long friend Armand Lunel, like Milhaud a descendant of a most ancient family from Provence. The opera was commissioned by the Koussevitzky Foundation to mark the three thousandth anniversary of the establishment of Jerusalem as the capital of Judea by King David. Lunel and
Milhaud visited Israel together to see the biblical locations and to breathe
the atmosphere of the Holy Land. Milhaud composed the five-act opera
(twelve scenes) in Aspen, Colorado, and at Mills College, Oakland, California, where he taught composition, in the summer and autumn of 1952
at a pace quicker than was possible in Israel to print the vocal score and
copy the orchestral parts from the full score. (Delays infuriated him, as letters to this author indicated.) It was given in oratorio form, authorized by
the composer, in Jerusalem on 1 June 1954 at the Twenty-eighth World
Music Festival of the International Society for Contemporary Music. It was
conducted by Georg Singer; Aharon Ashman had prepared a Hebrew version of Lunel's libretto. At the stage première at the Teatro alla Scala in

Darius Milhaud's opera, *David*, Teatro alla Scala, Milan, January 1954. Scene
design by Nicola Benois. (Photograph: Erio Piccagliani.)

Milan, it was sung in an Italian translation by Claudio Sartori; the first performance took place on 2 January 1955. Nino Sanzogno conducted; Margarete Wallmann was the producer.

The opera tells the biblical story of David from the first visit of the Prophet Samuel to the house of Isa'i, David's father, to the anointment of Solomon as King of Israel and successor to David's throne. A "Chorus of Israelites of the Year 1954" comments on the biblical story from the point of view of men and women of modern times and draws parallels to the recent history of the people of Israel in the Land of the Bible. Darius Milhaud had written to Lunel in March 1951 after having accepted the Koussevitzky commission: "Get deeply absorbed by the Bible, suck in the lyricism of the psalms, so that I may toot my most resounding trumpet." The score contains some of Milhaud's most inspired pages of music, especially in the choral prayers, culminating in the final scene "At the Holy Fountain at Gihon" with the anointment of Solomon and the Israelites—men, women, and children—praying for prosperity and peace for Israel and God's entire world.

Milhaud's religious and Jewish-inspired compositions also include settings of traditional Jewish texts and translated Jewish poetry, and liturgical and folkloristic melodies, a complete Sabbath Morning Service (1947), and a Psalm Cantata (1968). One of his last works, written two years before his death, was "Ode to Jerusalem" for orchestra (1972). Milhaud wrote his autobiography *Notes sans Musique* (Notes without Music) in French in 1949; the English version was published in 1952. In 1973 there followed his *Ma Vie heureuse*.

MILHAUD'S COMPOSITIONS with a Hebrew or Jewish background were often intentionally conceived with allusions to or inclusion of liturgical of folkloristic melody mainly of French-provençal-Jewish origin. Yet there are phenomena in the history of musical compositions that at first sight, at first hearing, may give an impression of casual coincidences, even when their appearances in the works of composers span centuries—for instance, the occurrence of sacred motifs in compositions that have no relevant connection with sacred functions. For Catholic composers examples have been cited for instrumental works of Franz Joseph Haydn. In the Jewish field the outstanding parallels are the Kol Nidre prayer cantillation motif one might not have expected in a Beethoven Quartet or in a String Quartet by Arnold Schoenberg. In Beethoven's C-sharp Minor Quartet, Op. 131, the motif opening the Ashkenazic Kol Nidre can distinctly be heard in the Adagio movement preceding the Finale; in Schoenberg's Fourth String Quartet Op. 37 it shapes the expressive Largo movement. In all of Beethoven's last string quartets the four-note characteristic intervals of the motifs are the main melodic cells of the compositions; in Schoenberg's work the same intervals form the melodic themes of all four movements and the extended prayer tune is played in the Largo *unisono* by all four string instruments to effect a deeper impact. There is an explanation for the compositions of both the Gentile and the Jewish composer. Beethoven wrote his last quartets at the time he had considered accepting the commission of the Jewish Community of Vienna to write a Cantata on Hebrew prayer texts for the consecration of their new synagogue and studied "the music of the Hebrews"; Schoenberg had heard his mother Pauline Nachod sing the old tunes in his childhood—she stemmed from a traditional Jewish family from Prague whose male members had for generations been cantors at the ancient synagogue. Schoenberg wrote his *Kol Nidre* composition for speaker, choir and orchestra two years after the Fourth String Quartet (1938). It is noteworthy also that in the sketches for an unfinished part of *Die Jakobsleiter* (1917) Schoenberg put down for the first time motives that are cells of twelve-tone melodies on the one hand and on the other hand contain the intervals characteristic for Hebrew liturgical chant, Kol Nidre.[8]

DARIUS MILHAUD had in addition to his love for Jewish-Hebrew themes a great fondness for exotic coloring, as is especially apparent in his Brazilian-inspired pieces and some of his operas. This was the impact of his nearly two-year sojourn (1917–18) in Rio de Janeiro as secretary to the poet Paul Claudel, who served as French minister to Brazil. In his exotic strains Milhaud followed earlier French composers: the nineteenth century had shown

---

[8]See P. Gradenwitz, "Beethoven op. 131–Schoenberg op. 37," in *Bericht über den Internationalen Musikwissenschaftlichen Kongress Berlin 1974*, Kassel 1980, pp. 369–372; and P. Gradenwitz, "Arnold Schoenberg's Streichquartett Nr. 4, Op. 37," *Meisterwerke der Musik*, No. 43, München, 1986.

Example 20. Beethoven's String Quartet Op. 131, 6th movement.

Example 21. Beethoven's String Quartet Op. 131, 1st movement.

Example 22. Beethoven's String Quartet Op. 132 (left), Op. 135 (right).

Example 23. Beethoven's String Quartet Op. 130.

Example 24. Schoenberg's *Kol Nidre* (Ashkenazic).

a new interest in the Orient, and French literature, painting, and music had been highly colored by Oriental or would-be-Oriental elements. The exotic had been a decisive element in impressionistic painting and music, and from Debussy onward French composers craved exotic effects. It is small wonder that Jewish artists were particularly attracted by the Oriental fashion—

Example 25. Schoenberg's Fourth String Quartet: 3rd movement (top), 1st movement (bottom).

Example 26. Schoenberg's *Die Jakobsleiter* (in a sketch for the 2nd part—unfinished).

which also showed its impact in Mahler's *Song of the Earth*—while at the same time the study of eastern music and of the ancient Hebrew chants stimulated interest in their Oriental heritage as well: many non-Jewish composers—foremost among them Mussorgsky in Russia and Ravel in France—adapted Jewish religious or folk tunes.

It was the charm of the exotic, too, that gained an overwhelming victory in the entire world for a new kind of music that came to Europe from the New World. This was the music of the exotic strains and the powerful rhythmic impulse of jazz, which—just like European music of modern times—was destined to bring new vitality into a world of decline. From modest attempts jazz developed into a powerful and stimulating force in contemporary music, and Jewish composers have been prominent in the field of jazz music as well as in its symphonic application. Irving Berlin (whose original name was Israel Baline) was one of the first writers of popular songs. George Gershwin created in his famous *Rhapsody in Blue* a remarkable concert-jazz symphonic composition and with his Negro folk-

Russian-Jewish melodic tradition in the works of Modest Mussorgsky. I. Modest
Mussorgsky (1839–81): melody from traditional Hebrew song in the cantata
"Joshua." (Biblical text from Joshua 10:12, ". . . and Joshua said in the sight of
Israel: Sun, stand still upon Gibeon, and thou, Moon, in the valley of Ajalong.")
II. "Hebrew Song" ("I am the rose of Sharon, and the lily of the valleys"; Russian
adaptation by L. Mey).

opera *Porgy and Bess* one of the greatest stage works in this style. His premature death robbed music of a genuine and versatile talent.

The influences of Yiddish popular songs from New York's East Side
and the American Yiddish operetta are clearly identifiable in Irving Berlin's
melodies. He was an immensely prolific writer of words and music, and on
his one-hundredth birthday the most distinguished American musicians
paid tribute to him at Carnegie Hall in New York (he lived from 1888 to
1989). He also wrote American patriotic songs, among them "God Bless
America" (1918), which became kind of an American national anthem; in
1954 he received a Congressional Medal. "White Christmas" (1942) was
another of his perennial songs.

George Gershwin (1898–1937), whose father had come to America
from Russia (his name was Gershovitz), also knew both Jewish liturgical
music and the Yiddish operetta; he was once asked to take over the musi-

cal direction of the New York Yiddish theater, which did not materialize. Albert Weisser, co-founder and president of the American Society for Jewish Music, quotes the composer Lazare Saminsky's recollection of a conversation with Gershwin in 1930: Gershwin indicated that he thought the clarinet solo that opens the *Rhapsody in Blue* (written in 1924) was related "to that particular type of Yiddish-Romanian folk instrumental soliloquy called *doyna* and other eastern-European klesmer practice." The Negro spirituals and Hebrew cantillation certainly have some similarities; there could also be suggestions of Jewish melody in the opera *Porgy and Bess* (1935).

AMONG THE FIRST European composers to grasp the possibilities of American jazz in serious music was Kurt Weill, pupil of Ferruccio Busoni and a composer of symphonic and operatic music before he succumbed to the impact of jazz. Weill created in modern music a new song style; again it can be no pure coincidence that a chant-like declamatory style of singing was introduced into music by a Jewish cantor's son. In various stage works, which met with an unprecedented success in central Europe, Weill practiced his new style and technique, and the number of his imitators soon became legion. On emigrating to the United States, Weill found in his new country ample opportunity to apply his singular gifts for stage music, and soon gained a prominent position among composers for the theater and for films. In the Franz Werfel–Max Reinhardt production of a biblical pageant, *The Eternal Way*, Weill could turn to a purely Jewish subject.

Kurt Weill, born in Dessau in 1900, settled in 1918 in Berlin, where he met considerable success with vocal and instrumental compositions before turning to music for the theater. He wrote music for plays by the foremost German playwrights of the time, including Georg Kaiser and Iwan Goll. Beginning in 1927 he collaborated with Bertold Brecht, and together they made music theater history: *Die Dreigroschenoper* (1928) which was *The Threepenny Opera* in Marc Blitzstein's American version; *Mahagonny* (1929); *Happy End* (1929); and *Die sieben Todsünden* (The Seven Deadly Sins, Paris, 1933) became worldwide successes. In 1935, after fleeing Nazi Germany and sojourning in Paris and London, he reached America, where he contributed significantly to the American musical theater. Only many

George Gershwin (1898–1937).

George Gershwin paints Arnold Schoenberg in Hollywood.

years after his death in New York in 1950 did the Jewish world take notice of his Jewish sacred works. He had been born into a family that included a long line of rabbis and cantors. His father (b. 1867), the Dessau synagogue cantor, published a volume of his own synagogal compositions in 1890 under the title of *Kol Avraham* for cantor and male choir, with Hebrew and German texts. In 1892 Weill's maternal grandfather also published a volume of synagogue songs, for solo voice, and a textbook. Throughout Kurt Weill's musical career, the liturgical heritage seems never to have been for-

Kurt Weill (1900–50).

gotten. As a 23-year old composer he had written a work based on the
Lamentations of Jeremiah, *Recordare* for mixed choir and boys' choir a
cappella (1923); this became known only after a performance at Utrecht in
1971 and in New York in 1980. Before this sacred piece he had already
composed a one-act opera, *Das hohe Lied*, after a novel by the German author Hermann Sudermann, and an oratorio based, like the opera, on The
Song of Songs; this was called *Shulamith*. Both were written during the
years 1919–20; one year later Weill wrote his Symphony No. 1 in one
movement, and in 1922 a Divertimento for chamber orchestra and male
choir. It is remarkable that both these instrumental compositions contain
liturgical reminiscences; the symphony has a section marked *Andante reli-
gioso*, the third part should be played *wie ein Choral* (like a chorale). The
fourth, final, movement of the Divertimento takes the form of a prayer to
the biblical God. All the works were conceived and written while Kurt Weill
was studying with Ferruccio Busoni, as was Weill's *Sinfonia Sacra* (Fanta-
sia-Passacaglia-Hymnus). Among Weill's later liturgical compositions and
music connected with biblical and Jewish themes were incidental music to
The Journey to Jerusalem by Maxwell Anderson (1940); the "dramatic oratorio" written by Franz Werfel and staged by Max Reinhardt entitled *The
Eternal Way* (1937); music for a Jewish political pageant, *We Will Never
Die*, by Ben-Hecht (1943); and a Friday evening *Kiddush for Mixed Chorus
and Organ* (1946). In 1947 he orchestrated the Jewish national anthem
"Hatikvah" on the occasion of a festive dinner for Israel's first president,
Dr. Chaim Weizmann, to be played by the Boston Symphony Orchestra.

IN GERMANY, Kurt Weill had been only one in a school of young composers among whom were Jewish musicians who had little interest in the
Jewish sphere as such but who made a name for themselves in the world of
new music in Germany and Austria. The most prominent of these composers—those who survived lived in America or England after the advent of
Nazism—were Erich Wolfgang Korngold, who made a meteoric ascent as
a child prodigy composer but later abandoned serious music for the theater and films; Hanns Eisler, the author of aggressive proletarian music and
of interesting concert music influenced by the Schoenberg style; Ernst
Toch, a modernist of great individuality; Egon Wellesz, composer and mu-

sicologist; Hans Gal, a sensitive musician; Adolf Schreiber, a romantic talent whose development was cut off by early death; and Franz Reizenstein, a pianist and composer of the Hindemith school who emigrated to England and there composed a Genesis oratorio in 1958. Mátyás Seiber, of Hungarian extraction, lived and taught in England; some of his compositions recall eastern modes and jazz influence. Both the Polish Josef Koffler and the Czech Erwin Schulhoff met premature death in the Nazi persecutions, as did the Czech composers Pavel Haas, Gideon Klein, Hans Krása, and the Viennese pupil of Schoenberg, Viktor Ullmann.

In addition to these central-European figures whose compositions contributed little, if anything, to Jewish music proper, there were musicians who devoted some of their efforts to the creation of music for the Jewish world. The most prominent and interesting among them included Paul Dessau, who composed a Haggadah oratorio to a text arranged by Max Brod; Karol Rathaus, who wrote, among other works of Jewish interest, the stage music for the Habimah Theater's performances of the Karl Ferdinand Gutzkow play *Uriel Acosta*; Berthold Goldschmidt; Hugo Kauder; and Mario Castelnuovo-Tedesco, the prolific Italian-Jewish composer who wrote numerous works on Hebrew and Jewish subjects. In France, Manuel Rosenthal, Daniel Lazarus, Marcel Mihalovici, and Tibor Harsanyi were the best-known Jewish composers of their times; Sem Dresden was a prominent figure in Dutch music, as was Benjamin Frankel in British music. Aaron Copland (1900–90) was the towering figure in twentieth-century American musical history. Leonard Bernstein and Lukas Foss belong in the context of "Hebrew music of our time." Among the many interesting Jewish composers in the United States must be listed Marc Blitzstein, Louis Gruenberg, Irving Fine, Harold Shapero, David Diamond, Israel Citkowitz, Nicolas Slonimsky (the indefatigable music historian, bibliographer, and editor, apart from his creative musical work), Arthur Cohn, Ellis B. Kohs, Nicolai Lopatnikoff—most of their music is part of the general repertoire of twentieth-century American music. A singular figure was Sholom Secunda, whose Yiddish song "Bei mir bistu shēn" (1933) became world famous and was popular in Nazi Germany (!), where it was thought to be an American folk song. Among the works of Erich Itor Kahn, who came to the U.S. from Germany, is a two-movement composition for violoncello and piano *Nenia Judaeis qui hac aetate perierunt* (In Memory of the Jews Who Perished in the Holocaust) written in a French concentration camp where he was interned 1940–41, and completed in New York in 1943. Prominent Jewish composers in Latin America were Jacobo Ficher of Argentina and Jacobo Kostakowsky of Mexico. An influential composer who was not very widely known in the U.S. was Stefan Wolpe, born in Germany, a composer and teacher in Jerusalem for several years, and teacher of David Tudor, Ezra Laderman, Ralph Shapey, Elmer Bernstein, and Morton Feldman in the U.S.[9]

THE ENTIRE JEWISH WORLD—and not only those communities immediately affected—was mobilized by the reactionary developments of the 1930s. The large-scale migration from central Europe and the decimation of Jewry from 1933 to the end of the Second World War had far-reaching effects on the structure of Jewish society throughout the world. For even those who believed that migration meant no more than a change of domicile could not but feel that one more chapter in Jewish history had been completed—a relatively happy chapter ending in a catastrophe of incomprehensible proportions. The great world became Jew-conscious again—no matter whether people stood for or against the Jews; and the works of art created by Jewish as well as by non-Jewish artists in the time preceding and following World War II are vivid testimony of the stirring experiences of the era. The utter destruction of the flourishing central European Jewry, the biblical precedents for events in modern history, and the tragically dramatic story of a people which reads stranger than fiction have occupied minds and struggled for artistic expression ever since the storm began, while the basic conception of the assimilated Jewish romanticists was proved fallacious and their works seemed but memories of a period that had passed forever.

---

[9]For more information on Stefan Wolpe, see Chapter 14, The Pioneer Generation of Israeli Composers and Teachers, p. 374.

CHAPTER NINE

THE BIBLE IN MUSIC

T HE BIBLE is known to all civilized nations, and its books have been translated into more than seven hundred languages. No wonder, then, that the world of the Bible has influenced the spirit of mankind to a greater degree than any other creation of the human mind. The Book of Books has attained its towering position by its unequaled universality: it not only embodies religious creed and ethics, a legal and moral code, and a philosophy of life, but also contains a treasury of legends and stories that are among the most beautiful and the most dramatic of the world. The Bible provided the foundation of all western civilizations; its stories are among the first a mother tells to her children, and its morals form the basis of all education. By translating the books of the Bible into the vernacular great thinkers have created new styles of expression in their own languages, and the poetry of the Psalms, the Lamentations, and the Song of Songs have decisively influenced the poets of all nations. A larger number of paintings, plays, and musical works have been based upon biblical scenes than on any other source; the historical, philosophical, and religious contents of the Bible as well as the innumerable dramatic incidents described have proved to be the greatest source of inspiration for poets, artists, and musicians alike.[1]

Not all musical works inspired by the Bible can be said to contribute to our knowledge of the music of Israel proper, but a short survey of biblical compositions is of more than passing interest, for in treating an ancient literary or pictorial theme composers have often tried to recapture the biblical spirit and have studied the ancient heritage preserved by its creators, the Jews. For the oratorios and operas and the symphonic works based on the world of the Bible, composers—Gentiles as well as Jewish—have often used traditional Hebrew melodies or have attempted a musical characterization of ancient Jerusalem and Judea and their inhabitants; and though the music of those composers mirrors, of course, the masters' own conception of the East and the state of music in their period, it is most fascinating to study not only the various ways in which they have attempted to bring the biblical subjects to life but also their actual reasons for falling back on the Bible for a European work of art.

WE NEED NOT ENLARGE upon the obvious fact that artists could always draw upon the Bible because of their own familiarity with the subjects and because of the popularity they have enjoyed with the public throughout the ages. Painters and sculptors began employing biblical motives in the earliest of the Christian centuries, and though the ancient aversion to pictorial representation at first led the Church Fathers to prohibit the creation of such images, they could not prevail. The Orient thought that the eternal and boundless in man would perish on being given external form, while the Occident could only do homage to the visible embodiment of the objects of their worship. The artists were indeed instrumental in popularizing the figures and stories of the Bible, and in their creative work they also satisfied their own religious zeal. While the New Testament provided them with the themes directly concerned with the Christian creed of the West, they often chose scenes from the Old Testament for their more colorful and dramatic aspects.

---

[1] The Haifa music historian Moshe Gorali has published a lavishly illustrated encyclopedic survey, *The Old Testament in Music*, Jerusalem, 1993, 602 pages, large format, with reproductions of paintings and music excerpts.

In music the creation of independent works of art began at a later stage of European history than in the pictorial arts and in literature. Earlier composers were almost exclusively concerned with setting biblical passages to music and elaborating traditional liturgical chants for the clergy and the religious community. The Psalms and the Lamentations were the texts most frequently composed for the Church, and they kept their prominent position throughout the centuries. For the Protestant Church Martin Luther wrote his songs paraphrasing psalms or psalm passages, and the Huguenots got their own Psalter from no less a poet than Clément Marot. The Protestant songs accounted for some of the most beautiful compositions of Heinrich Schütz and Johann Sebastian Bach, while the Huguenot Psalter was composed by Claude Goudimel and exerted its influence on many musical masters—the Dutch organist Sweelinck above all. There are few composers who have not written psalms—from the German and Swiss composers of the Reformation through Lasso and Palestrina to J. S. Bach in the early eighteenth century, and from the classical period down to our own days. Christoph Willibald Gluck and Philipp Emanuel Bach were psalm composers in the early classic era; Felix Mendelssohn gave a new impetus to psalm composition in the romantic age; Antonín Dvořák's psalms are sublime examples of religious music in the nineteenth-century national idiom; Liszt wrote psalms at the height of the romantic era, while Max Reger returned to the pure religious spirit of Bach in his psalm compositions; in modern times Igor Stravinsky and Ernest Bloch, the American composers Charles Martin Loeffler and Alec Wilder, the English masters Elgar and Walton, the Swiss Honegger, and a great many Israeli composers have cultivated the composition of psalm poetry. The delicate lyricism of the Song of Songs and the possibilities it offers for pastoral tone-painting began to attract the composers at a time when naturalness and pastoral atmosphere were favored by a society that had turned away from the rigidity of the medieval Church. Its first great setting was that of Palestrina, who wrote a cycle of twenty-nine pieces on verses from the poem (completed in 1584). A beautiful Serenata on the Song of Solomon was composed by William Boyce in eighteenth-century England, and in our own time remarkable works based on this lyrical book are by Ralph Vaughan Williams (*Flos Campi* for voices, viola solo, and small orchestra, 1925), Arthur

Honegger (*Cantique des Cantiques* for speaker and small orchestra, 1926), Marc Lavry (*Shir ha-shirim*, oratorio, 1944), Lukas Foss (*Song of Songs* for mezzo-soprano and orchestra, 1946), the American Carl Hugo Grimm (the oratorio *Song of Songs*, 1930), and Jean Martinon (*Le Lis de Sharon*, 1952). The Israeli composer Noam Sheriff wrote *Shir ha-Shirim* for flute solo and orchestra. The Israeli Dov Selzer set *Shir ha-Shirim* as a melodrama for two narrators and chamber orchestra.

THE PSALMS attracted the composers by their sheer poetical beauty and spiritual greatness; some of them were chosen because of their inherent musical character and for their designation as song of praise to the accompaniment of musical instruments. The Song of Songs, on the other hand, has proved to inspire especially those musicians with outspoken pastoral and lyrical leanings and at times in which naturalness was the foremost demand of an artist—such as in the Italian Renaissance and in the early eighteenth century or in twentieth-century trends opposed to the exalted romanticism of the preceding age.

Few are the western composers who attempted to give their setting of biblical poetry an actual eastern background; an exception is Carl Hugo Grimm, whose choral "Song of Songs" contains exotic elements.

But while the poetical sections of the Bible have been set to music without much regard for their original context and their essentially eastern character, the inspiration of the composers of opera, oratorio, and symphonic works was kindled by the biblical legends and stories and their characteristic background. They turned to the world of the Bible particularly in periods of an increased interest in the Orient and in the exotic—such as the romantic era—and it is interesting to follow their imaginative trends from the beginnings of dramatic music down to our days.

The oratorio originated in the sixteenth century from sacred services into which elements of the mystery play and biblical scenes were introduced to attract the worshippers. With the late-Renaissance attempts to combine music and drama there came into being not only the dramatic musical play for the stage—opera—but also the more contemplative and epic form of the oratorio. The early oratorio composers gave no pictorial background to the music, but simply attempted to bring the sacred stories of the Old Testament closer to the public by glorifying their heroes; these works are written in the operatic style of the period with the emphasis on vocal expression. The earliest biblical oratorios known are those by Giovanni Francesco Anerio (1567–1620), younger brother of Palestrina's successor at the Papal Chapel; his *Teatro armonico spirituale* (1619) contains settings of the Joseph story, of Abraham's sacrifice, Jacob and Esau, Adam and Eve, and David and Goliath. The most famous of early oratorio composers is Giacomo Carissimi (1604–1674), who increased the part of instrumental music in his vocal works—which made the music much more dramatic—and also introduced a narrator to link the different scenes; among the heroes of his works are Isaac, David and Goliath, King Solomon, Jephtha, Jonah, Hiskia, Belshazzar, and Job; he also wrote an oratorio, *The Great Flood*.

While few composers of opera turned their attention to the Bible before 1800, biblical stories accounted for the greater part of the oratorios written in the seventeenth and eighteenth centuries—among which Giovanni Battista Vitali's *Hagar*, Giovanni Legrenzi's *Esther*, Giovanni Paolo Colonna's *Moses* and *Samson*, Giovanni Bononcini's *Josua*, and Alessandro Scarlatti's *Hagar and Ismael*, *Judith*, and *Abraham's Sacrifice* are a few outstanding works among a multitude of almost-forgotten compositions.

The vocal and dramatic style of these compositions closely resembles that of the operas; the only difference between the Italian operas and oratorios of early times is the stageless character of the latter—though many of them were actually presented with action and in costumes, too. In Germany, however, the oratorio took on a purely religious, devotional character, and it is because of this that the composers there more often turned to the New Testament; only in the Enlightenment period and in early classicism do we find Old Testament oratorios in Germany; Carl Philipp Emanuel Bach's *Israelites in the Wilderness* (1775) is an early and outstanding example. The classics took up the operatic trends of the Italian oratorio but achieved greater instrumental freedom and dramatic expression; a characteristic work is Mozart's *La Betulia liberata* (composed in March and April 1771 on a text by Metastasio), in which the youthful master—fifteen years of age!—accomplished some ingenious dramatic characterization; he also introduced a psalm tune for one of the choruses. The same master's

Davidde penitente is nothing but a pasticcio made up in 1785 from some movements taken out of the Mass in C Minor of 1782–83 and two new arias; the text is probably by Lorenzo da Ponte, the librettist of *Figaro, Così fan tutte*, and *Don Giovanni*—the poet of Jewish descent. The classical oratorio reached sublime heights in the works of Franz Joseph Haydn. His earliest attempt in the field of Biblical oratorio had been *The Return of Tobias* (completed in 1775); his masterpiece was *The Creation* (1797–98), in which all means of Haydn's great symphonic art are applied to the dramatic setting of the first chapters of Genesis, while no special interest is shown in the eastern conception proper. Biblical episodes were also set to music by his younger brother, Michael Haydn. An eighteenth-century curiosity is the series *Biblical Sonatas* for the keyboard by Johann Kuhnau, J. S. Bach's predecessor at St. Thomas' in Leipzig—early examples of instrumental program music.

The rococo, with its emphasis on emotion and feeling and its love of ornament, rediscovered the Orient; but in music it so far expressed itself only in the "Turkish" strains introduced in operas dealing with Oriental subjects (such as Mozart's *Entführung aus dem Serail*) or for the sake of special instrumental effects (such as the "Turkish" Marches of Mozart and Beethoven, the Janissary music in the middle section of the "Ode" in Beethoven's Ninth Symphony). But with the rise of romanticism, the Orient and the world of the Bible were seen by artists in a new light. Symbolism and mysticism had lived on in the Freemasons' temples (Mozart's *Magic Flute* abounds in symbolic allusions of the Masonic kind) and in many other secret societies of a similar character. Journeys to the Orient were a great vogue, and the customs and manners of the Oriental countries were studied. Johann Gottfried Herder tried to conjure up Oriental moods in his German versions of eastern poetry and thus gave inspiration to a long line of poets, leading from Goethe's "West-Eastern Divan" to Heinrich Heine and Friedrich Rückert. The artists craved the exotic and the mystical in music just as in poetry, and much of the romantic coloring is due to eastern influence.

The biblical operas and oratorios of the romantic era are the creations of musicians who did not compose their works for the sake of their church and for the spiritual, religious elevation of their communities; theirs were compositions for the theater stage and concert hall. Dramatic effect and sharp musical characterization were their main concern, and they found many pretexts to exercise their faculties for colorful music in the biblical stories. George Frederick Handel—the earliest composer in history to have created music with a view to public appreciation—had already discovered the attracting power of the heroes of ancient Hebrew history when his Italian opera did not flourish in early eighteenth-century England; the new public that streamed to the theater showed little interest in the Italian and Greek heroes that were far removed in time and ideals from their own reality and were presented to them in a language (Italian) foreign to them. But with his dramatic oratorios based on the biblical stories with which the English were traditionally more familiar than most other Europeans Handel quickly regained public favor, and it has been said that another reason for his choice of subject was the considerable interest shown in his concerts by the Jewish community of the time. Handel used many different biblical stories for his oratorios: Esther, Deborah, Saul, Israel in Egypt, Samson, Joseph, Belshazzar, Judas Maccabaeus, Joshua, Solomon, and Jephthah are the subjects of the biblical works composed between 1720 and 1751. His example set a vogue in England that was to last till the end of the nineteenth century, but the later composers found contact with the general romantic trends and often gave their works a striking Oriental background. The Handelian oratorio not only influenced the composers of England and the European continent but also found its way to the New World. An Americanized German musician, Charles Zeuner (1795–1857), performed his lavish *Feast of Tabernacles* in Boston but later destroyed all copies of the work, his own manuscript included; his younger American contemporary John Hewitt (1801–90) composed a "Jephthah" oratorio.

IT IS IMPOSSIBLE to list in the frame of this survey all the biblical operas and oratorios written in the course of the nineteenth and twentieth centuries, but some outstanding works may be named to show how many of the great composers turned to the Bible for inspiration. A study of these works—no matter whether in the field of the oratorio proper or the acted musical drama—reveals a rather obvious development: the works of the romantic age make an ever-increasing use of exotic tone-painting and melismatic would-be Oriental melody, while in late nineteenth-century and contemporary compositions barbaric dramatic aspects of the ancient stories are stressed in particular. There is a world of a difference between the delicate Near Eastern sensibility in, say, Saint-Saëns's *Samson and Delilah* (which, by the way, could not be performed in Paris for many years after its première in Germany—for a biblical subject could not be staged at the Paris Opera till 1890!) and the clashes of moods and temperaments in Honegger's biblical works, or between the dramatic exoticism in Verdi's early *Nabucco* and the stirring barbarisms in Walton's *Belshazzar's Feast*. The modern composer—opposing the emotional ecstasy of romanticism by the strength of melodic expression and the compelling forces of rhythm—either shows the temperamental Jewish masses in their opposition to their spiritual, prophetic leaders or contrasts the Jews as bearers of an idea to the barbarous peoples that grudged them their power in Judea. In many works by Christian composers the prophetic spirit is taken to symbolize Christianity. Thus Honegger's dramatic psalm *Le Roi David*—together with Willy Burkhard's *Isaiah*, William Walton's *Belshazzar*, and Leonard Bernstein's *Jeremiah*—is among the most powerful biblical works of our time.

Biblical opera began with Johann Theile's *Adam and Eve*, with which the Hamburg Opera was opened in 1678, and with Nicolas Adam Strungk's *Esther*, produced there two years later. The earliest French biblical opera was Rameau's first operatic work, *Samson* (1732). The form reached a notable stage of development with Méhul's *Joseph in Egypt* (1807) and Saint-Saëns's *Samson and Delilah* (1877); the latter work abounds in scenes that are imbued with Hebraic flavor. The actual Near Eastern fashion had been introduced in France by Félicien David, who had collected impressions and tunes on his journey to Turkey, Egypt, and Palestine in 1833–35 and himself composed an oratorio, *Moses on Sinai* (1846). In Italy it was Rossini who first turned to biblical opera; he wrote his *Cyrus in Babylonia* in 1812 and his *Moses in Egypt* in 1818. The oratorios of Mendelssohn *(Elias)*, Schubert *(Song of Miriam, Lazarus)*, Spohr *(Fall of Babylon)*, Neukomm *(David, Mount Sinai)*, Costa *(Naaman, Eli)*, Sterndale Bennett *(The Woman of Samaria)*, Cowen *(Ruth)*, and Parry *(Judith, Job, King Saul)*, and Goldmark's opera *Queen of Sheba* were the most successful romantic contributions in the biblical field; but Mendelssohn's great work is the only one to have survived the period. Anton Rubinstein's *Lost Paradise, Tower of Babel, Sulamith,* and *Moses*—works that once enjoyed a great vogue—occupy a position between opera and oratorio.

A new trend was brought into biblical drama by Oscar Wilde's sensual dramatization of the Salome story; this found an ingenious musical setting in Richard Strauss's opera *Salome* (composed 1903). It also inspired an opera by Antoine Mariotte (written before but produced after the Strauss work), a ballet *La Tragédie de Salome* by Florent Schmitt (1907), a tone poem by Henry Hadley (1907), and a symphonic *Poem of Passion* by Alexander Krein (1913); a more recent work is Bernard Rogers's *Dance of Salome* (1940). The novelty in Richard Strauss's master opera was the lavish use of Oriental devices; the composer not only tries to recapture the Oriental sensuality of the heroine and the barbaric character of the king but also to depict in music the speech and behavior of the Jews, and precedes the dance of the princess with a short orchestral prelude that conjures up the playing of a group of Oriental musicians. Most composers of biblical works in modern times have followed Richard Strauss in his conception of the Orient, and particularly in his orchestral effects; with contemporary composers' predilection for and skillful use of percussion instruments— demonstrated in modern jazz—the exotic coloring could be further increased. It goes without saying, though, that all these composers see the Orient with their own, Occidental, eyes.

The means used by Arthur Honegger in his biblical works are much less spectacular than those of Richard Strauss, but their effect is no less striking. His *Roi David* was originally composed for a band of fifteen musicians only—six woodwinds, four brasses, harmonium, piano, kettledrums, gong and tam-tam, and double bass—and kept its strange coloring even after the composer had rescored the work for a larger orchestra. In his incidental music for André Gide's *Saul* (1922), in his *Cantique des cantiques* (1926), and in his opera *Judith* (1925) he also uses orchestral effects to underline the dynamic contrast between mass movement and idea and between primitive barbarism and divine spirit—the spiritual forces that are also opposed to each other in Arnold Schoenberg's biblical opera *Moses und Aron*. William Walton is nearest to Honegger's spirit and conception in his powerful *Belshazzar's Feast* (completed 1931), in which the barbarism of Babylon's king is contrasted in a stirring way with the grief of the exiled Jews in the beginning and their joyous praise of the Lord in the hour of their redemption; Walton employs a narrator who links the scenes in a declamatory-musical style reminiscent of the psalmody of the ancient Hebrews. Two additional oratorios of great spiritual impact are Lennox Berkeley's *Jonah* (1932) and Willy Burkhard's *Vision of Isaiah* (1935).

A FEW MORE outstanding works should be listed to complete the survey of the most important compositions in the field of biblical music. "Judith" operas were written, apart from Honegger, by George W. Chadwick, Max Ettinger, August Klughardt, Natanael Berg, Eugene Goossens, and Alexander Serov; a tone-poem "Judith" was composed by the American composer Philip James. The story of Joseph inspired Arthur Farwell to a symphonic suite (for a play), while Richard Strauss and Werner Josten wrote ballets on the theme; the Israeli composer Erich-Walter Sternberg's *Joseph and his Brethren* is a suite of variations for string orchestra. Moses is the hero of an oratorio by Max Ettinger, and the African-American composer R. Nathaniel Dett wrote an impressive choral work, *The Ordering of Moses.* Stefan Wolpe wrote a ballet suite, *The Man from Midian* (1942), which he later transformed into a symphony. The "Cain" drama was set to music by Eugen d'Albert and Felix Weingartner in Germany and by Marc Blitzstein (a ballet drama) and Rupert Hughes in America; the Exodus forms the subject of a symphonic-choreographic work by the Israeli composer Joseph Tal (1946); *Exodus II* was the same composer's first contribution to the medium of electronic music. *Deborah and Yaël* is an opera by Ildebrando Pizzetti. For this opera, composed in 1922, Pizzetti received the Mussolini Prize donated by the newspaper *Corriere della Sera* in 1931; the composer wrote the "Duce" how "proud" he felt to have the name of his work associated "with the name—so fateful for every Italian—of Benito Mussolini."[2] The tragic fate of the "Hiob"-like Joram inspired Paul Ben-Haim to write an oratorio to a text by Rudolf Borchardt in the years 1931–33, before he, Paul Frankenburger, settled in Tel Aviv and changed his name to Ben-Haim. Three biblical episodes figure in Frederick Jacoby's *Hagiographa.*

---

[2]See Harvey Sachs, *Music in Fascist Italy,* London, 1987.

Michael Gnessin composed an opera-poem, *The Youth of Abraham*, and a dramatic song, "Ruth"; Idelsohn wrote a "Jephthah" opera; a tone poem by Rubin Goldmark has Samson as its hero; and Rudi Stephan set to music the story of Adam and Eve (*Die ersten Menschen*). Aaron Copland wrote a choral work, *In the Beginning*; the Esther story figures in operas by Mariotte and Milhaud; and Henry Hadley composed a "Belshazzar" oratorio. The prophetic books form the basis for Frederick Shepherd Converse's *Prophecy* (on words from Isaiah), David Stanley Smith's *Vision of Israel*, and Randall Thompson's *Peaceable Kingdom*. Wayne Barlow wrote a cantata, *Zion in Exile*. In the symphonic field (with voices) the outstanding works are Stravinsky's *Symphony of Psalms*, *Jeremiah* by Leonard Bernstein, the *Biblical Symphony* by Nikolai Nabokoff, the *Biblical Symphony* by Juan José Castro, and *The Song of Songs* of Lukas Foss. Abraham Wolfe Binder wrote a children's oratorio on the story of Judas Maccabaeus and a dramatic narrative, *Esther, Queen of Persia*. David, the royal singer and poet, appears in an opera by the American composer Adolph Weiss (a student and friend of Arnold Schoenberg), in a piano work by Mario Castelnuovo-Tedesco, in a French ballet by Henri Sauguet, in Florent Schmitt's *Danse d'Abisag*, and in two Israeli works: Karl Salomon's little opera *David and Goliath* and Menahem Avidom's four-movement *David Symphony*. King Solomon is portrayed in Ernest Bloch's rhapsody for violoncello and orchestra *Shelomoh*; Lazare Saminsky has composed a "Jephthah" opera and a ballet, *Lament of Rachel*; a "Samson" opera, *The Warrior*, was written by the American composer of Jewish descent, Bernard Rogers.

THE BIBLICAL PSALMS prove a perennial source of inspiration for composers all over the world. These compositions include strains of liturgical cantillation, in Hebrew or Plain Chant; others are free of any eastern leanings. Quite a few works could be regarded as contributions to a Hebrew music of our time. Outstanding psalm settings include Igor Stravinsky's *Symphony of Psalms*, Paul Ben-Haim's symphonic *The Sweet Psalmist of Israel*, Leonard Bernstein's *Chichester Psalms*, and two works by Czech-Jewish composers who perished in Nazi concentration camps: "Psalm 29" for organ, baritone, female choir, and small orchestra (1931–32) by Pavel Haas; and "Die Erde ist des Herrn" (God's is the Earth) for solo choir and orchestra (1932) by Hans Krása. Israeli composers have written many musical works based on psalms, entitled "Psalm," or in Hebrew "Tehilim," "Mizmor," or "Mizmorim." Both the composers who immigrated to and settled in the land of the Bible and the younger generation born and raised in Israel are inspired by the biblical reminiscences abounding in the country. The long list of psalm settings or quotations contains compositions by Ben-Haim, Oedoen Partos, Alexander Uriah Boscovich, Zvi Avni, Ben-Zion Orgad, Ami Ma'ayani, Zvi Herbert Nagan, Arthur Gelbrun, Shlomoh Joffe, Noam Sheriff, Gabriel Iranyi, Menachem Zur, Mordechai Seter, Yeheskel Braun, and many younger composers.

Franz Schubert set to music the Hebrew words of Psalm 92, "Mah tov le-hodót" (It is a good thing to give thanks), for the Viennese Synagogue in 1828 a few months before his death. It was published in the cantorial anthology *Shir Zion* of Solomon Sulzer, together with Jewish liturgical compositions by musicians of all faiths. Nine years earlier Schubert began but did not quite complete a setting of Psalm 13, "Ach Herr, wie lange willst Du mich vergessen" (How long, O Lord, will you forget me?), to Moses Mendelssohn's German text, which was also used by Abbé Maximilan Stadler for his twelve psalm compositions; the music for Schubert's fragment with the adapted original Hebrew psalm text was completed and published in Israel in 1977.

A number of composers have been attracted by Marc Chagall's paintings and especially by his stained glass windows on biblical themes. The Israeli Jacob Gilboa wrote in 1966 *The Twelve Jerusalem Chagall Windows* for Voices and Instruments. The British composer John McNabe wrote *The Chagall Windows*, a symphonic work, in 1974. Petr Eben, a Czech composer of Jewish descent, wrote his four-movement suite *Vitraux* (Windows) for trumpet and organ; the parts are named after four of the twelve tribes pictured by Chagall at the Jerusalem Hadassah Synagogue at Ein Karem: "Ruben," "Issakar," "Zébulon," "Levi." The blessings for the twelve tribes of Israel are also the basis for Gilboa's work, and Erich-Walter Sternberg wrote *The Twelve Tribes of Israel*, a symphonic work, comprising twelve variations on a theme. Jacob Gilboa's *Chagall sur la Bible* for mezzosoprano, brass quartet, and organ, is based on sayings of Marc Chagall in different languages, offering his views of the Bible. The Divine

Covenant and God's blessing of Jacob, progenitor of Israel's twelve tribes, his twelve sons, was set to music by Theo Brandmüller in a cantata "Wie Du unsern Vätern geschworen hast" (As Thou hast promised to our Fathers), commissioned and performed for the consecration of the first of Chagall's stained glass windows for St. Stephan's Church in Mayence, Germany (1978).

The heroic period of early Jewish history is pictured in one of the few operas written by Israeli composers, *Alexandra the Hasmonean* by Menachem Avidom, to a libretto by Aharon Ashman.

A dramatic biblical legend served a contemporary German composer for a work that made history in its own way. It was one of the first musical compositions conceived and produced in the electronic medium—*Gesang der Jünglinge* (Song of the Youths) by Karlheinz Stockhausen, who was twenty-seven years old when he wrote it. He electronically dissected a biblical text into verbal particles, using the mystical, heroic, devotional legend depicting the steadfastness of the three Hebrew youths who were thrown into a fiery furnace by the Babylonians and were saved by an angel of God. At the first West German Radio Studio in Cologne on 30 May 1956, a devoted Catholic listener tried (unsuccessfully) to provoke a scandal, as he regarded the practice as blasphemous.

The legend, told in the biblical Book of Daniel, had been dramatized as a church play nine hundred years earlier. An eleventh-century manuscript of the Byzantine liturgical drama, signed by Kassenos Koronas, has been preserved in monastery libraries on Mount Sinai and Mount Athos. This play has frequently been performed throughout the centuries as a shining example of belief in God for Jews and Christians alike. In Athens in 1971, the Greek composer and scholar of Byzantine music Michael Adamis presented a reconstruction of the ancient drama. Benjamin Britten composed his "Church Parable," *The Burning Fiery Furnace* (1966), based on the same legend; here the performance of the dramatized story is preceded—and ended—by a procession of monks intoning Plain Chant, and the play itself is accompanied by ancient, partly medieval, musical instruments. *Ludus Danielis* also belongs to the repertoire of medieval liturgical dramas and mystery plays that has been reconstructed and performed in modern times. The Czech composer Zdeněk Pololánik wrote an opera-or-

Scene from the liturgical drama, *Three Youths in the Fiery Burning Furnace*, after the Book of Daniel, Chapter 3, reconstructed from a manuscript from the fifteenth century preserved at St. Katherine Mt. Sinai and at a monastery on Mt. Athos, Greece. The Mt. Athos manuscript contains the picture of the saving angel seen in the reconstructed staging in Athens in 1971. The music was transcribed from the eleventh century Byzantine melodies by the Greek composer and Byzantine scholar, Michael Adamis. A narrator, Domestikos, narrates the story and leads the choir. The candles represent the fire from which the youths are saved. (Photograph: Babis Constanstatos, Athens.)

atorio, *Shir ha-Shirim* (1969), as well as *Cantus Psalmorum* for bass, organ, harp, and percussion (1966), and *Nebuchadnezar* for chorus, three trumpets, and four timpani, the latter a youthful work of the twenty-five-year-old composer (1960).

Among the impressive liturgical works of Krzystof Penderecki are compositions on old Hebrew biblical verses and legendary events; yet even in his Christian devotional music, Old Testament Hebrew verses are sung in their original Hebrew language. The compositions inspired by the Hebrew Bible include *Psalmy Dawida* (Psalms of David) for chorus, two pianos, celesta, harp, double basses, and percussion, written when Penderecki was twenty-five years old (1958); the electronically produced *Psalmus* (1961); *Canticum canticorum Salomonis* (The Song of Songs) for sixteen-voice chorus, chamber orchestra, and dance pair (1970–73); and *Als Jakob erwachte* (Jacob's Dream) for voices, orchestra, and twelve ocarinas (1974).

Although of necessity incomplete, our bird's-eye survey lists an amazing number of subjects and composers, and while no detailed analysis has here been attempted, the general trends in biblical composition have been shown. But these trends differ in Jewish and non-Jewish composers. While for Christian composers the Bible mediated between their own creed and the ancient world with which education and imaginative thinking have made them familiar, the Bible is for the Jews the only great spiritual heritage that is quite unmistakably their own. For the Gentile in the western countries there remains something strange, exotic, unexplained in the biblical East; by painting sacred scenes and by giving them new lyrical, epic, dramatic, or musical expression, western masters attempted to give tangible form to the hidden and mystic and to impart to mankind their own notion of antiquity. For the Jews there is nothing strange in the biblical world, even if they are most remote from traditional Judaism; creating a work of art in the spirit of the Bible conjures up for them the past splendors of their history and inspires them with hopes for a bright future for their people. It is thus that in spite of many characteristic traits common to the biblical works of non-Jewish and Jewish artists, we can find one distinctive trend of evolution in the purely western works of Christian masters inspired by the Bible and quite another in the creations of Jewish composers. We have tried to show the development from the devotional biblical work by early Christian composers to the Orientally colored compositions of romanticism and the exotic dramas of our times; the contemporary Jewish contributions to biblical music have been mentioned in this general survey, but their singular position in Jewish music history demands a more detailed discussion in the chapter devoted to the Hebrew music of the present century.

CHAPTER TEN

TRENDS IN LITURGICAL MUSIC

IT WAS IN THE SYNAGOGUE that Israel's tradition lived on throughout the two millennia of dispersion, and it was on the high holy days that even the assimilated Jews of the nineteenth and twentieth centuries took part in the sacred service and were impressed by the cantor's songs, which were so different from the music heard in the western world. For though the period of emancipation also brought about a far-reaching westernization of the liturgical songs and their performance, enough characteristic traits remained to distinguish the music of the synagogue from other liturgies. Many stylistic features strike the ear as common in the Jewish synagogal music of communities that are otherwise greatly separated geographically and culturally. Much of the choral singing in the European and American synagogues of today is reminiscent of Mendelssohn's oratorios and romantic opera, and the hazan falls back for his chant on Italian operatic virtuosity; but complete assimilation could never be achieved and was indeed rarely attempted. And though musically the Occidental harmonic and polyphonic arrangement of the originally western chant proves satisfactory only in the rarest cases, the essentially "foreign" character of Hebrew synagogue music is obvious to the musician and the non-musician alike and has been noted by non-Jewish and Jewish observers throughout the ages.

The principal features of the sources of synagogue music as practiced in western Europe and America have been extensively covered in Eric Werner's admirably documented book *A Voice Still Heard. The Sacred Songs of the Ashkenazic Jews* (1976), which dismisses the misconceptions of Jewish traditions on the part of semiprofessional writers who found their way into renowned encylopedias. The Ashkenazic tradition *(Minhag Ashkenaz)* developed a number of musical forms, mainly (following Werner) Plain Psalmody, Ornate Psalmody, Plain Response, Refrain, Antiphony, Free Melismatic Recitative, and Missinai tunes and chants. In the latter may be seen "the most distinctive element of Minhag Ashkenaz"; they originated in the German Rhineland during the twelfth to fifteenth centuries at a time of a bloody persecution of Jews. The Missinai tunes were so much venerated by the Jews that they argued that they must have been given to Moses on Mt. Sinai (*Missinai* = *miSinai* = from Sinai). Most of their texts were older than the melodies; some of them were connected with the high festivals, like Kol Nidre, Kaddish on the eve of Rosh Hashana, Alenu on the high holy days. Kol Nidre was formally introduced into the synagogue—and probably sung—by R. Yehuda Ga'on in the eighth century: it is first referred to and "corrected" (as he found the text had been "corrupted") by R. Mordecai Jaffa of Prague (in his book *Ha-Lebush*, 1622–24).

The tunes preserved from the early times seem hardly related to each other but show similarities to medieval western European song models; the influx of "outside" song elements was severely criticized by the Jewish authorities, for instance in the Sefer Hassidim of the early thirteenth century.

The traditional sacred melodies of the synagogue are based on *modes*, melodic patterns. These have often been misunderstood and have been erroneously described as "scales." They are *not* scales in the modern sense of the term, for they do not always consist of stepwise intervals, as do scales, but frequently skip intervals. The prayer modes have become known by names taken from the Ashkenazic prayer book, the *Siddur,* by the beginnings of the prayers Adonai malach, Ahavah rabbah, Magen avot; the tunes based on the respective modes were sung on the days when the prayers beginning with the above words were recited.

Example 27. Some traditional prayer modes of the synagogue.

Systematizing of the traditional Hebrew modes led to a distinction of a Pentateuch mode, a Prophets mode, the Hiob mode, and the Psalm mode; the first two were based on Middle Eastern modes also found in ancient Greek music. These modes formed the foundations for the modes exemplified below. They underwent manifold variations and changes under the influence of eastern European liturgical and folk music on the western European synagogue music, but a large and recognizable portion of the ancient modal foundations is preserved in the Ashkenazic synagogue so that its music still sounds "foreign," "different" to musicians and listeners not accustomed to Jewish sacred song.

The synagogue chant developed differently in the western and the eastern European countries and in western Europe and America. When eastern Europe came under the influence of the Ashkenazic civilization, the hazanim introduced the Ashkenazic song into their synagogue but retained in their music the melodic and rhythmic freedom that had characterized their earlier, largely Near Eastern chant. The spirit of improvisation was never abandoned in eastern Jewish music; it created a special type of coloratura which combined a most brilliant virtuosity with the expression of an exalted emotion. While in central and western Europe the hazanim molded their song under the influence of the highly developed musical culture around them, the eastern Jewish communities were as isolated in their music as in their life; for until well into the nineteenth century there was no flourishing musical culture in the countries in which they lived.

The eastern European precentor held a prominent position in his community, and the emotional character of his singing became the greatest inspiration for the people. Seventeenth-century sources tell of hazanim whose singing had a profounder influence on the minds and hearts of worshippers than the preaching of the rabbis, and who moved the worshippers to tears. It is interesting that one such source source added that in other countries the hazanim "have neither melody nor emotion"; and it is also reported that at the time of the Chmelnitzki pogroms in 1648 a hazan, Hirsch of Ziviotov, chanted the memorial prayer El Mole Rachamim in so touching a manner that he was able to move the Tartars to save three thousand Jews from the hands of the raging Cossacks.

The Jewish communities in eastern Europe suffered decline in the eighteenth century after a period of pogroms and persecution, and many scholars and singers migrated to the West; yet enough hazanim remained to preserve the tradition of the liturgical style. The East disdained all the contemporary reform and assimilatory movements of the West and saw in them a destruction of the traditional values of Judaism. Emotional depth and vocal virtuosity remained the foremost requirements for the eastern hazan—in contrast to the musical technique and craftsmanship exercised by his western colleague—and they must have been found marvelously combined in the art of one of the first precentors whose tunes have come down to us, Salomon Kaschtan (1781–1829). Kaschtan was hazan at Dubno but traveled throughout the eastern countries all the year round, returning to his own city only for the high holy days; his influence on the communities he visited must have been overwhelming. His style of performance and composition served as a model to an entire school of hazanim in the East, while his most gifted pupil, his son Hirsch Weintraub, came under the spell of western reform when he occupied a position at Koenigsberg. Other famous nineteenth-century hazanim were Dovidl Brod Strelisker (1783–1848), Bezalel Schulsinger (ca. 1790–1860), Sender Polatschik (1786–1869), Joseph Altschul (1840–1908), Yoel Dovid Levinsohn (1816–50; a pupil and friend of the Polish composer Moniuszko), Boruch Kaliner (died 1879), Yeruchom Blindmann (1798–1891), and Nissan Spivak (1824–1906). The last-named hazan, who became famous under the name of Nissi Belzer, exemplifies one peculiar trend in eastern European hazanuth.

While touring the eastern countries he lost his voice through an accident, but his remarkable talents as a choral leader and liturgical composer let the community forget his vocal defects: though it would have been impossible for an eastern community to employ a musician as conductor and composer only (as often happened in the western sphere, where in the field of art music the separation of the creative from the performing artist had meanwhile asserted itself), even a voiceless hazan was able to maintain his position in the eastern synagogue. Nissi Belzer made a virtue out of necessity. He limited his solos to a minimum, making more use of the choir instead, and thus became the founder of a new musical style in eastern synagogue service: virtuosity and solo expression gave way to a well-planned responsorial.performance in which the solo parts played only a secondary role.

The ancient tradition was never forgotten in the eastern communities, though toward the end of the nineteenth century—when the work of the reform composers of the West became widely known and the musical culture of the eastern countries rose to great heights—the eastern hazanim absorbed much of the classical and romantic trends of western synagogue music. Among such hazanim were Nisson Blumenthal (1805–1903), David Nowakowsky (1848–1921), Wolf Shestapol (ca. 1832–72), Boruch Schorr (1823–1904), Elieser Gerovich (1844–1913), Boruch Leib Rosowsky (1841–1919), and Samuel Alman (1877–1947). The last-named introduced the eastern synagogal style into the English service.

WHILE IN THE EASTERN SYNAGOGUE the traditional bonds were so strong that they could inspire the Jewish renaissance movement in music (the hazanic chant, in fact, formed the root of all early Jewish art music), the assimilatory movement in the West led to a complete change in the religious services and rendered the origins of synagogue music almost unrecognizable. The translation of the prayers into the vernacular, the stricter rhythmization and melodic symmetrization of the ancient tunes, and the choral arrangement of the psalms and prayers mirror the gradual estrangement of the western Jew from tradition and the appeal the European church music exercised upon the hazan. Classical and romantic harmony is applied to the ancient chant, songs of other people find entrance into the synagogue, and the organ is employed to accompany the singing. The introduction of the organ—and of other musical instruments—into the synagogue had already been tried in Prague in 1594, at the time Salomone Rossi created in Italy the first synagogue music in the style of his time, and we have already recorded the abortive attempt to establish an organ in the synagogue in Renaissance Venice. But it was only in Germany, in the nineteenth century, that the "organ synagogue" gained ground and was able to defend its place against orthodox opposition.

The reform movement, which reached its first height of development about 1810, had started in Germany in the eighteenth century, and its earliest signs had been choral arrangements in the classical style and the organized employment of musical instruments in the synagogue. The admission of the latter had been stressed by the cabbalistic writer Isaac Luria (sixteenth century) and his pupils, and in addition the cantatas sung to instrumental accompaniment in the Protestant churches during the service on Sundays exerted great influence on the Jews. The musicians who had so far only preserved the tradition of the popular ghetto music performed at weddings and other ceremonies put their talents at the service of the synagogue and also influenced the hazanim by the popular style of their music. On the other hand, the institution of synagogue choirs, which became a common practice at the beginning of the eighteenth century, was largely due to the Protestant example; many of the Jewish hymn melodies sung by these choirs were—again following Protestant precedents—adapted from folk songs, Jewish or German.

The hazanim of the West generally had a good musical background and spent much labor—even research—on their synagogal compositions, much in contrast to the eastern singers, who drew their inspiration from the emotional mood of their prayers and left most of their creative work to improvisation; some of the German cantors are said to have been accomplished players of musical instruments as well. Of their earliest representatives the name of Solomon Lifshitz (died 1758) is worthy of note; among the important cantors about 1800 are Ahron Beer (1738–1821), Leon Singer (died 1800), and Israel Lovy (1773–1832).

It is only natural that the general assimilation and westernization of Judaism should have found expression in the synagogue as well as in Jewish life and thought; but the reform movement did not originate with the officials of the synagogue or other Jewish dignitaries, though among them there were many to join the preachers of enlightenment and progress. On the contrary, the keepers of the synagogal tradition and the learned rabbis were as fervently opposed to change and reform as had been their ancestors at the time of Salomone Rossi's modernization of the synagogue song. The first men to work for the reform of the liturgy were enlightened burghers who had been drawn into the process of emancipation and had lost much of their spiritual contact with ancient Judaism, and who now tried to establish a form of Jewish worship acceptable to modern society. They could not go to the extreme of creating an entirely new service and having original melodies composed for the prayers; but the prayers were translated into the vernacular, the chant was transformed into simple declamation, and the choral song was based on popular songs or on those of the traditional melodies that seemed to possess the qualities most suited to adaptation. These reforms strove to give Jewish worship a place in modern life and to make it attractive for those who tended to turn their backs on Judaism; they were also part of the general eighteenth-century trend to liberate society from clerical bonds and the feudal order.

The reform movement started in earnest with the translation into German of the prayer book by David Friedlaender, a wealthy Berlin merchant, whose version of 1787, though not immediately accepted, by its very idea exerted a far-reaching influence. In 1810 the first Reform Temple was built at Seesen, in Westphalia; it was dedicated by Israel Jacobsohn, a rich and influential merchant who enjoyed the support of the French government of the province and who had tried out his first reforms in the frame of a children's service. Jacobsohn did away with the hazan and introduced a reader instead, and the choir sang hymns on German chorale tunes. In 1815 he opened a similar temple in his private home in Berlin, and his example was followed by Jacob Herz Beer, Meyerbeer's father, in the private temple at his house. His son arranged the music for him; but Beer did not want to do without a cantor, for the Berlin community was accustomed to his singing and would have missed it greatly. He engaged as a hazan Ascher Lion, and among the preachers officiating in his temple was Leopold Zunz, a brilliant scholar, creator of the "Science of Judaism." Meyerbeer had ideas of his own regarding the musical part of the service and opposed the introduction of the organ, which he regarded as a typically Christian instrument: "I consider it my merit," he writes in a letter to the secretary of the Vienna community, "that, in accordance with Mendelssohn-Bartholdy, I arranged in Berlin an a cappella choir only. The praying man should approach God without any intermediary. The Jews have maintained that opinion since the destruction of the Temple, and we should not introduce any innovation. But if any music is required, then—according to my opinion—flutes and horns should be used, similar to those used in Solomon's Temple. However, the human voice is the most moving."

The German reforms brought forth stormy debates throughout the European Jewish world, and some of the younger rabbis—among them men like Abraham Geiger and Samuel Adler, of the elite of nineteenth-century Jewish scholars—arduously defended the innovations. But it took considerable time before the reforms met with general acceptance, for only singers and composers who could successfully blend the traditional values and the classic-romantic style were able to convince the Jewish worshippers. Such men rose in central European Jewry in the persons of Salomon Sulzer in Vienna, Samuel Naumbourg in Paris, and Louis Lewandowski in Berlin; their Europeanized Jewish liturgical music greatly impressed their communities, and it was similarly admired by non-Jewish musicians, who frequently adapted their religious tunes—a famous example being Max Bruch's "Kol Nidre" for violoncello.

Salomon Sulzer (1804–90) was a singer and composer of undisputed talents, and Franz Liszt, who heard him sing, was "deeply stirred by emotion, . . . so shaken that our soul was entirely given to meditation and to participation in the service." Though arranging his liturgical music in the choral style of the period, Sulzer did not discard the traditional tunes which—in his own words—had only to be "improved, selected, and adjusted to the rules of art." Sulzer felt it his duty

> to consider, as far as possible, the traditional tunes bequeathed to us, to cleanse the ancient and dignified type from the later accretions of tasteless embellishments, to bring them back to their original purity, and to reconstruct them in accordance with the text and with the rules of harmony. For obvious reasons, this could be more easily achieved with the songs of

the Festivals than with the Sabbath service, because for the latter there were frequently employed profane tunes which desecrated the holiness of the service . . . whereas the songs of the High Festivals have an inwardness and depth, a gripping and moving power, which they have preserved through the centuries.

Sulzer's music avoids all virtuosity and emotional emphasis; it is always dignified and serious and tends not so much to impress the worshippers as to create the spirit of holiness proper to a house of worship. Nothing is preserved in Sulzer's choral songs of the ancient Oriental and of the traditional eastern European style of hazanuth, but some elements of ancient Hebrew chant remained evident nevertheless—above all to non-Jews—though the classical style of choral harmony frequently covered its Near Eastern quality.

Two hazanim-composers of German descent were instrumental in reviving the musical heritage of southern-German Jewry, whose melodies had been preserved since the early Middle Ages; but they, too, gave their liturgical music contemporary dress. They were Maier Kohn (1802–75), who worked in Munich, and his most gifted pupil, Samuel Naumbourg (1815–80), who went to Paris and created there a synagogal style that was influenced by the operatic tendencies of his time; famous composers such as Jacques Fromental Halévy and Meyerbeer contributed to his two-volume synagogue service.

Sulzer's counterpart in Germany was Louis Lewandowski, who was born in 1821 in the eastern German province of Posen but came to Berlin, the future place of his activities, at the age of thirteen (he died there in 1894). He enjoyed a thorough musical training and became familiar with the trends of reform of which Berlin had become the center. A decisive experience for him, and the entire Berlin community, was the visit of Hirsch Weintraub, who was the hazan at Koenigsberg, and his cantoral performance in the emotional eastern style but to the background of European choral arrangements. Apprenticed to Ascher Lion, the cantor of the Reform Temple, and later to his successor Abraham Jacob Lichtenstein, young Lewandowski learned all aspects of hazanuth before he tried his hand at cantoral composition. Sulzer's music at that time exerted a great influence on the choral song everywhere, but Lewandowski succeeded in making his own independent contribution to synagogue music. His work—a complete service for the entire year is his main achievement—is distinguished by the fine melodious lyricism that permeates not only the choral songs but also the recitative based on traditional tunes. His musical settings soon conquered the synagogues, and Lewandowski himself became the idol and leader of an entire generation of hazanim and synagogue composers; indeed, few others succeeded as he did in blending the traditional and modern, the eastern European and western elements.

LEWANDOWSKI'S MUSIC proved to have a universal appeal. The service contained in his collection was accepted by cantors all over the Jewish world, and his hymns were sung by Christian communities as well; the style of his music was imitated and elaborated by later composers of liturgical music. Though the famous hazanim of the later nineteenth and the twentieth century—such as Joseph Rosenblatt, Mordecai Herschmann, Zavel Kvartin, and others—have shown a preference for the emotional virtuoso style of eastern character, Lewandowski's music has provided the foundations for the synagogal choral style; together with the works of Sulzer and Naumbourg his compositions still occupy a commanding place in the service of both eastern and western Europe and of the Americas and are even sung in some synagogues in Israel.

With the development of music in the late nineteenth and early twentieth centuries there rose new synagogue composers who sought to utilize for the liturgical service what was best in contemporary musical art. In the nineteenth century Lewandowski, Sulzer, and Naumbourg had written their music in the classical choral style; these were followed by other classicists and some composers in the romantic vein, such as Israel Meyer Japhet, Mombach, Wasserzug, Moritz Deutsch in Europe, and Alois Kaiser, William Sparger, and Edward Starck in America. As these composers added nineteenth-century contributions to the service, so twentieth-century composers sought to apply to the liturgy the achievements of modern harmony and counterpoint. At the same time composers tried to strip synagogal music of its romantic cloak and to give it a background more appropriate to its original ancient character. They reconstructed the ancient modes and underlined the foreignness of the service, and they reduced the harmonic accompaniment to a minimum. Their work is closely connected with the contemporary renaissance of Hebrew music and the compositions in Hebraic style by Jewish composers of modern times: Ernest Bloch, Frederick Jacoby, Lazare Saminsky, Isadore Freed, Jacob Weinberg, Abraham Wolfe Binder, Heinrich Schalit, and Chemja Winawer are among those who have written completely new services for practical or concert performance; Jewish and non-Jewish composers such as Roy Harris, Leonard Bernstein, Bernard Rogers, Darius Milhaud, Erich Itor Kahn, Arnold Schoenberg, and in Israel Mordechai Seter, Paul Ben-Haim, Sergiu Natra, and Marc Lavry have enriched liturgical music by works in which the ancient spirit is expressed in modern terms and Near Eastern tradition has left its unmistakable impact. Their liturgical style has exerted its influence, in turn, both on the masters of Hebrew music and on the composers inspired by the world of the Bible to independent musical works.[1]

During the last decades of the twentieth century there has been an ever-growing interest in modernizing the synagogue service, especially in the United States. The pioneers in the field were Lazare Saminsky at New York's Temple Emanu-El, Cantor David Putterman at the Park Avenue Synagogue in New York, Reuben Rinder of Temple Emanuel San Francisco, all of whom commissioned and performed a large number of new liturgical works for the synagogue by Jewish and non-Jewish—American, European, and Israeli—composers.

---

[1] The history of Jewish liturgical music is most extensively treated in two musicological classics: Abraham Zvi Idelsohn, *Jewish Music in Its Historical Development*, New York, 1929, and Eric Werner, *A Voice Still Heard. The Sacred Songs of the Ashkenazic Jews*, University Park and London, 1976.

CHAPTER ELEVEN

THE JEWISH NATIONAL MOVEMENT

IN EASTERN EUROPE

W HILE IN THE WESTERN COUNTRIES the Jews eagerly sought admission into society and renounced the traditional unity of religion and life for the sake of the liberty, equality, and fraternity preached by the French Revolution, the ideas of emancipation and of "liberal" Judaism and "reform" remained entirely foreign to their eastern brethren, whose number exceeded theirs manyfold. The very conditions—and restrictions—of life in the eastern states forced the Jewish population into isolation, and the development of an autonomous Jewish state in sixteenth-century Poland, the Messianic movement of the seventeenth century, and eighteenth-century Hassidism had greatly contributed to strengthening the bonds with traditional Judaism from within. With the assimilatory movement in the West a sharp dividing line was drawn between western and eastern Jewry: the emancipation was regarded by eastern Jewry as a betrayal of the spirit of Judaism, and when, on the other hand, the pogroms and massacres of the nineteenth century compelled masses of eastern Jews—who had kept their dress and customs of old—to migrate to the western countries and to America, the assimilated communities saw in them strangers from foreign lands.

The gulf between western and eastern Jewry was widened in the nineteenth century by the nationalistic trends which set in everywhere as a reaction against the cosmopolitanism of the idealistic period. In western Europe the assimilated Jews often espoused the nationalistic feeling and became fervent patriots for the cause of the countries in which they lived. In the East, where the greater and smaller nations rose to independence in the course of the nineteenth century and where the greatest emphasis was laid on the evolution of a national life and culture, the Jews were also much impressed by the renaissance movements around them; but there it led to a strengthening of the *Jewish* national idea. Just as the poets and composers of the eastern countries revived their national lore in the form of works of art, so did the Jews cultivate their own spiritual values and try to give them artistic expression; the national idea which in the countries of their dispersion expressed itself in political strength, inner unity, and national expansion inspired the Jews with a new longing for a homeland and cultural center of their own. The terrible sufferings of the Jews in Poland and Russia only strengthened their national bonds, and all attempts to convert them by ridiculing and suppressing their religious and cultural life were doomed to failure. The yearning for a return to Zion, which had hardly ever ceased in the souls of the eastern Jews, now developed a national as well as a religious character.

It is thus that the important contributions made by the eastern Jews to literature and the arts were not those created in a spirit of emancipation but were works designed to serve the Jewish national renaissance. Only a few assimilated artists can be found in the entire history of eastern Jewry, most of them flourishing at the time of Czar Alexander II (1855–81), when some Jewish scholars, writers, and musicians tended to a more cosmopolitan and universal art. In the field of music these artists characteristically joined the western trends—and not the national schools—in Russian composition. Outstanding among them was Anton Rubinstein (1829–94), who achieved world fame as a pianist, composer, and pedagogue; Tchaikovsky was among his pupils. Rubinstein was an influential figure in the musical life of St. Petersburg, where he founded the Conservatoire in 1862 [the Moscow Conservatoire was founded by his younger brother Nikolai (1835–81) in 1864]. The long list of Anton Rubinstein's compositions includes a number of operas and stage oratorios inspired by Jewish themes: *The Maccabeans*, *The Tower of Babel*, *The Shulamite*, *Moses*, and *Hagar in the Desert*.

TWO DIFFERENT spiritual movements were styled "enlightenment" in the nineteenth century: the one the "enlightenment" of the West, which led to the declaration of equal rights for all men and opened new vistas for the relations between the Jews and the world around them; and the other—the *Haskala* (Hebrew for "enlightenment")—which originated in the East and was intended to make Judaism a living force by reviving its language and culture. The western emancipation had obliterated the boundaries between Jew and Gentile, and the Jews tended to forget their religious and national heritage while rising to great heights of achievement in cultural fields; exactly the contrary happened in eastern Europe, where the Jews also endeavored to adopt as much as possible of the general knowledge and culture but did so in order to enrich their own spiritual experience. The Jewish national character of the eastern enlightenment—which was strongly opposed by the orthodox scholars and the hassidim on account of its inherently worldly character—expressed itself foremost in the renaissance of the Hebrew language. The revival and cultivation of the national language and lore had been the first step in the renaissance movements of all the eastern people in the nineteenth century. The Jews, too, recognized how strongly a common tongue and folklore distinguish a nation from its neighbors; they realized also that for a people that lived in dispersion throughout the countries of the earth the uniting bonds could become even more powerful. The revival of Hebrew soon showed its first results. Poets and writers cultivated the ancient-modern language in their works: in Abraham and Micha Josef Lebensohn the Jews got their first modern poets, while Abraham Mapu wrote the first novels in modern Hebrew. But as the new Hebrew literature began to flourish, Jewish writers also continued to cultivate the Yiddish language—that derivation from medieval German which the Jews had taken with them to the East on their migrations and which had become in the course of the centuries the language of millions of Jews.

WE HAVE TO KNOW the sociological and cultural conditions of nineteenth-century eastern Jewish life and of the background of the Jewish national movement in order to appreciate the efforts of those pioneers who laid the foundations for a renaissance of Hebrew music. The first steps in this field mirror all the different trends characterizing the revival of the Jewish spirit, the Hebrew language, and the national idea: the music reflects the traditional lore of the Yiddish dialect as well as the restoration of Hebrew, it expresses religious contemplation or national enthusiasm, it revives ancient melodies and acknowledges the trends in general nineteenth-century musical art.

All national renaissance movements in music begin with the collection and practical arrangement of folk tunes. The singing, playing, and dancing of the people, their rural and urban life, and their festivals inspired masters like Carl Maria von Weber in Germany, Smetana in Bohemia, Grieg in Norway, Gade in Denmark, and especially the Russian composers from the times of Mikhail Glinka. Characteristically it often occurred that foreign musicians kindled the interest of composers in their own national folklore; thus Glinka received his first impetus to write national operas from an Italian in St. Petersburg, Catterino Cavos, whose operas in popular style—making frequent use of Russian folk tunes—exerted a decisive influence on the Russian master; similarly Russian composers inspired Jewish musicians to devote their attention to the treasures of Jewish folk song and folklore. Balakirev and Rimsky-Korsakov, the leaders of the national movement in Russian music, were the first to recognize the qualities of Jewish folklore, and Taneiev and Ippolitov-Ivanov were the teachers of Yoel Engel, the pioneer of the Jewish national renaissance. The Imperial Ethnographic Society invited this critic and scholar to deliver a lecture before the most prominent musical writers of St. Petersburg, and in 1900 the thirty-two-year-old musician exhibited to them the first fruits of his research into Jewish folk song. For the first time the wider public became interested in the world of Jewish music, and a lively discussion in the Jewish as well as in the non-Jewish field followed Engel's first lectures, publications, and concerts. Engel himself continued his work: he collected and arranged folk tunes, propagated his idea in the spoken and printed word, and organized concerts of Jewish music in the capital and the provinces. He gained a considerable number of ardent followers, collaborators, and friends.

Out of Yoel Engel's circle came the men who founded the Jewish Folk

Music Society in St. Petersburg in 1908; Ephraim Schkliar, Michael Gnessin, Salomo Rosowsky, and Lazare Saminsky were its leading spirits. In the
ten years of its activities (which were brought to an end with the Russian
Revolution) thousands of songs were collected by the members of the society all over the Russian countries, in Latvia, Poland, Galicia, and elsewhere, and a large number of folk tune arrangements and of compositions
based on folklore were actually published. Branches of the society were established in other Russian cities, among them one in Moscow under the
leadership of David Schorr in 1913. The circle of writers, composers, and
musicians supporting the idea of the society quickly grew: in 1912—the
fifth year of its existence—it could boast of some four hundred members,
of whom almost two-thirds were active in St. Petersburg alone. Apart form
the men already named, the society attracted Joseph Achron, Moses Milner,
L. Schitomirsky, and the brothers Gregory and Alexander Krein as composers, the pianist Leo Nesviski-Abileah, the engineer and enthusiastic
music lover Israel Okun, and the collector N. Kisselhoff. Musicological research received a great stimulus through the expeditions of Baron Gins-
burg and later through the monumental work of Abraham Zvi Idelsohn,
who collected ancient Hebrew and medieval Jewish melodies in the countries of the Orient and in eastern Europe and who was instrumental in imparting to comparative musicology the tools for comparing Temple and
Synagogue music and early Christian chant.

The activity of the Russian society met with great interest in all European centers and in America, and Palestine gained its decisive contact with
the Jewish musical renaissance through the permanent settlement there of
some of the leaders of that organization, among them David Schorr, Salomo Rosowsky (in Palestine 1925–47), Arieh Abileah, and Yoel Engel
himself. Saminsky and Achron continued their work in the United States,
while Gnessin and the Kreins remained in Russia after the Revolution.

THE PIONEERS of Jewish music went different ways in their desire to give
a Jewish or Hebraic flavor to their musical expression. Yoel Engel (1862–
1927) conceived all his works in the popular idiom. Besides his piano arrangements of folk tunes proper (in which no new harmonic style was created to suit the peculiar features of the eastern Jewish melos), he composed

Yoel Engel.

fine lyrical songs on poems by Bialik, Tchernichowsky, Perez, and other Hebrew poets; his best-known work is the stage music for Ansky's dramatic legend *The Dybbuk*, which the Hebrew theater Habima performed with enormous success all over Europe and America. Engel's great achievement lies much less in his musical creations than in the fostering of the idea of the Jewish musical renaissance and in his unswerving struggle for the cause. There is nothing new in the stylistic foundations of his music, and his works possess no great inventive originality; but their theme, their spiritual content, and their emotional background give them a character entirely their own. The texts of his early songs are partly Yiddish, partly Hebrew, but his entire work is based on the Yiddish folk songs of Russia, the foundations of which have such widely different sources as the Russian and White Russian songs, Rumanian elements, and old German tunes which had been preserved by the Jews in their migration from West to East and adapted by them in the same way as the old German language. In Palestine, where Engel settled in 1924 after a sojourn of two years in Berlin, the composer experienced yet another decisive influence: that of the Near Eastern atmosphere. The maturing artist achieved a characteristic folk style that united the many heterogenous elements into a harmonious whole. Many of Engel's songs have become real folk tunes in modern Israel.

While Engel had never regarded it as his primary task to create musical art works, new tendencies began to take shape in the compositions of his younger colleagues in Russia. These composers also started their way as arrangers of folk tunes or liturgical music, but they soon utilized the traditional melodies for musical works on a larger scale. Moreover, when giving free rein to their own melodic invention they attempted to recreate in their themes the melos of the Yiddish or Hebrew song. Among the older leaders of this school was Salomo Rosowsky (born 1878 in Riga, died in New York, 1962), whose style strongly resembles Engel's and who wrote a large, musicologically disputable book on biblical cantillation—which also plays an important role in his compositions. Other composers of the Russian school —above all Lazare Saminsky (1882–1959), Alexander Krein (1883–1951), Michael Gnessin (1833–1957), Moses Milner (1886–1952), and Joseph Achron (1886–1943)—sought contact with the new developments in western music; they tried, each in his own particular way, to elaborate Jewish melos and Hebraic themes by means of contemporary musical technique.

Numerous characteristic features recur in the works of all these composers, and this fact (to be explained by their common background of education in the Jewish as well as in the Russian sphere) justifies our speaking of a Jewish school in music just as we talk collectively of the German romanticists or of a national Russian school. But the composers of the Jewish school, though perhaps more closely resembling one another in purpose, content, and style than the masters of other European schools, do not lack individual traits either. Lazare Saminsky—who made his second home in the United States and there became a prominent figure as a lecturer and writer, conductor and composer—wrote "general" as well as "Jewish" compositions and attempted to imbue with Hebraic traits works conceived in a modern musical style. Alexander Krein found contact with the Jewish national movement at a comparatively late stage of his creative development; his symphonic works are full of sensuous emotion, while his melodic invention clearly shows the imprint of Hebrew liturgical melos and orna-

Joseph Achron.

ment. His elder brother, Gregory (1879–1955), wrote music that is more meditative and profound in content but lacks the emotional passion that impresses the listener in Alexander Krein's work. Michael Gnessin's music is characterized by a cooler, more restrained temperament; he often shows feeling but rarely strong emotion, and he emphasized the national traits much more than Alexander and Gregory Krein, whose style never denies the influences of Scriabin and the French impressionist school. Moses Milner is the composer most rooted in the soil: his music mirrors little of contemporary developments; it always remains folk-like, lyrical, and of an immediate appeal. Joseph Achron, finally, the youngest of these Russian Jewish musicians, was perhaps the greatest creative talent among them; beside the somber Gnessin, the passionate and colorful Alexander Krein, the meditative Gregory Krein, and the naïve Milner, he stands out as a most original and vital personality. As a virtuoso of the violin Achron has written a great many works of virtuoso character; his violin concertos and the smaller pieces for his instrument combine Jewish melos, refined instrumental technique, and a novel style of elaboration. In his last phase the composer came much under the spell of Arnold Schoenberg and his music, and his last works are accomplished examples of a modern distinctively Jewish art that can vie with the creations of twentieth-century musical geniuses.

The composers of the Russian Jewish school prepared the ground for widespread activities in the field of Jewish music. In Russia a considerable number of Jewish musicians—and non-Jewish artists as well—became interested in Jewish folklore; a chamber music ensemble organized in 1918 and consisting of a string quartet (Jacob Mistechkin, Gregory Besrodney, Nicholas Moldavan, Josef Cherniavsky), the clarinetist Simon Bellison, and the pianist Leon Berdichevsky toured Europe, America, China, Japan, and Siberia, and finally Palestine, with a repertoire of Jewish music; and publishing companies printed arrangements of Jewish folk songs.

Alexander Veprik (1899–1952) belonged to the younger generation of Russian Jewish composers influenced by the Jewish Folk Music Society's work. Prokofiev's *Overture on Jewish Themes* is among the earliest compositions in a Jewish vein from the pen of a non-Jewish master; Ravel's *Deux melodies hébraïques* is another outstanding example. In the western European countries a number of musicians and composers took up the idea of Jewish music and propagated it by collection, performance, and composition. The most active leaders were Léon Algazi in Paris, Joachim Stutchevsky who came from Russia via Vienna and Zürich to Tel Aviv, Mario Castelnuovo-Tedesco in Italy and later in the U.S., Alice Jacob-Loewensohn in Berlin and then in Jerusalem, Marko Rothmüller in Yugoslavia and later in Zürich, and two composers who have done much to popularize Jewish folksong—Janot S. Roskin and the Lithuanian Arno Nadel, who worked in Berlin and was murdered by the Nazis at Auschwitz at the age of sixty-four.

COMPOSERS who were attracted by the exotic charm of Jewish liturgical or popular music, which became available in print everywhere after the First World War, can be found in almost all countries; at first they turned to the eastern Jewish folk song which had shaped the Russian composers' Jewish works, but then they went further back to the genuine roots of Hebrew music and its Near Eastern foundations. The movement which had started in a circle locally and spiritually confined to the eastern Jewish sphere spread throughout the musical world, and when the tragic history of European Jewry reached its heights with the pogroms and mass murders in the years of the Second World War many composers were deeply stirred by the ghastly tragedy and inspired to profound musical works in which the Jewish melos found personal expression.

Some of the work of the Russian pioneers was continued in the United States, where a few of the original members of the Jewish Folk Music Society eventually settled and exerted great influence on younger musicians. The National Jewish Music Council, sponsored by the National Jewish Welfare Board, was organized there to foster composition and research in the Jewish field and to propagate and distribute new material. Among the musicologists and writers in America, Eric Werner, Albert Weisser, and Joseph Yasser have been foremost in new research in the field, and of the many composers especially interested in Hebrew composition the outstanding names are Abraham Wolfe Binder, Jacob Weinberg, Julius Chajes, Herbert Fromm, Gershon Ephros, Max Helfman, Isadore Freed, Harry Coopersmith, Reuben Kosakoff, Rabbi Israel Goldfarb, Hugo Adler, and Zavel Zilberts. The traditional element is strong in all works of these contemporary composers, who belong stylistically—with few exceptions—in the world of late nineteenth-century and early twentieth-century Jewish music as created by the Russian school of Jewish composers.

Of the many compositions by the original Russian pioneers of Jewish music, perhaps only a few have an intrinsic musical value, yet they must all be credited with having drawn the attention of the world's musicians to treasures that without their initiative might have been irretrievably lost with the destruction of the eastern Jewish communities. A composer, conductor, and teacher who especially cultivated the heritage of Yiddish literature and song in his music was Lazar Weiner, of Russian birth (1897), who died in New York (where he had settled in 1914) in 1982.

THE INFLUENCE exerted by the eastern national school on the composers of the West expressed itself in many ways. The assimilated western musicians found the Jewish folk material as strange to them as it was to the non-Jews, and in their arrangements—made for performers and for a public that demanded Jewish music—they did not always strive for a true realization of the spirit that had created the original songs. The Jewish folk tunes had for them an exotic charm similar to that of Greek or Negro or Chinese songs: they approached them from without, as the national significance of the renaissance movement had not touched them so far. While the national Jewish school in the eastern countries had attempted a synthesis of Jewish melos, traditional song, and national expression, many western composers now introduced the Jewish tunes into musical works that had little to do with the national foundations. In the Germany of the 1920s and early 1930s a number of composers wrote music that showed a peculiar blend of Jewish melos and a modern musical language, while a typically French style permeates the Jewish works of composers in France—with Darius Milhaud as their foremost representative. The composers of the West also gave their Jewish music a stronger formal planning and toned down the emotional exaltation dominating the eastern song; it is thus that the music created by the Jewish composers of the West derived more inspiration from the ancient Hebrew melodies and hymns—which had helped to shape the earliest Christian music—than from eastern European Jewish folk music, which was made up of a great variety of ingredients, both Slavonic and Jewish.

Two main trends can thus be discerned in the field of modern Jewish music as a result of the Russian Jewish pioneers' decisive initiative: the eastern Jewish school, whose composers create their works on the soil of folklore and try to give musical expression to the life and sentiment of the Jewish people; and the composers of the old musical nations of the West—not united in a school proper—who add Jewish traits to the central European style of the time. The Jewish character is the most important concern of the eastern European composers, whose musical language follows the characteristics of Jewish folk music without any attempt at an original or novel contribution to the world's musical literature; the composers of the assimilated sphere struggle for an adequate incorporation of their Jewish spiritual experience into musical works conceived in a novel and progressive idiom. Both trends reverberate in the Hebrew music of our time; the first synthesis of the various traditional and modern elements was achieved by a genius of Hebrew music, Ernest Bloch.

CHAPTER TWELVE

TWENTIETH-CENTURY

HEBREW MUSIC

MONG THE MUSICIANS for whom the national renaissance movement proved a decisive experience in their early development the
outstanding figure is that of Ernest Bloch. Born in Switzerland in
1880, educated and musically trained in Belgium, France, and Germany,
strongly influenced in his later life by the American atmosphere, Bloch
could not but imbue his creations with a cosmopolitan and universal style.
After an early work entitled *Oriental Symphony*, his career as a composer
began with large-scale symphonic works and an opera after Shakespeare's
Macbeth—compositions that continued the nineteenth-century European
musical tradition. But shortly before the First World War, when the waves
of the Jewish renaissance movement reached the central European countries, Bloch was apparently caught by its spirit, and he turned out a number
of significant Hebrew works in quick succession: two psalms for soprano
and orchestra in 1912, three Jewish "Poems" for orchestra in 1913, another psalm—for baritone—in 1914, the rhapsody *Schelomo* for violoncello
and orchestra in 1915, and the *Israel Symphony* in 1916 (this large-scale
work for voices and orchestra had been begun in 1912). It is interesting to
reflect that Bloch seems to have been predestined as a composer of He-

Ernest Bloch (photograph by Anne P. Dewey).

brew music, for strange orientalisms had already puzzled the critics at the time of the first performance in Paris of his *Macbeth* opera. "This music is an indecipherable rebus, rhythmically as well as tonally . . . ," was the verdict of one of France's foremost music critics; ". . . as to harmonic sequences, they are no less extraordinary, and one can qualify them as savage. . . ." This was in 1910, when the world had already experienced the operatic dramas of Richard Strauss, who, by the way, exerted a profound influence on the compositions of the young Ernest Bloch.

Bloch's Hebrew music has little in common with the works of the eastern-European Jewish national school of composers, for he rejects their fundamental tendency to incorporate actual folk tunes in musical works of art. "It is not my purpose, nor my desire," the composer himself has said,

> to attempt a reconstruction of Jewish music, or to base my work on melodies more or less authentic. I am not an archeologist. I believe that the most important thing is to write good and sincere music—my own music. It is the Jewish soul that interests me, the complex, glowing, agitated soul that I feel vibrating throughout the Bible: the freshness and naïveté of the Patriarchs; the violence of the Prophetic Books; the savage Jewish love of justice; the despair of Ecclesiastes; the sorrow and the immense greatness of the Book of Job; the sensuality of the Song of Songs. All this is in us, all this is in me, and it is the better part of me. It is all this that I endeavor to hear in myself and to transcribe in my music: the venerable emotion of the race that slumbers way down in our souls.

And somewhere else Bloch has stated:

> In my works termed *Jewish* . . . I have not approached the problem from without—by employing melodies more or less authentic (frequently borrowed from or under the influence of other nations) or oriental formulae, rhythms, or intervals, more or less sacred! No! I have listened to an inner voice, deep, secret, insistent, ardent, an instinct much more than cold and dry reason, a voice which seemed to come from far beyond myself, far beyond my parents—a voice which surged up in me on reading certain passages in the Bible, Job, Ecclesiastes, the Psalms, the Prophets . . . ! It was this entire Jewish heritage that moved me deeply, and it was reborn in my music. To what extent it is Jewish, to what extent it is just Ernest Bloch, of that I know nothing—the future alone will decide.

Bloch's own words clearly show that his must be a purely emotional music, music born out of glowing passion and inner pathos, of lyrical contemplation and spiritual strength. Bloch indeed was a romantic at heart, and while his musical language reflects twentieth-century tonal developments in his own personal way, he was essentially heir to the confessional style of Gustav Mahler. In his late-period compositions—particularly the second string quartet—he comes very near to Schoenberg's expressive twelve-tone melodic invention, and the synthesis between Blochian exoticism and Schoenbergian twelve-tone influence produces a stimulating proof of the latent Oriental roots of the twelve-tone style. Yet while Schoenberg can hardly have been conscious of the Oriental heritage of his theory at the time of its formation, Bloch would possibly have denied relationship between his Oriental emphasis and Schoenberg's music; for fundamentally he stood as far from the new attempts at a strict tonal organization made by Schoenberg as from Hindemith's revival of communal music and polyphony and from Bartók's artistic sublimation of folklore; he perpetuated—in a way quite different from Schoenberg's—Mahler's ethos and search for truth, and he summarized his own faith when he composed the Twenty-Second Psalm and said that he saw in the biblical text the embodiment of an idea to which he had himself long wanted to give expression—"the idea of the suffering of humanity and of justice and happiness to be realized on earth—the vital cosmic element in the prophetic soul."

Almost all of Bloch's works are conceived in an essentially contemplative mood; they are imbued with a somber spirit of resignation in the beginning but turn to hope and confidence toward the end; only his rhapsody on the "Vanity of Vanities" concludes on a pessimistic note, the only rays of light and hope coming after a lyrical meditation of the royal preacher and philosopher Solomon. "I discovered its true sense fifteen years after I had written it," said the composer of this passage in *Schelomo* in 1933, "and I have used it to illustrate a page of my *Sacred Service*, where the words express the hope, the ardent desire, that one day men may at last recognize that they are all brethren and may live in harmony and peace."[1]

To the works that have already been named Bloch added more Jewish compositions in later years, among them *Baal Shem: Three Pictures of Hassidic Life* (for violin, 1923), *Abodah: A Melody for the Day of Atonement* (for violin, 1929), *From Jewish Life—Three Sketches* (for violoncello, 1925), *Méditation hébraïque* (violoncello and piano, 1925), and *The Voice in the Wilderness*, a symphonic poem for orchestra with violoncello obbligato (1936). His crowning achievement in the field of Hebrew music is his *Sacred Service* (Avodat Hakodesh), composed in 1932. But it seems that his works of the greatest intrinsic musical value are those written without a specific intention, the compositions in which Bloch forgot his role of

---

[1]The quotations from Bloch are taken from M. Tibaldi-Chiesa's article on the composer in *Musica Hebraica*, Jerusalem, 1938, and G. Gatti's biography in Thompson's *Cyclopedia of Music and Musicians*. See also P. Gradenwitz, "Ernest Bloch," in *Swiss Composers in the 20th Century*, ed. Andres Briner, Pro Helvetia, Zürich, 1990, pp. 15–20.

prophet or preacher and gave free rein to his fertile invention and orchestral fantasy; his Hebraisms—evident in the rhapsodic lyricism of his asymmetric melodies, the variety of his rhythmic schemes and the exotic coloring—are no less distinct in the works of pure and absolute music than in the compositions inspired by the Bible or by Jewish life. The two string quartets (1916 and 1945), the Quintet for Strings and Piano (1923), the Piano Sonata (1935), the Violin Concerto (1938), and the *Suite Symphonique* (1945) are genuinely great music conceived in the entirely personal idiom which is unmistakably Bloch's on the one hand and apparently Hebraic on the other. In the purely Jewish works the struggle for adequate expression often produces disagreement between purpose and artistic result; the abstract works, however, show Bloch's individual romantic talent at its best, with his musical invention unhampered by philosophical meditation. Ernest Bloch lived in the United States from 1916 with a nine-year sojourn in his native Switzerland 1930–39; in later years he lived in California till he acquired a house at Agate Beach, Oregon, where he died in 1959.

In speaking of the Hebraic character of Bloch's music we must not forget that it is the artist who creates a specific musical language and that the musical Hebraisms in Bloch's works are as much a personal creation of his own mind as the Czech flavor is Smetana's characteristic contribution to music and the Russian idiom Mussorgsky's. It is difficult to argue that there exist such things as national Russian or Bohemian or German musical traits: it is the great composers that have given musical expression to their people's character in the frame of works firmly rooted in their national soil; no national music was found by them ready-made for use. In the life of Diaspora Jews the place of national soil was taken by the traditional spirit of Judaism as preserved in worship and custom, prayer and popular life; the eastern-European Jewish composers had given tonal form to the more popular aspects; Ernest Bloch created a Hebraic idiom to express in music the awe-inspiring spirit of Israel's most ancient heritage. He thus holds in the history of Hebrew music the place Smetana and Dvořák hold in Bohemian, Grieg in Norwegian, and Mussorgsky in Russian music: he is the originator of a musical language which identifies his people's own character. Unlike the nineteenth-century masters, however, he has created not a *national*, but a purely *spiritual*, musical idiom—in accordance with the western nineteenth-century conception of Judaism as a spiritual force devoid of a national existence.

Ernest Bloch taught a great number of disciples in the United States, his second homeland: the most prominent composers among them are Roger Sessions, Douglas Moore, Bernard Rogers, Randall Thompson, Frederick Jacoby, Quincy Porter, Isadore Freed, Mark Brunswick, and George Antheil. In the works of many of these musicians, even the non-Jewish ones, the rhapsodic and Hebraic elements of Bloch's music are further elaborated. His characteristic style has also greatly influenced the work of other musicians who, consciously or unconsciously, have come under his spell. Moreover, by pointing out the deep spiritual significance of the Scriptures and particularly of the Psalms and the Prophetic Books, he has inspired a good many of the contemporary compositions mentioned in our survey of biblical music. His is as great and singular an influence in the sphere of music embodying ethical and spiritual ideas as is Schoenberg's in the renovation of purely musical values; he has created a tonal language which has come to be regarded as the most congenial expression of the biblical spirit and which continuously proves its great influence on the creations of Jewish and non-Jewish composers alike.

A NUMBER of important works of contemporary music are particular testimonies to the influence of Bloch. One of them is the *Jeremiah* symphony of Leonard Bernstein (1918–90), the versatile pianist-conductor-composer whose meteoric ascent startled the musical world in the early 1940s. The many-sidedness of his talents, his temperament, and his creative facility are strongly reminiscent of Felix Mendelssohn. Like the early romanticist, the young American composer also showed early interest in the religious sphere; but while Mendelssohn's thoughts were devoted to Christian religious music, Bernstein was concerned with the world of Hebrew thought and wisdom into which he was thoroughly introduced in his youth. His symphony does not follow any fixed program, for the composer's intention is "not of literalness but of emotional quality," and its three movements— "Prophecy," "Profanation," and "Lamentation"—are an epic, rhapsodic symphonic movement of profound depth, a grim scherzo, and a symphonic song for contralto and orchestra. The motto of the work is a broad lyrical

Example 28. From *Kol Nidre* by Arnold Schoenberg (1938). The traditional prayer melody of the Day of Atonement service in the woodwinds (lower voice). (Copyright 1948. Used by permission of Bomart Music Publications, Long Island City, New York.)

Example 29. Largo (third movement) from Schoenberg's Fourth String Quartet (1936). The main theme, played by all strings in strict unison, shows a remarkable likeness to the *Kol Nidre* tune. (Copyright 1939 by G. Schirmer, Inc., New York. Reprinted by permission.)

Example 30. (a) Beginning of Second String Quartet by Ernest Bloch (1947). (b) New motive, derived from main theme, in thirteenth measure of first movement. Schoenberg's influence as well as certain melodic turns characteristic of Hebrew prayer can be noticed in these excerpts. (Copyright 1947. Reprinted by permission of the copyright holder, Boosey & Hawkes, Inc., New York.)

theme of a Blochian Hebraic flavor: it gives the entire symphony a characteristic imprint and appears in various guises and variations in all three movements. The Scherzo is based on a traditional liturgical phrase which is most freely elaborated; its queer and exotic rhythms betray the influence of contemporary American jazz. The "Lamentation," based on a song Bernstein had put down on a biblical text at the age of seventeen, makes an impressive finale which opens in a spirit of resignation and despair but ends on a note of hope and confidence. The student of contemporary music in general and of modern Hebrew music in particular cannot fail to discern that in spite of the composer's romantic leanings this is a work of the 1940s as well as the creation of a composer belonging to a younger generation than Bloch's. The Hebraic idiom shaped by the older master appears now in modern melodic, rhythmic, and harmonic dress. No wonder, too, that a work written in the years of the Second World War is stronger and more concentrated in its emotional content than any similar composition of an earlier period.

Example 31. "Lamentation" (third movement) from Leonard Bernstein's *Jeremiah* symphony (1942). (Copyright 1943 by Harms, Inc. Used by permission.)

The *Jeremiah* symphony (1942) was Leonard Bernstein's first large-scale work; it was followed by an impressive list of compositions inspired by a religious theme and elaborating the composer's own personal religious philosophy. They are works by a composer who said of himself, "I suppose I could have become a passable good rabbi: However, there was no question of it, because music was the only thing that consumed me." The developments of his time, when disbelief and the loss of faith spread throughout the world, worried Bernstein's mind all his life; he compared them to the negation of tonality in contemporary music and pleaded for the rein-

Leonard Bernstein (photograph by Lauterwasser, DGG).

statement of belief in the Divine and of tonality in music. His very first
characteristic composition had been a setting of Psalm 148 for voice and
piano, written by the seventeen-year-old Bernstein in 1935. Then came
the *Jeremiah* symphony, Hebrew liturgical and folksong settings, and in
1963 the deeply moving *Kaddish* symphony for speaker, soprano, chorus,
boys' choir, and orchestra. In 1965 Bernstein composed *Chichester Psalms*
on the original Hebrew Psalms. In 1971 Bernstein completed *Mass*, a hotly
disputed "theater piece for singers, players, and dancers" with a colorful
mixture of Jewish, Christian, and Far-Eastern religious rituals and thoughts.
In 1974 he wrote music for Jerome Robbins' *Dybbuk* ballet; his last large-
scale symphonic work was *Jubilee Games* (concerto for orchestra), dedicated to the Israel Philharmonic Orchestra and abounding in cabbalistic
musical settings (1986–89). Bernstein was a versatile genius who excelled
as much as conductor, pianist, music lecturer, and educator as he did as
intriguing composer of both *serious* and *light* music, between which he
allowed no distinction to be made. The characteristic style of the ostenta-
tiously Hebrew works is felt in most of his compositions—in lyrical songs
in his musicals, in the more tender moments of his ballet music, and in the
"Dirge" in his second symphony, *The Age of Anxiety*, after W. H. Auden's
poem. Leonard Bernstein's death in October 1990 was mourned the world
over.[2]

A composer who had great influence on the musical development of
Bernstein and was his life-long friend was Aaron Copland, the eminent
American-Jewish composer who was born in Brooklyn in 1900 and died
only a few weeks after Bernstein's death in 1990. Both in Bernstein's ballet music and in his lyrical and contemplative moods, strains of Copland's
style may be felt, especially in his earliest and most youthful compositions.
In Copland's masterful contributions to American music, eastern-European Jewish and Blochian-Hebraic influences seem to meet, and in turn
Copland's style exerted great influence on generations of younger composers. His scores for the theater, film, and ballet and his symphonies are regarded as the most typically American compositions ever created, and have

---

[2]See P. Gradenwitz, *Leonard Bernstein. Unendliche Vielfalt eines Musikers*, Zürich/
Mainz, 1995.

Aaron Copland (photograph by Viktor Kraft).

proved to be successful all over the world. His contributions to Jewish music are a chamber music trio, *Vitebsk* (1929), and a choral work, *In the Beginning* (1947).

Works derived in some way from Bloch's Hebraic music abound in contemporary music literature. Important among them are Randall Thompson's *Peaceable Kingdom*—a sequence of sacred choruses, text from Isaiah (1936); Frederick Jacoby's Hagiographa for String Quartet and Piano—three biblical narratives: Job, Ruth, Joshua (1938); and the *Song of*

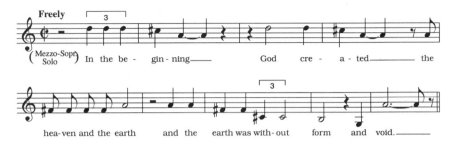

Example 32. Aaron Copland, *In the Beginning* (Genesis I) for mixed chorus a cappella with mezzo-soprano solo (1947). (Copyright 1947. Reprinted by permission of the copyright owner, Boosey & Hawkes, Inc., New York.)

Anguish—after Isaiah—for baritone and orchestra (1945) and *Song of Songs* for mezzosoprano and orchestra by Lukas Foss (born in Berlin in 1922, in the United States since 1937).

Lukas Foss—as composer, pianist, and conductor as versatile as Bernstein, in whose *Age of Anxiety* he often participated as piano soloist—wrote music in a more adventurous style than some of his contemporaries. His beautiful *Song of Songs* was counted among the most impressive new symphonic compositions when it was introduced in 1947. The style of expression and texture in this "biblical cantata" comes very near indeed to the eastern Mediterranean style sought by some modern Israeli composers. Lukas Foss captures something of the Near Eastern atmosphere without having experienced its immediate impact when he wrote it.

A singular figure among the older generation of contemporary composers in America is Russian-born Leo Ornstein, who has written music in most daring and experimental idioms and occupies a position between the Yiddish and Hebrew composers. Other works by composers of eastern European origin who came under the influence of Ernest Bloch are the biblical symphonies of Nikolai Nabokoff, Jacobo Ficher, and Jacobo Kostakowsky. The profound impression of Bloch's Hebraic style can also be found in the music of Bernard Rogers, who studied with Bloch for a number of years and has written a number of works with biblical themes.

A CROSS SECTION of the trends in Hebrew and biblical composition of our times appears in a singularly interesting work written by seven contemporary composers of great individuality—six Jewish and one non-Jewish: a seven-part symphonic suite based on passages from the early chapters of Genesis. It had been the idea of the conductor and composer Nathaniel Shilkret to commission a number of composers to contribute to a work that was to interpret the story of the Creation and of the first men, and the suite was completed at the end of 1945. The works are introduced by a narrator, and choral and orchestral music supplies the musical and interpretative background to the biblical narration. Nathaniel Shilkret himself wrote a piece entitled "Creation"; a miniature suite by the Polish Jewish composer Alexander Tansman follows as illustration of the tale of Adam and Eve; a dramatic movement by Darius Milhaud tells the story of Cain and Abel; the episode of Noah's Ark is told in music by the Italian-Jewish composer Mario Castelnuovo-Tedesco; the Covenant is the theme of Ernst Toch, the composer of German Jewish descent. The following cantata, "Babel," for chorus with orchestra and narrator was composed by Igor Stravinsky—an impressive work by the composer of the powerful *Symphony of Psalms*. The *Genesis Suite* is preceded by a contemplative symphonic Prelude by Arnold Schoenberg. The composers were completely free in their treatment of the biblical material and wrote their contributions entirely independently of each other. The work is of special interest as it unites musical masters of great individual note who had at one time or another treated Jewish or biblical subjects in compositions of general concern, and it thus mirrors a variety of trends in twentieth-century music.

THE JEWISH MASTERS of the western world, the pioneers of the national idea in eastern Europe, and Ernest Bloch as the creator of a Hebraic idiom in music represent the characteristic contemporary trends in the *Music of Israel*—but they all lack the firm roots without which an art of national aspirations can never flourish. Music conceived in complete freedom purely for the sake of art can rise to great spiritual heights and will be universal in character, while the artistic creations of composers inspired by national values may well elevate men throughout the wide world; but no man and no artist, however much a citizen of the world he may feel himself to be, can achieve a happy and sublime expression in art without having his place in society and a land he can call his own. It is thus that the Jewish features of the national Jewish music of eastern Europe and the Hebraic idiom in the works of Ernest Bloch and his school have something of a spiritually abstract and remote character and seem to lack ultimate inner satisfaction and happiness. With the return of the Jews to the ancient Land of Israel, the conditions were created for a new national and cultural center that not only has become the homeland for the new dwellers of Zion but also a great source of inspiration for Jewish culture and art throughout the world.

A UNIQUE MUSICAL FEAT, linking ancient Near Eastern traditions, biblical interpretation, and novel ways of introducing Near Eastern microtonality and twentieth-century nontonality into works inspired by the Bible was the composer Mordecai Sandberg's setting to music of the entire Book of Psalms and of large parts of the poetry and scriptures of the Bible. He composed the 150 psalms twice in different ways, and composed other texts separately or set in the form of oratorios. It is hard to understand why this interesting composer has escaped the attention of musicians, composers, musicologists, and lexicographers almost completely. Sandberg was born in Romania in 1897, studied medicine and music in Vienna, and settled in Jerusalem at the age of twenty-five in 1922. There he studied traditional Arabic and Jewish traditions, wrote his biblical music in microtonal notation, published a music journal, and was co-founder of the Institute for New Music, a forerunner of a section of the International Society for Contemporary Music. He stayed in Jerusalem until 1938 and then moved to the United States, where he died in 1973. His biblical works include a trilogy of oratorios: *Shelomoh*, *Ruth*, and *Ezkerah*.[3]

A DARINGLY ORIGINAL musical work was contributed to the week of concerts produced by the West-German Broadcasting Station (WDR)-Cologne for the Meeting of the Jewish Diaspora with Israel (Begegnung

---

[3]For one of the few evaluations of Sandberg's monumental and highly interesting life work see Roman Brotbeck, "Völkerverbindende Tondifferenzierung. Mordecai Sandberg—ein verkannter Pionier der Mikrotonalität," in *Neue Zeitschrift für Musik*, 1991, No. 4, pp. 38–44; also Charles Heller, "Mordecai Sandberg: His Compositions and His Ideas," in *Journal of Synagogue Music of the Cantors' Assembly*, 1984, and program notes for Luigi Nono's "Verso Prometeo," Milano, 1984, p. 10.

The composer Alvin Curran plays a shofar in his work for shofar and instruments at the 1990 Diaspora Israel at the West German Radio (WDR). (Photograph by Klaus Barisch, reproduced by permission.)

der Diaspora mit Israel), 29 October to 4 November 1990: *Shofar for Instruments and Electronic Sounds*, by the American Jewish composer Alvin Curran (born 1938), who also played the shofar in the performance himself. Curran describes the hallowed Jewish ram's horn as the "primeval trumpet *par excellence*"; he had used it already in his *Crystal Psalms* and *For Julian* before composing the virtuoso concerto featuring the instrument. At the Cologne performance he played a large shofar and some smaller models and added electronics based on chants of Yemenite Jews recorded at the Jerusalem Wailing Wall on the day of mourning for the destruction of the Holy Temple (*Tishah be-Av*). The composition, a parallel to the folkloristic-national solo works by Swiss composers for the Alphorn, was the opening work in the Diaspora-Israel concert week in which Jewish- or Hebrew-based compositions were performed by Mauricio Kagel *(Liturgien)*, Jonathan Berger, Richard L. Teitelbaum, and the Israelis Oedoen Partos and Ben-Zion Orgad, apart from works of a more general character by world-known and lesser-known Jewish composers.

IN MEMORIAM

The song is ended

but the melody lingers on . . .

THE BEAUTIFULLY NOSTALGIC LINE of Irving Berlin's unfading song of 1927 comes to mind when we look back at the murderous twelve years of the Nazi-Fascists' "Reich for a Thousand Years," in which so many millions of Jews and political opponents of the brutal regime were arrested, tortured, and exterminated, just because they came from an ancient and venerable race of people or believed in humanity. Among those executed were many scores of creative artists, composers, writers, poets, musicians, and entertainers; a few escaped the fangs of the persecutors, even miraculously got out of death camps, yet their lives were ruined. Only those who saw the evil coming and left the countries of their birth in time had a chance to start a new life on foreign soil, where only some felt themselves regarded as truly accepted citizens. In Israel, many remained haunted by the ghastly experiences they had lived through and by the fate of their families and friends to the extent they could not bear listening to the music of the German composers celebrated in the land they had fled.

However, for those who perished in those years and whose song is ended, as it was brutally cut down, the musical world pays tribute to their memory and cares that their "melody lingers on." Yet, alas, only after decades of silence about the fate of the scores left by the murdered composers, did musicians, many Gentiles among them, begin to collect biographical material, manuscripts of writings, and musical scores. Music written and performed in the composers' youth and during their incarceration, even up to the day they were transported to their death, has been resuscitated, studied, and newly performed. Thus a horrifying chapter in the story of Jewish music and of music written by Jews can be unveiled and valuable musical works added to the roster of twentieth-century compositions that deserve not to fall into oblivion. The tragic end of the musicians is mourned by everyone living; of the music preserved only the most outstanding works, judged by their intrinsic musical value, will achieve a lasting place in posterity.

The Nazi regime's concern about musical activities in the concentration camp ghettoes was infamous; they wanted to show off to the outside world "how well" the inmates lived there and "enjoyed" musical entertainment—even opera and cabaret. There were music activities in the camps of Buchenwald, Mauthausen, Flossenburg, Gleiwitz, Dachau, and others, but especially in Terezín (Theresienstadt), Birkenau-Auschwitz, and Sachsenhausen. Some of the camps had "resident" chamber groups, others only choirs; some had sizeable orchestras and opera "companies," and the interned composers wrote music for whatever musical groups were there to perform it. In May 1948 sixteen musicians who had survived from a full-size symphony orchestra of sixty-five players at the Dachau concentration camp—all the others had been killed—played with Leonard Bernstein on his visit to Landsberg and Feldafing near Dachau. At these concerts five thousand camp survivors and friends were present, as were the members of the Bavarian State Orchestra (whose conductor after the war was Georg Solti); Bernstein called it "an unforgettable experience."

Documentation exists on music in the camp ghettos, some by first-hand observers who survived, some reported by writers who interviewed survivors and had access to preserved sources. Most extensive are the book by Joža Karas, *Music in Terezín 1941–1945*, New York, 1985, containing biographical sketches of composers and musicians, and a list of existing compositions written in Terezín by twelve composers; the monumental work of a survivor, Hans-Günther Adler, *Theresienstadt 1941–1945. Das Antlitz einer Zwangsgemeinschaft: Geschichte, Soziologie, Psychologie,* Tübingen, 1960; Fania Fénélon, a survivor, *Sursis pour l'Orchestre,* Paris, 1976, in German *Das Mädchenorchester in Auschwitz,* Frankfurt/M., 1980; Hermann Langbein, *Menschen in Auschwitz,* Europaverlag, 1972. For a shorter but comprehensive survey with extensive bibliography see Eckhard John, "Musik und Konzentrationslager. Eine Annäherung" in *Archiv für Musikwissenschaft,* 48, Heft 1, 1991, pp. 1–36. For an extensive story on the "Dachau Symphony Orchestra" concerts, see Gradenwitz, *Leonard Bernstein.*

Heart-rending accounts of musical life in the camps have been given by Fania Fénelon, a violinist who survived Auschwitz, where there was a girls' orchestra led by Alma Maria Rosé, a niece of Gustav Mahler and daughter of the eminent violinist Arnold Rosé, who was concertmaster of the Vienna Philharmonic Orchestra and leader of the world-known Rosé Quartet. The father succeeded in reaching England in 1938 after having been with the Vienna Philharmonic intermittently for fifty-seven years, but the daughter was captured in France and became conductor of the Auschwitz Orchestra, whose members were women between the ages of sixteen and twenty—Germans, French, Belgians, Russians, Poles, Hungarians, and Greeks. She demanded the highest discipline and extraordinary devotion to their musical tasks; they had to perform for high-ranking Nazi officers, for the infamous Himmler, for Dr. Mengele, the medical murderer, and others. Alma Rosé died of a "normal disease" in the camp, and her death "moved" the camp commanders. Ghastly indeed was the story of the violinist Henry Meyer's camp life, told at the "Visit from the Exile" conference at Essen, Germany, in 1989. Meyer had survived the horrors and later joined the Lasalle String Quartet based in the U.S., which toured the world and devoted much of its repertoire to music that had been "banned" in the Fascist countries; its primarius was Walter Levin, of German-Jewish descent, who was raised and had his first musical education in Tel Aviv.[1]

---

[1] The fate of musicians in exile is vividly told in two German-language books: *Musiktradition im Exil,* ed. Juan Allende-Blin, Köln, 1993; and *Musik im Exil. Folgen des Nazismus für die internationale Musikkultur,* ed. Hanns-Werner Heister, Claudia Maurer Zenck, and Peter Petersen, Frankfurt, 1993. Monographies and documentary material on composers driven into exile and musicians who perished are published in the series *Verdrängte Musik* (in German) by von Bockel Verlag, Hamburg. See also Bibliography, pp. 457–458.

In Israel, many composers have written works devoted to the memory of those who perished. A few are musicians who survived concentration-camp barbarity; others lost their most dear ones in the Nazi hell. Of particular impact are the works of Eddy Halpern who was born in Krakow in 1921 and reached Israel in 1951, where he died in 1991. A number of his compositions memorialize the Holocaust; among them the most moving are *The Auschwitz Orchestra Is Playing* (1970) and *Words on an Auschwitz Tombstone* for orchestra (1983). The earlier work includes recorded testimonies of the Auschwitz camp and memories of survivors. Leon Schidlowsky, of Chilean-Jewish birth (1931; since 1969 in Israel), wrote *La Noche de Cristal* for tenor, male chorus, and symphony orchestra, to commemorate the martyrdom of the Jews on the Crystal Night of November 1938 when the Nazis burned and destroyed synagogues and Jewish property. This work was written in 1961; among Schidlowsky's later compositions of commemoration are *Kaddish* for violoncello and orchestra (1967), *Babi Yar* for string orchestra, piano, and percussion (1970), and various works composed in Israel including *In Memoriam, De profundis*, and *Requiem*.

A list of compositions written by composers at the Terezín (Theresienstadt) concentration camp and preserved (contained in Joža Karas book; op. cit.) contains fifty works—solo and chamber music, choruses, cantatas, and two operas—by twelve composers, only two of whom survived: Karel Berman, also a bass singer, born in Bohemia in 1919, of whose music are preserved two song cycles in Czech, and "Terezín," a suite for piano; and František Domažlicky (born in 1913) of whose Theresienstadt music a "May Song" for men's voices, in Czech, and "Song Without Words" for string quartet are extant. After the war some of his symphonic compositions were performed in Europe and in the United States. Other survivors of Terezín were the great Czech conductor Karel Ančerl and the pianists Edith Steiner-Kraus and Alice Herz-Sommer, both of whom started new lives in Israel after the war.

Among the composers who perished at Terezín were Pavel Haas, Gideon Klein, Viktor Kohn, Hans Krása, Egon Ledec, Carlo Taube, Zikmund Schul, and Viktor Ullmann. Of the music by Egon Ledec, who was leader of a string quartet, only a Gavotte for Strings has been found. From Carlo Taube a song in German, "Ein jüdisches Kind" for soprano and piano, has been saved. Of Viktor Kohn, also, only a Prelude for string quartet is preserved.

Ledec was born in Bohemia and was violinist in various orchestras before his imprisonment; he was transported to the Auschwitz death camp in 1944. Little is known about the violist Viktor Kohn, who was in his early forties when he died at Terezín. Among the youngest of the Terezín composers was Zikmund Schul, who was born in Germany in 1916 and at a very young age had enjoyed composition lessons with Paul Hindemith in Berlin. He fled the Nazis to Prague where he studied with the composer Alois Hába, who introduced him to quarter-tone and sixth-tone music. He also conducted research at the venerable Altneuschul Synagogue, where he found medieval Hebrew manuscripts. After the Nazi invasion of Prague he was arrested and sent to Terezín, where he died in 1943, weakened physically and psychically by tuberculosis, only twenty-seven years old. It is probably due to the influence of his studies with Hindemith that his music is of stark polyphonic, dissonant character—as is Paul Hindemith's early music. Schul was also possessed by mystical cabbalist religious ideas, which made their impact felt in his compositions. Among the works saved are the Finale (no more) from *Cantata Judaica* for men's chorus and tenor solo, in Hebrew; "Schicksal" (Fate) for contralto voice, flute, viola, and violoncello (in German); "Two Hassidic Dances" for viola and cello; and Duo for Violin and Viola.

The largest number of compositions preserved from Terezín prisoners, all of whom were transported to Auschwitz in 1944, were by Pavel Haas, Hans Krása, and Viktor Ullmann, and by Gideon Klein who died at the Fürstengrube Camp in 1945, only twenty-five years old.

Pavel Haas was born in Brno in 1899 and studied with two erstwhile students of Leos Janáček whose instruction he also enjoyed at a master class for composition at the Brno State Conservatory. The list of his works is not large, and he left many pieces incomplete. For a time he was curiously attracted by archaic Czech chorales which he combined in some works with ancient Hebraic elements, till he was drawn to Hebrew and Jewish themes in his Terezín years. He was taken to Terezín in December 1941, a short time after the establishment of the camp, and there wrote a choral piece for men's chorus "Al S'fod" on a Hebrew poem by the Israeli poet Ya'acov Shimoni, written during the Arab-Jewish disturbances of 1936–39: "Do not lament, do not cry, when things are bad, do not lose your heart, but work, work, work!" Here again, related strains of the St. Wenceslaus chorale and of Hebraic melody have been detected. Not too different in style are "Four Songs to the Text of Chinese Poetry" (in Czech translation) for bass and piano; the words are by Chinese poets, all expressing loneliness, homesickness, and hope for a happy return home. The composer Viktor Ullmann, who also wrote music reviews for the camp inmates (twenty-one such reviews have been preserved) wrote that

> the eloquent, courageous, all-round talented artist, singer, composer, conductor Karel Berman . . . has delivered his masterpiece . . . enthusiastic thanks also to Pavel Haas for his beautiful gift: his "Four Songs to Chinese Poetry". . . . Once one has heard them, one would not want to miss Haas' topical songs so full of life. . . . This way new art can succeed in the course of time: it becomes house music and an indispensable friend.

The songs premièred in May 1944, a month after their completion, and Bermann's recital was repeated several times. Another extant work by Pavel Haas is his Study for String Orchestra (1943). Both the study and the Chinese poems were newly performed in the first series of concerts entitled "Music at Theresienstadt" given in early May 1991 by the association Musica Reanimata at a colloquium on music by composers who were persecuted and murdered in the death camps. The colloquium's lectures and concerts took place at Dresden, Germany; previously the association had presented music by the composer at the Berlin Akademie der Künste in September 1990.

Before his incarceration Pavel Haas had already written three string quartets, piano works, music for wind instruments, solo songs and choruses, orchestral music, and an opera *Der Scharlatan* (The Charlatan). The "charlatan" is the baroque quack, miracle doctor, and surgeon Johann Andreas Eisenbart (in France known as "Le Docteur Isembert"). The opera premièred at the Brno Theater in April 1938. Pavel Haas used for his libretto a novel by the German physician and writer Josef Winckler; the "Eisenbart" figure was named Pustrpalk. The composer also translated the Czech libretto into German, hoping for a German performance of the opera, which he did not live to see. After three years at the Terezín camp,

Pavel Haas was transported to Auschwitz and died in its gas chambers in October 1944 at the age of forty-five.

Gideon Klein was born in 1919 in a Moravian town. His parents arranged for early instruction in music, and he graduated from the Prague Conservatory's master class for pianists at the age of twenty. At just twenty-two years of age, he was arrested and brought to the newly opened Terezín camp where he stayed for three years before being deported to Auschwitz. At Terezín he organized chamber music concerts and choral evenings, as well as performances of plays and operas, and participated in a "Studio for New Music" established at the camp. Gideon Klein had started composing at a young age, mainly chamber music and choral works. At Terezín he wrote two madrigals on Czech translations of poetry by François Villon and Friedrich Hölderlin, a piano sonata, chamber music, and arrangements of Hebrew songs. His String Trio, Piano Sonata, and String Quartet were performed at the 1991 "In Memoriam" concerts. His String Trio (1944) included variations on an old Moravian folk song, and Klein's knowledge of Arnold Schoenberg's music is evident in the Piano Sonata (1943). Before his deportation Gideon Klein had also written music in quarter-tones, influenced by Alois Hába with whom the young composer had studied for two years. A song cycle entitled "Die Pest" (The Plague) on poetry by Petr Kien, a talented opera librettist, poet, and painter, seems to have been lost. Kien is best known for his opera *Der Kaiser von Atlantis*, composed by Viktor Ullmann. Like Gideon Klein, Kien came from Moravia and was deported to Terezín at the age of twenty-two in 1941, and perished at Auschwitz with his wife and his parents in October 1944. Some of Kien's portrait drawings of Terezín composers have been preserved (and are reproduced in Joža Karas' book). One of Gideon Klein's dramatic efforts is known only through survivors' accounts; it was a monodrama entitled *Velky Stín* (The Great Shadow) written by Gonda (Egon) Redlich depicting "memories of an old Jewish widow who found herself suddenly in a concentration camp, unable to answer the burning question WHY?" (Káras 1985, p. 75). Text and music have not been preserved. All that is known about the work comes from two survivors of Terezín who performed at the première of the monodrama—the actress Vlasta Schönova, who recited the reminiscences, and the dancer Helena Harrmannova, who translated the memories of the old woman into choreography to Gideon Klein's music. Like Gideon Klein, the author Redlich perished at Auschwitz.

A frequently discussed Terezín composition was by Hans Krása, born in Prague in 1895, composition student of the eminent conductor and composer Alexander von Zemlinsky. One year before Krása's deportation to Terezín the Jewish Orphanage of Prague produced his children's opera *Brundibár*, to a libretto by Adolf Hoffmeister. The orphanage had become a meeting place for Jewish and anti-Fascist poets, painters, and musicians. A children's choir had already performed Paul Hindemith's *Wir bauen eine Stadt* (Let's Build a Town, 1930) and *Tlusty pradedecek* (It Turned Out Well or The Fat Great-Grandfather) by Jaroslav Kricka to a libretto by Karel Čapek (1932). Hans Krása's *Brundibár* score dates from 1938. For a performance at Terezín to be possible, he had to reduce the original full score for a smaller group of instruments; the scores, with Czech and English texts, have survived. The opera became immensely popular with the inmates of Terezín, where it was first performed in September 1943 and played fifty-five times in smaller and larger auditoriums; the cast changed a number of times as participants, including children performers, were sent to their deaths. In the opera, two little children, Little Joe and Annette, have no money to buy milk for their sick mother. They see and hear the organ-grinder Brundibár playing at the street corner and annoy him by singing. They get help from a dog, a cat, and a sparrow singing with them and are given money from passers-by to buy milk for the mother. But when Brundibár manages to steal the money; the children and the animals all chase him and the money is recovered. The opera ends with a victorious song "Brundibár Is Defeated, We Got Him Already," and the tormented audiences surely gained hope that the evil-doers who had imprisoned them would also one day be defeated. A poignant review circulated in the camp, written by Kurt Singer, a medical doctor and musicologist, general intendant of Berlin's Charlottenburg Opera House until the advent of the Nazi regime, then director of the Berlin Jüdischer Kulturbund (Cultural Activities Association for Jews) and president of the organization of German Jewish cultural associations. Imprisoned in Terezín after the Nazis had caught him in Holland where he had fled in 1939, Singer wrote, before his death there in February 1944, that "Brundibár shows how a short opera of

Brundibár. Photo of the actual performance of Krása's children's opera in Terezín for the International Red Cross Committee. (Reproduced with permission from Joža Karas, *Music in Terezín 1941–1945.*)

today should look and sound, how it can unite the highest in artistic taste with originality of concept, and modern character with viable tunes" (Karas, p. 101). *Brundibár* (in Czech language) premièred in the U.S. in West Hartford, Connecticut, in April 1975, and an English version prepared by Joža Karas and Milada Javora was first given in Ottawa, Canada, in November 1977; Joža Karas conducted both performances.

Hans Krása's compositions written at Terezín are few in number, but he also composed several important works that enjoyed successful performances before his deportation. They include an opera *Verlobung im*

Sketch of the set for *Brundibár* by the stage director from the National Theater, architect František Zelenka. (Reproduced with permission from Joža Karas, *Music in Terezín 1941–1945.*)

Traum (Betrothal in a Dream) based on Dostoyevsky's short story, "The Uncle's Dream" (1933). It was performed at the Prague German Theater in 1933 under the baton of George Szell and earned Krása the Czechoslovak State Prize for Composition the same year. Before that his Symphony was performed by the Boston Symphony Orchestra, conducted by Serge Koussevitzky, in November 1926 when Krása was only twenty-seven years old, and a year later Zemlinsky conducted it in Prague. In Paris, Zürich, and other European cities the name of Hans Krása was soon well-known. European publishers started printing his works, among them the psalm cantata *Die Erde ist des Herrn* (The Earth Is the Lord's) for solo, choir, and orchestra (1932). His *Chamber Music for Harpsichord and Seven Instruments* (1936), dedicated to the pianist and harpsichordist Frank Pollak (who after settling in Palestine-Israel changed his name to Frank Pelleg) used a popular song by Krása. At the memorial concerts in 1991 Krása's String Quartet, Op. 2, composed when Krása was twenty-four years old, his *Dance for String Trio* (Terezín 1944), and five of his early lieder where performed.

   Der Kaiser von Atlantis (The Emperor of Atlantis) is an opera which Petr Kien and Viktor Ullmann wrote for the groups performing operas at Terezín, but its presentation was prohibited by the camp commanders just when the rehearsals had finished, and most of the performers as well as Ullmann himself were sent to their deaths. The work aroused interest in the music activities in the Nazi camps and especially in the composer Viktor Ullmann; it was relatively widely performed after Kerry Woodward first conducted it in Amsterdam on 16 December 1975, the world première. Performances followed in San Francisco (1977), Israel (1982), and Stuttgart (1985); the writer and producer Georg Tabori staged it in Vienna in 1987, and additional performances were given in other German cities and elsewhere. The opera also led musicians and music historians to study whatever of Ullmann's compositions have been preserved—actually a great deal of his life's work in music.

   It may be incomprehensible today that the concentration-camp inmates—living under horrible conditions in daily expectation of torture and of transport to their final destination, death—could plan and stage opera performances. Terezín was the Nazis' "showplace"; they did everything to demonstrate how attractively the prisoners in their ghettoes could spend their "leisure time" by reading, painting, playing, making music, and staging plays and operas. In Terezín the great actor Kurt Gerron of pre-Nazi-Berlin fame had to organize a cabaret and to make a propaganda movie *Der Führer schenkt den Juden eine Stadt* (The Führer Donates a Town to the Jews), which was completed but survives only in archives. The composer Theodor Otto Beer wrote an operetta, *Das Ghettomädel*; there was a dance orchestra, the Ghetto Swingers, and—tactlessly, as some observers termed it—Johann Strauss's *Die Fledermaus* was performed by a large cast of singer-actor inmates, accompanied by piano and reed-organ. Theater plays were given from the works of Molière, Rostand, Gogol, Shakespeare, Schiller, Hofmannsthal, and the Czech repertoire; operas performed were by Mozart, Pergolesi, Smetana (*The Bartered Bride*, *The Kiss*), Puccini, Offenbach (*Les Contes d'Hoffmann*), and even *Carmen* and *Aida*, mostly with piano accompaniment. Oratorios were also sung, with the tragic choice of Giuseppe Verdi's *Requiem*: the conductor Rafael Schächter had succeeded in September 1943 in finding four soloists and enlisting a choir of some one hundred and fifty singers, and all were taken away and murdered after the performance. The conductor tried again, another performance followed, and the choristers were again transported to death. Another attempt, with only sixty singers in the choir, succeeded in singing the great work fifteen times. The last performance, attended by high officers and Adolf Eichmann, moved and shocked singers and audience deeply when the final *"Libera me"* was sung, almost shouted, by the singers, who were then immediately taken to their extermination.

Petr Kien and Viktor Ullmann were encouraged by the nearly professional ways in which oratorio and opera were handled in the camp to attempt an opera production of their own, in which they also hoped to hide by play on words and music some feelings of hope for salvation, which, alas, they were not to live and see. In their *Emperor of Atlantis*, with the subtitle *Der Tod dankt ab* (*Death Abdicates*), they depict a tyrannical monarch who outlaws Death but later feels remorse and begs Death to return so that humanity can be saved from the horrors of life. The Emperor, whom the authors named "Überall" (Everywhere, Above All), rules an empire full of wicked and corrupt people. He orders Death to fight a war for him. But when the personified Death refuses to obey him and goes on strike so that no one in the country will die, a horrible chaos ensues; when Death agrees to return to duty, the Emperor has to become his first victim.

Viktor Ullmann scored the opera for a cast of five singers representing the Emperor, Death, a Pierrot, a Girl, and a Drummer, with an orchestra consisting of thirteen players, including a saxophone, a banjo, and harpsichord. There are many hidden musical allusions in Ullmann's score, as for instance the quotation of a trumpet call, a Death theme from the *Asrael Symphony* by Josef Suk (*Asrael* is the Angel of Death), a variation of the German national anthem in a minor key, and a Finale based on the German reformator Martin Luther's chorale "Ein' feste Burg ist unser Gott" (A Mighty Fortress Is Our God). Tragedy, tragicomedy, despair and hope, signs of resistance, and an abortive will to fight are mirrored in Petr Kien's libretto and Viktor Ullmann's music. It is astonishing and moving—and one reads it with mixed feelings—that Ullmann wrote in notes found after his death that he was "not impeded but *encouraged*" in his musical work by Theresienstadt, for "we did in no way only sit at Babylon's rivers and lament but our cultural will was adequate to our will to live; and I am convinced that all those who wanted in life and art [to] wring form out of [the resisting] matter will say I am right" (as quoted by H. G. Adler, 1960, p. 661). He argued that Theresienstadt was and is for him

> the school for form . . . when it was easy formerly to create the beautiful form, here where also in daily life the matter has to be overcome by form, where the muses are in diatrimetical contrast to the environment: here is the true master school—to eradicate matter through form (in Schiller's sense), this being the mission of man, not only of the aesthetic but also the ethical man.

Viktor Ullmann planned to write a second opera at the camp, based on the legendary Joan of Arc; he wrote the libretto but could not even start composing the music. When he was told that he would leave Terezín, Ullmann packed all his belongings but instead of taking them along with him, he gave his writings and his music to his friend Dr. Emil Utitz, who had once been professor of philosophy at the German University of Prague (this writer's revered teacher). Utitz, and the chronicler of Terezín, Dr. Hans-Günther Adler, survived and thus also saved Ullmann's legacy for posterity. This includes some twenty compositions of the Terezín years:

Piano Sonatas Nos. 5, 6, and 7; the Third String Quartet; a large number of vocal works (solo and choral) with German, Yiddish, Hebrew, or French texts; and the full score and vocal score of the opera, with German and English libretto. Many works from Ullmann's pre-Theresienstadt years are extant in manuscript or published form: opera, four earlier piano sonatas; Variations and Double Fugue on a Theme of Arnold Schoenberg (from Schoenberg's Op. 19, No. 4), for piano, also orchestrated for full orchestra; *Slavonic Rhapsody* for orchestra with obbligato alto-saxophone; a piano concerto; and a large number of vocal compositions. Ullmann also wrote a Sonata for a Quarter-note Clarinet and Piano in B-flat minor.

An unusual interest in Ullmann's music derives from the fact that for some time early in his musical development he studied composition with Arnold Schoenberg. Viktor Ullmann was born in Têsin (Teschen) near the Polish-Moravian border on 1 January 1898, and joined the piano class of Eduard Steuermann and the composition classes of Arnold Schoenberg and his students Josef Polnauer and Heinrich Jalowetz in Vienna in the years 1918–19. Schoenberg recommended him to his brother-in-law Alexander Zemlinsky, then musical director of the German Opera of Prague. Ullmann became assistant conductor to Zemlinsky, and as a twenty-three-year-old already conducted opera there. He also conducted in Aussig and Zürich, gave music lessons in Prague, and worked at an anthroposophical bookshop in Stuttgart, Germany. The shop closed because of the Nazi antagonism to anthroposophy in 1933. Ullmann returned to Prague, where he lived on the proceeds from lectures, radio work, music journalism, and private teaching. He also studied quarter-tone music with Alois Hába. When he received the deportation order in 1942, he left all his musical works to a friend, who then handed them over to the Karlova University Library in Prague. One of the last works he wrote at Terezín was a setting of Rainer Maria Rilke's "Weise von Liebe und Tod des Cornets Christoph Rilke" (which a year earlier had been set to music for contralto voice and orchestra by the Swiss composer Frank Martin). Ullmann wrote music for a selection of twelve chapters of Rilke's epic poem for narrator and orchestra or piano, dated July 1944, three months before his deportation to Auschwitz. At the Musica Reanimata memorial concerts in 1991, Viktor Ullmann's musical work was represented by the Third String Quartet, the

Piano Sonata No. 5, and the set of twelve songs, *Der Mensch und sein Tag* (Man and His Day), written at Terezín in 1943 to words by Hans-Günther Adler, for baritone and piano.

POSTERITY may be able to lift many poets and musicians from oblivion— those who perished in the most tragic years of Jewish history and Jewish music history and those who were not able to write and sing any more after Auschwitz. Among the composers whose works have been rediscovered after decades of undeserved neglect, even after the end of the war, is the Czech-German-Jewish pianist and composer Erwin Schulhoff, who was born in Prague in 1894 and died at the Bavarian concentration camp of Wülzburg in 1942. He studied with Max Reger in Leipzig in the years 1908–10 and after returning to Prague embarked on a career as concert pianist. Like many of his contemporaries he studied quarter-tone music with Alois Hába. He travelled to Moscow in 1933 and was influenced by the Communist ideas of social revolution; after the Nazi occupation of Czechoslovakia he was granted Soviet citizenship which protected him from arrest, yet when the Nazis marched against Russia in 1941, he was interned at the concentration camp and died there the following year.

Erwin Schulhoff was a versatile and prolific artist who followed the current trends between the two world wars with personal engagement. Shortly after the First World War he became interested in the dada movement in the arts and joined the International Pacifist Organization, Clarté. He corresponded with Schoenberg and Alban Berg in a rather polemic tone but could not convince them of his ideas. As a pianist he studied the techniques of jazz playing, and jazz rhythms also became a characteristic of many of his compositions. In the 1920s Schulhoff tried his hand at many different forms and styles, including Schoenberg's twelve-tone writing, Slavic folklorism, and neo-classicism; some works also contain Jewish elements. In the 1930s his conviction was that the epoch of the bourgeoisie should come to an end, and he composed a cantata for thirteen voices, solos and double mixed chorus, with wind band accompaniment, based on the complete text of the Communist Manifesto of Marx and Engels. The long list of his works comprises vocal works, chamber music, a great many compositions for piano solo, including jazz pieces, an opera and two ballets, and six symphonies, as well as solo concertos. Shortly before his incarceration he had written his Sixth Symphony with a choral finale based on Adalbert von Chamisso's "Lied an die Freiheit" (Ode to Freedom) and had begun to compose a seventh symphony, his "Eroica," which remained unfinished, as was an eighth symphony (1942).

APART from the Jewish composers interned in concentration camps, there were also among the political and war prisoners other musicians and composers who wrote important works during their isolation. The greatest among them was Olivier Messiaen, who served in the French army at the outbreak of war in 1939 when he was thirty-one years old and held the office of organist at the Trinity Church in Paris. He was captured by the Germans and sent to Stalag VIII prison camp at Görlitz, Silesia, where he was imprisoned for two years. There he composed his *Quatuor pour la fin du Temps* and played the piano at its first performance on 15 January 1941. It is scored for violin, clarinet, violoncello, and piano; as its name indicates (Quartet for the End of Time) and like many of Messiaen's compositions of his entire creative life, it has a deeply religious background. A "Divine Message from the Angels of Heaven" serves as musical and liturgical inspiration.

A Czech composer, Rudolf Karel, thought to have been the last composition student of Antonín Dvořák, suffered the same fate as did Messiaen. Karel was arrested by the Nazis, for he had been active in the Czech resistance movement during the First World War. He was taken to Terezín and died there in 1945, sixty-four years old. In the camp he composed "a musical fairy tale" entitled "Třivlasy děda Vševěda" (Three Hairs of the Wise Old Man); the unfinished work was completed for posthumous performance by his student Zbyněk Vostřák.

The somber story of twelve years of music under conditions of coercion, terror, and mass murder is not complete without a memoir of intrepid resistance on the part of a very few, too few, prominent musicians. Foremost among them was the German composer Karl Amadeus Hartmann, who was twenty-eight years old when the Nazis came to power. Already at the brink of a most promising musical career, Hartmann was commissioned by the Munich Nazi rulers to compose a chamber music work for a representative festival. Although wanting to refuse, he felt his life was in danger and accepted. He wrote a string quartet ("Carillon") that same year (1933). On a visit to a Polish Jew whom a friend of his had hidden from the Nazis at his house he had noted traditional Jewish folksongs, and he incorporated them into each of the three movements of his work. His work was awarded a prize at the Nazi festival and first prize by the Geneva Society for Contemporary Chamber Music, surely as outstanding "German music" (1936), and it represented Germany at the international Festival of the International Society for Contemporary Music in London in June 1938! Most of Karl Amadeus Hartmann's following compositions expressed, more or less directly, his feelings about what happened in Nazi Germany. Among them was "Miserae," a symphonic poem for orchestra, the German contribution to the Festival of the International Society for Contemporary Music in Prague 1935. The composer dedicated the work "to my friends who had to die a hundred times, who sleep for eternity, we do not forget you," which he wrote after a visit to Dachau 1933–34. In 1939, when the Germans rejoiced that the war began "against the enemies," Hartmann composed a work for violin and string orchestra which is known by the name "Concerto funèbre" or "Musik der Trauer," documenting, in the composer's words, "the hopelessness for everything spiritual expressed in the two chorales of the first movements and an expression of a glimmer of hope in the fourth, final movement," which is also a chorale[2]. In 1936–37 he wrote a vocal work with accompaniment entitled "Friede Anno '48" (Peace in 1648) after Andreas Gryphius's "30-Years' War"; a cantata, a kind of requiem after Walt Whitman; a symphony *Klagegesang* (Song of Lament, 1944) dedicated to the philosopher Robert Havemann, an opponent of the regime (1944); and Piano Sonata No. 2, inspired by the sight of 20,000 prisoners from the Dachau camp witnessed by Hartmann in April 1945. This sonata counts with the most stirring musical documents of the times. After the war, in 1960, Hartmann contributed a scene entitled "Ghetto" to the work *Jüdische Chronik* written by Jens Gerlach. It consists of the parts contributed by several composers: "Prologue" (composed by Boris Blacher), "Will the silent call, will the lame walk, will the deaf hear,

---

[2]See the Hartmann biography by Andrew D. McCredie (in German), Wilhelmshaven, 1980, and *Thematisches Verzeichnis der Werke von Karl Amadeus Hartmann*, Wilhelmshaven, 1981.

will the blind see?" (Rudolf Wagner-Régeny), "Ghetto" (Hartmann), a prison horror scene (Paul Dessau), "Rebellion" (Hans Werner Henze), and Epilogue (Dessau). Karl Amadeus Hartmann died in Munich in 1963.

Fighting for the ideals of freedom of thought in Fascist Italy was Italy's great composer Luigi Dallapiccola (1904–75), who composed the opera *Il Prigioniero* (The Prisoner) (begun 1944, completed 1948), and the choral *Canti di Prigionia* (Songs in Captivity): "Prayer of Maria Stuart," "Invocation of Boethius," and "Farewell of Girolamo Savonarola" (1938–41).

Among other works of remembrance may be singled out the "Ballad of Mauthausen" by the Greek composer Mikis Theodorakis for solo voice and instrumental ensemble, opening with verses from "Shir haShirim"; Hanns Eisler's *Deutsche Sinfonie* for solos, narrators, chorus, and orchestra; Kurt Weill's "We Will Never Die," Luigi Nono's "Ricorda cosa ti hanno fatto in Auschwitz," the Thirteenth Symphony of Dmitri Shostakovich for bass solo, chorus, and orchestra; Franz Waxman's (Wachsmann) "The Song of Terezín"; Max Neikrug's "Through Roses"; and Steve Reich's "Different Trains." The list is by far incomplete, for composers have not rested from remembering as well as reminding their contemporaries of what passed in the middle of the century and what also continues to haunt the minds even of those who did not live in the hell of those times.

The most evocative, most stirring, and surely the greatest of all works of remembrance is Arnold Schoenberg's *A Survivor from Warsaw* for narrator, chorus, and orchestra, composed during the composer's American exile in 1947. It concludes with the chorus intoning the Hebrew Sh'ma Yisrael (Hearken o Israel), the prayer that is ever-present for the devoted Jew and also recited when death approaches.

SONGS, words alone, and words with music, written in the camps by the inmates and later by writers and composers in memory of the Holocaust, are legion; some of the camp texts have been published in a book by the German lecturer in history, sociology, and music, Ulrike Migdal, born in 1948[3]. Millions were the martyrs to be remembered in Jewish history. Few

---

[3]Ulrike Migdal, ed., *Und die Musik spielt dazu. Chansons und Satiren aus dem KZ Theresienstadt,* with a preface by Ulrike Migdal, Munich, 1986.

and far between were the heroes who were ready to help them, at a danger to their own lives. Yet the world of music remembers the most charming of Viennese operetta and melody composers Robert Stolz (1880–1975), to whom the Nazi echelon in Berlin promised the highest distinctions if he were to return to Germany, which he had left although not persecuted. Robert Stolz not only declined—for he would not cease writing music to words of his Jewish friends and text collaborators who had to leave Germany and his native Austria—he also drove several times from Berlin to the Austrian frontier, although he had not yet left Berlin and Austria had not yet been occupied by the Nazis, let his driver fly the swastika flag, and greeted the frontier guards with the "Deutschem Gruß"; yet inside his car he had valuable carpets, and rolled in them were Jewish fugitives whose lives he thus saved—one of them he met at one of his visits to Israel as conductor of the Israel Philharmonic Orchestra. In diametrical contrast to Stolz was the famous operetta composer Franz Léhar, who owed many of his successes to his Jewish librettists and to the eminent Jewish tenor Richard Tauber (who emigrated to England) but nevertheless declined to use his influence on Hitler, who loved Léhar, in order to secure freedom for his main librettist Dr. Fritz Löhner-Beda, who perished at Auschwitz.

Nazi Germany lost not only some of the greatest composers for "racial" or political reasons; the most eminent musicologists emigrated—while others, faithful to the Nazi doctrines, falsified the values and ethics of their profession. In the sphere of lighter music almost all of the successful composers of the 1920s and 1930s were Jews or of Jewish decent or married to Jewesses, and they left Germany and Austria. Among them were Paul Abraham, Leo Ascher, Ralph Benatzky, Edmund Eysler (he was hidden and survived), Leon Jessel, Emmerich Kálmán, Oscar Straus, Jean Gilbert, and Bruno Granichstätten. Exempted from Nazi boycott were the waltzes and operettas of Johann Strauss (the son), although his birth register (at St. Stephen's Cathedral in Vienna) shows that he was of Jewish descent; the Nazis confiscated the documents and falsified copies as it was believed unthinkable to forbid his music to be played or that *Die Fledermaus,* based on a text by two French-Jewish authors, not be performed.[4]

---

[4]See Peter Kemp, *The Strauss Family,* London, 1985.

The emigration from Germany, Austria, and other fascist and communist countries drained the cultural scene in those countries and benefitted Israel and the United States. In their new homelands most of the musicians exerted no mean influence on musical developments, even where some of them, especially in America, did not become truly acculturated. For the music in pre-1948 Palestine and in the State of Israel, the settling of musicians and composers from the countries of the West meant the opening of a completely new chapter in the history of the Music of Israel.

CHAPTER THIRTEEN

THE RETURN TO ZION

THE POLITICAL AND ECONOMIC CONDITIONS prevailing toward the end of the nineteenth century had demanded decisive resolutions from the central European and eastern Jews, as the (voluntary) cultural assimilation in the West and the (enforced) isolation in the East provoked sharp reaction in the Jewish as well as in the Gentile world. The national renascence was borne by the strong belief in the living values of Judaism; and while the first *ideal* aims led to a recognition of the latent qualities of folk life and customs and to a gathering of forces, there soon also began attempts at a *real* centralization and a reorientation of Jewish life. In Leo Pinsker's treatise *Auto-Emancipation* (1882) it is for the first time frankly declared that the Diaspora is the cause of all evil; and the author demands that the Jews concentrate in two great countries: in America, which had already become a great center of Jewish settlement, and in Palestine—primarily the country of future potentialities, where the Jews would have to take real possession of the soil, the cultivation of which they would have to learn anew. Pinsker's treatise preceded by fourteen years that other famous book of identical purpose—Dr. Theodor Herzl's *Jewish State* (1896). The author of the latter work was also undecided at first what country would prove most suitable for large-scale Jewish settlement: he proposed Argentina in addition to Palestine. It is significant that the call for centralization should have come from two completely different camps: Pinsker's from the east of Europe, where oppression and persecution made the life of the Jews miserable, Herzl's from the assimilated circles of the West. And though both men at first failed to recognize that the creation of even an autonomous Jewish colony among other people could never provide a completely satisfactory solution in face of the traditional love and longing for Zion, it soon became clear that only one country offered both the material and the spiritual conditions for the foundation of a Jewish state. Only in the ancient Land of Israel, the Holy Land of their ancestors, could a new community prosper; for throughout the two millennia of its dispersion Jewry had never forgotten the ancient splendors of Zion and had never ceased praying that the coming year would find them in a newly built Jerusalem. The religious authorities turned against the purely national zeal of the new movement; but Zionism derived its great impact from the very promise of a political, national gathering of the dispersed people in the ancient beloved land of the Bible.

The first pioneers set out for Palestine in 1882, the very year in which Leo Pinsker's treatise was published, and since then many waves of immigration have brought settlers to the Land of Israel from all parts of the globe. Colonization was begun by the pioneers of the "Bilu" and "Hovevei Zion" groups, which came from the countries of the European East in the 1880s, and the same Jewish centers provided the bulk of settlers till in the 1930s there set in the large-scale immigration from central Europe. The settlers not only hailed from different lands and had diverging notions of how to realize the national life, they also differed greatly in their cultural standards, their languages, their forms and ideals of life, and their educational and professional backgrounds. But all groups and individuals were united in their wish to create a new community and to become a people tied together by the bonds of land, creed, language, and common work—and the first step to achieve their goal was the recognition of Hebrew as the common tongue in the old-new country.

The beginnings of the new national home are mirrored in the development of the country's cultural life and thus in its early music history as well. With their language and literature, with their customs and ways of life, the pioneers brought along their songs, their music. The early pioneer songs, sung in the hours of sweat and toil, some surviving in modern Israel, were songs in a Russian, Polish, Ukrainian, Rumanian, or Caucasian idiom; central and western European, Turkish, Egyptian, and Yemenite influences mingled with them freely at a later stage, and the folklore collected by the Society for Jewish Folk Music formed an important part of the early song repertoire. The first working songs, dance tunes, and nursery rhymes that were actually created in Palestine were modeled on those melodies which the immigrants had brought with them, but they soon showed the first signs of an independent character with the beginning of an amalgamation of European and Near Eastern traits. It is interesting to note that this amalgamation was much more quickly achieved by the eastern European immigrants than by western European Jewry, the explanation being that eastern European music had generally greater affinities with the Near Eastern character than the creations of central and western European masters of music, and that the old Jewish tradition was much more alive in eastern countries than in the assimilated western world.

The first function of the new Palestinian center was that of a vast melting pot in which—much as in the early history of the United States of America—cultural heritages and traditions were recast to form raw material for a new and independent civilization. The Yiddish-Jewish Diaspora song, Hebraic expression, Oriental elements, and modern musical techniques became the foundations of early Palestinian music; the process of amalgamation and crystallization has shaped the step-by-step development of a characteristic Israeli art music.

THE SONGS sung by the pioneers while working in the fields or paving the roads, the tunes accompanying the merry dance, the ditties sung by the children in kindergarten and school provide everywhere the foundations of community life and form the starting point for the creators of art music. In Palestine, as in other countries during a period of colonization, they remained the only means of musical expression for many decades. It is with the growth of the villages and the foundation of urban centers that art music gained a foothold in the country and that the Palestinian soil was prepared for artists as well as for composers of music reaching beyond the popular sphere.

Early musical life in the Land of Israel followed European patterns as much as the songs of its settlers. The larger rural communities and the inhabitants of the first Jewish city, Tel Aviv (founded in 1909), felt the desire to enjoy organized public performances of music as they knew them from European concerts. Musically gifted settlers were the artists for the earliest musical evenings, but with the growth of the communities it soon became worth the while of international artists touring the Mediterranean countries and the East to halt in Palestine and to sing or play for its enthusiastic audiences. Music schools had in the meantime sprung up in the cities and prepared the youth to appreciate good music, and in the 1920s the country could boast of a many-colored musical life—with music institutes and concerts in the towns, choirs and popular instrumental groups active in the villages and settlements, and a general enthusiasm for music that astounded visiting artists.

Palestine's first school of music was established in Tel Aviv in 1910, a year after the city had been founded as a suburb of the ancient Arab town of Jaffa. The initiator of the school was Mrs. Shulamith Ruppin, wife of the noted Jewish sociologist, Arthur Ruppin, and it was named Shulamith School after her; M. Hopenko was appointed to lead the affairs of the institution. After one year, seventy-five pupils were studying at the institute, and Tel Aviv's first concerts were the "public examinations" of its youth in the hall of the first Hebrew grammar school, the Herzliah Gymnasium. A school orchestra was later organized to give concerts in Tel Aviv as well as elsewhere in the country and to entertain the British forces there in the First World War. A second music school was opened in Tel Aviv in 1914 by Miriam Levit. Jerusalem got a music institute through the initiative of its first British governor, Sir Ronald Storrs, in 1918, while Haifa followed in the early 1920s with an institute led by Mrs. Dunia-Weizmann.

The conditions of life in those early years did not allow for any but rather primitive musical entertainment, as contact with the great world was still limited and the endeavors of an enthusiastic few did not yet find the soil as fertile as it became after the mass immigrations of the 1920s and 1930s. The Jerusalem governor himself encountered these difficulties when he attempted to introduce music to his people by arranging concerts at Government House. On one occasion he had invited two pianists from Jaffa to play classical piano duets. Though the performers had made a journey of many hours on donkey-back to give the concert, the audience was rather apathetic; Storrs records in his memoirs (*Orientations*) that "the only item that was applauded and had to be encored was the buffet provided during the intermission." For the music institute Storrs selected an interconfessional committee and himself procured the teachers as well as the musical instruments. In the ranks of the army he found the violin virtuoso Tchaikov and appointed him principal of the school; the first funds were collected by Tchaikov on an Egyptian concert tour. The institute was open to Christians, Jews, and Moslems alike, but as 90 percent of the pupils and 75 percent of the teachers were Jews, and as the Christians and Moslems did not actively support the venture, Storrs handed the school over to the Jewish authorities; they assumed responsibility for its affairs for a short interim period till, after Tchaikov's departure, it became an independent establishment under the directorship of Sidney Seal, a British pianist on active service in Palestine at that time and its principal until his death.

The first large-scale musical organization came into life in 1923 with Mordecai Golinkin's foundation of the Palestine Opera. A year before, attempts at forming an opera company had already been made by Storrs in Jerusalem, but nothing had come of the plan. Golinkin was a conductor who had dreamed of a national opera for Palestine while he was still in Russia and who now realized his vision with the support of an enthusiastic troupe of singers and musicians. The Palestine Opera was opened in Tel Aviv on 28 July 28 1923, with a performance in Hebrew (translated by Aaron Ashman) of Verdi's *La Traviata,* and in the course of the four years of its existence the opera presented some twenty works in Hebrew versions by Ashman, Meir Freidmann, and Abraham Schlonsky. The company performed in Tel Aviv, Haifa, and Jerusalem; Golinkin also used its orchestra and chorus for separate symphonic and choral concerts. In 1927, when the opera had to cease activities for lack of funds, a symphony orchestra was founded by Fordhaus ben-Tsissy, who later devoted most of his time to oratorio and became musical director of the Habima Theater, which in 1932 permanently settled in Palestine. A truly remarkable feat was the Beethoven Centenary celebration in 1927 under the auspices of the Hebrew University: the symphony orchestra performed the *Eroica* and Fifth Symphonies at the 2000-seat amphitheater of the University in Jerusalem on Mount Scopus, and a series of chamber music evenings was also arranged. In the same year the Institute for New Music was founded in Jerusalem by Mordecai Sandberg. In 1929 a smaller instrumental ensemble made its appearance under the baton of Zvi Kumpaneetz; the ensemble stayed in the country till 1932 and gave some sixty concerts during the three years of its activities. But Palestine did not remain without an orchestra once the beginnings had been made in the concert field, and in 1933 a Philharmonic Society was founded which gave regular concerts under the conductors Golinkin (who also tried at various times to revive his opera company), A. D. Jakobsohn, Wolfgang Friedlaender, and Michael Taube, who instituted subscription concerts in December 1934. Other important musical groups of the early 1930s were a chamber opera founded by Benno Fraenkel; a chamber orchestra and academic choir conducted by Karel Salomon; a musical society in Jerusalem; and the first organized string quartet, led by Emil Hauser, who had in 1933 established the Palestine Conservatory of Music and Dramatic Art in collaboration with the Department of Education of the British Administration in Palestine and the Extension Department of Music then operated by the Hebrew University.

The artists—conductors, musicians, and composers—who visited Palestine in the early years of its musical development make a long and impressive list. They include the composers Michael Gnessin (who spent many months composing in a small wayside house fifteen miles from Jerusalem), Lazare Saminsky, and Joseph Achron; the conductor Oscar Fried; the violinists Jan Kubelik, Henri Marteau, Jascha Heifetz (after whom Tel Aviv called the concert hall in the Shulamith Conservatoire), Jacques Thibaut, Joseph Szigeti, and Bronislaw Huberman; the singer Joseph Schmidt; the pianists Leopold Godowsky, Emil von Sauer, Artur Schnabel, Artur Rubinstein, Alexander Borowsky, Imre Ungar, Alexander Brailowsky, Bruno Eisner, and Franz Osborn; the Casadesus family; and the cellists Arnold Földessy and Emanuel Feuermann. For most of these artists their sojourn in Palestine proved a singular experience, and many returned to the country several times. The settlers received their concerts enthusiastically, and large audiences greeted their appearances in the towns. Their programs were the same as those they presented to their listeners in New York and London, Paris and Berlin, Rome and Moscow, Cairo and Tokyo. Western middle-class concert life was thus transplanted to a country in which pioneer spirit and labor reigned foremost, and the musical organizations and the symphonic and operatic groups also imparted to the urban and rural communities the foundations of musical art taught and appreciated all over the western world. The activities of the local groups and the visiting performers thus combined in linking Palestine with the outside musical world; the evolution of a musical culture rooted in the soil and in the atmosphere of the land began in entirely different quarters.

THE CULTIVATION and composition of specific Jewish or Hebrew music was furthered by various factors. Concerts devoted solely to Jewish composers or to popular works were instituted in Jerusalem by the composer Jacob Weinberg—who in October 1924 completed the first opera on a Palestinian subject, *The Pioneers* (fragments in Hebrew performed in Jerusalem in 1925, complete performance in New York in 1934, where the composer later made his home, under the title *The Pioneers of Israel*)—and in Tel Aviv by Yoel Engel; in the colonies and among the workers united in the Labor Federation (Histadruth) since 1920 there were organized choruses and instrumental groups; a Popular Music Institute was founded by David Schorr; in 1929 a musical form that became most popular—community singing in the frame of Sabbath festivals—was launched by Menashe Rabinovitz (Ravina) with the support of the Hebrew poet laureate Haim Nachman Bialik. In 1925 a first gathering of the country's choirs was held in the Jesreel Valley; the meeting gave a great stimulus to choral singing and choral compositions, and the distribution of suitable material to the many groups, especially in the settlements, became the concern both of the Popular Music Institute and of the cultural divisions of the national organizations. Yehuda Shertok (Sharett), conductor and composer at Yagour settlement, was the first to publish sheets and booklets regularly for the use of the choirs; this task was taken up on a larger scale in the 1940s by the Cultural Department of the Labor Federation.

Another stimulus to composers and at the same time to the possibility of a widespread distribution of specifically Jewish music was given by the Hebrew theaters, particularly by the Workers' Theater Ohel ("Tent") and by the Habima ("The Stage"), both of which specially commissioned music for their plays from famous Jewish composers and local musicians. As many of their early performances—apart from the Hebrew versions of world literature—depicted scenes from Jewish Diaspora life, it was mostly the Yiddish trend in music that dominated the compositions; only gradually did Palestinian plays come to be written, confronting the composer with the problem of an adequate expression in music of the old-new country's recreation. This theater music—contributed in the early years especially by Yoel Engel, Salomo Rosowsky, Verdina Schlonsky, and Yedidya Gorohov—represents the second stage in the evolution of Palestinian music, for here the composer was forced by the substance of the play to search for a new style breathing something of the Palestinian atmosphere.

The decisive year in Palestinian music history was 1936. In April of that year the British administration opened the Palestine Broadcasting Service—operating an English, Hebrew, and Arabic section—and put at the head of the music division a musician of many talents and interests, Karel Salomon. In December 1936, the greatest and artistically most perfect musical organization yet created was launched when Arturo Toscanini raised his baton—in the largest hall on the Levant Fair Grounds in North Tel Aviv—for the first concert of the Palestine Orchestra (which in 1946 was renamed the Palestine Philharmonic Orchestra and became the Israel Philharmonic Orchestra with the foundation of the State of Israel in 1948). The establishment of a first-class symphony orchestra had been the vision of an artist who, like many others, had paid concert visits to Palestine and had taken away with him the impression of an unusually enthusiastic audience and a most fertile soil for good music. This was Bronislaw Huberman, who devoted many months of organizational work, auditioning, and fund-raising to realize his idea, and whose own enthusiasm infected musicians and conductors all over the world. Many of the musicians were first-desk players from orchestras in Germany, Poland, Russia, and other European countries; by securing their leave from those countries and an immigration permit for them from the British administrators in Palestine, Huberman also saved them from persecution and possible extermination in

Arturo Toscanini and Bronislaw Huberman after the general rehearsal for the opening concert of the Palestine Orchestra, 26 December 1936 (R. Weissenstein).

the holocaust of the 1930s. After the ensemble had had several months of preparation under the guidance of Hans Wilhelm (later William) Steinberg, Toscanini offered his services to the new venture; his concerts with the Palestine Orchestra in the opening season and on a subsequent visit one and a half years later, have gone down as historic events in the up-building of the country.

The foundation of a first-class symphonic ensemble attracted a number of outstanding musicians to settle in the country, and their orchestral concerts as well as their chamber concerts and pedagogic activities raised the standard of music appreciation and music-making to high levels. Masterpieces of old and modern music, virtuoso concertos, and chamber works could be enjoyed by audiences all over the country, and special care was taken that the workers were given concerts of their own. The youth of the country could rely for their musical training on teachers of highest standing and were now able to get a first-hand knowledge of the world's great music. The results were soon felt with the rise of a generation of young artists who mounted the concert platforms side by side with world-famous performers and who could also hold their own before the critical audiences of Europe and America.

The Philharmonic invited conductors and soloists from all parts of the free world to visit the country; many of them followed the call without asking for remuneration, following Toscanini's example. Among the conductors who led the Palestine Orchestra in the first ten years of its existence were Felix Weingartner (who also traveled with the orchestra to Egypt in the middle of the Second World War), Malcolm Sargent, Issai Dobrowen, Eugen Szenkar, Hermann Scherchen, Jascha Horenstein, Bernardino Molinari, Charles Münch, Manuel Rosenthal, Izler Solomon, Ignaz Neumark, Josef Rosenstock, Eduard Lindenberg, and Simon Parmet. Of the conductors resident in Palestine, Michael Taube, Georg Singer, Otto Selberg, Jonel Patin, Karel Salomon, Marc Lavry, Otto Lustig, Paul Ben-Haim, Bronislaw Sculz, and Wolfgang Friedlaender (youth concerts) appeared regularly. Among the soloists of the first decade were Adolf Busch, Ignace Friedmann, Alice Ehlers, Magda Tagliafero, Harriet Cohen, Sabine Kalter, Oda Slobodskaya, Simon Goldberg, Stefan Aschkenase, Jacob Gimpel, Imre Ungar, Shulamith Schafir, Monique Haas, and Nicole Henriot. Many soloists were drawn from the ranks of the orchestra, and young artists took their bow with the organization before embarking on an international career—foremost among them the pianists Pnina Salzmann, Ella Goldstein, Sigi (later Alexis) Weissenberg, and Menahem Pressler.

The broadcasting station began its musical programs with modest chamber music offerings and solo appearances but gradually enlarged the scope of its activities till it founded a small-scale symphony orchestra of its own—with Karel Salomon and Hanan Schlesinger as permanent conductors. The trilingual structure of the service was from the very beginnings instrumental in imparting to the many communities in the country the music of the Oriental and European spheres and thus greatly contributed to the mutual knowledge of the Palestinian people. With the years the Palestine Broadcasting Service became the greatest consumer of music in the country and offered a hearing to every composer who had something to say. Competitions and commissions gave an additional stimulus to the creators of music. While the Philharmonic was slow in recognizing the importance of furthering local composers, the music division of the broadcasting station encouraged them to create and present their music; in November–December 1947 it presented a "Month of Jewish Music" for the first time. With Israel becoming a state in May 1948, a state broadcasting service—named Kol Israel ("The Voice of Israel")—took over the organization and musicians from the British-administrated service.

Various musical organizations utilized the possibilities given by the permanent settlement in the country of the great number of artists serving the orchestral bodies. The Tel Aviv Museum instituted regular chamber music evenings on Saturday nights. Musical societies sprang up in Jerusalem, Haifa, and some of the colonies—notably Rehovoth. The idea of concerts of Jewish music was revived by Joachim Stutchevsky. The Palestine Section of the International Society for Contemporary Music (first recognized in 1928) renewed its activities. The Cultural Department of the Labor Federation developed the concerts in the settlements. Interest in ancient music was aroused by the concerts of the harpsichordist Frank Pelleg. Youth orchestras and workers' ensembles came into existence to provide training centers for future members of the Philharmonic. Even the dream of a Palestine Opera materialized again. After a number of short-lived attempts in the field, the Palestine Folk Opera was founded in 1941, with Georg Singer, Lev Mirsky, Mordecai Golinkin, and Wolfgang Friedlaender as operatic conductors, Marc Lavry as leader of operetta and ballet, and with Gertrud Kraus as choreographer. A considerable number of serious and light musical stage works were produced in the five years of this group's existence, and in 1945 it produced a work especially written for the organization, an opera from Palestinian folk life, *Dan the Guard,* with a libretto by Sh. Schalom and Max Brod and music by Marc Lavry. After a two-year break, opera came to the fore again in 1948 with the American singer Edis de Philippe founding and directing the Israel National Opera (which in 1959 performed one of the few opera compositions by Israelis then extant—Menahem Avidom's *Alexandra the Hasmonean* to a libretto by Aharon Ashman). Performances took place in a house on the Tel Aviv–Mediterranean seashore which had served as seat of the first Parliament, the Knesset, of the State of Israel before moving to Jerusalem. The National Opera existed until 1982; in 1985, a new operatic venture came into being, the New Israeli Opera. Financial means and artistic professionalism for opera are not easy to find anywhere; in her time, Edis de Philippe took great pride in the fact that a young and still rather unknown Spanish tenor spent two and a half years with her company—together with his wife, also a singer—and acquired a repertoire for which he became world-famous soon after: Plácido Domingo. [He devotes many pages in his autobiography *My First Forty Years* (1983) to life in Israel and at the Israeli Opera from 1963 to 1965.] The New Israeli Opera moved into an opera house specially built for opera and ballet in Tel Aviv in the fall of 1994.

Among the organizations that had sprung up in pre-Israel-Palestine were the Archive of Oriental Music at the Hebrew University of Jerusalem and the World Center for Jewish Music in Palestine. The Archive of Oriental Music was established by the German scholar Robert Lachmann in 1935 with the aim to revive and continue the work of Abraham Zvi Idel-

Scene from the New Israeli Opera's production of Verdi's *Nabucco* at Tel Aviv's new opera house (1995).

sohn, who had founded an Institute for Jewish Music in Jerusalem in 1910. Idelsohn's main objective, followed by Robert Lachmann, was the recording, collecting, and studying of the traditional music of Near Eastern and North African Jews—and their regional neighbors. Dr. Lachmann was joined by Edith (Esther) Gerson-Kiwi, who continued Lachmann's work after his death (1939) and soon became the internationally acknowledged foremost authority in the field of ethnomusicology; she was appointed director of an ethnological center for Jewish music at the Music Department of the Israeli Ministry of Education and Culture in 1950. The Idelsohn and Lachmann recordings and archives were out of reach during the Jordanian occupation of the Hebrew University campus on Mount Scopus from 1948 to 1967 but came then into possession of the Phonotheque of the Jewish Music Research Center, which was established at the Department of Musicology of the Hebrew University under the direction of Israel Adler. The Jewish Music Research Center attracted a number of scholars and students in Israel and from many parts of the world and started in 1968 issuing a periodical publication, *Yuval*, with articles mainly in English, Hebrew, and French. Parallel research was conducted at the Institute for Sacred Music (since 1958), for which Avigdor Herzog edited a series of traditional liturgical music *Reganot*; for the religious kibbutz movement Michael Perlman collected and edited liturgical chants *(Zemirot)*.

The short-lived World Center for Jewish Music in Palestine was founded in 1936 by an immigrant from Germany, Salli Levi, a dental surgeon by profession and an enthusiastic music amateur with a special interest in Jewish music. In his hometown, Frankfurt on Main, he had organized choral activities and planned concerts of "Jewish music," even writing an essay on "Judaism in Music." In Jerusalem he was joined by another enthusiastic music fan, the amateur music-journalist Hermann (Gershon) Swet, of Russian descent. The World Center had a predecessor in an International Jewish Music Society, founded in Paris in 1957 under the initiative of Leon Algazi, who invited scholars from Israel and all over the world to a Congress where papers were read and discussed under the chairmanship of Eric Werner, the eminent musicologist from the Hebrew Union College of Cincinnati, Ohio, where he occupied the post once held by Idelsohn (he later organized and directed the Department of Musicology at the University of Tel Aviv). Concerts were presented and a series of "Monumenta" was planned, publications to continue Idelsohn's collection of traditional music. However, the Society never really got active. Even before that, in July 1933, also in Paris, which had become a temporary refuge for Jewish composers and musicians before the Nazi echelon destroyed Jewish property there and threatened and persecuted French and emigré Jews, Arnold Schoenberg—dismissed from his post as director of master classes for composition at the Prussian Academy of the Arts at Berlin—drew up a declaration to call for the foundation of a national Hebrew music institute for the dissemination of a specifically Hebrew musical culture. The declaration was signed by Bronislaw Huberman, Misha Elman, Arthur Schnabel, Jascha Heifetz, Leopold Godowsky, Bruno Walter, Ossip Gabrilowitsch, Oskar Fried, Ernst Toch, Darius Milhaud; additional prominent Jewish musicians were expected to sign. Schoenberg had originally planned to attend the Zionist Congress in Prague that same year to present his ideas, but he was not given a mandate and thus refused to go, not wanting to speak solely as an individual. In the end, his plan of a national Hebrew music institute fell victim to the turbulent times and the emigration from Europe of the signatories. Many of Schoenberg's principles and ideas were noted down by him in the numerous articles and speeches found in his legacy.

The World Center for Jewish Music in Palestine was started at a not particularly favorable period of Palestinian history. The late 1930s were a time of fervent, belligerent hostilities of parts of the Arab population directed against the ever-growing Jewish immigration caused by the brutal persecution in central Europe; in 1939, with the outbreak of war, the contacts between Jerusalem and the outside world were seriously interrupted, which also meant an almost complete stop of correspondence and mutual exchange of ideas with Jewish musicians in the wide world. In the course of 1936 Salli Levi printed a first memorandum, drawn up in collaboration with the composer, writer, and music librarian Alice Jacob-Loewenson. This described the goals of the organization and was circulated among personalities in the country and abroad. It met with acceptance and refusal, willingness of cooperation as well as scepticism, as many Jewish composers and musicians felt that the initiators' enthusiasm was not matched by pro-

fessionalism in the field. While a Gentile composer, himself an ethnomusi-
cological authority, like Béla Bartók, "welcomed the action with sympathy," the Nobel-prize scientist and amateur violinist Albert Einstein sent a
rhymed response, reading:

> *Lieblich ist ja, was Sie tun,*
> *Doch Ihr Vorbild sei das Huhn:*
> *Brav legt es zuerst sein Ei,*
> *Dann erst folget das Geschrei.*

> While it's lovely what you plan,
> Let your model be the hen:
> First she lays her egg, she's wise,
> Only after that she cries.
> (Translation, P. Gradenwitz)

The quotation, from Albert Einstein's letter in the archives of the
World Center, is contained in a survey on the history and the archives of the
World Center written by Philip V. Bohlman for the *Abraham Zvi Idelsohn
Memorial Volume* of *Yuval*, Vol. 5, Jerusalem, 1986, pp. 238–264.
Bohlman extended his study into a full-length book on the World Center
in 1994.

Darius Milhaud and Ernest Bloch welcomed the establishment of
the Center; Milhaud contributed an essay to *Musica Hebraica*, Vol. 1–2,
the only publication (1938) of the planned periodical. A number of international scholars sent articles for future (never published) editions of the
journal.

The Palestine Broadcasting Service assisted in the organization of concerts, noteworthy among them the performances on 21 June 1938 of the
oratorio *Balat and Bilam* by Hugo Adler, who then still officiated as Cantor at Mannheim, Germany, and on 18 June 1940 of Ernest Bloch's *Avodat HaKodesh*. Soon after this concert, the World Center found no means
for continued activity; the nationalistic enthusiasm of its organizers proved
to be no equivalent to a professionalism that might have attracted larger circles and the support of organizations like the Palestine Symphony Orchestra and its resident and eminent guest musicians.

Great conductors had led the orchestra in its early years. With the foundation of the State of Israel in 1948 and a somewhat stabler political balance

in the region, a never-ceasing flow of the world's most distinguished conductors and instrumental and vocal soloists came to Israel as guests of the
Israel Philharmonic Orchestra. In 1951 it embarked on its first North-
American concert tour, led by Serge Koussevitzky, who had earlier come to
Israel for the first time and was assisted by Leonard Bernstein, who since
1947 had become the most frequent and most beloved guest conductor of
the Israel Philharmonic, and by Eleazar de Carvalho. The first European
concert tour, four years later, was conducted by Leonard Bernstein, Paul
Kletzki, and Paul Paray, who for some years was chief conductor of the orchestra. Carlo Maria Giulini took the Israel Philharmonic to the United
States, Canada, Japan, and India in 1960, and many additional world tours
followed in the course of the years. In the 1956–57 season the orchestra
had some 17,000 subscribers (of an Israeli population of about 1.8 million)
and each concert had to be performed for them seven times in Tel Aviv,
twice in Haifa, and once in Jerusalem. In Tel Aviv it played in the 1000-seat
Ohel Shem Theater till in 1957 it received its own almost 3000-seat hall,
the Fredric R. Mann Auditorium, named for the American maecenas who
was instrumental in donating the cultural center to the city of Tel Aviv and
its orchestra. In 1960 the number of subscribers rose to 26,000 (of a population of about two million); in the 1980s a series of twelve concerts had
to be given for the almost 36,000 regular subscribers (of a population of
about four million). Although the builders of the auditorium had not devised its stage suitably for operatic performances—much to the regret of
Koussevitzky, who was one of the advisors to the planners—the Philharmonic also included in its yearly schedules (primitively) full-staged, half-
staged, and concert performances of operas at regular intervals, some of
them presented by operatic ensembles from foreign countries, others with
guest protagonists and local singers. Hardly a prominent name of conductors and soloists is missing in the list of the Philharmonic's guest performers—from Georg Solti to Rafael Kubelík, from Lorin Maazel to Kurt
Masur, from Jennie Tourel to Montserrat Caballé, from Dietrich Fischer-
Dieskau to Plácido Domingo, from Arthur Rubinstein to Glenn Gould
and Arturo Benedetto Michelangeli, to name but a few. Jascha Heifetz and
Yehudi Menuhin, Isaac Stern and Mstislav Rostropovich played with them,
and Helmuth Rilling conducted oratorios with his Gächinger Kantorei as

choir. Itzhak Perlman, Daniel Barenboim, Shlomoh Mintz, and Pinchas Zukerman joined the roster of Israeli soloists of world renown. Zubin Mehta accepted the post of music director and chief conductor (for life) in 1967. Leonard Bernstein was named laureate conductor.

In the course of time, a number of smaller orchestras, each important in its own way, came into being in Israel, while the Israel Philharmonic and the Jerusalem Radio Symphony Orchestra remained the most important orchestral bodies in the country. Haifa received its symphony orchestra, the Beersheva Orchestra was established, a Kibbutz Symphony Orchestra and Kibbutz Chamber Orchestra (of kibbutz members) were founded, chamber orchestras sprang up in smaller cities such as Holon, Ramat-Gan, Herzliah. The important Israel Chamber Orchestra was founded by Gary Bertini and later led by Rudolf Barshai and, in the 1990s, by Shlomoh Mintz. With the influx of professional musicians from Russia, the composer-conductor Noam Sheriff established the Rishon-le-Zion Symphony Orchestra in the city of Rishon-le-Zion and made it a point to perform rarely heard masterworks and contemporary orchestral music by Israeli composers, some of whom were commissioned to write works especially for this orchestra. Orchestral and vocal ensembles were also formed at the country's music academies and at the Haifa Technical Academy. Various youth orchestras also sprang up in the country, some of them connected with the music schools. One youth orchestra, the Gadna Orchestra—comprised of young girls and boys of a pre-military training organization—played at the 1958 Brussels World Exposition under Shalom Ronly-Riklis and won first prize at the international meeting of youth orchestras in Holland.

The Israeli broadcasting station Kol Israel developed the instrumental ensemble of the Palestine Broadcasting Service into a full symphony orchestra which also attracted eminent artists from Europe and the Americas. Permanent conductors during its first years were Heinz Freudenthal and Georg Singer; Otto Klemperer, Walter Goehr, René Leibowitz were among its early guest conductors. In later years the orchestra was led by Lukas Foss, Yehudi Menuhin (who conducted the Israeli Jacob Gilboa's *Kathros U-Psantherin*, which he had commissioned), and Krzysztof Penderecki, among other luminaries of the musical world. A tradition of combining choral with orchestral concerts started with the foundation of a choir of Christians, Moslems, and Jews by Crawford McNair, director of the Palestine Broadcasting Service during the time of the British Mandate, himself a conductor of note. A series of concerts of sacred music of all confessions, named "Liturgica," was initiated by Gary Bertini in the 1980s; they are given yearly for an entire week at the end of December when the Jewish Hanukka festival and Christmas week often coincide.

Choirs were formed in cities, villages and the kibbutzim. The first large-scale choir was organized by the conductors Shlomoh Kaplan (the United Chorus) and Israel Brandmann (Workers' Choir); both were formed in pre-Israel Palestine with the aim to cultivate the Palestinian-Jewish, classical, traditional, and socialist song in contrast to the large-scale oratorios and classical and modern chamber-choral music offered by the Palestine Oratorio (Fordhaus ben-Tsissy) and the Tel Aviv Chamber Chorus (conductor Otto-Eytan Lustig), respectively; the latter eventually developed into the Philharmonic Choir. The choral organizations of various kinds were the first to stimulate composers to write works at a time when the possibilities for them to write symphonic music for acceptance by the symphony orchestras were still limited. Encouragement and first recognition of local composers came with the establishment of the Yoel Engel Prize by the Tel Aviv municipality (1945). The Israeli Performing Rights Society (Acum) later instituted prizes for writers, composers, and interpreters; some composers were honored by the State of Israel on Independence Day with the grant of the Israel Prize, others by the Prime Minister's Prize.

A number of music festivals came into being as early as 1944. In that year twenty-four choirs formed a chorus of one thousand and sang at a choir festival at the kibbutz Ein Charod in the Jesreel Valley; two years before a convention had been held to discuss the various aspects of the Palestinian song. In 1944, also, the folk dance movement was launched; its first large-scale festival (a smaller one had been organized earlier) was held at Dahlia in the Ephraim Mountains in 1947, when some five hundred dancers presented their popular creations—accompanied by traditional folk music—and there came some twenty thousand spectators. A Bach-Handel Festival was held in Jerusalem twice; at Ein Gev on the shores of Lake Kinneret a Passover Chamber Music Week became a yearly attraction—with the donation of an auditorium by the American Esco-Foundation it

Israel Festival: concert at the Roman amphitheater of Caesarea.

became a popular music-and-dance festival. Riccardo Muti brought the
Philadelphia Orchestra, and Daniel Barenboim and Claudio Abbado the
Berlin Philharmonic Orchestra to Israel. Folk festivals were temporarily organized at the artists' colony at Zikhron Ja'acow, and festive events were
held at the amphitheater on Mount Scopus above Jerusalem, interrupted
only by the nineteen years of Jordanian aggression and occupation of East

Jerusalem. Since 1952, an international gathering of professional and amateur choirs has regularly been held in Israel; its planner and first director, Aharon Zvi Propes, entitled it Zimriah. A. Z. Propes also directed the first Israel-government-sponsored Israel Festival, held since 1961. In 1954 the first International Festival of Contemporary Music took place in Haifa and Jerusalem, with composers and delegates of the International Society for Contemporary Music attending from many countries; its highlight was the world première, in concert form, of the opera *David* by Armand Lunel and Darius Milhaud, conducted in Jerusalem by Georg Singer.

The visits to Israel by prominent creative musicians and interpreters as guests of the festivals, the orchestras, choirs, and music schools occasioned the holding of seminars. The Brazilian composer Heitor Villa-Lobos was guest lecturer at the Music Teachers' Training School of Tel Aviv; Aaron Copland met composers at Beit Daniel at Zikhron Ja'acow; master classes by guest composers and interpreters were held at the music academies and

In the open-air "Green Room" at the Caesarea Israel Festival: *(right to left)* Pablo Casals, Mrs. Casals, violinist Alexander Schneider, pianist Rudolf Serkin. (Photograph by Israel Government Press Office.)

also at Beit Daniel—where guests included Eduard Steuermann, Rudolf Kolisch, Maurice Gendron, Matyas Seiber, and the musicologist Alphons Silbermann.

THE STEADY RISE in number and scope of music-performing bodies—choral, chamber music, orchestral—and the improvement in the quality of teaching in the music schools, along with the establishment of music-publication facilities and the growth of European and American interest in Israel's musical life, musical development, and musical creation, all contributed to a growing self-confidence of the Israeli composer, who was led to a belief that he might be called to contribute to the cultural upbuilding of the old-new country. The question was asked—abroad more than in Israel, proper—whether there is, whether there *could be* a characteristic Israeli music, and if so what might its recognizable traits be. Are composers trying to look for regional-liturgical or folk-music-traditional melodic, rhythmic, formal, sonic qualities to inspire their compositions; do they combine Near Eastern musical characteristics with conventional or modernist western aesthetics, styles, and techniques? Can eastern music be approached at all with western perceptions? Do the language and speech of an immigrant to a Near Eastern country reflect in his musical compositions; does their character change in musical language and speech where Hebrew is spoken and Hebrew is sung?

The composers of pre-Israel Palestine and of Israel have given different individual answers to these basic questions. The composers of the Jewish national school in eastern Europe and their followers had tried to derive a typical Jewish musical style from the folk tunes of the Jewish Diaspora; their idiom was closely bound to that of their environment. The Hebraic idiom of Ernest Bloch—which considerably influenced a great number of composers, especially in the United States but also in South American countries—had been inspired by the spirit of Judaism as preserved in the Bible and the prayers; there was no connection in this music with actual contemporary Jewish life. In new Israel the composer lives in a newly formed society and in an environment full of historical and sacred associations and pregnant with promises of the future, he sees a landscape he loves, he feels the pulse of his own people's life, and he speaks the language of the land—a modern form of the Hebrew of the Bible. Living has achieved a meaning for the Jew who has become a master of his own life on his own soil but who has to start shaping his existence anew from the very beginnings. The immigrant must learn to cultivate the fields that will yield their harvest to his people and to conquer the spirit of the language in which he will speak to his neighbors; the creative artist must likewise acquire the roots of a new language and attempt to absorb the spirit and atmosphere of the country. In judging the first efforts of Israeli composers in the various fields of music we must not forget that only civilizations boasting of a long and unbroken tradition and supported by strong national foundations have been able to produce sublime, lasting works of art of supernational impact, and that composers who are creating under conditions new to them and in a country that only gradually reveals its singular beauty must needs overcome a stage of struggling, experimenting, and search before achieving the first height of artistic expression.

MANY DIFFERENT TENDENCIES might be observed in the output of the country's composers. A great number are utterly unconscious of the influence exerted by the new medium, yet their music mirrors the unique atmosphere in one way or another; one group pretends that no truly Israeli music can ever be created without the elaboration or imitation of the melodies typical of the old Orient or the new country; yet another opinion is expressed by those saying that not the melodic material but the spirit of the country should characterize the new compositions—that is to say, the spirit of the glorious Biblical past or of the modern pioneer work. It need not be stressed that great music has never developed by way of *tendencies* and that a composer's success depends not so much on his material, his sympathies and ideas, and his artistic desire as on the greatness and originality of his invention and the craftsmanship underlying the presentation of his musical inspiration. But young nationalistic communities do not always heed such deliberations, and very often a poor work is applauded on account of its national trends or the appearance of a favorite tune. In fact, such a work might even inspire composers of stature to better and greater music. Many Israeli musicians were once led to believe that a "set of variations on a Palestinian folk song" must needs represent Palestinian music, or that musical craftsmanship is less important than national enthusiasm clad in sounds. The country has to its credit a great number of composers in whose creations a faithful and natural musical expression is found—in the frame of a purely musically conceived composition—of the work and feast, the sorrow and mirth, the song and dance, the tradition and youth of the country.

CHAPTER FOURTEEN

THE PIONEER GENERATION

OF ISRAELI COMPOSERS AND TEACHERS

S IN ALL NATIONAL RENASCENCE MOVEMENTS, the most important composer in early Palestine music was "Anon." His songs
and dance tunes appear in kindergarten and schools, in the fields,
on the village green, and at rural festivities, and he still inspires song writers throughout the country. Nursery song literature in Hebrew had its origin in the works of Yoel Engel, who based the bulk of his children's songs
on texts of Haim Nachman Bialik; later writers of popular tunes sung in
modern Israel include Mordecai Ze'ira, Daniel Sambursky, Yehuda Shertok
= Sharett, Shalom Postolsky, Menashe Ravina, Nahum Nardi, Ephraim
Ben-Haim, Moshe Wilensky, Zvi Kaplan, Ya'ariv Esrahi, Yoel Walbe, Itzhak Edel, David Sahavi, Nissan Cohen-Melamed, Benjamin Hatulli, Marc
Lavry, Emanuel Pugatchov-Amiran, and Yedidya Gorohov-Admon, many
of whose songs show a particularly interesting synthesis of East and West,
as do those of Sarah Levy-Tana'i (who founded the Israeli-Yemenite dance
theater, Inbal). None of these composers had a western, say western European, background, but for most of them modern Hebrew was a new language, different in pronunciation, prosody, inflection, accentuation, and
sound from both the Russian or Polish of their original homeland and their

The Inbal Dance Theater. (Photograph by Israel Government Press Office.)

popular language, Yiddish. New, also, were the themes of their songs. The Jews whose ancestors, or who had themselves, lived in the ghetto, in the Jewish *shtetel*, had not known songs as did the world surrounding them, songs of nature, flowers in the fields, hunting, pet animals, drinking, marching songs, and gay dance tunes. The Jews of the shtetel and ghetto did not see flowers and trees, rivulets and fields. They did no have carefree love songs; they danced at weddings, but their texts and melodies always had some religious connotation, some mystic feeling. In the new country, they enjoyed the history-laden atmosphere, with place names known from the biblical stories, plants and flowers mentioned in the Bible, and experiences their biblical forefathers must have known. Most of the new settlers led a life that was distinctly more secular than religiously minded, and when composers set to music verses from the Psalms or The Song of Songs, they did not necessarily create a prayer song of religious devotion but rather were attracted by the naturalness and lyrical poetry of the biblical language. The new Palestinian and Israeli dancing tunes showed the heritage of Hasidic dancing, while the eastern European Jewish operetta song found a continuation in the couplets written in Israel for the Army entertainment troupes and satirical stage shows in the cities; the popularity of the early ditties seemed never to wane. The westernization of Israeli civilization and a growing influence of western musical trends brought about a novel kind of popular music in an East-West song style; Naomi Shemer, Israeli-born, who wrote the lyrics and music of the internationally known *Jerusalem of Gold* (Yerushalayim shel Sahav), was the first to write songs that became true Israeli evergreens.

Some of the folk-style composers of the earliest period in "Palestinian music" also created works on a larger scale; they wrote art songs, artistic folk-tune arrangements and variations, and instrumental compositions of merit. Israel Brandmann, who was born in Russia in 1901, studied in Vienna, and settled in Palestine in 1921, wrote instrumental works based on music by Yoel Engel and local folklore. His *Variations on a Theme by Engel* for piano and orchestra (1934) and his *Variations on a Hebrew Dance Tune* for strings (1928) have been widely played. His Sonata for Violin and Piano (1927) is the first valuable work in an abstract form with a distinctly local color in its thematic invention. In his later years, Brandmann devoted most of his time to choral conducting and neglected musical composition. Itzhak Edel (1896–1973), having pondered the possibilities and necessities of modern Hebrew music, concluded that European scales and harmonies should have no place in the work of the Israeli musician but that the structural forms of sonata, rondo, and aria are the highest possible achievements and can well be filled with entirely new contents. He thus used them as "frames" for his Sonatina for Oboe and Piano (1943) and for two string quartets, while basing his themes on synagogal or ancient modal scales. His Capriccio (1946—in a version for piano solo and in an orchestral arrangement) elaborates a Jewish dance tune in rondo form.

The local atmosphere is salient in the two suites for string orchestra and Variations for String Quartet by Ya'ariv Esrahi and the piano and chamber music of Aviassaf Baernea (1908–57). The most popular, and most frequently played, among Israel's "light symphonic" works is Marc Lavry's symphonic poem based on his own popular song *Emek* (1937). Marc Lavry (1903–67), composer of the folk-style opera *Dan the Guard* (1944–45), also composed an oratorio *Song of Songs*, a concert overture *From Dan to Beersheva* (1947) and, among other works, two piano concertos (1945, 1947). His *Country Dances from Israel* (1952) and *Israeli Dances* are also widely performed.

A composer whose life story and musical development show the impact, more than any other's, of his living in Israel by completely changing his outlook and style is Joachim Stutchewsky, violoncellist, pedagogue, writer, and composer. Born in Russia in 1891, he lived in Vienna and Zürich before settling in Tel Aviv in 1938. His earliest compositions, and again some of his later works, follow the trends of the eastern European (Russian) national Jewish musical movement; in Vienna—where he served for some time as cellist in the famed Kolisch Quartet (the friends and promoters of Arnold Schoenberg)—Stutchewsky was strongly influenced by the progressive Viennese musical modernism. He had already started thinking of how to rejuvenate Jewish music and had published some early small-scale compositions in Vienna and Zürich. In Tel Aviv he organized concerts of Jewish music and developed into a prolific composer of piano, chamber, vocal, and orchestral music in a style linked, alternatively, to Near Eastern Israeli and eastern European Jewish folklore. He wrote *Israeli Melodies* and an *Israeli Suite* as well as a *Hasidic Suite* for violoncello (his instrument) and piano and *Four Jewish Dances* and *Hasidic Dance* for piano. The foremost characteristics of his style, in the "Israeli" as much as in the "Jewish" compositions, are the lyrical expression pervading throughout, coupled with a strong sense of rhythm and a fine sense of the properties of each musical instrument; among his most notable works are *Kol Korèh* (A Voice Is Calling) for French horn and a Concertino for Clarinet and String Orchestra. Stutchewsky died in Tel Aviv in 1982.

Also of eastern European descent were Shalom Aharoni (1893–1972), the violinist and composer Baruch Liftman (1905–70), and Dan Aharonovicz (1909–81), all of whom were attracted by eastern Jewish as well as Israeli folklore. Outstanding among the eastern Jewish generation of musicians was Joseph Kaminski (1903–72), one of the leaders of the violin section of the Israel Philharmonic Orchestra. His most original composi-

Composer-conductor Joseph Kaminski conducting the Palestine Orchestra in the middle of the desert for British, Arab, and Palestinian (Jewish) soldiers during World War II. (Photograph by the Israel Philharmonic Orchestra.)

tion is his Concertino for Trumpet and Orchestra (1940–41) comprising an opening movement "Un Poco Vivaldi," the theme of which is a travesty of the most hackneyed of Antonio Vivaldi's violin concertos which no young violinist can afford to ignore. The slow lyrical movement that follows, "Improvisazione," opens and closes with a cadenza of liturgical character answered by the orchestral "choir" with an "Amen" response. The Finale is a boisterous and colorful tarantella. Among other important works are Kaminski's String Quartet (1945), his *Comedy Overture* (1944), *Three Israeli Sketches* (1955), *Variations* for English horn and strings (1958), his Violin Concerto (1950), and *Triptych* for piano (1958). Smaller-scale compositions are his *Ballade* for harp and orchestra (1945) and *Legend and Dance* for strings.

A prolific composer also of eastern European descent was Verdina Shlonsky—sister of the poet Abraham Shlonsky and Israel's first woman composer. Born in the Ukraine in 1905, she came to live in Tel Aviv in 1929, after having studied in Paris. She wrote a considerable number of interesting small-scale works—songs, piano music, compositions for one or more instruments and piano, and music for the Hebrew theater. Her "Eleven Musical Postcards" for piano (1955) is a charming and very valuable contribution to the roster of easy educational piano music. Among her larger works, her three-movement String Quartet (1948) was accorded a Béla Bartók Prize. An interesting chamber orchestra piece is entitled *Euphony* (1967); *Space and Esprit* (1969) is scored for vocalise, bassoon, and piano. Verdina Shlonsky also wrote a number of symphonic works and a piano concerto. A most ambitious symphonic composition is *Meditations*, originally written in 1971 and several times revised by the composer, who died in Tel Aviv in 1990.

THE RISE, growth, and development of modern Israeli civilization, culture, literature, art, and music are closely linked to the consecutive waves of immigration from different regions of the world and the attitude, understanding, and sympathy of the new immigrants toward the country's inhabitants of long standing and their ancient traditions. The population of Palestine has never been and will never be homogenous, as throughout the centuries people of many beliefs, religions, sects, and nationalities have wished to make their home in the Holy Land. Christians, Muslims, and Jews revere holy sites in the country. There had always been a considerable Jewish presence all over the country, most especially in Jerusalem, where toward the end of the fifteenth century 1000 Christians and 500 Jewish inhabitants were counted; statistics of 1818 show 5000 Muslims, 5000 Christians of various denominations, and 10,000 Jews living in Jerusalem; in 1838 there were equal numbers (10,000) of Muslims, Christians, and Jews in the city; and ten years later there were 15,000 Muslims, 10,000 Christians, and 7500 Jews living side by side. Sizeable Jewish communities existed also in Hebron, Safed, Jaffa, and Tiberias. Then, as now, there were Christian Greek, Roman, Armenian, Coptic, Syriac, and other churches with their characteristic rites and prayer intonation; Muslim mosques with a Muezzin calling to prayer from their minarets; and Jewish synagogues and schools of religious learning with Sephardic and Ashkenazic traditions. When the earliest large-scale Jewish immigration began in the 1880s in the wake of the brutal pogroms in Russia, and later when the second immigration came between 1905 and 1914, most of the immigrant Jews tended toward the creation of a socialist-oriented community in the old-new country, and the same held true for the third wave of immigration between 1919 and 1924 that brought fugitives from the Ukraine pogroms to the country following the encouraging Balfour Declaration of the British government supporting the building of a national home for the Jews in Palestine, which after the defeat of the Turks came under British mandate.

The foremost aim of the early groups and individuals settling in Palestine had to be the recolonization of the land—freeing swamps of malaria, building roads, ploughing, sowing, making the dry desert fertile, establishing elementary and vocational schools. The settlers, real pioneers, brought their languages, customs, and Jewish backgrounds with them and also their songs and their dances. The traditional rites and singing in the synagogues of Jerusalem were as foreign, as exotic to them as the Christian and Muslim religious services, as indeed was also the Near Eastern Hebrew, based on the Sephardic Mediterranean tradition whereas the Jews from Russia and Poland spoke Yiddish and prayed in the Ashkenazic Hebrew tone and pronunciation. The Near Eastern style of singing and playing of musical instruments in the oriental communities also sounded exotic to the immigrant Jews, as it does to western Europeans and Americans today.

In 1834 precisely that exotic style kindled the interest and musical imagination of a French composer, Félicien David, who on a pilgrimage to the Near East noted down Arabic tunes and elaborated them later in songs, piano pieces, and a "symphonic ode" entitled *Le Désert*, thereby initiating an entire movement of "musical orientalism" in European music.[1]

In the later 1920s—with a fourth wave of immigration from about 1924 to 1927—the cultural aspects of recolonization had grown in scope and intensity. The Jewish population had established grammar schools, there were stages for theater and opera, the Hebrew University was founded in 1925. A number of writers and poets created a new Hebrew literary style. For the Jewish composers the old musical traditions alive in the country became of growing interest. The fifth immigration began in 1927 and grew immensely after 1933 with the rise of the National-Socialist regime in Germany and the growth of Fascism in almost all European countries; it brought to Palestine for the first time a majority of settlers reared in western European civilization and culture, science and learning, arts and music. For most of them, Hebrew was a completely new language and it took them a long time to be able to express themselves adequately. For the musicians and composers among them, the world of Near Eastern singing and instrumental playing proved as stimulating as the acceptance of a new language. The contacts with Jews of Near Eastern or North African descent and with Arab singers and musicians were sought as presenting chances for imaginative composers to create a completely novel kind of music under the impact of a new musical experience. As had Félicien David in 1834, a number of composers noted down, studied, and elaborated Near Eastern melodies and were inspired by them to write compositions combining Mediterranean and western-style musical structures and forms of

---

[1]For the data on the population in Palestine see Gradenwitz *Das Heilige Land in Augenzeugenberichten*, Munich, 1984. On musical orientalism see Ralph P. Locke, "Félicien David, compositeur saint-simonien et orientalisant," in *Les Saint-Simoniens et l'Orient Vers la modernité*, ed. Magali Morsy, Aix-en-Provence, 1989; P. Gradenwitz, *Musik zwischen Orient und Okzident*, Wilhelmshaven, 1977; and "Félicien David and French Romantic Orientalism," *The Musical Quarterly*, Vol. 62, No. 4, 1976, pp. 471–506.

expression. The special sounds of traditional Near Eastern musical instruments and ensembles also reverberate in many of the works for which the term *Eastern-Mediterranean music* was widely used. With the establishment of the already cited Archives of Oriental Music and later the phonograph library at the Hebrew University Jewish Music Center, composers could easily listen to recorded ancient Christian liturgical singing, Muslim calls to prayer, and eastern synagogue services, as well as to the playing, improvised or bound by traditional forms, of Near Eastern musicians with their special stringed, wind, and percussion instruments. A rescue operation called Magic Carpet brought a large contingent of Jews from Yemen to the country; Operation Solomon saved Ethiopian Jews from oppression in the country from whence had once come the Queen of Sheba to visit Israel's King Solomon; and in the late 1980s and the 1990s an ever-growing immigration from the former Soviet Union changed the numerical balance between East- and West-born Israelis, the Oriental communities and Israeli-born generations, respectively. The demographical fluctuations and changes brought with them a wealth of divergent streams of musical traditions interesting to ethnomusicologists and stimulating to Israel's composers. Many works of Israeli music reflect the changes in the musical scenery of the country; others are characterized by the very absence of an influence from liturgical or folkloristic sources; but it may be said that the majority of compositions of intrinsic value beyond space and time are those in which the composer succeeded in letting reverberate strains of traditional melismas and sounds in music of a distinct individual character and superior mastery.

FIVE COMPOSERS can well be regarded as founding fathers of modern Israeli music, each of them a creative musician of great individuality as well as a composition teacher of influence to more than one generation of younger Israelis. This is most especially true of the oldest of them, Paul Ben-Haim, first in a line of creators of Eastern-Mediterranean music.

"I am of the West by birth and education," wrote Ben-Haim in 1961,

> but I stem from the East and live in the East. I regard this as a great blessing indeed and it makes me feel grateful. The problem of a synthesis of East and West occupies musicians all over the world. If we—thanks to our liv-

Paul Ben-Haim.

ing in a country that forms a bridge between East and West—can provide a modest contribution to such a synthesis in music, we shall be very happy.

Ben-Haim was introduced to the traditions of the region when soon after coming to Palestine he met the singer and folklore-collector Braha Zefira and through her became closely acquainted with Near Eastern chants and folk music, which previously he had known only more theoretically from the published collections of A. Z. Idelsohn. Ben-Haim accompanied Braha Zefira at the piano in many of her concerts and made congenial arrangements of folk material for her; he then also composed original songs in the vein of Near Eastern folklore. In most of the composer's later great music reverberate the melodic strains, the rhythms, and the coloring of this music. When in the 1940s composers and writers—Max Brod most prominent among them—began speaking of an Eastern-Mediterranean school of music, it was obvious that Ben-Haim was regarded as the earliest and foremost creator of a musical style, the melismatic melodies, intricate rhythms, and characteristic coloring of which had come to reflect the very special atmosphere of the Land of Israel—its geographical region, its spiritual leanings, and the unique blend of heritage and innovation that is also found in other countries bordering the eastern Mediterranean Sea, such as Greece and Turkey.

Paul Ben-Haim was born in Munich, Germany, in 1897; his original family name was Frankenburger but he took the Hebrew name when he started concertizing in Palestine. He was a graduate of the Munich Music Academy and became known in Germany as a pianist and conductor before settling in Tel Aviv in 1933, where he lived, worked, and taught till his death in 1984. His early works betray the influence of central European modernism. Among these works are songs, chamber music, and music for orchestra. The outstanding chamber work is a String Trio, Op. 10 (1927), impressive in its pregnant themes, their concise development, and the distinct lyrical undertones even in the passionate first Allegro and the gaily moving Finale; a melodious Andante forms the middle movement. Two early symphonic compositions which are still occasionally performed are a Concerto grosso in three movements—Overture, Aria, and Chaconne—Op. 15 (1931), and *Pan*, a symphonic poem for soprano and orchestra (1931), after Heinrich Lautensack. A beautiful early choral work is the composition of Psalm 126 ("When the Lord turned again the captivity of Zion") for unaccompanied eight-part male chorus.

Ben-Haim's most important early work is the three-part large-scale oratorio *Joram* completed in Munich in February 1933 just before his leaving Germany—a very forcefully dramatic composition for solos, chorus, and orchestra on a poem by Rudolf Borchardt telling a moving story in archaic biblical language of a man whose character and tragic fate are reminiscent of the biblical Job.

The first music Paul Ben-Haim composed after coming to Palestine was a series of melodic arrangements and songs of his own for the concerts of Braha Zefira. In the later 1930s he completed the first of an important line of chamber music compositions, a realm in which he found his very best medium of expression in lyrical, colorful, and pensive compositions. A four-movement string quartet (1937) was the first of his works in this medium;

it was followed two years later by a piano trio. In the string quartet may already be felt the impact of a singular Near Eastern atmosphere deriving from traditional folkloristic melismas.

Paul Ben-Haim's considerable creative output included music for solo instruments, chamber music, fine lyrical songs, choral works, liturgical music, compositions for piano, and symphonic works with or without soloists. Most important among the latter are the two symphonies of a relatively early period, written before the foundation of the State of Israel. The two symphonies offer complete contrasts. The First Symphony (1939–40) contains two dramatic movements of tragic quality, while the second of the three movements is a contemplative, lyrical piece of rare beauty, possessed of an inner calm that can leave no listener unimpressed. The Second Symphony (1943–45), in four movements, is pastoral throughout and bears the stamp of folkloristic influence; contemplation of the landscape and the beauties of nature have occupied the composer's mind. The opening theme of the flute sets the pastoral mood of the first movement and of the entire symphony. The work is delicately scored, especially in the Notturno, which forms the third movement. A symphonic work on a smaller scale is Ben-Haim's poem for violin and orchestra, *In Memoriam* (1942), a requiem without words that takes the shape of a one-movement piece in three interlinked parts: an introduction, an invocation, and a dramatic allegro ("Remembrance"), after which an epilogue calls back the theme of the introduction and brings the work to a solemn conclusion. A Concerto for Strings (1947) and a Piano Concerto (1948) followed the style of the composer's Second Symphony. The titles the composer has given to the three movements of the Piano Concerto are characteristic of Ben-Haim's

Example 33. Beginning of second movement from Ben-Haim's First Symphony (1939–40). (Copyright Israeli Music Publications, Ltd.)

predilection for imaginative lyricism: the opening movement, a calm prelude and a sonata-form temperamental allegro, is entitled "Visions"; a dainty and poetic nocturne "Voices in the Night" contains a solo for viola d'amore; the finale, "Dance," follows without break and creates the feeling of an ecstatic Oriental dance.

Among Ben-Haim's later orchestral compositions the outstanding work is *The Sweet Psalmist of Israel*, a sinfonia concertante with solo instruments leading the orchestra in each of the three movements. Commissioned by the Koussevitzky Foundation and composed in 1953, the work has been widely performed throughout the world and was recorded by the New York Philharmonic Orchestra conducted by Leonard Bernstein. The world première of the work took place in Tel Aviv in December 1956, with Georg Singer conducting, Clari Szarvas as harpist, and Arieh Sachs at the harpsichord. In 1957 Ben-Haim was awarded the prestigious Israel Prize for his work. The "Sweet Psalmist" is David, the royal poet and musician of Israel, and is seen in each of the three movements from a different angle. The first movement, for orchestra with harpsichord solo (imitating King David's kinnor, the stringed lyre) and wind instruments, was inspired by the biblical passage from Samuel I, 16:23:"And it came to pass, when the evil spirit from God was upon Saul that David took a lyre and played with his hand, so Saul refreshed, and was well, and the evil spirit departed from him." For the middle movement, for harp solo and strings, Ben-Haim quotes Samuel II, 23:1–2: "The sweet Psalmist of Israel said, The spirit of the Lord spake by me, and His word was in my tongue." The final movement, entitled "A Song of Degrees," is scored for harpsichord and harp solo and the full orchestra and quotes Psalm 134: "Behold, bless ye the Lord, all ye servants of the Lord, which by night stand in the house of the Lord. Lift your hands in the sanctuary and bless the Lord. The Lord that made heaven and earth bless thee out of Zion."

Other important works of Ben-Haim are the composition written for the Louisville Orchestra, *To the Chief Musician—Metamorphoses for Orchestra* (1958), again quoting a biblical psalm (Psalm 49); the Violin Concerto (1959–60); *Dance and Invocation* (1960); *Capriccio* for piano and orchestra (also 1960) inspired by a Sephardi love song ("In the sea there is a tower, In the tower there is a window, In the window there is a dove, She loves sailors"); a Violoncello Concerto (1962); and *The Eternal Theme. Music for Orchestra,* six interlinked sections quoting a saying of Rabbi Nachman of Bratzlav: "In the days to come when the Lord will be the language known to all nations, then from sublime heights you will behold the sublime belief, which is song, its eternal theme being the song of all songs." Written during 1963–65, the work, is characterized, like *The Sweet Psalmist,* by concertante parts. The composer has said of it that "it tries to speak a musical language of its own and to steer clear of the many divergent stylistic tendencies dominating the musical scene of our day."

Paul Ben-Haim's last orchestral compositions were *Symphonic Metamorphoses on a Bach Chorale* (1967–68); *Sonata per Stromenti a Corde* (1969); Divertimento Concertante for solo flute, harp, celesta, glockenspiel, vibraphone, and strings (1972); and Rhapsody for Piano and String Orchestra (1971). In a popular vein he wrote a suite *From Israel* in 1951 and the frequently performed *Fanfare to Israel* for either full orchestra or symphonic band (1950). For string orchestra Ben-Haim composed Concerto for Strings (1947) and *Music for Strings* (1956).

An impressive list of compositions for piano and chamber music combinations includes Serenade for Flute and String Trio (1967); *Songs Without Words* which may be performed by various instruments with piano or with orchestra (also written for voice and accompaniment), written in 1952; Prelude for String Quartet (1973); *Music for the Piano 1957* and *Music for the Piano 1967* composed for Varda Nishry, and some more light piano works. Among the finest works ever written for solo instruments are Ben-Haim's Sonata in G for violin solo composed for and widely performed by Yehudi Menuhin (1951) and *Music for Violoncello Solo* written for Uzi Wiesel (1974). *Studies* for violin solo was Paul Ben-Haim's very last composition, also dedicated to Yehudi Menuhin. The Sonata in G blends the improvisatory art familiar to Near Eastern musicians with sublime western craftsmanship; the slow middle movement played *con sordino* throughout, produces a Fata-Morgana-like atmosphere with its coloring by way of grace notes, trills, and echo effects—an example of true Eastern-Mediterraneanism.

Paul Ben-Haim never wrote an opera; his only really dramatic work was the early oratorio *Joram.* But in the vocal field he left an impressive number of lyrical songs, psalm compositions, and larger scale choral works, among them *Vision of a Prophet* (1958–59); *Three Psalms* for soloists, choir, and orchestra (or organ) completed in 1962; *Hymn from the Desert* (1962–63); *Liturgical Cantata* (1950); and the Friday evening service *Kabbalat Shabbat* (1966–67). The solo song compositions include a cycle *Melodies from the East* (1970), echoes of the composer's early work with the singer Braha Zefira; *Myrtle Blossoms from Eden,* five songs for soprano (or tenor), contralto (or baritone), and piano or orchestra (1965–66); and *Kochav na-fal* (A Star Fell Down) on poems by the Israeli poet Matti Katz, a victim of Israel's defense wars. These songs, composed in 1969–70, rank with the finest lyrical contributions to the modern lieder. The three songs of the cycle were recorded by contralto Ursula Mayer-Reinach with the composer at the piano—the only preserved recording of the playing of Ben-Haim himself.

LIKE PAUL BEN-HAIM, other composers of the earliest generation important in the growth and development of Israeli music hailed from European countries with a musical culture of their own, but, unlike him, were from eastern and southeastern Europe and were also ten to twenty years younger.

Oedoen Partos (1907–77), a violist and composer native to Hungary but since 1938 a resident of Tel Aviv, was solo violist of the Philharmonic Orchestra from 1938 to 1956 and in 1951 became director of the Tel Aviv Music Academy. An early work of his, Concertino for String Quartet (1934), was written before the composer's immigration to Palestine. It is conceived in a fierce and buoyant temper, and the spirit of the Bartók-Kodály school cannot be easily mistaken; even with the very different style of the later Partos, this remains a forceful piece, with a craftsmanship and inner power which stirs at each hearing. Partos is among those composers who recognized the charm of the Oriental folksong through the efforts of Braha Zefira, who sang to him the unaccompanied melodies and commissioned him to write an instrumental background to these songs. Partos has written a good many such arrangements, as did Ben-Haim, and absorbed in his later works much of the inherent characteristics of Near Eastern melody and rhythm. In his *Four Israeli Melodies* for violin and piano he transcribed such songs for the young violinist, while in his *Choral Fantasia*

Oedoen Partos.

(with orchestra) Oriental folkloristic material was treated in the frame of a small-scale symphonic cantata.

Yizkor (In Memoriam) for solo viola and string orchestra or for viola (or violin, or violoncello) and piano, was written in 1946 to accompany an expressive mimic dance conceived by Deborah Bertonoff and dedicated to the memory of the victims in the war of extinction against the Jews in Central Europe during the Second World War; Partos later extended and elaborated his original work.

A most impressive work by Partos is his first concerto for viola and orchestra, called *Song of Praise* and played by the composer for the first time with the Israel Philharmonic Orchestra in December 1949, Paul Paray conducting. The title was inspired by the psalm-like character of the Prelude and the exalted mood reigning throughout the huge main movement; describing the composition simply as a viola concerto would unduly minimize its symphonic character. In musical form, the work presents itself as a symphonic Prelude on two related themes and a Sonata movement comprising nine variations on a theme derived from the Prelude; emotionally, the composition takes us from the meditative and epic mood of the Prelude through all shades of exalted feeling to the vehement passion of the final variations, till meditation reigns again in the Epilogue. The composer was soloist in his work when Serge Koussevitzky took the Israel Philharmonic Orchestra on its first American tour in 1951; Partos' *Song of Praise* was conducted by Leonard Bernstein.

In 1951 Partos wrote his first purely symphonic work, dedicated to the music-loving settlement of Ein Gev on the shores of Lake Kinneret: the symphonic fantasy *Ein Gev*, for which Partos was awarded the Israel Prize 1954. It is inspired by the landscape, character, and history of the communal settlement bearing the same name, situated near the Syrian border of Israel. Partos had been a regular guest and participant in the annual music events arranged at Ein Gev during Passover week, and it was there after a concert (years before the Esco Music Center and Auditorium were opened there) that musicians and listeners celebrated in the dining hall and the guest book was passed from hand to hand—a book filled with illustrious names of many celebrities in the fields of science, arts and letters, and politics. The spiritual and programmatic background of the work is shaped by the scenery and the recent history of Ein Gev; idyllic peacefulness is disturbed by wars and tragedy, the mourning for fallen heroes must give way to fresh efforts and planning for a happier future.

In 1957 Partos completed his Second Concerto for Viola and Orchestra, a one-movement composition written at Ein Hashofet, dedicated to

Example 34. Opening of *Yizkor* (In Memoriam) by Oedoen Partos (1946) for solo viola and string orchestra. (Copyright 1948, Israeli Music Publications, Tel-Aviv.)

and first performed at this kibbutz. In 1958 Partos' Concerto for Violin and Orchestra was completed; this work, commissioned by Yehudi Menuhin and the Fromm Foundation, had occupied him for many years. The composer had assembled so much material for this work that it seemed impossible to use it all for a single composition: the Second Viola Concerto, *Visions*, and the song *Kivrat Adama* were meanwhile composed from musical material originally conceived for the Violin Concerto. In its final form, the three-movement Violin Concerto is still a work of large symphonic dimensions, a difficult but highly rewarding challenge for violinist and orchestra alike. *Mourning Music* for violoncello and piano, earlier entitled *Oriental Ballad*, belongs to a series of compositions in which Partos tries to achieve a synthesis of Oriental and Occidental musical elements and techniques.

In January 1957 Partos wrote his orchestral composition *Visions*. The interlinked movements of the work—which is scored for solo flute, piano, and string orchestra—are described by the composer as "Recitative," "Invocation", and "Dance"; the latter is followed by an Epilogue. The thematic material is based on a motive of Yemenite origin and is elaborated in a way that points to the ever-growing influence of eastern elements on the musical inspiration as well as on the technique and coloring of the thematic development in Partos' work.

In 1958, Partos completed an important chamber music work, a quintet for flute and strings in three movements, in which Partos developed further his idea of linking the concepts of dodecaphonic organization and *māqām* style. He entitled the quintet *Māqamāt*. Māqamāt are the Arabic–Near Eastern equivalents of the Indian râgas, the Greek nomoi, or the Far Eastern patet, combining the functions of basic tonal and melodic material, rows of notes, the basis for elaboration and variation, with a spiritual meaning.

Around 1960 a change occurred in Partos's musical outlook and style; he became more deeply involved in the study of western dodecaphonic and serial techniques while also learning more about the structure and meaning of Near Eastern musical forms. Works of transition include the orchestral composition *Demuyot* (Figures), which was composed in 1960 and first performed by the Israel Philharmonic Orchestra under Antal Doráti in 1963; String Quartet No. 2 entitled *Tehilim* (Psalms) written in 1961; and

Agadah (Legend) for piano, viola, and percussion instruments (1960) pre-mièred by Frank Pelleg with the composer and percussionist Yoel Thome at the London Festival of the International Society for Contemporary Music 1962.

In his compositions of the later 1960s and the 1970s he seemed to be more involved in the technical problems of composition; the complexity of his thoughts overshadowed the spontaneous musicality that distinguished his earlier works. Partos found his way back to spontaneous expression in his *Music for Oboe and Chamber Orchestra* written for and first performed by Heinz Holliger in 1976. Complex works of his last years were the Third Viola Concerto (*Sinfonia concertante*, 1962), *Shiluwim* (Combinations) for viola and chamber orchestra (1970), and various works for symphony and chamber orchestra. *Nebulae* (1966) for wind quintet, a Concertino for Flute and Piano (1969), and a piano piece *Metamorphoses* (1971) are among Partos' latest chamber music compositions.

ALEXANDER URIA BOSCOVICH was born in Transsylvania in the same year as Partos, 1907. He settled in Tel Aviv in 1938 and died there in 1964. Also one of the first composers to strive for "Mediterranean" expression in music, he had been most concerned with eastern European Jewish music before coming to Palestine, and had composed a seven-movement suite for orchestra, *Chansons populaires juives* (The Golden Chain), on which in a program note he commented as follows:

> In this music I have tried to distill the essence of Jewish melodies. The musical material of the songs in this suite is drawn entirely from eastern European Jewish folksongs. I have not tried to arrange these songs in the in-dividualistic-romantic way which characterized, for instance, the time of Liszt who transferred songs by Schubert and others into another world of ideas and feelings quite foreign to the atmosphere of the original songs. I have tried as far as possible to keep to the spirit of the original folksongs which are the expression of an entire people—and I might call this way of arrangement, in contrast to the individualistic conception, a collectivistic one, an attitude which has also been taken by such masters as Bartók and Kodály. I have changed nothing in the melodic structure of the songs and used orchestral color and thematic elaboration only as a medium to express the different psychological contents of the poems.

Alexander Uria Boscovich.

In his Violin Concerto (1942) Boscovich aimed at "expressing by musical means the experience of our land and our soul, the Bible. These are the two candles which will burn as long as one Jew remains on the earth"; the work is based on psalm intonation.

The composer's most characteristic work is the Concerto for Oboe and Orchestra composed 1943 and revised 1950. This is a three-movement concerto tinged with Mediterranean color, a difficult but rewarding task for a virtuoso oboist. Genuine eastern elements in the work have become an integral part of the composer's style, not only in his melodic and rhythmic foundations but also in his instrumental expression and scoring. The fine work had its first performance with Bram Blez and the Palestine Orchestra in 1944; the 1950 revision concerned mainly the originally somewhat over-laden orchestration.

A work in a lighter vein is Boscovich's *Semitic Suite* (1947), a series of dances and songs in which the composer tries to convey something of the regional atmosphere by means of an unusual style of scoring. After the *Semitic Suite* and a set of piano pieces, *Album for the Young*, Boscovich did not make known any new works for many years; except for some music for the theater and some short vocal compositions. He lived through a period of depression in which he mainly devoted his time to teaching and study; he analyzed the music of contemporary western composers and read philosophic treatises of eastern and western thinkers and mystics. When he started composing again, he had left his folkloristic leanings far behind. Only four completed compositions are known of the short last period of the composer's life: *Canto di Ma'alot* (Song of Degrees) composed in 1960, a work on which biblical cantillation has had discernible influence; a cantata *Bat Israel*; a *Concerto da camera* for violin and chamber orchestra; and *Ornaments* for flute and orchestra (1964). In all these works, biblical psalmody in Near Eastern style influenced the shaping of melodic themes, rhythmical organization, and melismatic writing; the orchestral texture seems not always convincing. The composer's intensive study and analysis of the music of Anton Webern had also left its mark on his very last works. His striving for a synthesis of the Near Eastern impact and the European avant-garde music of the time must have proved a challenge—a struggle too hard to master in his sad, last years of malignant disease, depression, and ever-declining physical power.

THE FOURTH COMPOSER in the line of important early creators of music in Palestine-Israel, and also of marked influence on the younger generations of musicians, is Josef Tal, the first Israeli composer who sought to rejuvenate the musical theater and who studied and used electronically produced tapes for his compositions. Josef Tal, pianist, pedagogue, and composer, was born in the Province of Posen in 1910 and graduated from the Berlin Musikhochschule. He came to the country in 1934 and, after living some time at a Kibbutz, settled in Jerusalem. In many of his musical works he sought inspiration in the world of the Bible and ancient legend, and he also especially studied the problems of choreographic music. The composer's most important works of his early period are a symphonic cantata *A Mother Rejoices* and the choreographic poem *Exodus* (1945–46), which was inspired by a dance poem on the story of the Exodus from Egypt by Deborah Bertonoff, the mimic dancer.

In 1961 Tal founded the first studio in Israel for the production of electronic music and ever since has made use of electronically produced sound. In 1958 he had already conceived and produced an electronic version of the "Exodus" theme. *Exodus II* is an electronic composition which Tal created after studying this new field of musical creation in the studios of Paris, Cologne, Gravesano, and Milan; in this work Tal goes back to the theme and form of his earlier choreographic poem for symphony orchestra and again uses the human voice to create a link between the different sections of the biblical dramatic tale.

In the symphonic cantata *A Mother Rejoices* (1948–49), Tal recreates the Maccabean legend of Hannah and her seven sons. The heroic mother sees all her sons killed by a cruel king because they refuse to bow before the Christian cross, but she rejoices over their steadfastness and does not want them to renounce their holy ancient belief. She takes her own life in an exalted spirit, praising the one and only God. A piano solo in Tal's composition symbolizes the task of narrator and commentator, while the story itself unfolds in a setting for solos, chorus, and orchestra; a jubilant "Hallelujah" concludes the work, at the climax of which two boys' voices join the chorus to intone an ancient Oriental psalm tune.

Among Tal's other early works there are three piano concertos (1944, 1953, 1956—the latter with tenor solo on a short text by Eleasar Kallir), *Visions* (Mar'oth) for string orchestra, piano works, songs, and chamber music. His Piano Sonata (1950) is a concentrated and highly expressive three-movement work, in the second movement of which a popular tune by Yehuda Sharett appears in the bass. *Lament and Dance* provide two attractive pieces for violoncello and harp; for harp solo, Tal wrote *Intrada*.

In 1951, the composer produced a short Violin Sonata, the three movements of which treat the thematic material as does a classical first-movement form. In 1959 followed the First String Quartet, a one-movement work dedicated to the memory of the cellist Joseph Weissgerber and developing around a lament-like expressive violoncello theme. Tal's Second String Quartet (1964) already belongs to his electronic period and proves the impact which a composer's preoccupation with electronically produced sounds must necessarily have also on music he creates for traditional musical instruments.

In the symphonic work *Festive Vision* (1957) Tal tries to give musical form to the outstanding architecture of the Fredric R. Mann Auditorium in Tel Aviv, home of the Israel Philharmonic Orchestra since October 1957. The vast open space of the hall unsupported by pillars is musically depicted by way of a themeless sound; the breadth and width of the hall, as suspended from the roof, are translated into the musical form of a fugue.

Josef Tal is among the few composers of Israel who have always been strongly interested in opera; with his first work in the operatic medium, the biblical drama *Saul at EnDor,* he gained an immediate, resounding success. Not concerned—as have been composers before him—with the magic and supernatural aspects of the biblical episode, Josef Tal was attracted by the human tragedy behind the dramatic tale. The Prophetess of EnDor is not a witch, as she is described in most modern literary and musical versions of the biblical scene, but a priestess, full of dignity and human insight. When Saul comes to her hiding place, he is still the mighty king, conscious of his authority and commanding power. But after hearing Samuel the Prophet pronounce the dire fate that is in store for him, Saul breaks down and becomes miserable and helpless. The Prophetess of EnDor then shows her warm, almost motherly, understanding. She prepares a meal for him and does not permit him to proceed on his way toward the inevitable before he has rested and gathered new strength. Her charity is in stark contrast to the severity shown by Samuel imparting to Saul the voice of the Lord whose commands the King has not followed.

Tal's next operatic work was the short opera *Amnon and Tamar* (book by Recha Freier), based on the tragic relations between King David's son and his stepsister; this work was completed in May 1958 and in dramatic style and expression is related to the earlier operatic composition.

Tal's First Symphony was written in Jerusalem in 1952 and first performed under the baton of Heinz Freudenthal in various European countries in 1956; the first performance in Israel took place in an Israel Philharmonic subscription concert in February 1957, with the same conductor. The Second Symphony followed the First after eight years; composed in 1960 it was premièred by the Jerusalem Radio Symphony Orchestra, Shalom Ronly-Riklis conducting, and thereafter played by many orchestras all over the world. Like the First Symphony, it is a one-movement symphony in which the musical material is presented and developed in pregnantly concise form. The very colorful orchestration contributes to making this work one of the most interesting, effective, and successful Israeli contributions to the contemporary symphonic repertoire.

At the International Festival for Contemporary Music in Haifa 1954, Tal's Concerto for Viola and Orchestra was accorded the South African Prize; this concerto takes its special character from the use of motives drawn from traditional Persian-Jewish tunes. Tal returned to the viola in 1960 when he wrote a Sonata for Viola and Piano.

Josef Tal's later concerted works are obviously influenced by electronic sounds; some of them even incorporate electronic music in their scores—such as Concerto No. 4 (1962), Concerto No. 5 (1964), and Concerto No. 6 (1970), all for piano and electronic tape, and Concerto for Harpsichord and Electronic Tape (1964).

Tal's four large-scale musical dramatic works are the oratorio *The Death of Moses* (1967) and the operas *Ashmeda'i* (1970), *Massada 967* (1972), and *The Experiment* (1975)—alternatively called in English *The Temptation*. *The Death of Moses* was composed to a text of Yehuda Ya'ari for solo voices, choir, orchestra, and magnetic tape. *Ashmeda'i*, *Massada 967*, and *The Experiment* have libretti by Israel Eliraz; *Ashmeda'i* and *The Experiment* are full-scale operas in which electronic sounds play some illustrative roles. In *Massada 967* narration and singing are accompanied only by electronically produced music.

Ashmeda'i, premièred by the Hamburg State Opera in 1971 with Leopold Lindtberg directing and Gary Bertini conducting, and produced by the New York City Opera in 1976, is based on the talmudic legend of the demon who usurps the reign of a kingdom and as dictator becomes the personification of evil. *Massada 967* recreates the tragic events of the year 73 C.E. when the Romans captured the last stronghold defended by Jewish heroes, who finally preferred taking their own lives to captivity. History proved, however, that the Jewish spirit survived when nothing remained of the Roman Empire.

For *The Experiment*, commissioned and premièred by the Bavarian State Opera in 1976 with Götz Friedrich directing and Gary Bertini conducting, Israel Eliraz wrote a symbolical story around a group of people who leave their city in search of new ideals and in the mountains find a man who has never encountered human civilization but soon grasps the blessings of knowledge, money, love, and power; he returns to the city with the group and as elected leader becomes a ruthless dictator who drives his people to madness—those of the group who remained alive leave the city again on a new search of a better world.

In the three operas Tal's music makes a much less dramatic impact than in the earlier short operatic works, for the music is mostly illustrative, simply accompanying events on the stage, where the action is also only symbolical for the underlying idea—and that must be why some of the audience and many critics praised the dramas above the music. In his style Tal is here much more indebted to musical tradition and convention than in the vocal and instrumental compositions of his late creative period. For the New Israeli Opera's first season at the newly built opera house in Tel Aviv (inaugurated 1994), Tal was commissioned to write a new opera; he wrote his probably dramatically and musically strongest opera, *Josef*, on a Kafka-esque libretto by Israel Eliraz. It was premièred in July 1995.

Vocal works in a chamber-music style are Tal's cycle of songs on verses by Heinrich Heine (a collage, 1971) for voice and four instruments; *Else*, written in memory of the poetess Else Lasker-Schüler on a text by Israel Eliraz (1975) set for voice, speaker, and instruments; and *The Garden*, a chamber opera in seven scenes (Israel Eliraz, 1987). The opera *Der Turm* (The Tower) was composed in 1983 on a libretto by Hans Keller. In 1987 Tal wrote another dramatic scene, for voice and soprano, *The Hand*, to a text by Eliraz. By 1995 Tal had composed six symphonies and an additional number of works for solo instruments and chamber orchestra or chamber ensembles.

If Josef Tal may well be described as Israel's most intellectual, most searching composer—to which his many composition students and the listeners to his lectures can attest—then Mordecai Seter, the fifth influential early composer and six years younger than Tal, is the most introverted—an almost ascetic thinker and composer. Mordecai Seter (born at Novorsijk, Russia, in 1916; his original name was Starominsky) came to Tel Aviv with his parents in 1926, and studied piano and composition in Paris 1932–37. He wrote some of the most interesting works produced by Israeli composers. His first composition to draw attention to his unusual style of writing was the *Cantata for the Sabbat* for solos, chorus, and string orchestra, written to psalm texts and passages from the Song of Songs. The impressive cantata is based on modal counterpoint throughout but the effect is not archaic at all, since Plain Chant and synagogue music were derived from a common source, and the composer reaches at times a most personal style. The same composer's *Folk-Chorus Suite* is not quite so original and deeply felt as the earlier work, but it contains many novel choral effects and an authentic Hebrew touch; it is in three movements, using traditional texts of popular character.

After composing a series of *Motets* in which he further developed a style combining ancient liturgical and modal elements, Seter became interested in instrumental music and wrote a few compositions for various combinations of stringed instruments, among which a Sonata for Two Violins (1952) and a Sonata for Violin alone (1953) seem to be the outstanding works. *A due e a tre* is a series of duos and trios for violins in a rather dry instructional style. A composition that has been performed in various instrumental guises is the *Ricercar* written in 1956 for three solo string players and string ensemble, also reduced in instrumentation for a string quartet.

The director of the Inbal Dance Theater, Sarah Levy-Tana'i, awakened Seter's interest in the traditions of Yemenite rites, dances, and music. His ballet music based on Yemenite folklore written for the Inbal Dance Theater's production *Midnight Vigil* seems to be the important turning-point in the development of Seter's musical style. His Yemenite rhapsody (1959) entitled *Midnight Vigil* and the large-scale oratorio *Tikkun Chatzot* (Hebrew for "Midnight Vigil") of 1961, partly based on the earlier work and written on a text by Mordecai Tabib, strive to unite Near Eastern liturgical and folkloristic elements with contemporary western styles of expression. The oratorio's radio version produced by the Jerusalem Broadcasting Service earned the producers the coveted Prix Italia 1962.

In the 1960s Seter composed two scores for choreographic productions by Martha Graham: *Judith* (1962) and *Part Real—Part Dream* (1964). A Chaconne for Orchestra is based on the music for *Judith*, a "Fantasy" on the music for the latter ballet. Seter's most ambitious work after *Midnight Vigil* is the symphony *Jerusalem* for choir, brass instruments, and strings, composed between 1966 and 1968 and first performed at the Israel Festival in August 1976; the three movements of the large-scale work are based on biblical texts from the Book of Lamentations, the Psalms, and Isaiah.

Among Seter's later-period compositions are Variations for Orchestra (1959), chamber music works for various combinations (*Monodrama* for clarinet and piano, 1970; *Epigrams* for flute and violoncello, 1970; Quartet for Flute, Clarinet, Violoncello, and Piano, 1971; *Janus* for piano, 1972; Capricci for Piano,1973) and *Expressivo* for thirteen stringed instruments (1971). In these compositions Seter experiments with modal scales and motifs of individual character. The modal scales invented for such compositions may contain any number of notes—up to twelve-note scales—but Seter does not necessarily develop a musical work out of such scales as other composers do with twelve-note rows.

Mordecai Seter was doubtlessly one of the most interesting composers of his generation in Israel; he seems most original in his vocal compositions and especially his treatment of cantillation in liturgically inspired works, yet less convincing in some of the purely orchestral scores. He died in 1994.

SOMEHOW REMOTE from the mainstream of Israeli music and its composers' search for *couleur locale* are two composers of German-Jewish descent who wrote some important musical works but cannot be said to have wielded much influence on younger generations: Erich-Walter Sternberg and Hanoch (Heinrich) Jacoby.

Sternberg (1891–1974) was a well-known figure in contemporary German music before settling in Israel, and his independent style changed lit-

tle, if at all, in his years in the National Home. Jewish subjects interested
Sternberg long before he decided to settle in Palestine. In his First String
Quartet he introduced a Sh'ma Yisrael prayer tune, while eastern Jewish
folktunes are used in the First as well as the Second String Quartet. In Israel, Sternberg turned especially to biblical compositions. His most important symphonic work is called *The Twelve Tribes of Israel* (1942), which
is a set of variations on an original theme. Each of the biblical tribes is characterized by one variation of the basic theme which represents the common
root and the common belief of the Israelite tribes. The final variation, dedicated to Benjamin, the chosen tribe, described in Genesis 40:27 as "the
ravenous wolf," takes the form of a mighty quadruple fugue to crown an
impressive and finely conceived work. Of similar stature is the string orchestra suite *Joseph and His Brethren* (1939) in which various episodes from
the Bible stories are welded into a harmonious musical whole.

Example 35. Opening of the First String Quartet by Erich-Walter Sternberg (1924).
(Copyright Israeli Music Publications, Ltd.)

Sternberg's earlier orchestral works included a suite from the children's
opera *Dr. Doolittle* (1932), a comedy overture (1933, revised 1943), and
a suite from his music to Habimah's production of Shalom Aleichem's popular comedy *Amha* (1935)—humorous episodes from life in a small eastern
European community. After the completion of his *Twelve Tribes of Israel*,
Sternberg began to turn back to his earlier scores in rather a strange way, re-
vising many and using material from others for new compositions. In his
symphonic poem *Hearken, O Israel* (1947) he fell back upon an idea that
had already occupied him in his first quartet written more than 20 years before. He employed in it the Sh'ma Yisrael prayer tune in a nineteenth century German setting and built a symphonic composition in rondo form

Erich-Walter Sternberg.

around it; the music sounds like an echo from times long gone by. Later orchestral works by Sternberg include *Contrapuntal Studies* for large orchestra and *Little Suite* for small orchestra.

Sternberg's vocal compositions include a set of songs with small instrumental ensemble, on texts of the poetess Elisheva; Peasants' Songs for Chorus and Piano; *The Raven* (Edgar Allan Poe) for baritone and orchestra; and a song cycle for soprano and orchestra on poems by Elsa Lasker-Schüler, *My People*. His chamber music includes two string quartets (1924, 1926): the one is built on the eastern Jewish tune "Bai a Teich, woss sie ist tief un breit" and uses, as a short episode, the Sh'ma Yisrael in the second and third movements; and the other quotes in its second movement the popular Jewish song "Trag Dein Peckele, Yudele." Other chamber works are Trio for Piano, Violin, and Violoncello (1941) in four movements; a Quintet for Wind Instruments (1942); and a Quodlibet for Strings (1936), in which the composer contrapuntally treats three Palestinian folksongs and the Hanuka hymn "Maoz Tzur." *The Story of Goliath and David* for baritone and eleven instruments is based on a rather humorous treatment of the biblical story by Matthias Claudius. Popular among pianists are the well-written Toccata, Capriccio, and Allegro for Piano.

Praise Ye ("Yishtabach") is among the most important choral works written by Israeli composers. It is based on hymns by Yehuda Halevy and set for baritone and mixed chorus. Among Sternbergs' later works are the oratorio *Die Wiederauferstehung Israels* for baritone solo, chorus, and orchestra (1959), not performed during the composer's lifetime, and the symphonic work *Die Arche Noah,* which the Jerusalem Symphony Orchestra played in 1961.

HANOCH (HEINRICH) JACOBY (1909–91) was a pupil of Hindemith in Germany and like his teacher was also a violist. He settled in Jerusalem in 1934 and taught at the Conservatoire, later the Academy of Music, till he joined The Israel Philharmonic Orchestra in 1958. His earlier works are driven by the same motoric rhythm and playful polyphony which characterizes Hindemith's works of the 1920s and early 1930s, while Jacoby was also influenced by the romanticism that later crept into the music of the erstwhile "anti-romantic" German composer. A decisive change in Jacoby's style came in the years of the Israeli war, when the composer began to write simple songs and easy pieces for orchestra. Jacoby composed a Concertino for Viola and Orchestra (1939) and a Concerto for Violin and Orchestra (1942), both of which are somewhat dry and impersonal in style though they contain some fine music.

An important work is his First Symphony Op. 17 (1944) in four movements based on identical thematic material. In the Second Symphony (1951) the composer also based all movements on identical musical material. The Third Symphony (1960) is somewhat freer in conception and elaboration. The Sinfonietta (1960) contains the four traditional contrasting movements of a symphony in concise form within a single movement. Another symphonic work of note is Jacoby's *Symphonic Prologue* (1948), a short orchestral piece opened by woodwind and horns in a calm mood; the characteristic rhythm of the opening theme recurs throughout the work.

King David's Lyre, written for small orchestra (1948) and also available in the composer's own versions for violin and piano and for viola and piano, is a variation work based on an ancient talmudic legend retold by Joheved Dostrovsky. Above David's couch near the open window hung his lyre. At midnight the breeze would blow from the north, and the strings of the lyre would softly begin to play under his spoken psalms. The melodies emerging from his wondrous instrument are never to be forgotten—echoing down through the ages in manifold shapes and forms. In the beginning it was a shepherd's tune, the music of the royal shepherd himself, and then it became a song of war. Later it turned into the mourning song of the exiles on the waters of Babylon. It became the lullaby sung by the Hebrew mother praying for the Messiah to come and redeem his people; then a Hasidic dance and song which stirred the pious to ecstasy and happiness in the Lord. With the return to Zion of the first Bilu settlers the tune becomes a fervent call; it echoes in the pioneers' song of work and building. When the independent State of Israel is founded, the melody of King David's lyre is at last allowed to return to the city of David as a proud song of victory. Jacoby's work takes the form of theme and variations, each variation characterizing one of the stages in the history of Israel and of the royal tune. Jacoby's main subject fits the words of God's promise to Jacob (Genesis 28:15) "And behold, I am with thee and will keep thee in all places whither thou goest, and will bring thee again into this land," while the mourning song (Variation 8) is based on the words of the Psalm 137 (By the Rivers of Babylon), and the Hassidic dance (Variation 5) can be sung to a popular song from eastern Europe.

Capriccio Israélien (1951) is a light symphonic work influenced by but composed independently of Israeli folklore. Among Jacoby's chamber works are two string quartets (1937, 1938), songs for contralto with viola solo, and the Variations and Finale for Piano, Violin, Cello (1942), from which latter work Jacoby derived the material for his First Symphony. *Seven Miniatures* for piano were also orchestrated (1945). A Canzona for Harp was composed for Israel's first International Harp Contest in 1961. His Wind Quintet (1946) is a fine work, the three movements of which combine romantic melodiousness with strict contrapuntal character.

Among the later works were *Partita Israeliana* for string orchestra (1959), *Serio-Giocoso* for symphony orchestra (1964), and *Partita concer-*

tante written for the Israel Philharmonic. *Popular Suite* and *Little Suite* are unpretentious, easy-going compositions for small orchestra.

A VERY IMPORTANT EPISODE in the musical life of Jerusalem was the all-too-short period which the great composer and teacher Stefan Wolpe spent in the city. Stefan Wolpe was born in Berlin in 1902 and came to Palestine in 1933. He had absolved studies with Paul Juon, Franz Schreker, and Anton Webern and had achieved a highly personal style of composition. Hebrew poetry exerted a great influence on him and he was much attracted also by traditional eastern folklore. In 1929 he had written a cantata *The Passion of Man* for singers, dancers, chorus, and orchestra. In Jerusalem 1936 he composed starkly expressive *Twelve Palestinian Songs*; these were followed in 1939 by an oratorio *Israel and His Land*; in New York he wrote a choreographic score *The Man from Midian* (1942).

In Jerusalem, Wolpe had assembled around him a number of talented young musicians and encouraged performance of their works; however, he found little understanding with the majority of the established music pedagogues and he left Jerusalem, to the regret of the more progressive forces in music, only five years after his arrival. He settled in the United States in 1938 and died in New York in 1972.

Among his pupils in Jerusalem were Herbert Brün, Haim Alexander, Peter Jona Korn, Zvi Kaplan, Wolf Rosenberg and Werner Fabian Süssmann, all of them in their early twenties. Although some of them left the country not long after their master, emigrating to the United States or to central Europe, none of them followed the philosophy of composition of Wolpe himself.

Zvi Kaplan, born in Berlin in 1916, came to Palestine in 1935 and became a serious and successful music teacher and composer of charming songs for children in Jerusalem. Peter Jona Korn, born in Berlin in 1922, lived from 1936 to 1939 in Jerusalem and emigrated to Los Angeles in 1939. He returned to West Germany after World War II and became director of Munich's Richard Strauss Conservatoire, but he turned against all his teacher's musical beliefs and what they stood for, and in his own works and his aggressive writings sides openly and dangerously with the reactionary forces of past and present. His own music, post-romantic and epigonal though it is, is the work of a musical craftsman and not all devoid of charm. Wolf Rosenberg, born at Dresden 1915, came to Jerusalem in the 1930s, where he studied with Stefan Wolpe. He was a teacher at the Sidney-Seal Conservatoire 1942–44 and a private teacher in Jerusalem until 1950, when he went to Munich as an independent writer and composer. Some of his theoretical and analytical essays have received attention, but few of his musical works have become widely known—among them are compositions for chamber music combinations and electronic compositions. Like Peter Jona Korn's works, Wolf Rosenberg's music no longer had a connection with Israel.

A strange case is that of Werner Fabian Süssmann, who was born in Berlin in 1910 and had lived in Jerusalem since the 1930s. He was among the most serious and most interesting young composers of the Wolpe School and had remained in Jerusalem, but after his first few chamber music compositions no other works are known. He later joined the Jerusalem Police Band and died in 1972.

Haim Alexander and Herbert Brün remain the only musicians of the Wolpe circle who made careers as composers—Alexander in Jerusalem and Herbert Brün first in Israel and later in the United States.

Haim Alexander, a pianist, pedagogue, and composer, was born in Berlin in 1915 and studied at the Stern Conservatoire there before settling in Jerusalem in 1936, where he finished his studies at the (then) Palestine Conservatoire and became a teacher at the Rubin Academy of Music. Alexander belonged to the original group of Stefan Wolpe's pupils, though Wolpe's influence is felt little in his early works; most of them are distinguished by an easy flow and are of an immediate appeal. Though his musical outlook and style changed considerably in the 1960s after a period of study with Wolfgang Fortner at Freiburg/Breisgau and his meetings with avant-gardist composers at the International Vacation Courses for Contemporary Music of Darmstadt, the *Six Israeli Dances*, composed in 1951, remains his best-known and most frequently performed work. The six movements of this charming suite, entitled "Pastoral," "Shepherds' Round," "Spring Dance," "Farmers' Dance," "Reapers' Dance," and "Dance of the Sabras," exist in versions for piano, for piano duet (four hands, one piano; four hands, two pianos), and for orchestra. Other early works of Alexander are a suite for orchestra, quartet for two flutes, cello, and piano, and songs. His first compositions in a new vein were *Sonata Brevis* for two pianos (1960) and *Sound Figures* for piano in variation form. Here Haim Alexander unites a musical organization based on a twelve-note row with caesuras of a quasi-harmonic effect. Similar in conception and style are *Four Quatrains* for voice and chamber ensemble based on poems of Omar Khayyam 1963). In his later compositions, Alexander expresses himself best in the concise, smaller forms.

Herbert Brün, born in Berlin in 1918, entered Stefan Wolpe's circle of pupils in Jerusalem in 1936 and was much influenced by the independent thinking and original style of the elder composer. Long-time interest in the dance gave Brün's music its singular freshness of attack and rhythm which in his works is coupled with clear-cut formal design and concise expression. Among his best early works is a Concertino for Orchestra (1947) in three movements. A forceful theme—based on a twelve-note row—is sounded from the beginning of the work by the strings and continued and answered by the woodwind section; theme and elaboration are marked by strong and characteristic rhythms. A sort of second theme comes up in the oboe and trumpet and is later developed in combination with the main subject. As second movement an Andante con moto follows, built on instrumental contrasts. The theme is first presented in three-part writing by flute, oboe, and bassoon and then taken up by various other instruments; the entire movement is scored in chamber music style. The Finale is opened by an energetic first subject characterized by wide melodic leaps and played by oboe and trumpet; after a short treatment of the theme, the middle section of the movement concentrates on polyphonic play in varying dynamic degrees and instrumental density. Strong dynamic contrasts dominate the development of this Finale, till a last forceful restatement of the main subject by an unaccompanied trumpet ushers in a very short stretta leading to the conclusion of the interesting and original work. Another orchestral work of this composer is the *Dedication Overture* (1949) commissioned by Leonard Bernstein for the dinner given in 1949 at the Waldorf-Astoria Hotel in honor of Israel's first president, Dr. Chaim Weizmann. This short overture is made up of a gay, freshly celebrating theme and an elegiac section in the mood of a funeral march, the latter written in memory of the tragic history of world Jewry before the State of Israel became a reality. Among Brün's early chamber music works are a Sonatina for Violin (1948), a Sonatina for Viola (1950), a Sonatina for Flute (1949), and a *Poem* for low voice and string quartet (1949) to words by Natan Alterman. He has also written *Five Piano Pieces*, music for ballets, dance movements for piano, and songs.

In 1953 Brün composed his First String Quartet; the three-movement work is based on a series of twelve notes out of which two subjects are formed for each movement. The work was performed at the World Music Festival of the International Society for Contemporary Music, Baden-Baden in 1955. At the same society's 1958 Strassburg Festival, Brün's Second String Quartet attracted much attention; it derives its form and character from the permutation of rows of motives and of time durations. Its single movement consists of eight sections, each giving predominance to a different component of music, varying from melodic design to serial structure. As the last section is almost identical with the first, it reminds one of the traditional form of theme–variation–theme. The work was completed in March 1957 during the composer's stay in West Germany, where he wrote theater music for Fritz Kortner's stage productions and studied electronic music. Another, strongly individual, work is the Piano Sonata in which piano virtuoso and strict thematic construction are successfully welded.

After several study trips to West Germany and the United States, Brün finally settled in the United States and produced a number of electronic works, while also studying the possibilities of computer-produced music.

A PROLIFIC ISRAELI COMPOSER of the elder generation who is difficult to place in the frame of a survey of trends and styles in the growth of Israeli music is Menahem Avidom. During a long life and musical career, he experienced the influences of many-sided developments in European, Israeli-Mediterranean, and western avant-garde musical techniques and styles and adopted them to his personal style of musical expression. Menahem Avidom was born in 1908 at Stanislawow, Poland. His original name was Mendel Mahler-Kalkstein. He came to Palestine for the first time in 1925, lived and studied in Paris and Egypt, and settled permanently in Tel Aviv in

Menahem Avidom.

1935, where he served various public bodies till becoming director-general of Israel's Performing Rights Society, Acum, in 1955. He wrote his earlier works under the influence of the lucid style of modern French music, but turned to Eastern-Mediterraneanism in his early Palestinian compositions. Avidom believed that all music must be within easy reach of the people—easy to perform and to hear. In 1945 he wrote a five-movement symphony, which he called *Folk Symphony* to indicate that it might be performed by any kind of orchestra and for any sort of audience.

In a similar vein he wrote a Concertino for Strings and Flute (1944) in three movements, and *Music for Strings* (1950) which can be played by a string quartet or by string orchestra and contains a Fantasia in slow tempo, a Divertimento (Allegro), an Andante ostinato, and a "Dance" Finale. In the field of chamber music, the composer tried to give expression to Near Eastern elements in a String Quartet (1945), a work using classical forms in all of its four movements, and in *Yemenite Songs* for strings and voice. In an easy style are also two Sonatinas for Piano. Original early chamber works are Avidom's Concertino for Violin and Piano (1950–51) and Concertino for Cello and Piano (1950).

Avidom's first opera, *Alexandra the Hasmonean*, was written to a libretto by Aharon Ashman. The subject of the opera is the heroic struggle of the Hasmoneans against the tyranny of Herod. The choral writing for the mass scenes is musically expressive, and the "Bacchanale" in the Third Act is very effective. The opera was produced by the Israel Opera, Georg Singer conducting, in 1959 and revived in 1976.

A very ambitious symphonic work is Avidom's Second Symphony, the *David Symphony*, written between January 1947 and December 1948. Though this composition lacks the substantial depth of a real symphonic creation, it nevertheless has a charm of its own; in fact, it is just another *Folk Symphony*. As one of the works created in the Holy Land under the influence of the country's great historic past and message, this work shows that the experience of the Israeli composer creating in the newly built land of yore is still too fresh and dynamic to enable him to do full justice to the greatness of the biblical themes. This *David Symphony* is not a biographical or descriptive symphony; it is not even concerned with David the King. The composer was primarily interested in the human progress of David from boyhood to kingship, and the four movements of what would better be described as a symphonic suite mark four decisive stages in David's psychological development. The dedication of the work "To the Brave and Clever in Israel" clearly shows in which light the contemporary composer saw his ancient hero. The listener is left with the impression that he has heard a popular version of a great and moving story—"digested" for the people and the children. Serge Koussevitzky chose this work for the Israel Philharmonic's U.S. tour in 1951. The first performance had taken place a year before in Vienna with the Wiener Symphoniker conducted by Georg Singer.

Avidom's *Mediterranean Sinfonietta* (1951) is a fresh and lightly scored work. His Symphony No. 4, composed in 1955, has traits of a light symphonic suite. It opens with a movement based on two contrasting sections—one slow and lyrical, the other fast and lively, both using identical thematic material. Next comes a Scherzo movement on hora-rhythms. The third movement resembles the first with its contrasting slow and fast sections. The Finale is in rondo form and makes use of a debka dance tune of the Druses; the tune is heard in its entirety only toward the conclusion of the work, after the composer has built it up out of its motives in gradually increasing intensity from repeat to repeat. This symphony had its première at Sofia, Bulgaria, under the baton of Georg Singer in 1956.

The Fifth Symphony, completed in the spring of 1957, is entitled *The Song of Eilat* and takes the form of a symphonic song cycle, its movements corresponding to the Allegro, Adagio, Scherzo, and Finale of a four-movement symphony. Four poems by the poetess Ora Attaria are sung by a low voice, with frequent orchestral interludes in which the symphonic material is elaborated. In I. M. Lask's English version the movements are entitled "The first who dared," "Eilat," "With Petra lying yonder," and "A prayer and hymn for Eilat." Each poem is devoted to another aspect of Eilat on the shores of the Red Sea Gulf—its awakening to new life, its singular scenery, and its biblical and historical associations. This symphonic work, which is among the composer's most mature and serious compositions, is musically based on a single motive, consisting of two syncopated notes and recurring in ever-changing contexts. Avidom's Sixth Symphony, written 1958, is composed in the same concentrated and tightly constructed way as the *Song of Eilat*, but otherwise it takes up again the lighter vein of the preceding symphonies. Quite an original work is Avidom's *Suite 1962 on the Name of B. A. C. H.*—scored for a small orchestra of single woodwinds, piano, vibraphone, xylophone, gong, and strings.

The Seventh Symphony, composed in 1961 for the 25th anniversary of the Israel Philharmonic Orchestra, is entitled *The Philharmonic* and was played by that orchestra under Paul Klecki that year. The *Festival Symphony* (No. 8) was written for the 1966 Israel Festival. In these works Avidom attempted a synthesis of stricter structural organization and logical musical development without abandoning his ideals of a lurid style. The same is true of his Symphony No. 9, *Symphonie Variée* for chamber orchestra (1968), based on a twelve-note theme arrived at by three transposed statements of a four-note motif based on letters contained in the composer's name. In 1981 Avidom completed his Tenth Symphony, *Sinfonia Brevis*, for symphony orchestra. The composer described the work as "a cyclic composition, based on one basic dodecaphonic theme that shapes all of its four movements": Passacaglia, Adagio, Scherzo (Quodlibet) with two trios, Finale.

Avidom uses twelve-note series in quite a number of his later compositions, but usually assumes a freedom of variation and elaboration with his twelve-note themes. He is most consistent in the working-out of a dodecaphonic theme in his *Enigma* for wind quintet, percussion, and piano written in 1962; here he makes use of the traditional ways of transforming and transposing a row of notes in retrograde and mirror forms while reminding the listener of a cantillation motive.

Menahem Avidom enriched Israeli piano literature with some compositions that are especially attractive for young pianists. Early works are *First Pieces for Miriam* and *Little Ballet for Daniela*. In 1972 he wrote *Yemenite Wedding Suite* consisting of an allegretto Prologue; an andante "Come, oh bride"; an allegretto "Come, my beloved"; an allegro giocoso "Rejoicing"; and an epilogue, Allegretto giocoso. Characteristic scenes from the wedding rites and celebrations in the Yemenite-Jewish communities are depicted in a light vein in a style that links Avidom's early French-influenced Mediterranean style with a more advanced chromaticism and lucid contrapuntal writing.

In addition to the large-scale opera *Alexandra*, Avidom composed a few chamber operas. In 1955 he wrote *From Generation to Generation* on a libretto by Leah Goldberg for the Ein Gev Passover Festival. In 1967 there followed *The Swindler* on a two-act satire by Ephraim Kishon. In 1971 he set to music an expressionistic libretto by Daliah Hertz, *The Farewell*. At the Israel Festival 1976 followed the première of *The King's New Clothes* on a text by Michael Ohad. For the Inbal Dance Theater of Sara Levy-Tana'i, Avidom wrote music for a ballet *The Pearl and the Coral*, a score for an ensemble of eleven instrumentalists.

Among the few vocal works of this composer is a cycle of five psalms based on Psalms 48 ("Great is the Lord"), 149 ("Sing unto the Lord a new song"), 127 ("Except the Lord build the house"), 1 ("Blessed is the

Man"), and 148 ("Praise ye the Lord"). This cycle was composed in Jerusalem in the summer of 1976; it is written for low voice with accompaniment of two clarinets and percussion instruments. The composer notes that the instruments may be replaced by other woodwinds of similar register; the percussion is ad libitum.

Menahem Avidom died in 1995. His last completed composition (1994) he named "Peace Cantata."

AMONG THE MOST VERSATILE of the older generation of Israel's composers was Karel Salomon (Salmon, 1897–1974), who was appointed musical director of the broadcasting system of the country at its inauguration in 1936. He was responsible for the music department of the Palestine Broadcasting Service under the British Mandate and continued as musical director of Kol Yisrael after the creation of the State of Israel; in 1958 he became head of Kol Yisrael's transcription service. Coming from Germany in 1933 with the reputation of a well-versed conductor, singer, and composer, Salomon soon gained a foothold in the new country and wrote songs, chamber works, and orchestral compositions to suit its needs. The most original among his early works for orchestra is *Ali Be'er, Variations on a Hebrew Folksong* (1937). Another fine orchestral composition is called *Four Greek Folkdances*. Here, Salomon treats Greek traditional tunes in symphonic form, stressing the Mediterranean relation of these tunes to modern Palestinian folksongs—the final movement is called "Hora Hellenica." The work also exists in the composer's own arrangement for two pianos, four hands. An amusing occasional work is *The Top*—variations on a children's Hanuka song, extant in a version for coloratura soprano or for violin solo and small orchestra. *Nights of Canaan* (1949) is a four-movement symphony of romantic character.

Partita for Strings (1948) opens with an interesting movement ("Jerba") based on tunes found in the collection of the late Dr. Robert Lachmann, who studied the cantillation of the ancient Jewish community of Jerba off the coast of Tunis. An easy piece extant in a piano solo version as well as a trio for violin, viola, and violoncello and a string orchestra instrumentation is *Israel Lives,* bagatelles on a popular theme (1948). Salomon's miniature opera *David and Goliath* to a libretto by Albert Baer has been used for puppet theater and television presentations. It was written in 1930 while the composer was still in Germany.

A work of great practical interest, and also of rare musical charm, is Salomon's *Israeli Youth Symphony* (1950)—a composition that may be performed by small or large instrumental forces and by a great variety of interchangeable instruments; thus, the four-movement symphony is suitable for performance by youth and amateur orchestras. Melodic and rhythmic elements of Oriental traditions combine with instruments of Near Eastern orchestras in the colorful rhapsody *Dahlia*, composed under the impact of the dance festivals in the Hills of Ephraim (1954). Among other compositions, special mention is due to the cantatas *Kibbutz HaGaluyoth* on biblical texts (1952), *Le-Ma'an Yerushalayim*, also on texts from the Bible (1958), and *Chaye'i Adam* (The Life of Man) composed in 1967 on the psalm verse, "The days of our years are threescore years and ten" (Psalm 90:10; the composer himself was 70 when he wrote the cantata) and also using a poem by the medieval Judeo-Spanish poet Abraham ibn Ezra. From music written for a festival at Kibbutz Yavneh comes the *Yavneh Overture* for orchestra, based on motives of biblical cantillation and sacred songs. A symphonic, four-movement piano concerto dates from 1947.

An unusual little work is "Elegy and Dance," which may be performed by soprano with two flutes or two violins, but the soprano part may also be played by an oboe or a violin. The "Elegy" has as its motto the verse "Rachel is weeping for her children" (Jeremiah 31:14), and the motto of the "Dance" is "Go forth in the dances of them that make merry" (Jeremiah 31:3). For high voice and piano or orchestral accompaniment are the very beautiful "Two Songs of Faith" on medieval Hebrew poems. An instrumental piece for an unusual combination is the *Jerusalem Concertino* for carillon and orchestra (composed in 1948).

An important work of great originality is the cantata *Doth Not Wisdom Cry* based on Proverbs 8:1–13. Composed in Jerusalem in 1962 for medium voice and organ and dedicated to a staunch friend of Israel, Prelate D. Dr. Hermann Maas of Heidelberg in Germany, the cantata was premièred in Heidelberg in 1964 by contralto Ursula Mayer-Reinach and organist Bruno Penzien; in 1967 the composer also orchestrated the organ part for string orchestra. Voice and instruments alternate in the performance of the work in real antiphonal style, and only at the climax and conclusion of the composition do voice and organ (or orchestra) join each other. Salomon's opera *Nedarim* (Vows) on a libretto by the composer has as subject an episode in the life of the great poet Yehuda HaLevy. It was completed in 1955 and performed in concert form at Ein Gev, conducted by Georg Singer. Another opera, *Viermal Methusalem* (completed 1966), was written for the medium of television and produced by the Second German TV Network in 1969; the libretto was written by the composer and follows the ancient comedy practices of disguises and confusion. Karel Salomon also composed music for organ, among which is a series of pieces on traditional Hebrew tunes.

ABRAHAM DAUS (1902–74) was a composer of German descent whose early contacts with the countryside, children, and community life in the Land of Israel greatly influenced his music; the rather moderate modernism in his earlier musical style soon gave way to a simplified and rather direct expression. Daus, who was an orchestral and choral conductor in addition to being a versatile composer, settled in Tel Aviv in 1936 but lived and worked in various kibbutzim between 1940 and 1963, teaching as well as writing and conducting. Of his orchestral works, two have justly aroused attention: *Legend and Scherzo* (1950) for string orchestra consisting of a passionate, romantic movement and a wild scherzo with strangely pathetic undertones; and an overture to the cantata *Gate to the Sea* (1937), a symphonic elaboration of themes used in a cantata composed for the third anniversary of Tel Aviv's harbor. Among Daus's early chamber works are two charming suites for recorder duet, a Sonata for Violin and Piano, and an original "Little String Quartet."

A remarkable work is Variations on a Yemenite Song (1940) for flute and piano, which is an original attempt at presenting a tune in various styles; its melodic line hardly changes in the course of the variations but it assumes the character of various dance and song types in the framework of a rondo form; the conclusion is reached with an impressive passacaglia. Each variation is written in a different "folk" style. The composer's most beautiful works are a chamber composition for contralto, viola, and flute: *Songs of Rachel*, the Hebrew poetess of Kinneret, and his *Twelfth Sonnet* for violoncello solo. In the *Songs of Rachel* (1938) Daus set to music five poems of the poetess in congenial musical lyricism; the songs in this cycle are "Barrier," "Shabbat," "Nights of Old," "Evening Mood," and "Are You the End?" In a lighter vein, Daus wrote a little grotesque for piano and pieces for violin and piano.

In the 1950s, travels abroad and contacts with avant-gardist western composers led Daus to study and absorb new musical techniques and means of expression. Although the basically lyrical and expressive foundations of his music remain characteristic features also of his later music, a change of style, melodic expression, structure, and vocal and instrumental writing is evident in all his compositions since 1953. The *Twelfth Sonnet* (1969) and the piano piece *Au Moins* (1972) are the most mature sublimations of the musical lifework of this composer. As a motto for the piano composition, Daus quotes the Israeli poetess Leah Goldberg: "Whoever keeps his eyes wide open, sees at least a hundred wonderful things each day."

The Twelfth Sonnet for violoncello solo was written for the great cellist Siegfried Palm, a friend of long standing of the composer. Daus said at the time of composition that he did not want to write a mere virtuoso piece; thinking of a guiding idea he found formal inspiration in the twelfth of the *Sonnets to Orpheus* by Rainer Maria Rilke, without, however, attempting a musical illustration or interpretation of the poem. The melodic material of the four parts of the composition is related just as the four stanzas of Rilke's poem are dominated by one basic idea. As motto the composer quotes Rilke's opening line:"Blessed be the spirit that may bind us together" ("Heil dem Geist, der uns verbinden mag").

Among other works from the last creative period of Abraham Daus, the most important are the *Five Sonnets after Shakespeare* for soprano, lute, and flute (1963); *Arabesques after Paintings of Paul Klee* (1961) for soprano and chamber ensemble; *Confession of an Angry Man* in the form of a piano sonata (1967); and, on a smaller scale, *Four Dialogues* for violin and violoncello, written in 1957 for friends, a young musical couple in a kibbutz, in four movements—"First Encounter," "Wedding Song," "Problems," "Cradle Song"—all thematically based on a series of twelve notes (four plus eight) played by violin and cello in the opening bars of the first movement. A *Simple String Quartet* completes the list of Daus' late-period compositions.

BERND BERGEL (1909–69) was an Israeli composer who avoided the lime-light and devoted himself to his music in seclusion. Some of his works, which were performed by the Israel Philharmonic Orchestra and the Palestine Broadcasting Service Symphony, point to an original and independent musical mind. Bergel was born in Hohensalza in 1909 and studied at the Berlin Music Academy, attending Arnold Schoenberg's master classes in composition and also working for the experimental broadcasting studio. He settled in Tel Aviv in 1938 and worked in schools, settlements, and various musical institutes. In 1954, he was one of twelve composers commissioned by the Music of the Twentieth Century Festival to compose a work for the international meeting in Rome; the composition was entitled *Prayer of a Man in the Year 2100* and set for solo voice and eleven instruments (including three pianos and organ). Bergel also wrote his own lyrics for this "Prayer," in the spirit of philosophical meditations that had occupied him for a number of years. For orchestra, Bergel wrote a sprightly Divertimento for Small Orchestra and the impressive Variations for Orchestra, which won a prize from the Israel Philharmonic.

The last years of his life he devoted to philosophical studies, which he developed in a 702-page book *Von der Krankheit und Genesung des Seienden oder Der Zweite Sündenfall*, which Bergel explained both as "a draft of a hypothesis and its dialectic development on the metaphysical foundations of what happens in the world as well as confessions of a Jewish musician in the era of earthly atom splitting." The book was printed privately in 250 copies and not made available on sale; the author distributed it to "such personalities whom he wants to read it." The treatise is full of interesting ideas put forward by an author familiar with the important philosophers' theories, but it also has an autobiographical character. Bergel, who was pessimistically inclined, also gives an insight into the creative process, the difficulties of a composer, and his own personal and creative problems.

The great musical work of this last period is an opera *Ja'acob's Traum* (Ja'acob's Dream) composed after the drama of the same name by Richard Beer-Hofmann. From the music of the opera Bergel composed an orchestral suite which attracted much attention in Israel and Europe when conducted by Georg Singer, who also premièred a concert performance of Act One of the opera at a Jerusalem Radio Symphony concert.

CHAPTER FIFTEEN

COMPOSERS IN MODERN ISRAEL

I N THE LATER 1940s a younger generation of composers came to the fore who were less concerned with the problematic sides of Israeli music than were the musicians of the older generations. Some of them had come to Palestine at a young age, where they were then brought up and musically trained. As a consequence they absorbed the conditions and way of living and the spirit of the country in a much more immediate way than the immigrants of former generations—the composers who had come from various cultural spheres, had studied the traditions of the Near East, and become the teachers of the new generations. The composers who first created music that may be recognized as Israeli in certain characteristics and who became influential teachers of the younger Israeli musicians—such as Paul Ben-Haim, Alexander Uriah Boscovich, Oedoen Partos, Mordecai Seter—achieved an East-West synthesis in their mature works, all of them in their own ways. The next generation continued somewhat in their footsteps but then assimilated more closely, even more naturally, contemporary western innovations, the newly developed media of communication and recording, and the fruits of ethnomusical research.

Without belittling the contributions to Israeli music by other composers of their age, it may safely be said that the most successful among the middle generation of composers—those born before the 1930s—are Abel Ehrlich (born 1915), Jacob Gilboa (1920), Ben-Zion Orgad (1926), and Zvi Avni (1927). Of Ben-Zion Orgad may be said that, coming to Palestine at school-boy age and thus growing up with Hebrew as a natural idiom of thinking, he became the first Israeli composer to write vocal as well as instrumental music moulded by the particular word-and-sound melody of Hebrew poetry and prose. Abel Ehrlich, while the oldest of these four composers, has been foremost at applying western avant-garde musical ways, discoveries, and techniques to structures and traditional styles found in the Near East. Jacob Gilboa is the Israeli composer whose inventiveness stands out especially in the writing for voice, in the opalescence of his instrumentation, and in the use of tape-recorded musical material drawn from his scores. Zvi Avni, the youngest of the four, is the most lyrical among them and has most successfully blended electronic sounds—which are also usually of a lyrically expressive quality and not just of the often-encountered noise-effect kind—with the human voice or musical instruments. Abel Ehrlich has also exerted much influence on an ever-growing number of composition students, some of whom have already made mature contributions to Israeli music.

Other composers of note in this generation have contributed music to the early repertoire of Israeli music, among them Moshe Lustig (1922–58), who wrote a Sonata for Harp and French Horn (1943–45), a Quintet for Flute and Strings (1945), a lyrical piano piece (1946), and an orchestral fantasy on two Palestinian tunes, entitled *Kinnereth*; and Daniel Friedlaender (1918–36) to whose memory a retreat for artists—the nucleus of an artists' colony—was dedicated in Zikhron Ya'acov by his mother.

Yehoshua Lakner (born in 1924 in Bratislava) came to Israel in 1941 and had to leave for family reasons in 1965, settling in Zürich. His Sonata for Flute and Piano (1948) is frequently played. In Zürich he composed mainly music for the theater. For the Testimonium he wrote a highly original work entitled *The Dream of Mohammed*, based on an old Muslim legend and weaving into the choral and orchestral texture sounds of a pre-recorded electronic tape. Bible cantillation and muezzin calls combine in this symbolic work, performed in reunited Jerusalem in 1968. Robert Starer, born in Vienna in 1924, likewise emigrated after studies in Jerusalem 1938–43 and settled in New York, completing his studies at the Julliard School of Music; he became a successful composer and composition teacher in a conservative way.

Of the same generation are the composer and pedagogue Yeheskel Braun (born in Breslau 1922 and brought to Palestine at the age of two), Sergiu Natra (a native of Bucharest, 1924, in Israel since 1961), and Ram Da-Oz (born in Berlin 1929; came to Tel Aviv with his parents in 1934). Yeheskel Braun has written music of a predominantly lyrical character. Sergiu Natra's masterwork is *The Song of Deborah* for mezzosoprano and orchestra (1967). Natra is among Israel's prominent teachers of composition, and some of his works have been featured in European and American concerts. Ram Da-Oz, who had joined the Israel Defense Forces while still a student in the War of Independence in 1948, was wounded and lost his eyesight. He gallantly continued his studies nevertheless, made a living as a piano tuner, and wrote some intriguing vocal and instrumental works. Also of this generation of composers is Asher Ben-Yohanan of Greek-Macedonian parentage (born 1929), composition student of Ben-Haim, oboe and piano player, and a prolific, versatile composer of works both in somewhat traditional and modernistic styles.

ABEL EHRLICH was born at Cranz, East Prussia, in 1915, and left Germany after finishing school. He spent five years in Yugoslavia, where he studied at the Zagreb Music Academy, and came to Palestine in 1939, devoting his time to composition and teaching. Frequent study trips to western Europe broadened his musical outlook. Ehrlich is an extremely prolific composer; most of his works are short and concise and, though differing in quality, are always interesting and original. Some of them are written on unusual ancient or modern texts and use unfamiliar combinations of voices and instruments. Near Eastern structures, melismatic melodic lines, and short motivic phrases such as found in Arabic and Hebrew traditional music have influenced the evolution of Ehrlich's style as much as eastern biblical cantillation and the rhythmical complexity of eastern music, while the composer has also thoroughly absorbed modern western musical developments.

One of his earliest characteristic works, and still one of his most arresting and original compositions, is entitled *Bashrav*. This work is among the most interesting pieces written in Israel. The title is taken from Near East-ern folklore and describes a kind of rondo form in which the recapitulations of a basic theme steadily undergo variations. In this work, Ehrlich tries to employ the basic elements of eastern music and musical structure in the frame of a composition written in modern western style and technique. In the development of the melodic theme, the composer follows the principles of the māqām: the melodic line starts from a basic note and develops in ever-changing intervals till it finally returns to its "root." Ehrlich also uses micro-intervals common to Oriental music, such as 1/4- and 3/4-steps. In the rhythmical texture the "breathing rhythm" of monodic chant has in-fluenced the composer, while he regards harmony from the point of view that melody and sound cannot be separated from each other. In re-creating a traditional form of folk-music, Ehrlich does not follow it strictly but only uses it as starting-point; he is especially attracted by the "mosaic" tech-nique dominating the music of the Near East.

Bashrav was composed in 1953 as a piece for unaccompanied violin and premièred by Avram Melamed at the Royal Festival Hall, London, in 1954. In 1956 Ehrlich wrote a version for violin solo and a choir of strings; in 1958 there followed a symphonic *Bashrav*, and in the same year Ehrlich also completed a large-scale *Work for Orchestra* in which he worked along the same principles as in his *Bashrav*.

The catalog of Abel Ehrlich's compositions comprises more than four hundred vocal and instrumental works, the majority of which are of less than ten minutes' duration in performance. A short cantata, originally written for soprano, violin, oboe, and bassoon, "The Writing of Hezekiah," com-posed 1962 and rewritten for soprano and chamber orchestra in 1970, is based on a text from Isaiah 38:10–12, 14–16, and 18–20. The composer says that he was guided in this work by the sound of biblical Hebrew: the consonants found musical equivalents in the varying pitch, dynamics, and tempo of the thematic material, while the vowels inspired the sound-colors of the vocal and instrumental combinations. A choral piece, written in 1964, is set on a text from the Prophet Zechariah 1:4–5: "Be ye not as your fathers, unto whom the former prophets have cried, saying, Thus saith the Lord of hosts: Turn ye, now from your evil ways, and from your evil doings."

A serious composer with a refreshing sense of humor, Ehrlich has written some short musical plays and chamber operas and a series of *Wine Songs* for contralto, flute, violoncello, and piano on texts from the Bible ("King Solomon on Drinking"), the Archipoeta ("Meum est propositum in taverna mori"), and the Greek poet Alkaios. The Hebrew lines of King Solomon are scored for voice, flute, and piano (with an introduction for the instruments alone); the Latin piece is for voice and violoncello solo (this movement begins with a violoncello introduction and is followed by a flute episode); the Greek Finale is scored for voice and the three instruments. The cycle of songs (composed 1971–75) was premièred at a Tel Aviv Museum concert of the Israel Broadcasting Service, with the mezzosoprano Ursula Mayer-Reinach and an instrumental ensemble in 1975. An orchestral work full of humor is Ehrlich's divertimento "The Young and the Old," written for clarinet, double bass, and small orchestra (1975).

JACOB GILBOA was born in Czechoslovakia in 1920 and grew up in Vienna, where he pursued technical studies before getting interested in the study of music. It was only in Israel (he came to Tel Aviv in 1938) that he started seriously studying composition. His teachers were Josef Tal in Jerusalem and Paul Ben-Haim in Tel Aviv. In 1965 he took part in the Cologne courses for new music, where he experienced his first contacts with the musical avant-garde of the time. His earlier musical works had shown conservatively modern writing. After his return to Israel he put his new experiences to individual use. His *Twelve Jerusalem Chagall Windows, Crystals* for five players, *Thistles* for chamber ensemble, and *Pastels* for two pianos were proof of the workings of an original mind; Gilboa followed up these compositions with *From the Dead Sea Scrolls* and *Cedars* for orchestra, the orchestral *Lament of Kalonymos*, various works for chamber ensembles, the worldwide success of his *Fourteen Epigrams for Oscar Wilde*, and *Kathros U-Psanterin* for orchestra. A common trait of all these compositions is Gilboa's talent of exploiting all the possibilities of vocal and instrumental expression in a most colorfully shaded style. It is the attractively original coloring of his scores coupled with a fresh musical outspokenness and sense of humor that has earned Jacob Gilboa much success in Israel and abroad, where he has been chosen by international musical juries several times to represent Israel at international festivals of contemporary music.

Seven Little Insects, miniatures for piano, opens with "Prelude—the Ant"; there follow "Waltz in the Air—the Dragonfly," "Walk in the Moon-light—the Spider," "Sad Interlude—the Grasshopper," "Dialogue with the Lilac Blossoms—the Cockchafer," "Funeral March in the Grass—the Caterpillar," "Thoughts of Spring—the Butterfly." The style of effective and original writing for the piano evident in the "Insect" miniatures is fur-ther developed in two later piano compositions: the *Epigrams for Oscar Wilde* and "Micro-Toccata." The *Epigrams for Oscar Wilde* were first writ-ten for piano solo; each of the pieces had a motto taken from Oscar Wilde's sophisticated witticisms. In 1973 the composer rewrote and rescored the *Fourteen Epigrams for Oscar Wilde* for voice (reciting and singing) with piano and magnetic tape; this version had its world première at the Rejk-yavik, Iceland, Festival of the International Society for Contemporary Music in June 1973 with Ursula Mayer-Reinach as soloist. The magnetic tape is prerecorded; the pianist records his part as written—with sections in which part of the inside of the piano is "prepared" and sections in which the pianist plucks or strikes strings inside—and at the actual performance of the work the "live" pianist accompanies the reciter and singer while the magnetic tape accompanies them at given places being played at double speed. This is a device Jacob Gilboa often uses in his later works: prere-cording the playing of an instrument or of a group of instruments and then letting the tape run at double speed.

Two compositions were written by Gilboa in connection with paintings of his own: *Pastels* (1969) for two pianos, four hands, inspired by the play-ing of Aloys and Alfons Kontarsky (first performed by Regina and Gideon Steiner) and translating into music four pastel drawings he had made; and *Red Sea Impressions* (1976)—"Seastars," "Corals," "Tiger Mussels"—for a small instrumental ensemble accompanied by a prerecorded tape played at double speed, a work for which Jacob Gilboa devised nine colored paintings (three for each of the pieces), which he likes to have screened as slides to ac-company the musical performance. Paintings and music may be described as abstract neo-impressionistic in color, style, and impact.

Most of Jacob Gilboa's compositions follow pictorial or literary mo-tives; however, none of them can be regarded as program music that merely illustrates the subject alluded to in the title or motto of a work. Gilboa entitled a cycle of works *Symphonic Paintings to the Bible*. When he was commissioned by the Israeli Composers' Fund to write a piece for orchestra, he composed *Cedars* as a first work in the projected cycle. He chose five passages from the Bible in which the cedar tree is mentioned and quoted these as sources of inspiration for the five movements of the symphonic composition. *Cedars* was completed in 1972; the first performance in 1973 was played by the Israel Philharmonic Orchestra and conducted by Zubin Mehta.

The second of the Symphonic Paintings to the Bible is entitled *From the Dead Sea Scrolls* and is written for mixed choir, children's choir, two organs, a large symphony orchestra, and magnetic tape. The work had been commissioned by the Northwest German Radio and was first performed at a Hamburg concert and broadcast in January 1972 by the Hamburg Radio Choirs and Orchestra conducted by Ladislav Kupkovic. Part One of the work is entitled "Lines," Part Two "Mosaic." The words intoned by the choirs are taken from texts found in the Dead Sea Scrolls:

> I give thanks unto thee, and for thy doing wonders with me. . . . These things go to my heart and touch me to the bone that I raise a bitter lament and make doleful moan and groan and play my harp in moanful dirge and bitter lamentation till injustice be brought to an end, plague and sickness are no more.

The children's choir sings in psalmodic manner, while the manifold, divided mixed choir develops the psalmody in expanded lines. Many passages are sung on vocalises; a falsetto tenor solo toward the conclusion of the piece is meant to create the feeling of a tune sung by a son of the desert.

An earlier work than the extant Symphonic Paintings to the Bible first made Gilboa's name known in the world: the *Twelve Jerusalem Chagall Windows*—"2 x 12 miniatures" for high mezzo-soprano solo, five female voices, six recorders, harp, four violas, keyboard instruments, and percussion—in fact, kind of a baroque ensemble used in a modern way. The work was composed in 1966 and first performed in Jerusalem in 1968. The composer notes that the stained glass windows created by Marc Chagall for the synagogue of the Hadassah Hospital at Ein Karem near Jerusalem—which represent the twelve sons of the patriarch Jacob, the twelve tribes of Israel—do not attempt to illustrate realistically the biblical texts quoted: the blessings by Jacob of his sons (Genesis 49) and the blessing of the tribes by Moses (Deuteronomy 33). Gilboa interprets Chagall's work as a symbolic transposition in which animal, fish, flowers, and trees stand for human figures. The symbolism of the windows is elusive, Gilboa argues: "Each window may evoke many, even widely diverging, feelings and ideas, and every viewer will thus bring his own personal interpretation as to the poetic meaning of these radiant works of art." Gilboa conceived his composition in a similar symbolist vein. The composer attempts "to interpret in sound the impression created by the colorful evocative art of Chagall as lingering in an individual composer's mind and heart."

Jacob Gilboa likes to think in terms of cycles of works, and as a second musical piece dedicated to "Synagogues" he wrote *The Beth Alpha Mosaic* for voice, chamber ensemble, and pre-recorded tape. This piece was composed in response to a commission given by the Israeli National Council for Culture and Art for the Contemporary Chamber Players of the University of Chicago in celebration of the bicentennial of the United States of America; completed in 1975 it was first performed at the University of Chicago in February 1976 with Ralph Shapley conducting the ensemble. Here the composer conveys an interpretation in sound of the impression created by the unique mosaic floor discovered in the ancient synagogue dating from the 6th century at Beit Alpha in the Valley of Jesreel.

Three other chamber music compositions by Jacob Gilboa have pictorial associations. *Crystals*, eleven miniatures for flute, violin, violoncello, piano, and percussion (1967), is a colorful piece of about six-and-a-half minutes' duration that "imitates" in music the mirror-like symmetry of crystals. *Thistles* is inspired by Genesis 3:14–19. A pictorial inspiration is also evident in *Horizons in Violet and Blue* (1970), nine short sketches for a ballet, for flute and piccolo, clarinet alternating with bass-clarinet, violin, violoncello, percussion, piano, electric organ, celesta, and magnetic tape.

A work for which Shoshana Gilboa, the composer's wife, provided a poem is *Thaw* for a speaking children's chorus and harp; the composition was awarded the Acum Prize in 1968. An original idea inspired Gilboa's *Bedu* for baritone and instrumental ensemble for which the composer used a tune of Bedouin origin. The composition was commissioned for the Israel Festival 1975 and was chosen as the Israeli work for the 1978 International

Society for Contemporary Music Festival in Helsinki. The Bedouin tune is stylized; in the accompanying ensemble of flute, violin, viola, violoncello, and pianoforte, the viola is tuned a quarter-tone above the ordinary pitch of the instrument. The fourteen-minute work may be performed with a magnetic tape recorded during rehearsals at double speed and then added to the ensemble at a given moment.

For the 1974 Testimonium Gilboa wrote *The Lament of Kalonymos,* "a lament without words for symphonic orchestra without solo parts." The motto of the piece is taken from a poem by Kalonymos bar Yehuda, member of a noted family of rabbis, scholars, and poets in the southwestern German city of Mainz between the early tenth and thirteenth centuries. Kalonymos bar Yehuda was witness to the massacre of the Jews of Mainz at the hand of marauding Crusaders in May 1096; he was among the few survivors of this holocaust."Could that my head were water and a fountain of tears my eyes," he wrote, "that I might weep night and day for the dead of my people, young and gray, and weep for the people of the Lord, for the House of Israel who fell by the sword."

To fill a commission by the Yehudi Menuhin Israeli Music Project, Jacob Gilboa completed in 1977 his *Kathros u-Psantherin—Theme and Meditations in Four Moods* for orchestra. Here, Gilboa exploits the basically parallel foundations of Oriental motif models and chant structures on the one hand and early church liturgical chant on the other. The "Theme" is followed by a "Râga Meditation," a "Maqam-Meditation," and meditations on "Gregorian Chant" and "Bible Cantillation." As in the earlier orchestral compositions, the string bodies are divided manifold, while harpsichord, harp, and celesta provide a Near Eastern coloring to the score.

For a CD recording *Hommage à Chagall* (1990), with first recordings by Wladimir Vogel, Theo Brandmüller, and Petr Eben, Gilboa contributed *Chagall sur la Bible*, for mezzosoprano (singing and reciting), brass quartet, and organ. Words of Marc Chagall on the Bible were chosen by the composer for this original work; they are sung and recited in French, English, German, and Hebrew. For the festival week "Encounter Diaspora-Israel" of the West-German Radio Cologne (1990), Gilboa contributed a four-movement work entitled *The Gray Colors of Käthe Kollwitz,* taking inspiration from four drawings of the great German artist (1867–1945) whose art showed a visionary prescience of the horrid times that were to come. The first piece in the cycle, "Selbstbild" (self-portrait), uses the chamber ensemble with a female voice, synthesizer, and magnetic tape to draw a gray picture of the social misery between the two World Wars. "The Poster with the Hungry Children" points to nostalgic remembrances of a lost youth. For the third piece Gilboa quotes a saying by Oscar Wilde: "To live is the rarest thing in the world. Most people exist, that is all." The piece is entitled "Bettelnde" (Beggars) and has an ascetic character. The cycle closes with "Dance Around the Guillotine." Gilboa here draws on the march rhythms from Gustav Mahler's Sixth Symphony, music of a composer who gives the impression that he saw the tragedy of coming revolutions, and also quotes Hector Berlioz's "March to the Guillotine" from *Symphonie Phantastique*. Resignation as well as contemplation and meditation reign at the conclusion of the work with the expression of a glimmer of hope and a quietening atmosphere.

BEN-ZION ORGAD (born at Gelsenkirchen, Germany, in 1926; original name Büschel) came to Palestine with his parents in 1933 and showed interest in music at an early age. He took lessons in violin playing—with, among others, Rudolf Bergmann, then concertmaster of the Palestine Orchestra—and studied composition with Paul Ben-Haim in Tel Aviv and Josef Tal in Jerusalem. From the very beginning he took special interest in the prosody of the Hebrew language and how it could be congenially used to create musical melodic lines; he may be seen as the first Israeli composer to grow up as a child in school with Hebrew as his main language—even if it was not his mother tongue—and thus to approach Hebrew poetry and prose from quite a different level of comprehension than musicians who learned Hebrew at a late stage in their life and career. This is already felt in Orgad's very early compositions such as his *Tagore Songs* for soprano and flute (even though they are based on texts that are not originally Hebrew; he used a translation by Reuben Grossman), a solo instrumental piece Ballad for Violin (1949), and his *Hatzvi Israel* (1949), four movements based on David's elegy over the death of Jonathan (II Samuel 1:19) for baritone and orchestra, a work the composer revised and rewrote in 1958. In 1948 Orgad also first tried his hand at a purely orchestral com-

Ben-Zion Orgad.

position: *Movements*, a suite with descriptive parts styled "Steps in the Night" (prelude), "Awakening" (rondo), and "Prayer in the Rain" (passacaglia). His motet for male voices "O Lord, o Lord" (1947) is a serious and impressive setting of Psalm 8 in the chromatic-modal style that became a hallmark of Ben-Zion Orgad's personal manner of writing. *A Soldier's Prayer* (1948) for baritone and small orchestra, a Fantasy for Violoncello and Piano, and two biblical cantatas *The Story of the Spies* (1952) and *The Vision of Isaiah* (1953) complete the list of Orgad's early compositions.

Between 1949 and 1952 Orgad spent some time in the United States, where he pursued studies at the Berkshire Music Center, Tanglewood, and took lessons with Aaron Copland; later he attended classes at Brandeis University in Waltham, Massachusetts, where he graduated with a Master of Fine Arts in 1961. In Israel he became Inspector of Music Studies in the Ministry of Education and Culture.

Orgad's personal style found most felicitous expression in compositions for solo instruments in which vocal Hebrew prosody and strains of Bible cantillation are transferred to the instrumental medium, and in vocal works, while some of the purely symphonic works carry less conviction. A characteristic solo piece is the *Monologue* for viola alone (composed in 1957), written for and first performed by Oedoen Partos on the occasion of Orgad's receiving the Acum Chamber Music Prize for his local work *Out of the Dust* (1956) for mezzosoprano, flute, and strings after three poems by Erella Ur.

Seven Variations on C for piano was written during Orgad's stay at Brandeis University in 1961 and dedicated to the composer Irving Fine. The world of sound characteristics of Near Eastern instrumental performance reverberates in Orgad's *Taksim* for harp solo (1962); it is later also found in many of the orchestral compositions in which queer combinations of instruments and instrumental groups often dominate the musical structure.

In the 1960s Orgad completed *Music for Orchestra with Horn Solo*, Trio for Strings (1961), *Mismorim* for solo voices and chamber orchestra (completed 1968), a number of works called *Ballade, Songs in the Early Morning* (1968), *The First Night Watch* (1969) for string orchestra, and chamber music.

The ideas Orgad expressed in his piano work *Variations on C* recur in his *Movements Around A* for orchestra (1965) and *Kaleidoscope* for orchestra (1966). Ballads include the compositions "Death Searches for the Wooden Horse Michael" (1968), after a text of Nathan Sach, for two mezzosopranos, two trumpets, two trombones, oboe and bassoon, viola and double bass, and percussion; *Ballade* for orchestra (1971) in three movements, premièred by the Israel Philharmonic Orchestra conducted by Lukas Foss in 1972; *The Story of a Pipe* (1971) for vocal solos, female choir, and chamber orchestra, ten movements after a religiously inspired mystical story by Samuel Josef (Shai) Agnon; and *Story of a Night* for soloists, choir, and orchestra (1972). The earlier orchestral work *Building Heights for the King* (1957), based on stage music Orgad wrote in 1953 for the Habimah-Theater's production of the play *Most Cruel Is the King* by Nissim Aloni, also belongs to this category of works; Jean Martinon conducted the first performance of this piece with the Israel Philharmonic in 1959.

Mismorim (Psalms) contains three movements based on Psalm verses preceded by a prologue and ending with an epilogue. In each of these five sections one soloist dominates, symbolizing a precentor, while the other singers represent the community at prayer.

In *The First Night Watch* (1969) for string orchestra and *Second Night Watch* for full orchestra (1973) Orgad conveys musical impressions of nights in old Jerusalem. In the second of these pieces, as well as in the *Ballad for Orchestra* of 1971, Orgad places some instruments in the concert auditorium. Chamber music of the 1970s includes *Songs without Words* for six instruments (1970) a quintet for wind instruments *Panorama* (1970), and *Two Preludes in an Impressionistic Mood* for piano solo. Two large-scale works deserve special mention: *Suffering for Redemption* and *The Old Decrees*.

The Old Decrees, composed for the 1971 Testimonium, which had as a theme "The Middle Ages," is a kind of "passion oratorio" for soloists, choir, and orchestra based on five documented witness stories about the cruelties committed by crusaders against Jews in the year 1096, as laid down in a Hebrew manuscript preserved in Darmstadt in West Germany. Orgad also used passages from a decree of Pope Urban II in Latin and documents in the Middle–High German language that lives on in today's Yiddish. *Suffering for Redemption* was commissioned for the 1974 Testimonium *"De profundis"* and is a cantata for solo voices and orchestra based on eight poems written by Recha Freier, all expressing hope for the coming of the Messiah; the poetic texts are sung partly in alternation and partly simultaneously interwoven. At the "Encounter Diaspora-Israel" of Cologne Radio in 1990 *The Old Jewish Decrees* was performed in a revised version of 1989.

Other important works of this interesting composer are his cantata *Hymn to the Goddess, Hallel* for symphony orchestra (1979), and *Individ-*

uations for clarinet and chamber orchestra (1981). In a private edition (Tel Aviv, 1989), Ben-Zion Orgad published a 318-page autobiographical/philosophical book entitled *Colmontage—a Partita for Solo Voice.*

ZVI (TZVI) AVNI, born at Saarbrücken in 1927 and living in Tel Aviv since 1933, is the most lyrical among the Israeli composers of his generation. Judging from his vocal compositions he is less concerned with characteristic Hebrew prosody or cantillation models than Ben-Zion Orgad; their musical attractiveness stems from different qualities. He studied composition with such different personalities as Paul Ben-Haim, Mordecai Seter, and Abel Ehrlich in Israel and with Aaron Copland and Lukas Foss at the Berkshire Music Center, Tanglewood, Massachusetts (1962, 1964). His musical outlook and style of composition took a decisive turn after he was introduced into the world of electronic music production at New York's Columbia University, where he studied with Vladimir Ussachevsky. Avni's interest in poetic texts was furthered especially by his Polish-born wife Pnina, a poetess in her own right (who died in 1973), some of whose lyrics and poems he also set to music. Returning from the United States, Avni served as music teacher for several Israeli schools and was for fifteen years director of the Tel Aviv Central Music Library. In the 1970s he became more and more involved in the field of electronic music and established a special electronic music department at the Rubin Music Academy of Jerusalem.

In the works of Avni's early period of composition, the influence of Paul Ben-Haim's Eastern-Mediterraneanism may certainly be discerned. In this period he composed a song cycle for soprano and orchestra, a Wind Quintet (1959), works for piano, choral pieces, a *Prayer* for soprano and orchestra (1961), and a Chaconne for Harp Solo (1962). The best-known of his early works is the string quartet entitled *Summer Strings* (1962). His first electronic production was a vocalise, in which a soprano voice is moulded into the electronic sounds; this work (produced 1964) was recorded by Turnabout–New York with the composer's wife Pnina Avni as vocalist; Avni tried to apply classical sonata form to this electronic composition.

Lyricism pervades Avni's instrumental and vocal compositions; his conception of sound—in free tonal harmony—is as lyrical as his melodic invention. Characteristic orchestral works are his *Meditation on a Drama*

Zvi Avni.

(1966) and *On the Waters of Babylon* (1971). *Meditation on a Drama* is not based on an actual dramatic subject or text; Avni describes the composition as metamorphoses on a theme. It is written for chamber orchestra and scored in inventively changing dynamic and sound shades of color. *On the Waters of Babylon* is based on prayer chants of Babylonian Jews as noted by Abraham Zvi Idelsohn in his *Thesaurus of Hebrew Oriental Melodies*; Avni scored two versions of this work—one for five wind instruments, piano and string orchestra, the other for full symphonic orchestra.

Avni is quite a prolific composer, and his musical output comprises works for many kinds of vocal and instrumental combinations. Some of his compositions were successfully used by ballet companies for new choreography. In these compositions for ballet Avni combines, juxtaposes, and mixes electronic sounds, *musique concrète*, vocal and instrumental music. In *Requiem for Sounds* (1970) Avni's recorded tape contains a mixture of animal cries and percussion sounds.

For the first Testimonium of Recha Freier in 1968, Avni wrote two commissioned pieces: *The Destruction of the Temple of Jerusalem* and *The Heavenly Jerusalem*; the works were premièred at David's Citadel in Jerusalem by the Jerusalem Radio Choir and Orchestra under the direction of Mendi Rodan. *The Destruction of the Temple* is, in the composer's own description, "a narrative piece with dramatic outbursts, moments of crisis, and a lamentation to end. . . ." The words of the choral score are taken from the Apocalypse of Baruch. The text for the second piece, *The Heavenly Jerusalem,* comes from the cabbalist Zohar and is sung in Aramaic. Here, as in the first work, the literary content provides the outline for the musical development; it is based on three motifs:

> A description of the generation of the wilderness who need to cleanse themselves of original sin through grave-digging by day, their self-interment by night, and their resurrection in new bodies every morning; the description of a hidden spring which has its source in the Garden of Eden and then flows to the Temple, on the floor of which it leaves traces of mysterious drawings from the hand of God; a description of 350 columns in the Temple, decorated with all types of brilliant gems . . . between the columns are 2100 lamps and in each of these 2100 candles shine by day and are extinguished by night for the sorrows of Israel.

Both compositions are based on preconceived tone-rows which are used freely; in the first work the orchestra dominates the vocal forces, while in the second work words and choral singing are dominant over the orchestra.

At the time of the 1968 Testimonium, Zvi Avni gave a description in a recorded interview of his own leanings and musical style:

> I don't consider myself to be an avant-gardist. What is most pronounced in my attitude toward music today as compared with the period eight years

ago is that I have thrown off the bonds of definitions as regards form, orchestration, and the whole general conception. I live in a freer world.

Avni admitted that he was especially attracted by contemporary Japanese music and by the works of the Polish composers Witold Lutoslawski and Tadeusz Baird and it may well be said that in his entire *oeuvre* even the most complex compositions of Zvi Avni seem in keeping with the attitude expressed in 1968.

The list of Avni's compositions comprises an *Elegy* for violoncello solo (premièred by Joachim Stutchewsky in 1968), a Woodwind Quintet, *Collage* for voice, flute, percussion, and magnetic tape (1968), *Five Pantomimes* for eight instruments (1968), *Akeda* (Sacrifice) for four chamber groups with narration after a text by Yehuda Amichai (1969), solo songs and choral music, chamber music, and instrumental solos, *De profundis* for string orchestra (1969), *Prayer* for orchestra (after a poem by Pnina Avni; 1973); *Metaphor for a Festive Day* for symphony orchestra (1970); *Programme Music* (as the composer said, not to be taken in the 19th-century sense) for symphony orchestra (1980). In 1982 Avni wrote a concertante work for the zither-like oriental *santur* (of Persian origin) played with mallets like the xylophone, which Avni also proposes as alternate solo instrument; the work is entitled *Mizmor* (Psalm) and the solo is accompanied by full orchestra.

An important later work is *Desert Scenes*, premièred by the Israel Philharmonic Orchestra conducted by Zubin Mehta in 1992. The composer commented on the work on this occasion:

> The symphony *Desert Scenes* has undergone many transformations in the process of its creation. It was conceived after my first encounter with the desert, when I was sent, in the late 1960s, to lecture on music to an army unit in the Sinai Desert. The moment of sunrise on the barren wilderness, the feeling of the infinite and the biblical myths connected with the desert, have become in my conciousness something which had to find its musical expression. . . . In "Awakening" I tried to describe the feeling of wide spaces, the silence, the vibrating inner voices and the ancient echoes aroused in us by the desert. Woodwinds and percussion are the leading instruments in this movement. Some of the rhythmic elements here are based on texts from the book of Exodus. The movement ends with a short epilogue for bass-clarinet, leading directly into the next movement "Communion." Here, a lyric, prayer-like element is apparent, echoing rhythms

and melodic contours of biblical cantillations. In this movement the string instruments are dominant. However, the rhythmic recitative-like elements are also emphasized by the percussion section. These two relatively short movements form together the first section of the work. The third movement, "Dance Festivities," is the second section. At first I planned to concentrate on the sensualism of the Dance of the Golden Calf, but in the process of composing I saw before my eyes the vision of a variety of dances: dances of joy, dances of fury, dances of passion and excitement.

IT IS EVIDENTLY IMPOSSIBLE to offer in a historical survey of living Israeli music a complete account of the creative work of the ever growing number of active Israeli composers (the Israel Composers' League counted more than two hundred members in 1993) and to assess their contributions to Israeli music. In five decades of rise, growth, and development of new music in Israel, many composers—including some who were still young near the turn of the century—made novel contributions to world music and have conquered a place in the "concert of nations." Only time will tell whether the promising talents of rising stature of the 1980s and 1990s fulfill their promise and enter the records of memorable twentieth century Israeli music in times to come.

Among the immigrant composers who were born in pre-statehood times and made notable contributions to music education in Israel and to Israeli music are Mark Kopytman and Joseph Dorfman, who came to Israel around 1970 and were already accomplished musicians in what was then Soviet Russia; Jan Radzynski, who came from Poland; and Leon Schidlowsky and Ruben Seroussi, who came from Latin-American countries. Another important pedagogue and composer, Yizhak Sadai, came from Bulgaria at the age of fourteen and enjoyed his music education in Israel.

Mark Kopytman was born at Kamentez-Podolsky, U.S.S.R., in 1929. After finishing school and music education at the conservatory, he studied both medicine and music at Tchernowzy (Czernowitz) in the Ukraine, graduating from the musical college (piano) in 1950 and from medical school in 1952. After serving as physician in a hospital near Lwow for two years, during which time he also studied composition at the Lwow Academy of Music, he pursued additional music studies in Moscow in 1958 and wrote a doctoral dissertation on polyphony. He taught theory, composition, and twentieth century musical techniques in various Soviet music

Mark Kopytman.

academies till he came to Israel in 1972. Mark Kopytman is quite a prolific composer and in the U.S.S.R. was recipient of many coveted prizes for theoretical and musical works, among them the opera *Kasa Mare* (composed in 1966; won a prize in a competition for opera and ballet, Moscow, 1971). He presented his *Dodecaphonic Graphs* (1973), an attempt at noting dodecaphonic music in a novel, comprehensibly analytical system, to the participants of the First International Schoenberg Congress in Vienna in 1974. When his composition . . . *this is a gate without a wall* . . . was completed and performed in 1975, Kopytman wrote on the general style of his later works that he tries

> to employ as germs of composition the micro-intonations of Jewish folklore, mostly those originating in the Yemen region, the peculiar thematic motifs of which seem best adaptable to my creative purposes. This tendency is also linked with the use of heterophony as practised by the performers of traditional music in the region. . . . My technique of composition can be described as a blending of stability and mobility, between determination and indetermination known as the 'changing technique.' While trying to follow this principle, I limit freedom of transmission of my music by the performers in order to maintain the intended musical struc-

ture in its total and in its separate parts. The performers are at liberty to choose for themselves the single elements of the structural units and produce their own diverse combinations—such as selecting the sequences and the duration of separate notes from a given group of sounds. The other feature, the method of spreading several musical ideas like layers, produces an unimpeded flow of different melodic layers, either attuned to each other or confronting each other in opposition and as a result producing a lively sound pulsation, a distinctly musical sphere which departs from classical tonal harmony.

Kopytman has composed music for various solo instruments: *Lamentation* for flute solo (1973), *For Trombone* (1974), *For Piano I* (1972), *For Piano II* (the same year), *For Percussion* (1975), *For Harpsichord* (1975), *Monodrama* for ballet performance (1976). *Voices* for orchestra with flute and voice solos (1974–75), a Piano Concerto (1972), and *About an Old Tune* for chamber ensemble (1977) are the more ambitious compositions of Kopytman's first years in Israel. *About an Old Tune* was, in the words of the composer, "influenced by the high poetic and musical quality of Yemenite folklore." No actual Yemenite tunes or sections of tunes were used, but the composer tried to "grasp the spirit of the micro-intonations characteristic of the Yemenite melodic structures."

In a series of compositions entitled *Cantus* Mark Kopytman has tried to incorporate elements of Jewish folklore melodic strains, of synagogal cantillation, and of microtonal Near Eastern music. "Cantus I" for three oboes and "Cantus II" for string trio were followed by "Cantus III" for bass clarinet and orchestra (1984) and "Cantus IV," "Dedication," for violin solo (1986). In 1990 the composer wrote "Cantus V," kind of a one-movement concerto for viola and orchestra in which lyrical and dramatic episodes are contrasted with each other in ever-changing moods. The work was premièred by Tabea Zimmermann at the "Encounter Diaspora-Israel" in Cologne in November 1990, Gary Bertini conducting.

Other important works of this interesting composer are *Rotations* for mezzosoprano and orchestra (1979); *Memory* for symphony orchestra with a Yemenite voice (1981); *Life of the World to Come* to a text by A. Abulafia for mezzosoprano, clarinet, and violoncello (1985); *Letters of Creation* for voice and strings (1986), and *Variable Structures* for piano solo (1984).

Joseph Dorfman, born at Odessa in 1940, graduated from the Conservatoire in music history, composition, and piano, and completed his studies at the Gnessin Pedagogical Institute in Moscow 1968–71, having written a doctoral dissertation on aspects of Paul Hindemith's chamber music works. Dorfman settled in Tel Aviv in 1973 and joined the musicological department of Tel Aviv University. After composing for traditional media Dorfman became interested in graphical music notation and the use of magnetic tape. Some of these new works have been performed in Israel. Dorfman has written easy (educational) pieces for the piano, two Piano Sonatas, and a String Quartet. Two important trios are the *Piano Trio in Memoriam Dimitri Schostakovich* (1976) in seven movements—"Symphony," "Memory," "Interlude," "Prayer," "Movement," Capriccio, and "Cantus firmus"—and a Trio for Flute, Violin, and Piano (1977). *Kol Nidrei* for violin solo (1975) is original in content and notation: it is partly noted in conventional notation and partly with graphic signs explained for performing practice by the composer; the work demands from the violinist a few exclamations of text during performance. *Tribes of Israel* (1974) is music for percussion to accompany a showing of slides of the Chagall glass windows in Jerusalem; the graphic score is noted within frames resembling the Chagall window frames and the work may be performed by one percussionist or by two, three, four, or six performers. *Sic et non* (1974) is written for violoncello and piano; *Viribus unitis* is for piano, three tapes, and ring modulator; *Spectres* is a score in colored graphic notation for string instruments (1974); *Ascent* is composed for piano and percussion (1974).

Among Dorfman's works composed in the 1980s may be singled out his opera *The Dragon* to a libretto by Grigori Gerenstein and the composer (1982–83); *A Cantillorio*, written from 1978 to 1983 and revised in 1990 (five soloists, boys' choir, mixed choir, and orchestra); Concertos for Piano (1981), Violin (1984) and Violoncello (1985). Dorfman has also composed a series of vocal works (most with solo instruments), and music based on klezmer tunes and playing style.

A Cantillorio opened a first International Festival of Jewish Art Music at Vilnius, capital of Lithuania, in May 1992, where Dorfman's aim was to show works of Jewish art music of past and present in a town which itself has a venerable Jewish history. Dorfman's own work, based on biblical texts and Jewish poems from many centuries, centered around the salient questions of man's—and the Jews'—existence on the planet earth.

Leon Schidlowsky (born in 1931 in Santiago de Chile; living in Israel since 1969) made a name for himself as a theoretician, composer, and teacher in Chile and Germany before coming to Israel, where he was appointed professor at the Rubin Academy of Music in Tel Aviv. Among the more than a hundred musical compositions of Schidlowsky's pre-Israel and Israeli period of writing are some works of an incomparably stark impact and others in which the pleasure of experimenting seems greater than the artistic depth. Many of his musical works have themes connected with early or recent Jewish history and events. Among them are the four-movement symphonic work in memoriam *Die Kristallnacht* (1961), *Invocation* to remind the world of the victims of Nazism (1964), *Kaddish* for violoncello and orchestra (1967), *Babi Yar* for strings, percussion, and piano (1970), *In eius memoriam* for orchestra in memory of the heroes of Israel's Yom-Kippur-War (1974), *Akiba ben Yoseph* after a text by Recha Freier for solo voices, children's choir, mixed choir, and orchestra (1974), and *Eleven Tombstones* for contralto, brass quintet, percussion, and electronic tape written under the impact of the massacre by anti-Israel Arab terrorists of the eleven members of the Israeli sports delegation at the 1972 Olympic Games of Munich. Most of the works of the late 1970s are written in graphic notation, which makes good-looking pages for the viewer and provides singers and/or players many widely different options for production, but not always with a convincing result for the listener.

Golem for seven voices and magnetic tape (1975) was produced at Testimonium IV in 1976 with a film by Aryeh Mambush and Nina Mayo. An earlier work of note, like *Golem* written in graphic notation, was *Tombstone for Else Lasker-Schüler* for voice and six percussionists (1969). In the years 1982–85 Schidlowsky composed a "pentology," remembering his land of birth and upbringing, Chile and its continent: *Amerindia*, consisting of a Prologue, a piece for narrator and instruments on a text by Cesar Vallejo, a work for wind instruments and percussionists, a scene for narrator and orchestra on words of Pablo Neruda, and another Neruda setting for narrator and orchestra. An *Ode* for female voices, trombone, piano, celesta, harp, harmonium, and strings was written in 1982; in 1984 Schidlowsky composed two choral works for mixed choir and instruments: *Missa in Nomine Bach* and *Laude*—the first on a Latin sacred text, the latter on the words of Psalm 130. Two orchestral works were completed between 1988 and 1990: *Elegy* (1988) and Prelude (1990). Among Schidlowsky's chamber music works is a trio for viola, violoncello, and double bass *In Memoriam Luigi Nono* (1990).

Jan Radzynski, born in Warsaw in 1950, came to Israel in 1969. He studied theory and violoncello performance at the Rubin Academy of Music in Tel Aviv, taking composition lessons with Leon Schidlowsky. In 1975 an early major work of his, *The Third Face*, written after a text of the Polish avant-gardist lyricist, Tadeusz Rózewicz, was performed at a Composers' Workshop concert in Tel Aviv. The composition is scored for an ensemble of two sopranos, two mezzosopranos, flute, violoncello, trumpet, piano, and percussion, with the participation of an actor. An extended Sonata for Violin solo was written in 1984 and a year later Radzynski composed a Divertimento for Clarinet, Violoncello, Percussion, and Piano. For choreographic performance the composer wrote *Homage to Manger*, set to a poem of Itzik Manger for nine players (1979). A Mazurka for Piano (1988) was commissioned by and set as an obligatory piece for the sixth Arthur Rubinstein International Piano Master Competition of 1989.

Radzynski went to the United States to study with Krysztof Penderecki and Jacob Druckman. He graduated from Yale University, which appointed him associate professor for composition. In the U.S. his *David Symphony, Kaddish* for orchestra (dedicated to the victims of the holocaust), and chamber music were performed; the *David Symphony* and *Mizmorim* (Psalms) for violin solo and eight violoncelli were performed in Poland—the symphony was conducted by Penderecki in Kraków. The orchestral work *Time's Other Beat* was premièred at the "Encounter Diaspora-Israel" in Cologne, Germany, in 1990. The title of this one-movement piece is taken from a sonnet "Music" by the Jewish poet Dannie Abse from Wales, in which are combined a series of metaphors and poetic images of music, all related to a central unifying idea. The composer has tried to mirror in his music the dramatic tensions originating from his understanding of the poem.

Jan Radzynski, Mark Kopytman, and Joseph Dorfman were followed in the late 1980s and early 1990s by many eastern European musicians, composers among them, who were able to settle in Israel when the eastern European countries took a more liberal course and became more democratic, thus making emigration from the countries possible after the many decades of oppression, especially of the minorities. The performing musicians joined already existing orchestras in Israel, new orchestral ensembles and chamber music groups were formed, and the composers found the opportunity to present their compositions.

An immigrant from Uruguay, Ruben Seroussi was born in Montevideo in 1959 and has been in Israel since 1974. He studied composition with Sergiu Natra in Tel Aviv, where he graduated from the Rubin Music Academy in 1986. Seroussi is an accomplished guitarist, concertizing in Israel and abroad, so in addition to other works he has composed music for his instrument, both solos and chamber music. He continued to study composition with Jan Radzynski.

Early works of Seroussi that attracted attention were his "Ludi" for two trombones and a Partita for Two Guitars. In 1984 he wrote a cantata for mixed choir and three percussionists based on traditional Hebrew texts. A year later he composed two additional vocal works, *Jacob and Esau*, incidental music to a play by I. Neeman, for voice, oboe, violin, and two percussionists; and *Two Poems by Antonio Machado* for voice with flute and guitar. From Antoine Saint-Exupéry's *The Little Prince* he chose a text for a piece for children's choir, entitled *Echo* (1987). In 1988 Seroussi composed a virtuoso woodwind quintet (Rondo). *Differencias* is written for guitar and chamber orchestra and bears the subtitle "A Still Unanswered Question" (1990). Also written in 1990 is an "Hommage à Luis Bu'nuel" with the title *Ce discret charme,* for clarinet, viola, and piano. At the "Encounter Diaspora-Israel," Cologne 1990, Seroussi's *Canto Al Antiguo Sol,* composed in 1982, was performed. Seroussi was inspired to write this piece, scored for two oboes (tuned a quarter-tone out of pitch), xylomarimba, timpani, harp, and double bass, by documents from the time of the conquest of Mexico and the music of the native Indians. Seroussi tried here to "combine the endless streams of primitive music with the so-called modern structures of western music and to juxtapose contrasting concepts of time with each other in a clearly organized piece."

Seroussi's Nocturne for orchestra, a work juxtaposing romantic-sounding "nocturnal" sounds with somewhat ironic, sarcastic, nightmarish impressions, won third prize in a competition for Israeli composers held by the Israel Philharmonic Orchestra jointly with the Israel Music Institute in 1993. First prize in this competition went to Ari Ben-Shabetai, born in Jerusalem in 1954, a composition student of Mark Kopytman in Jerusalem and of George Crumb and Richard Wernick in Philadelphia. His work was entitled *Sinfonia Chromatica;* "chroma" alludes to Aleksandr Scriabin's color symbolism. Eitan Steinberg, born in Jerusalem in 1955, a student of Mark Kopytman, Franco Donatoni, and Peter Maxwell Davies, received second prize for his *Shanti*. This work was the most Eastern-Mediterranean composition of the four works in the competition. Performed in the semifinal concert but not accorded a prize was the *Desert Symphony* of Benny Nagari, born in Tel Aviv in 1950, composer of concert music and works for the musical theater.

Yizhak Sada'i (original name Sidi, born in Sofia 1935, in Israel since 1949) first attracted attention when two of his compositions were broadcast in the state broadcasting service's "Music of Our Time" series in the winter of 1955 as part of a concert by the Israel Academy of Music, Tel Aviv. Sada'i studied at the Academy with A. U. Boscovich and later continued studies for a short time with Roman Haubenstock-Ramati; his development as a composer was greatly influenced by the work of the dodecaphonists and especially by the music of Alban Berg. He takes great interest in the parallels that exist between modern "serial technique" and traditional Oriental "tone-rows," and his music strives toward a synthesis of Oriental and western elements. His first published work was *Piccola Fantasia* for piano (1956). For Frank Pelleg he composed *Impressions of a Chorale* for harpsichord—a free fantasy on a chorale melody by J. S. Bach. Other early works of this interesting composer are a *Chamber Cantata* for contralto, baritone, flute, clarinet, viola, violoncello, and harp; an *Ecclesiastes* cantata; Chaconne for Solo Violin; Divertimento for Contralto Voice and Three Instruments (on words from "The Song of Songs"); a Serenade for Three Instruments; and *Ricercar sinfonico* for orchestra, written for and performed by Michael Taube and the Ramat-Gan Chamber Orchestra (1957)—a work which the composer later rewrote and revised.

Of decisive influence for Sada'i were his studies at the Paris studios for *musique concrète* and electronic music; he produced several works in these media, and his style of writing for conventional instruments was greatly influenced by them. He also opened a studio for electronic music at the music academy connected with Tel Aviv University. His later compositions include *Interpolation variée* for string quartet and harpsichord; *Nuances* for chamber orchestra with a "mobile" section (premièred at Hilversum on the occasion of Gaudeamus Week in 1966); *Aria da capo* for six instrumentalists and two magnetophones (1966); *Preludes for Jerusalem* for the Testimonium 1968 for voices and instruments; *Anagrama* for orchestra with magnetic tape, first performed by the Israel Chamber Orchestra in 1974. In 1984 Sadai wrote a string quartet, *Anamorphoses; Reprises* (1986) is written for eight instruments. An extraordinary electronic production is Sadai's work *The Interrupted Prayer*, an echo of the Yom Kippur War against Israel (1979). Two compositions written in 1985 are *Canti fermi* for orchestra and synclavier and *Antiphones* for chamber orchestra and synclavier.

Sadai devotes much time to theoretical studies and to teaching. Several of his students have become known as full-fledged composers of note, among them Yossef Mar-Chaim, Uri Sharvit (who is also a musicologist and ethnomusicologist of distinction), Ron Lewy, and Ron Kolton (who has also worked with electronic devices). In 1980 Sadai's important book *Harmony and Its Systemic and Phenomenological Aspects* was published.

Yoram Paporisz was a Polish-born composer whose tragic fate cut short a promising career as a brilliant pianist. He was born in 1944 and came to Israel at thirteen years of age in 1957. He received his musical education at the Rubin Academy of Music in Tel Aviv and graduated as a full-fledged pianist and composer, a student of A. U. Boscovich. He pursued further studies in Italy and with the composer Wolfgang Fortner in Germany. The beginning of a paralyzing disease did not permit him to return to Israel; when multiple sclerosis was diagnosed he was taken to a permanent nursing-home in Freiburg/Breisgau. As long as his eyesight permitted, he used several devices that enabled him to write music. His creative work comprises compositions for many instrumental combinations. His *Florianata* for flute solo was written for and recorded by Aurèle Nicolet. His most important work remains a five-volume collection of piano pieces, entitled *Discoveries at the Piano*—an introduction to historical, modern, European, primitive, and exotic forms and styles in an ascent from very easy pieces for beginners to difficult virtuoso recital works. It encompasses a world of techniques and sounds from strains of African native folklore to Japanese melodic and tonal impressions and experiments with dodecaphonic organization and cluster sounds, introducing the student to Gregorian Plain Chant melodies and to exotically colored twentieth-century styles. It is no wonder that this series has enjoyed such success with piano teachers and students worldwide. Yoram Paporisz died in Freiburg in 1992.

A controversial figure in Israeli music is André Haydu, who, after already leading an apparently adventurous life, arrived in France and then Tunis in the years 1959–61; in 1966 he settled in Israel. He tells that in Hungary, where he was born in 1932, he collected gypsy tunes and was awarded a prize for a gypsy cantata in 1955. In Israel Haydu began to investigate the field of Hassidic music and to teach at various institutes. The music he writes mirrors the world of the religious and folk music he studies; much of it is of an eclectic nature. On the occasion of the performance of his Piano Concerto No. 2 at the Cologne " Encounter Diaspora-Israel," he admitted frankly that he understands the rejection by the musical public of modernism and rather risks "to fall between two stools" in writing a "great romantic concerto," writing "with the heart of a Chopin and the temperament of a Bartók . . . what seems to be already taboo." Haydu has written a number of vocal and instrumental works, some of them with a declared educational aim. *Ludus Pascalis,* written for the 1970 Testimonium, is a kind of Jewish "Passion Play" based on medieval and Mishna sources, and is regarded by many as being in rather bad taste.

A few of the composers born in Israel acquired an international reputation in a comparatively short time, often with a help of study sojourns in European countries or America, where some of them also gained posts as assistant lecturers of composition or were even appointed professors in their fields. New outlooks and horizons benefitted their knowledge of world music and aesthetics; not only was their own music thus enriched but they could also teach a new, still younger generation of Israeli composers.

A work of Noam Sheriff (born in Tel Aviv, 1935), composer and conductor, was approved by the musicians' jury examination for performance at the inauguration of the Israel Philharmonic Orchestra's Fredric R. Mann Auditorium; his *Festival Prelude* was chosen for the opening concert in October 1957 and conducted by Leonard Bernstein. The piece has since been widely performed by orchestras all over the world. The thematic invention in this work was inspired by psalm intonation in the solemn sections that open and close the prelude and by folklore in the lively polyphonic middle section. Melodic and rhythmic freshness and a brilliant orchestration make Sheriff's work a very successful concert piece. Chamber music for oboe and strings, a Sonata for Clarinet and Piano, and songs are other early compositions of this talented composer, who was 22 years old when the *Festival Prelude* had its first performance. It was followed by yet another very successful orchestral composition *Songs of Degree* (1959), which the Israel Philharmonic played on a tour of the United States and the Far East in 1960.

Sheriff was a conducting student of Ze'ev Friedländer-Priell and studied composition with Paul Ben-Haim. A scholarship enabled him to go to Berlin to study composition with Boris Blacher and also work with conductor Igor Markevich in Salzburg. A Piano Sonata was written in Berlin under the influence of Blacher (1961). There followed a series of chamber music works, including *Music for Woodwind, Trombone, Piano and Double Bass* (1961), a work which he also arranged for the trombonist Ray Parnes as *Piece for Ray* for trombone and piano (1962). In many of his later works Sheriff uses Hebrew-liturgical motives or stylized cantillation and also stylizes sounds heard from Near Eastern instruments and instrumental combinations. His Chaconne for Orchestra (1968) was premièred by the Israel Philharmonic Orchestra, Zubin Mehta conducting, in 1969. For the chamber orchestra Sheriff composed a Sonata for Chamber Orchestra in 1973, the première performances of which the composer conducted himself. Although some of Sheriff's later works—for solo instruments as well as for instrumental combinations—are very demanding in performance, the lyrical verve characterizing his early successful pieces is always dominant in them and makes them more easily comprehensible to the listener—often superficially easy, it may seem—than many works of other composers of his generation.

For the twelve solo cellists of the Berlin Philharmonic Orchestra Sheriff composed *Trei-Assar-Dodecalogue* in 1978; eight years later he returned to the violoncello ensemble and wrote *Meeting for Six*, for six celli solos. In the same year, 1986, he completed a symphonic work *A Vision of David*.

What may be seen as a climax in Noam Sheriff's career as a composer was the commission, by the Belgian maecenas Bernard Gutman, of a work for the Israel Philharmonic Orchestra's festive concert to commemorate in Spain the 500th anniversary of the expulsion of the Jews, who for centuries had lived in peace on the Iberian peninsula with their Christian and Muslim neighbors, principally in the city of Toledo. Sheriff's work, entitled *Pasion Sefardi* (Spanish Passion), was performed in May 1992 in the courtyard of Toledo's Military Academy overlooking the town; the event was hosted by the Spanish actress Nuria Espert and the actor Gregory Peck. The French chief rabbi Joseph Sitruk lit a torch which set aflame seven smaller torches that represented the countries in which the Jews from Spain found refuge: Morocco, France, Italy, Greece, Turkey, Bulgaria, and Yugoslavia. Prayers were intoned by the rabbi and by Christian and Muslim religious leaders; among some two thousand guests of the event from all over the world was the concert's honorary president, Queen Sofia of Spain.

The Sheriff *Pasion Sefardi* consists of eight movements for soprano, mezzosoprano, two tenors, and bass, choir, and orchestra; Zubin Mehta conducted the Israel Philharmonic and the choir of the Spanish television; the Israeli violinist Gil Shaham played the Mendelssohn Violin Concerto. Plácido Domingo was the principal soloist in Sheriff's work; the other singers were Esther Kenan Ofri, Esperanza Rumbau, Jorge Lujua, and Julio Fernández. Isaac Stern was a guest soloist.

The movements of the *Pasion Sefardi* are an Introduction, "Those Who Ascend to Jerusalem," Intermezzo, Allegory, another Intermezzo, "Inquisition," "Romancero-Allegory," and "Jerusalem," returning to the "Canción de las Subidas" ("Those who ascend") of the beginning.

PASION SEFARDI, Noam Sheriff
Obra dedicada al Patrón de las Artes Bernard Guttman-Bruselas

I. Introducción

II. Canción de las Subidas

I was glad when they said unto me,
Let us go into the house of the Lord.

Our feet shall stand within thy gates,
O Jerusalem.
Jerusalem is builded as a city that is
compact together;
Salmo: 122:1–3 (en Hebreo)

III. Intermezzo

Kuandos son los unos
unos es El Criador
Baruch Hu uvaruch Shmo

IV. Alegoría

Pregoneros pos las plasas
Ijo del rey ken veria
Si se lo trayian bivo
ombres grandes los aria
Si se lo trayian muerto
Sus presentes les daria

Mas ariva i mas ariva
Por la sivdad di Silevria
Ay avia peshkadores
Peshkando sus proverias

Vieron vinir tres en kavayo
aziendo gran polveria
viniron serka del vio
Echo ganchos i gancheras
Por ver lo ke le salia
le salio un duke de oro
ijo del rey parecia

V. Intermezzo

VI. Inquisición

Chico: Christe Domine
Narrador I: En el día de hoy trenta de enero
de mil quatro sientos ochenta y
quatro en ciudad real La Santa Inquisicion
investiga en los sotanos de tortura
Narrator II: Parte do los investigador ha
muerto
Narrador I: Y otros han sucumbido y confesado

Chico: Christe Domine
Inquisidores: Num quid et tu Judaeus es?
Judío: Num quid ego Judaeus sum?
Non sum!
Chico: Christe Domine
Inquisidor: Quam accusationem affertis
adversus hominem hunc?
Coro: Si non esset hic malefactor,
non tibi tradidissemus ecum.
Num quid et tu Judaeus es?
Judío: Num quid ego Judaeus sum?
Non sum.
Inquisidores: Tu es Judaeus.
Judío: Non sum.
Coro: Tu es Judaeus.
Judío: Shma Israel Adonai Eloheinu Adonai
echad Dio de Los Cielos Patron del mundo
de las alturas Azeme konoser muy muy
presto lami ventura
Coro: Shma Israel . . .
Narrador I: En el día de hoy quince de
octubre de mil quatro ciento o noventa y
dos en la plaza de zodocover en Toledo,
Fuequemada en la hoguera
Leonor Gonzales

VII. Romancero-Alegoría

Durme durme, mi alma donzella
Durme durme, sin ansia y dolor
Siente siente, al son de mi gitarra
Siente hermoza mis males cantar.

VIII. Jerusalén

Ir me kero madre a Yerushalayim
En El m'arimoyo, En El m'enfiguzio yo
En el Patron d'el mundo, en el Singnor del
mundo.

Our feet shall stand within thy gates,
O Jerusalem, *(en Hebreo)*

Amen, Amen

Canción de las Subidas *(en Hebreo)*

Ami Ma'ayani (born at Ramat Gan near Tel Aviv in 1936), like Noam Sheriff, is a composer who has had the benefit of studying both in Israel and abroad; he also resembles the slightly older composer in the cosmopolitan musical style of his works and the easy-going character of even the difficult-seeming structural conceptions. Ma'ayani studied composition with Paul Ben-Haim and conducting with Eytan Lustig, and gained experience while working with the Gadna (Israeli Youth) Symphony Orchestra, the Orchestra of the Haifa Conservatoire of Music, and the Wind Band of the Tel Aviv Municipality. At the same time, he studied architecture at the Haifa Technion, from which he graduated in 1960. He continued his studies in architecture at Columbia University, New York, and during his stay there composed ballet music for the Juilliard School of Music. Ma'ayani first gained prominence when his compositions for harp became known—and won the Engel Prize of the City of Tel Aviv in 1963—and when the Gadna (Israeli Youth) Symphony Orchestra chose his orchestral work *Te'amim* to represent Israeli music in the programs of the youth orchestra's tour of the United States of America and Canada in 1964. For a concert of Israeli music at Philharmonic Hall, Lincoln Center, New York, in March 1965, the Composers' Showcase, New York, and Israeli Music Publications, Tel Aviv, commissioned Ma'ayani to write a work for solo voice and chamber orchestra based on biblical psalms. His *Mismorim,* premièred at this concert and was singled out for high praise by critics and public alike. Ma'ayani's works include *Toccata* for harp (first prize at International Harp Festival competition, Jerusalem, 1962), Concerto No. 1 for harp and orchestra (chosen as contemporary work for the 1963 International Harp Festival in Holland), *Te'amim* for orchestra (1964), *The Songs of Solomon* for string orchestra (1963–64), *Concerto da camera* for solo violin and strings or chamber orchestra (1964), *Māqamāt* for harp solo (1964), Trio for Flute, Violin, and Harp (1965), and *Mismorim* for high voice and chamber orchestra (1965). From his earliest period date a Divertimento for Chamber Orchestra and ballet music. The trio *Improvisation variée* for flute, violin (or viola), and harp takes the form of free variations on a theme of improvisatory character. The work is made up of two main sections: the first comprises the improvisation and seven variations, each of which is cast in a different mood. The character of improvisation pervades the variations as

Ami Ma'ayani.

well, with the melismas and ornamentation influenced by Near Eastern chant. The second section consists of another, independent, set of improvisatory variations that are closely interlinked with each other. Their theme is based on motifs from the opening subject (first section) but takes on a character of its own; its coloring may be termed Eastern-Mediterranean. The work was commissioned by Temple Israel, Johannesburg, South Africa for the Lucien Grujon–Walter Mony–Kathleen Alister Trio.

Continued composition studies in New York and his preoccupation with electronic music production did not lead to a fundamentally different style of musical composition. Ma'ayani still developed his predilection for melismatically flowering melodic motifs (so dominant in his characteristic orchestral piece *Te'amim* of 1963 and his various harp pieces) and intricate rhythms that lend his music its exotic flavor. Apart from two harp concertos, Ma'ayani wrote *Regalim* for solo soprano or tenor and large orchestra in five movements on the Pilgrims' Festivals of the Jewish year (1966), a symphonic poem *Qumran* on the caves of the Dead Sea Scrolls near the Dead Sea (1971), a Sinfonia Concertante for wind quintet and orchestra (1972), a cycle *Yiddish Songs* for mezzosoprano and orchestra (1974), a Viola Concerto, and a *Psalm Symphony* for voices and orchestra (1974).

Two important works by Ami Ma'ayani are his *Hebrew Requiem* and Concerto for Percussion and Eight Wind Instruments, with the percussionist performing on thirty-nine different instruments; the "accompanists" are flute, oboe, clarinet, bassoon, French horn, two trumpets, and trombone. The concerto consists of three movements. The first, "Lent," a fantasy, is dominated by eastern, Arabic ornamentation, short motifs, and small intervals, creating a very tight and tense harmony representing the conception of the first movement. The second movement, "Vite et Vif," takes the form of a scherzo of varying rhythms. The third movement, "Cadence," is ruled by the idea of improvisation, an opportunity given to each player to exhibit his powers as soloist. At the end, the opening passage of the work returns and serves as a coda. According to the composer, the concerto demonstrates the unlimited use of percussion instruments—technically, musically, and rhythmically—while preserving the special color of Oriental and Mediterranean music, its traditional uses of Oriental motifs, the eastern dreams, and a song and prayer so characteristic of this type of musical folklore. Furthermore, while attempting to treat the material in a strictly classical music manner, improvisation, which was common and developed in the classical period, is used in the spirit of our time and in our progressive conceptions of the world of sound. The concerto was premièred in April 1967 in Paris at the end of the International Chamber Music Festival, organized by the Casino de Divonne with Jean-Charles François, soloist, and Edgar Cosma, conductor.

The *Hebrew Requiem* was composed in 1977 for an international competition on the subject of the Holocaust and the Rebirth of the Nation.

This competition was held in honor of the 30th anniversary of the State of Israel in 1978. The *Hebrew Requiem* is written for contralto solo, mixed choir, and symphony orchestra, and was awarded first prize in the competition. The original idea was to create a requiem in the traditional western European form and style. The *Hebrew Requiem* is based on poems by Yitzhak Orpaz, interwoven with the Latin text of the requiem mass.

Yinam Leef, born in Jerusalem in 1953, studied piano at the Rubin Music Academy in his home-town and studied composition with Mark Kopytman. In the United States he continued his studies with Richard Wernick, George Rochberg, and George Crumb at the University of Pennsylvania, from which he holds a doctorate, and with Luciano Berio at Tanglewood. Scholarships from various sources enabled him to stay in America for six years, where he also taught composition at various universities and colleges. Returning to Jerusalem he assumed a post as composition and theory teacher at the Rubin Academy, at which he had once studied.

His early works include *Turns* for woodwind trio, piano pieces, and *Fireflies* for soprano, flute, and harpsichord (after Rabindranat Tagore). In 1984 he composed an octet, "after Kandinsky," eight miniatures for flute, clarinet, French horn, percussion, and four string instruments. A more extensive work, *A Place of Fire*, was composed in 1985 for mezzosoprano and chamber ensemble. A year later Yinam Leef wrote a piece for trumpet solo and string orchestra, entitled *Fanfares and Whispers*. His choral work *Sounds, Shadows* (1987) attracted attention at the International Society for Contemporary Music Festival in Oslo. In the years 1988 to 1990 the composer wrote a light-hearted orchestral work *Scherzos and Serenades,* which was premièred at the 1990 "Encounter Diaspora-Israel" in Cologne. An earlier composition for symphony orchestra is his Violin Concerto. For piano Leef wrote a short piece "How Far East, How Further West" (1988), for harpsichord three "Canaanite Fantasies" (No. 3, 1990).

Among Israel's female composers who made a name for themselves, especially outside their country of birth, are Shulamit Ran and Betty Olivero. Shulamit Ran was born in Tel Aviv in 1947, where she studied piano with Emma Gorochov and composition with Paul Ben-Haim and A. U. Boscovich. A scholarship enabled her to continue her studies at the Mannes College of Music in New York from 1963 to 1967, where she studied composition with Norman dello Joio and piano with Nadia Reisenberg; she also attended the Tanglewood courses of Aaron Copland and Lukas Foss. At the age of sixteen, in 1963, she performed her Capriccio for Piano and Orchestra at the invitation of Leonard Bernstein with the New York Philharmonic under his direction. She played the piano solo in her *Symphonic Poem* with the Jerusalem Symphony Orchestra in 1967 and a *Concert Piece* for piano and orchestra in Tel Aviv 1971. Shulamit Ran wrote numerous works for piano, also for harpsichord, and chamber music with piano. A song cycle *O, the Chimneys,* settings of poems by Nelly Sachs, was written and performed in New York 1970; the mezzosoprano solo is accompanied by an instrumental chamber ensemble. Her musical style, which is characterized by post-romantic as well as modernist traits, tends toward direct impact and effectiveness; the composer can thus count on appreciative performers and listeners. In 1991 a symphony commissioned by the Philadelphia Orchestra and its conductor Riccardo Muti earned Shulamit Ran the coveted Pulitzer Prize.

Betty Olivero was born in Tel Aviv in 1954 and studied piano and composition at the Rubin Music Academy and at the Yale University School of Music, where her composition teachers were Jacob Druckman and Gilbert Amy. After graduating from Yale in 1981 she received a scholarship for study at the Berkshire Music Center, Tanglewood, with Luciano Berio, and the Italian government supported a continuation of studies with Berio in Italy. There the Maggio Musicale Fiorentino commissioned two works from Betty Olivero in 1984: *Cantes Amargos* for voice and orchestra and *Horizons.* Another work commissioned from her—by the Fromm Music Foundation for the Aspen Music Festival, 1987, in Colorado—she entitled *Presenze*; it is written for ten players. In 1986 the composer wrote a piece for double bass and chamber orchestra, *Batnun,* and a Duo for Violin and Piano.

At the "Encounter Diaspora-Israel," and subsequently also in Israel, Betty Olivero's *Tenuot* (Hebrew for "Movements") written in 1990, was first performed. The work juxtaposes small chamber groups and the full orchestra, at times also solo instruments. The composer indicates: "Individual sonorous structures placed at various points of the acoustic space are linked with the device of melodic fragments. . . . These come and go and disappear in space and lend the massive symphonic structures continuous movement."

Ettel Sussman, an accomplished singer, has some musically appealing lyrical compositions to her credit, among them *Le Bien-aimé* (passages from the Song of Songs) for narrator, soprano, and small orchestra; songs for voice and harpsichord on classical Chinese poetry; and a triptych *Caesarea* for orchestra.

A COMPOSER of unusual interest is Habib Hassan Touma, born 1934 in Nazareth and a graduate of the Nazareth High School. He worked as a teacher in Arab and Bedouin settlements in Galilee and in his home town. He studied music at the Haifa Conservatoire and later at the Oranim Institute, till he entered the composition class of A. U. Boscovich at the Israel Conservatoire and Academy of Music in Tel Aviv. He then became a teacher at the French Mission School and the American Baptist Children's Village near Ramatayim. Explaining his musical outlook, Habib Touma stresses that in embarking upon a career in music he had to fight against the prejudices of a society that holds no regard for the professional musician. But he believes that Arabic music is in need of a renaissance and only a real master of his art can solve its problems in our time. The modern Arabic repertoire is spoiled by "popular" musicians who try to translate cheap western crooning melodies into the idiom of the East. In Touma's opinion, traditional Arabic melody and orchestration should exercise their influence on the modern musician of the East even when he applies the technical knowledge of the western musician. Touma considers himself to be the first Arabic musician in Israel "to risk studying western music in order to write good Oriental music that can be performed and appreciated by artists who so far may have regarded Arabic music as primitive and monotonous." His *Oriental Rhapsody* for two flutes and Oriental drum, composed and first performed at an Academy concert in 1957, is based on melodic material which is original but derived from the style of Arabic melodies and developed in accordance with western ideas of texture and form. Similar tendencies dominate Touma's later works—his *Arabic Suite* for piano solo, Study No. 1 and Study No. 2 for flute solo, *Sama'i* for oboe and piano, and *Taqsim* for piano. An interesting instrumental work is *Reflexus I* for twelve strings.

After graduating from the Free University of Berlin with a Ph.D. in musicology, Dr. Touma became a member of the International Institute for Comparative Music Studies in Berlin. He has published a number of important treatises and a book on the history, theory, and forms of Arabic music.

JEWISH COMPOSERS—and not only Jewish musicians—all over the world have written, and are still writing, musical works incorporating or influenced by strains of traditional or popular Jewish music as known especially from the eastern European scene. Even in Israel, composers, of early and younger generations, have not lost interest in Yiddish-Jewish melodies and popular Jewish instruments; many composers are attracted by the Sephardic-Mediterranean musical heritage and the Near Eastern cantillation and folk instruments. A late trend is the attempt by composers also to incorporate in their music the forms, tunes, and styles of their Arab neighbors. Foremost among them may be named Moroccan-born Avraham Amzallag (1941), who came to Israel at eleven years of age in 1952, and Tsippi Fleischer, born in Haifa in 1946. Amzallag studied flute with Uri (Erich) Toeplitz in Tel Aviv and also attended musicology classes at Tel Aviv University. He is very well-versed in the Near Eastern–Mediterranean musical traditions and tries to adapt traditional melody forms, rhythms, and musical structures for conventional western instruments. Among his typical compositions are *Taqsim* for flute (1968), *Midbarit* (Desolation) also for flute solo (1973); Sextet for Flute and Five Percussionists (1970); *Dulab* for oboe, *Dulab* for flute (1979); *The Jar* and *Achoti Kalah* (My Sister My Bride) for the Yemenite Inbal Dance Theater; *Mizmor* for oboe and strings (1979); and in the same year another *Taqsim* for flute.

Tsippi Fleischer goes further than Amzallag in her attempts to link Arab and Jewish-Israeli elements, setting to music Arab poems and using traditional Arab musical instruments. She studied both music and Arab language, history, and literature, and after graduating from university became a teacher at various institutes of learning. Among her musical works based on Arabic poems are a song cycle *Girl, Butterfly, Girl* (composed to Hebrew texts after Arabic originals) for voice and chamber ensemble (1977), a choral work based on a part of this work; solo music for guitar and for violoncello; *In Chromatic Mood* for piano and contact microphone (1986); *Ballad of Expected Death in Cairo* to an Arabic text, for tenor, piano, and three violins (1987); *The Gown of Night*—a collage of voices of Bedouin children, for magnetic tape, with a text by Muhammad Gana'im (1987); *Like Two Branches*—a chamber cantata with choir, two oboes, psaltery, and tar drums; *War* for a combination of bass-clarinet, A-clarinet, alto-saxophone, marimba, vibraphone, tom-toms, cymbals, electronic drums, triangle, gongs, and bow (1988).

TWO ASPECTS of music in modern Israel must still be considered for the completion of our survey. One concerns young and budding composers who must devote some years of their life to the military service that is so vital for the defense of the country, whose security is threatened from all sides; in later life they have to be ready for periods of reservist duties. For the first time in history a national Jewish army was formed, which needed its own stirring songs and march tunes. Composers on active service during Israel's defensive wars and their leaders and friends reacted to the exigencies of the time in various ways: they tried to contribute new songs to the folk repertoire which had never hitherto included marches and soldiers' songs; they wrote ditties of a new kind for the entertainment ensembles created to relieve soldiers at the front. The composers also wrote choral and instrumental works in simplified mediums, and they turned increasingly to the books of the Bible, especially to those episodes offering parallels between Israel's struggles and victories of old and the fight for the new State of Israel. Many of the compositions—some of which have been named in this chapter—reflect the spirit of the times alongside those that mourn the fate of the Jews in the Holocaust and those that keep the memory alive of the gallant defenders who lost their lives in Israel's wars.

Also, the student of music in modern Israel will note the rather curious lack of interest on the part of Israeli composers in music for the synagogue service; composers who wrote synagogue music mostly did so on commission from American synagogues. The reason lies in the very structure of Israeli Judaism. The bulk of the youth is organized in the Labor Federation; many grew up in socialist settlements in which the traditional feasts assume new forms of celebration, while the Jewish orthodox tradition finds itself in a state of opposition. In order to perpetuate the law as it has guided world Jewry for thousands of years, the Israeli authorities have to contend with many obstacles; and in the fight to preserve the very existence of tradition and traditional law the religious leader cannot be expected to adopt progressive views and to develop synagogue service and liturgical forms as they were developed in all countries of the Diaspora. Thus the liturgical style in the local synagogues still presents a rather chaotic mixture of tendencies and forms, and no real attempts at unification and modernization are evident. The composer has thus no interest in contributing to its literature, and the Israeli musician is not drawn to the liturgy at all. In a wider sense this was also why Israeli composers found the way to Biblical texts and poetry much later than their colleagues in other countries, a paradoxical situation that only a new order in Israel's religious life can be expected to improve. On the other hand, the new forms of ceremonial and celebration developed in the rural settlements and villages—in the early state still independent in their ways and means—are important musically, for the composers of the country are eager to contribute their share to the musical life of the communities and have often written elaborate works—for whatever choral and instrumental forces are available in the settlements that needed them—that revive the spirit of the ancient feasts born out of the cycles of nature, and of national elevation. Yehuda Sharett, Matthityahu Shelem, and Nissim Nissimov—all active in rural settlements—were the first to compose musical "services" for the community feast. In the oratorio-like works of this kind, in which all solo singers, chorus, and instrumental players that are locally available are the actual performers of the music in addition to speakers or narrators, the bulk of the community is generally asked to participate in the choral singing at the climaxes of the service; ancient practice is thus revived in the struggle for new forms of life and expression. It may well be that these rural "services" will become the nucleus for a new organization of communal life in the entire Land of Israel and greatly influence the reorganization of religious life as well as the musical forms to be developed by Israeli composers.

In the communal settlements (kibbutzim), musically gifted members of the community are given opportunities to study instrument playing, singing, and composing at the Israeli music institutions. As members of a community they have no day-to-day problems of livelihood and so they can devote the necessary time to making music and composing. For the feasts they contribute appropriate music but otherwise they are independent in their musical work. Quite a number of "kibbutz composers" have made a name for themselves in the concert life of Israel as well as in other countries, and some of their compositions have also been recorded on disk. A most versatile composer among them is Meir Mindel, born at Lwow in 1946, in Israel at Kibbutz Negba since 1958, a composition student of Abel Ehrlich. Dov Carmel, born in Budapest in 1933, came to Israel in 1949 and joined Kibbutz Daliah. He studied composition with Ehrlich, Seter, and Yitzhak Sadai. Also from Budapest (born 1934) came David Ory; since 1946 he has lived in Israel and since 1960 at Kibbutz Beit Alpha. He also studied composition with Sadai and Ehrlich. Yuval Shaked was born in 1955 at Kvutzat Geser; he studied with Sergiu Natra and Ehrlich in Israel and with Maurizio Kagel in Cologne. Arie Shapira, who was awarded the prestigious Israel Prize in 1994, is a native of Kibbutz Affikim; he is a student of Partos, Seter, and Ehrlich. Arie Rufeisen, Moshe Kilon, Moshe Gasner, and Shlomoh Yoffe are other kibbutz composers of note.

Among many composers in modern Israel who came to the fore especially in the last decade of the century, it must suffice to name a few creators of unusual musical works. Menahem Zur, born in Tel Aviv in 1942, studied in Israel and at various U.S. music colleges. He started, during his studies with Yizhak Sadai, in the field of light music before turning to large-scale orchestral works and interesting vocal and chamber music compositions. Other composers include Dror Elemelech (born in 1956), Israel-born composer and producer of electronic compositions; Ron Weidberg, born in Tel Aviv (1953), a student of Leon Schidlowsky; Haifa-born Moshe Rasiuk (1954), student of Ehrlich and Josef Tal; Oded Assaf, writer and composer (1948); Aharon Harlap, born in Canada (1941), since 1964 in Israel, composer and conductor; Steve Horenstein from the United States; Jerusalem-born Noah Guy; Dan Yuhas (1947); and Max Stern (1947)—who studied with Boris Blacher in Berlin, Erhard Karkoschka in Stuttgart, and also for some time with Luciano Berio, Milton Babbitt, and Karlheinz Stockhausen—a composer and double bass player who has made interesting musical contributions linking Near Eastern traditions and western music.

THE FUTURE of Israel's musical art depends on a great many factors, including how the country and its resources are developed, the degree to which the State of Israel recognizes and furthers the work of its creative artists, and whether and how deeply the composers themselves acknowledge the task allotted to them. The composers of modern Israel not only serve their own newly created nation—theirs may be a historic position. Throughout their ancient and modern history the Jews have played a role of mediator between the civilizations—from the time of the Patriarchs down to the most recent centuries; with their return to Zion the Jews have brought the modern West to the ancient East and perform a twofold mediation. Israeli artists and composers may play a decisive part in the age-long and ever-topical search for a synthesis between East and West. By taking their tasks seriously, they may by their own work and imagination exert a far-reaching influence throughout the world on a new art and on the great masters of music to come.

BETWEEN EAST AND WEST

A FTER ALMOST two thousand years of dispersion the Jews have begun to create a new national and cultural center on the very same spot that once saw their most splendid achievements in national life, science, and art. They have brought Occidental civilization to their Oriental brethren; they have applied modern agricultural techniques to a soil that had been plowed in the same way since time immemorial, they have irrigated the desert and made it bloom again by means of modern scientific knowledge, and they have imported the rich heritage of European art into a country that had preserved a most ancient tradition.

Under the influence of European music, Near Eastern musicians are rapidly adapting their tunes to western harmonization and abandoning their own instruments in favor of the piano and the modern orchestral instrumentarium. Comparative musicology and Oriental music research have to make great strides to record the last remnants of ancient Oriental (Near Eastern) musical culture. The song of the Bedouin, the shepherd, the muezzin, and the teller of epic tales, the synagogue chant of the Yemenite, Samaritan, and Persian Jews—all of them preserved since biblical times with probably little variation, if any at all—will soon be irretrievably lost; for

communities that have lived in seclusion and isolation since the beginning
of the Christian Era are now exposed to the influence of western civilization
through their direct contact with the western world as well as through listening to broadcasts and viewing television from all over the globe.

In the song of the Near Eastern communities the early Jewish settlers
of Palestine meet the last echoes of the ancient Hebrew tradition, while
the actual sounds of the Near Eastern world are still present in the music of
their Arab neighbors and of other Near Eastern communities. Arab music
in this area is in a state of flux too; no truly great musician seems to have
arisen as yet to give expression to the impact of East and West. Arab orchestras—brought into being by the Palestine Broadcasting Service and
continued independently by the Israeli and Jordanian stations after the end

East meets West: Ravi Shankar, prominent Indian sitar player, improvises with
Yehudi Menuhin at the Menuhin Festival at Gstaad, Switzerland.

of the British Mandate—have been experimenting in this direction; a number of Arab school choruses of remarkable standing cultivate Occidental as well as Oriental music. The considerable Armenian community, with a venerable tradition of religious music of its own, has produced a number of interesting musicians, and so have other Near Eastern groups. In the midst of this world the composers of modern Israel set to work—burdened with the heritage of the great musical traditions of Europe, disturbed by the twentieth-century changes in the social status and artistic creed of the composer, haunted by nostalgic memories, and placing all their faith in a new and hopeful future. Commanding a musical technique based on the principles of harmony and counterpoint, they are confronted in the new country with melodic patterns that do not naturally lend themselves to harmonization or polyphony. To them, Oriental melodies at first seem monotonous, lacking in variety, primitive; and they are inclined to forget that the Orientals, on their part, can as little tell the difference between a Bach chorale, a Mozart symphony, and a Schoenberg quartet (thinking all of these monotonous, lacking variety, primitive) as the Occidentals can distinguish among an Oriental Call to Prayer, a shepherd tune, and an ecstatic dance. Yet the unique atmosphere of the country, the continuous contact with rural life of all those who do not confine themselves within the walls of the cities, and the feeling that only with difficulty could musicians continue to create as they have done in a radically different world combine to make themselves felt in the works of almost all serious composers—pioneers all in their own particular way.

IT IS INTERESTING to compare Jewry's position in Israel today with that of thousands of years ago. Today, as then, immigrants are coming from many different countries, bringing along with them the habits and customs, the civilizations and tastes of their former surroundings. Today, as then, Israel represents a large crucible and its inhabitants wish to create a culture and an art of their own. In early times, Jerusalem was a spiritual center and a center of philosophy, art, and science that fed not only Judaism alone but all surrounding cultural centers. The Temple, symbol of ancient Judaism, has not been rebuilt, and Jerusalem, with its holy sites of three world religions and of a multitude of sects, with its new Givat Ram campus and the proud

academic buildings on Mount Scopus, is claimed by many creeds and nations all over the civilized world. The Hebrew University on Mount Scopus
overlooking venerable old Jerusalem as well as the width of the Jordan Valley and the Dead Sea, the stony vastness of the desert and the Judean
Mountains, is rapidly developing into a spiritual center. Authors, poets and
novelists, scientists and research workers are active all over the country,
and Israel's musicians and composers are regarded wherever they appear in
the wide world as "musical ambassadors" of a rising culture.

EAST AND WEST meet in the works of the composers of modern Israel; not
all of them may be conscious of their position in music history. The need for
a fresh musical impetus has long been felt in contemporary music in general; composers of many countries are looking to the East or to the songs
and dances of the "primitives" for new inspiration. From the exotic elements in Debussy and in Mahler to the eastern European sources of Béla
Bartók's great works and to the Schoenbergian twelve-tone scale with its
ancient *māqām* character, from the earliest invasion of Spanish, African,
and American rhythms into art music to the influence of jazz and swing elements on the masters of today, there is an unbroken chain of musicians
who are dissatisfied with the highly developed musical art of the West. It is
thus that the example of Israel—whose modern city of Tel Aviv has been
aptly described as a "show-window to Europe"—is already regarded by
western musicians as a prototype for possible ways to infuse new elements
into the art of contemporary music. It is thus that some textbooks of musical history devote a special chapter to contemporary music in the Land of
Israel just as they carry in their first pages a survey of the music of the ancient Hebrews. It is thus that a fascinating story unrolls before the eyes of
the historian who visits that Eternal Land and listens to the song of its shepherds in the deserts and the newly plowed fields and greening meadows, to
the exquisite music carried by the light breeze over the Sea of Galilee, and
to the sounds of the many-voiced chorus and orchestra reverberated by the
mountains of Judea. . . .

CHRONOLOGICAL TABLE

OF JEWISH GENERAL

AND CULTURAL HISTORY

Approximate dates are enclosed in parentheses.

GENERAL HISTORY	CULTURAL HISTORY

From the beginnings to the destruction of Jerusalem and Israel's dispersion

BEFORE THE COMMON ERA:

3761 Beginning of the Jewish calendar (fixed in 344 of the Common Era)	
(2000–1600) The Patriarchs	
(2000: Abraham)	
13th Century Moses	
1200–1050 The Judges	(1150) Deborah's Song
1050–586 The Kings	1000–450 The Prophets
(1000) David	
(950) Solomon	
933 Partition of the Kingdom	
722 Assyrian Exile	(725) Isaiah
587 Fall of Jerusalem to	(600) Jeremiah
Nebuchadnezzar	(575) Ezekiel
Babylonian Exile—to 538	(700) The earliest Hebrew script
538–332 The Persian period	known: The Siloah inscription

GENERAL HISTORY	CULTURAL HISTORY
332–166 The pre-Maccabaean Greek period	(621) The discovery of the Torah
331 Foundation of Alexandria	(450) Completion of the writing of the Torah (Ezra)
320 Judea passes under Egyptian rule	(300) The Greek version of the Scriptures: Septuaginta
203 Antiochus takes Jerusalem Judea under Syrian rule	(450–250) The Sofrim—learned writers
167 Maccabaean revolt, headed by Mattathias	(250) Simon the scholar
165 Victory of the Jews at Beth-Zur Rededication of the Temple	(180) The Book of Ben-Sira written (Hebrew)
104 Kingdom of the Hasmoneans	30 to (10 C.E.) Hillel the Great (from Babylon) teaches in Jerusalem
63 Pompey conquers Jerusalem and puts an end to Jewish independence	(300–100 C.E.) Influence of Hellenism on Jewish culture
48 Death of Pompey	40 to (20 C.E.) Philo of Alexandria
37–34 Herod "The Great," King of Judea	

THE COMMON ERA:

GENERAL HISTORY	CULTURAL HISTORY
6 Judea becomes a Roman province	10–220 The Tannaites, whose teachings are collected in the Mishna
4 B.C.E.–39 C.E. Herod Antipas ruler of Galilee and Peraea	
29 (?) Crucifixion of Jesus	
30 (or 35) Conversion of St. Paul	
37 Birth of Josephus	
38 Persecution of Jews in Alexandria	
41–54 Claudius Emperor	
54–68 Nero Emperor	
64 Burning of Rome and persecution of Christians	
66 Jewish revolt in Palestine	
69–79 Vespasian Emperor	
70 Titus destroys Jerusalem and the Temple	70 Jochanan ben Zakkai establishes a rabbinical school at Jamnia (Yavneh)

The Jews under Hellas and Rome

GENERAL HISTORY	CULTURAL HISTORY
79–81 Titus Emperor	76–79 Josephus completes his history of the "Jewish War"
81–96 Domitian Emperor	
96–98 Nerva Emperor	93–94 Josephus completes his "Antiquities"
98–117 Trajan Emperor	

GENERAL HISTORY

117–138 Hadrian Emperor
117–118 Jewish revolt in Palestine
132–135 Revolt of Bar-Kochba
138–161 Antonius Pius Emperor
161–168 Marcus Aurelius
(180–250) Soldier Kings and
decline of the Roman Empire
(250) and 303 Persecution of the
Christians on a large scale
c. 250–650 Babylon under Persian
rule
284–305 Diocletian Emperor
323–337 Constantine the Great,
who makes Christianity the state
religion
325 First Church Council at Nicaea
330 Constantinople (formerly
Byzantium) becomes capital of the
Roman Empire
(350) Jewish revolt in Galilee
361–363 Julian the Apostate
375 Beginning of the Great
Migration of People
395 Partion of the Roman Empire
after the death of Theodosius
    395–1453 Byzantine (Eastern)
    Empire
    395–476 Western Empire
    (conquered by the Goths)
614 Persian troops conquer
Palestine
629 Restoration of Byzantine rule in
Palestine

CULTURAL HISTORY

(100) Synod of Yavneh; Old
Testament canon finally fixed
(125) Rabbi Akiba
(135) Martyrdom of Rabbi Akiba
140–175 Revival of the Jewish
schools in Palestine
(190) Official text of Mishna fixed
by Rabbi Yuda ha-Nassi
219 Babylonian schools founded at
Sura and Nehardea by Rab and
Samuel, respectively, later at
Pumbeditha
220–500 Period of Amoraim, the
interpreters and teachers of
Scriptures and Mishna after the
Tannaites
320–370 Decay of the Palestinian
schools; completion of Palestinian
Talmud; fixing of the Jewish
calendar by Hillel II

499 Completion of the Babylonian
Talmud
589–1038 Period of the Ge'onim
(heads of the Babylonian schools at
Sura and Pumbeditha)

The Settlement of the West and Medieval History

321 The first Jews in Cologne
711 The Arabs conquer Spain
8th–13th Century The Jews flourish
in Islamic Spain
640 Bostanai, founder of the
Dynasty of the Babylonian Exilarchs

761 Rise of Karaite sect
892–942 Sa'adyah ha-Gaon
998–1038 Hai, the last of the
Geonim
(800) Massora
900–1400 Flourishing of Jewish

GENERAL HISTORY	CULTURAL HISTORY
1096 The first Crusade, followed by persecution of Jews	philosophy of religion
The first Privileges for the Jews in Germany: Speyer and Worms	1075–1105 The commentaries of Raschi
1236 Privileges for the Jews in all German countries	1050 Ibn Gabirol
1296 Expulsion of the Jews from England	1080–1145 Yehuda ha-Levi
1298 Expulsion of the Jews from Franconia	1135–1204 Maimonides
1306 Expulsion of the Jews from France	1165–1173 The travels of Benjamin of Tudela
1348–1349 "The Black Death" in Europe	1200–1600 Flourishing of the Cabbala1233 The writings of Maimonides burned in Paris
1394 Second expulsion from France	1242 Copies of the Talmud burned in Paris
1453 Constantinople falls to the Turks	(1310) Publication of the Zohar, the Cabbalist compendium
1492 The Arabs driven from Spain, expulsion of the Jews	1340 Turim Law Code completed by R. Jacob ben-Asher
1497 Expulsion of the Jews from Portugal	1437–1509 Don Isaac Abarbanel
1525 Josel von Rosheim defends the Jews in his writings	1455–1522 The humanist Reuchlin
1591 Spanish Jews settle in Holland	1475 The first Hebrew books printed
1500–1700 The Messianic movement	1492 First printed edition of Mishna with commentary of Maimonides issued at Naples
1657 Resettlement of the Jews in England	1520–1523 First complete edition of the Babylonian Talmud in 12 vols. folio
	1523–1524 First printed edition of the Jerusalem Talmud in one volume
	(1560) Shulchan Aruch compiled
	1626–1676 Sabbatai Zvi, the Pseudo-Messiah
	1632–1677 Baruch Spinoza

Renaissance Italy

1516 The Ghetto of Venice	1513–1578 Asarja dei Rossi, the Jewish humanist
	1571–1648 Leone da Modena
(1600) Privileges for Jewish scholars and artists in Renaissance Italy	(1587–1628) Flourishing of dance and music in the golden age of

GENERAL HISTORY	CULTURAL HISTORY
	Italian music. Salomone Rossi and other Jewish musicians at the Court of Mantua 1629 A Jewish music academy in Venice
1740 Israel Baal Shem, Hassidic movement 1787 Declaration of freedom of religion in America	1729–1786 Moses Mendelssohn (1800) Beginnings of the reform movement (1823) Science of Judaism

A Century of Emancipation and the National Movement in Eastern Europe

1790 Declaration of equality of the Jews by the French National Assembly 1812 The Jews recognized as citizens in Prussia 1840 Pogroms in Damascus 1869 Conclusion of the European emancipation: the "North German Union" 1881 (and after) Large-scale pogroms in Russia	(1800–1933) Flourishing of the Jews in European culture and the arts (1800–1918) Flourishing of the cantoral art in the eastern European countries 1877 Abraham Goldfaden founds his Jewish (Yiddish) Theater in Jassy 1908 Foundation of the Society for Jewish Folk Music in St. Petersburg

The Return to Zion

1882–1905 First wave of immigration into Palestine 1905–1914 Second Immigration and creation of a labor movement in Palestine 1914–1918 First World War 1917 Russian Revolution 1917 Balfour Declaration: England supports the building of a National Home for the Jews in Palestine 1919–1920 Pogroms in the Ukraine 1919–1924 Third Immigration 1922–1948 England's mandatory power in Palestine 1924–1927 Fourth Immigration	1874 Chaim Weizmann born near Pinsk 1882 Pinsker: *Auto-Emancipation* 1896 Herzl: *The Jewish State* 1897 First Zionist Congress (in Basle) 1916 Habima Theater founded in Moscow 1924 The first Hebrew opera in Palestine 1925 Opening of the Hebrew University in Jerusalem 1926 Foundation of a Palestine Section of the International Society for Contemporary Music

GENERAL HISTORY

1927 Beginning of Fifth
Immigration, growing after 1933
and including children and youth on
a large scale
1933 Rise of the National-Socialist
regime in Germany and growth of
Fascism in all central Europe
1936–1939 Arab riots in Palestine
1939–1945 Second World War and
destruction of Jewish communities
in central and eastern Europe—
pogroms and mass murders till the
fall of the Nazi regime
1947 The United Nations decrees
the partition of Palestine and the
establishment of an independent
Jewish State
1948 Great Britain ends Palestine
Mandate.
   David Ben-Gurion proclaims
the establishment of the State of
Israel.
   The neighboring Arab states
attack Israel, Transjordan occupies
the Old City of Jerusalem and
devastates synagogues and buildings
in the Jewish Quarter
1949 Truce declared. The United
Nations accepts Israel as a member
state
   Dr. Chaim Weizmann first
President of Israel
1950–1951 Mass immigration from
Oriental countries. Operation
"Magic Carpet" from Yemen
1956 Second Near East war, the
Suez War, after Britain's retreat
from the Canal Zone and Egypt's
nationalization of the Suez Canal
Company
1964 Arab guerilla groups found

CULTURAL HISTORY

1927 Mordecai Sandberg establishes
the Institute for New Music in
Jerusalem
1933 (and later) Emigration of
Jewish artists from the central
European countries
1936 Opening of Palestine
Broadcasting Station and
inauguration of Palestine Orchestra
(Toscanini), renamed Israel
Philharmonic Orchestra in 1948
   World Center for Jewish Music
in Jerusalem

1948–1949 International music
publishing starts in Israel

1951 First U.S. tour of Israel
Philharmonic Orchestra
1952 Restitution agreement
between West Germany and Israel.
Cultural relations with European
and overseas countries
   First International Choral
Festival in Israel (Zimriah)
1954 Festival of the International

GENERAL HISTORY

Palestine Liberation Organization
1967 Third Near East war, the Six-Day War, after repeated attacks and Arab threats against Israel. Israel regains the Jordan-occupied Old City of Jerusalem and occupies areas of previously mandated-Palestinian country
1973 Egyptian-Syrian surprise attack on Israel (Yom Kippur War)
1977 Egyptian President Anwar Sadat in Jerusalem
1979 Peace agreement between Egypt–Israel
    Continuation of guerilla war against Israel
1987–1991 *Intifada*—riots and attacks protesting Israeli presence in the occupied areas
1991 The Gulf War—U.S. and allies fight Iraq for its occupation of Kuwait. Dictator Saddam remains in office. Israel is attacked but not permitted to retaliate
1992 First peace talks between Arab states and Israel
1994 Peace agreement between Israel and King Hussein of Jordan

CULTURAL HISTORY

Society for Contemporary Music in Haifa and Jerusalem
1957 Opening of the Fredric R. Mann Auditorium, new home for the Israel Philharmonic Orchestra, in Tel Aviv
1959 First Television station in Israel
1965 Diplomatic relations with West Germany
1966 Foundation of Israel Chamber Ensemble, since 1977 called Israel Chamber Orchestra
1968 The Jerusalem poet and writer Recha Freier initiates a triennial series of commissions to Israeli and internationally known composers to commemorate themes and events in Jewish history (Testimonium)
1980 World Music Days of the International Society for Contemporary Music in Israel
1990 Musical Encounter Diaspora-Israel at West-German Radio Station, Cologne
1994 Inauguration of Israel's first opera house in Tel Aviv

MOST IMPORTANT BIBLICAL REFERENCES

TO MUSIC AND MUSICAL INSTRUMENTS

Old Testament (Hebrew)

Genesis—4:21 (Kinnor, 'Ugab)
  31:27 (Kinnor, Tof)
Exodus—15:20 (Tof)
  19:17, 19; 20:18 (Shofar)
Leviticus—25:9 (Shofar)
Numbers—10:2, 8, 9, 10 (Hazozra)
Joshua—6:4, 5, 6, 8, 9, 13 (Shofar,
  Keren)
Judges—3:27, 6:34; 7:8, 15, 18,
  19, 20 (Shofar)
  11:34 (Tof)
I Samuel—10:4 (Nevel, Tof, Halil,
  Kinnor)
  13:3 (Shofar)
  17:17, 23 (Kinnor)
  18:6 (Tof, Shalishim)
II Samuel—2:28 (Shofar)
  6:5 (Kinnor, Nevel, Tof,
  Mna'anim, Zelzelim)
  6:15; 15:10; 18:17; 20:1 and 22

(Shofar)
I Kings—1:34, 39, 41 (Shofar)
I Kings—1:40 (Halil)
  10:12 (Kinnor, Nevel)
II Kings—3:15 (Minstrel)
  9:13 (Shofar)
  11:14, and 12:13 (Hazozra)
I Chronicles—13:8 (Kinnor, Nevel,
  Tof, Zelzelim, Shofar)
  15:16 and 20 (Nevel, Kinnor,
  Zelzelim)
  15:19–28 (Miziltaim, Nevel,
  Kinnor, Hazozra, Shofar,
  Zelzelim)
  16:5–7, 28 (Nevel, Kinnor,
  Zelzelim, Hazozra)
  23:5 (Players on musical
  instruments)
  25:1 ff. (Kinnor, Nevel, Keren,
  Zelzelim)

II Chronicles—5:12, 13 (Zelzelim, Nevel, Kinnor, Hazozra)
7:5 (Instruments of music)
9:11 (Kinnor, Nevel)
13:12, 14 (Hazozra)
15:14 (Shofar, Hazozra)
20:28 (Nevel, Kinnor, Hazozra)
23:13 (Hazozra)
29:25 ff. (Zelzelim, Nevel, Kinnor, Hazozra)
35:15 (Singers)
Ezra—2:65 (Singers)
3:10 (Hazozra, Zelzelim)
Nehemiah—4:18, 20 (Shofar)
7:44, 67 (Singers)
10:40 (Singers)
12:27, 35, 41, 45, 47 (Zelzelim, Nevel, Kinnor, Hazozra, Singers)
39:24 and 25 (Shofar)
Job—21:12 and 33:31 (Tof, Kinnor, 'Ugab)
Isaiah—5:12 (Kinnor, Nevel, Tof, Halil)
14:11 (Nevel)
16:11 Kinnor)
18:3 (Shofar)
23:16 (Kinnor)
24:8 (Tof, Kinnor)
27:19 (Shofar)
30:29 (Halil) and 32 (Tof, Halil)
50:1 (Shofar)
Jeremiah—4:5, 19, 21, 5:1, 17 (Shofar)
31:4 (Tof)
42:14 (Shofar)

48:36 (Halil)
51:27 (Shofar)
Ezekeil—26:13 (Kinnor)
28:13 (Tof and Pipes)
33:3 ff. (Shofar)
Daniel—3:5 ff. (Keren, Mashrokita, Katros, Sabca, Psanterin, Sumponia)
Hosea—5:8 (Hazozra, Shofar)
Joel—2:1, 15 (Shofar)
Amos—2:2 and 3:6 (Shofar)
5:23 and 6:5 (Nevel)
Zephaniah—1:16 (Shofar)
Zechariah—9:14 (Shofar)
14:20 (Zelzelim)
Psalms—33:2 (Nevel-Assor)
44:8 (Minnim)
47:5 (Shofar)
49:4 (Kinnor)
57:8 (Nevel, Kinnor)
68:25 (Kinnor)
71:22 (Nevel, Kinnor)
81:2, 3 (Nevel, Tof, Kinnor, Shofar)
92:3 (Nevel, Kinnor)
98:5 and 6 (Kinnor, Nevel, Shofar, Hazozra)
108:3 (Nevel, Kinnor)
137:2 (Kinnor)
144:9 (Nevel-Assor)
149:3 (Tof, Kinnor)
150 (Shofar, Nevel, Kinnor, Tof, Minnim, 'Ugab, Zelzelei-Shema, Zelzelei-Truah)
Ben-Sira—9:4 and 32:5–8

New Testament (Greek)

Matthew—9:23 Aulos (oboe)
I Corinthians—13:1 Kumbalon (cymbals)
I Corinthians—14:7 Aulos, Kithara

Revelation—1:10; 4:1; 9:14 Salpinx (trumpet)
Revelation—18:22 Kithara, Aulos, Salpinx

"HATIKVAH," THE JEWISH

NATIONAL ANTHEM

In 1897 the song named "Hatikvah" (Hebrew for "The Hope") was adopted as the Jewish national anthem. The author of the poem is Naphtali Herz Imber (born 1856 in Zloczow, died 1909 in New York), a poet and writer who had much interest in music and who also published some essays on musical folklore and music in the ghetto. The poem "Hatikvah" appeared in 1886 in a collection *Barkai* published by Imber in Jerusalem (this was in the very first years of Jewish recolonization in Palestine). Tradition has it—but the authenticity of the story is difficult to prove—that Imber wrote the poem in the colony Rishon-le-Zion (one of the first new settlements on the coastal plain) and that a farmer of Bohemian descent adapted for the song an old Bohemian folk tune (sung today as in No. 10 of the music table). Another possibility is that Imber used phrases of the traditional "Yigdal" prayer melody (one version of which is given in No. 7). Rabbi Israel Goldfarb, Brooklyn, New York, who when he was still a young student knew Imber, says in a communication to the author of this book:

> I feel that Mr. Imber borrowed it [the music] from a cantorial composition by the famous Cantor Nissan Belzer of Odessa. Imber, who was contemporaneous with that well-known hazzan, must have heard the composition sung and took over the part which begins with "We'Havi'ēnu leZion Irēcha" (and bring us to Zion, Your City). I examined that composition in manuscript and found the music to tally note for note with the Hatikvah melody. It is not likely that Nissan Belzer copied from Imber because it was

the custom in those days to borrow synagogue melodies for secular songs. We have many such examples of Goldfaden borrowing from well-known cantorial compositions for his Yiddish operettas when the Yiddish stage was young (letter from Rabbi Goldfarb, 16 July 1948).

The author has not been able to examine the said composition himself, but it must clearly be of the "Yigdal" type (No. 7).

The words and music were adopted as the Jewish national anthem by the First Zionist Congress in Basel in 1897, following the suggestion of the Zionist leader David Wolffsohn, which was unanimously accepted by the assembly.

The tune of the "Hatikvah" is one of the so-called "wandering melodies," which appear in many forms and variations as folk songs of many peoples and which have consciously or unconsciously inspired composers to melodic invention of their own (see Wilhelm Tappert: *Wandernde Melodien. Eine musikalische Studie*, Berlin, 1889, from which some of the examples illustrated have also been taken).

The "Hatikvah" melody can be found in a great number of folk tunes and musical works: our selection of twelve tunes—transposed for the purpose of easier comparison—lists only the most characteristic examples.

"Hatikvah," the Jewish national anthem

No. 1. Beginning of the hymn as sung in Israel today.

No. 2. A tune contained in the Prayer for Dew ("Tal") of Sephardic Jews (Noskowski Collection, p. 218—after Idelsohn).

No. 3. Beginning of a Polish folk song (after Idelsohn).

No. 4. Basque folk song (after Salaberry, *Chants populaires du pays basque*, 1870, p. 260).

No. 5. Basque folk song (after Salaberry, *op. cit.*, p. 236).

No. 6. Spanish cancio (Felipe Pedrell, *Cancionero popular español*, Vol. II, P. 186).

No. 7. Beginning and cadence of the "Yigdal" tune as composed by the English singer and composer Leon Singer at the end of the eighteenth century; it inspired Thomas Olivers, a Welshman and Wesleyan minister, to write a hymn, "The God of Abraham, Praise," on the same melody (this hymn became very popular after its publication in 1772). See Idelsohn, *Jewish Music*, New York, 1929, pp. 220 ff.

No. 8. The form given to the ancient Bohemian folk tune in Smetana's symphonic poem "Vltava" (1874): it first appears there in the key of E minor, later in E major; for purposes of comparison it is here noted in G.

No. 9. Part of the beginning of Mahler's "Song of a Wayfarer" (1884); Mahler hailed from a small Bohemian town.

No. 10. A Bohemian folk song (after Martinowski, *Böhmische Volkslieder*, No. 22, quoted by Tappert, 1889, p. 18).

No. 11. A German nursery song.

No. 12. A German nursery song.

BIBLIOGRAPHY

The subjects discussed in this book have attracted many hundreds of scholars and writers throughout the centuries, and a complete bibliography of Hebrew, Jewish, and Israeli music would fill a volume by itself. The following selection lists the most conclusive books and scholarly articles and those which have been especially helpful to the present author in his work and which contain detailed biographies and lists of sources. We have not included the sometimes remarkable material contained in the encyclopedias (general, musical, and Jewish) such as the *Jewish Encyclopedia, Jüdisches Lexikon, Dictionary of the Bible, Encyclopedia Britannica, Grove's Dictionary of Music and Musicians, Oxford Companion to Music, Harvard Dictionary of Music*, Lavignac's *Encyclopédie de la musique et dictionnaire du conservatoire, Musik in Geschichte und Gegenwart, Encyclopedia Judaica*, Guido Adler's *Handbuch der Musikgeschichte*, nor have we listed biographies of musicians, which are included in every musical book of reference. The biblical sources (listed in Appendix Two and throughout the book itself) and the talmudic sources (frequently quoted in Chapter Three) are not listed in this bibliography either.

For the historical part of the book the author has used the works of Simon Dubnow, Heinrich Graetz, Josef Kastein, Josef Klausner, and Arthur Ruppin (*Sociology of the Jews*).

GENERAL BASIC REFERENCE BOOKS

Adler, Israel. *Hebrew Writings Concerning Music in Manuscripts and Printed Books, from Geonic Times up to 1800*. RISM, B/9, 2, 1975.

————. *Hebrew Notated Manuscript Sources up to Circa 1840.* RISM, 9/1, 1986.

Gorali, Moshe. *The Old Testament in Music.* Jerusalem, Maron, 1993.

Hofman, Shlomo. *Music in the Talmud.* Tel Aviv, Israel Music Inst., 1989.

————. *Miqraéh Musica, Biblical References to Music.* Tel Aviv, Israel Music Inst., 1974.

————. *Music in the Midrashim. Midrashic References to Music* (Hebrew). Tel Aviv, Mif'am, 1984.

Idelsohn, A.Z. *Hebräisch-Orientalischer Melodienschatz.* 10 Vols. Leipzig, 1914–1932, reprint 1973.

General Jewish Musical History

A number of important contributions have been added to the ever grow-ing literature on the music of the Jews since the author's *The Music of Israel* was published in 1949 and his German version *Die Musikgeschichte Israels* appeared in 1961. For the earliest period covered by our book the fundamental com-prehensive study is Eric Werner's *The Sacred Bridge. The Interdependence of Liturgy in Synagogue and Church During the First Millennium,* Volumes 1, 2, London/New York, 1959, 1984. An attempt by Suzanne Haik Vantoura *La Musique de la Bible révélée,* Paris, 1976, must be regarded with caution—simi-lar attempts at reconstruction of the Jerusalem Temple chant had already made been by the German Conrad Gottlob Anton in 1790–91, by Leopold Haupt in 1854, by Leopold Alexander Friedrich Arends in 1867, and by Otto Glaser in 1932. The entire extant literature of Jewish cult music up to the year 1967 is critically reviewed by the theologian-musicologist Dieter Wohlenberg in his dissertation *Kultmusik in Israel. Eine forschungsgeschichtliche Untersuchung,* Hamburg, 1967, in which the reconstructions of Anton, Haupt, Arends, and Glaser are also described and evaluated in detail. The development of cantor-ial music is covered by another significant work by Eric Werner, *A Voice Still Heard. The Sacred Songs of the Ashkenazic Jews,* Pennsylvania State University Press, 1976.

Ethnological studies on various Jewish communities have been published by Edith Gerson-Kiwi in scholarly journals, while Amnon Shiloah and Hanoch Avenary have contributed to our knowledge of medieval theory and practice. Israel Adler's important reference volumes in the series *International Inventory of Musical Sources* (RISM; op. cit. above) contain a wealth of material on He-brew music and musical theory; the same scholar published an extensive study on the music practiced in the European Jewish communities in *La Pratique Musicale Savante dans quelques Communautés Juives en Europe at XVIIe et XVIIIe siècles,* Paris/La Haye, 1966, 2 volumes. In a series published by Israeli Music Publications, Tel Aviv, *Early Hebrew Art Music,* some early cantatas for Jewish festivals were edited by Adler as was his transcription of *Melodies Notated in the 12th Century*—the three earliest known Hebrew chants written down by

Obadiah the Proselyte in neumatic notation.

Since 1968 the Jewish Music Research Center at the Hebrew University, Jerusalem, has periodically published the *Yuval* collections of scholarly studies. Twelve historical essays by various authors are contained in *Contributions to a Historical Study of Jewish Music,* edited by Eric Werner, New York, 1976, and a number of other studies, accompanied by a synopsis of discussions, is found in *Proceedings of the World Congress of Jewish Music, Jerusalem 1978,* edited by Judith Cohen, Tel Aviv, 1982. The American Society for Jewish Music, founded in 1974, started publishing the journal *Musica Judaica* in 1975. Articles of wide interest were published in Hebrew (with short English abstracts) in *Tazlil,* edited by Moshe Gorali for the Haifa Music Museum, for a number of years. The Israel Music Institute and Information Center (I.M.I.) in Tel Aviv started in 1990 to issue a quarterly review of musical activities in Israel and abroad for the promotion of music by Israeli composers; it contains biographical material, work lists, and directories of music institutions in Israel.

HISTORICAL SURVEYS

Anshen, Ruth Nanda, ed. *Mid-East: World Center* (Science and Culture Series). New York, 1956.

Berl, Heinrich. *Das Judentum in der Musik.* Berlin, 1926.

Cohen, A. Irma. *An Introduction to Jewish Music.* New York, 1923.

Cohen, Maxwell T. *The Jews in Music.* New York, 1939.

David, E. *La Musique chez les juifs.* Paris, 1873.

Ewen, David. *Hebrew Music.* New York, 1931.

Gradenwitz, Peter. *So singet uns von Zijons Sang. Jüdische Musik und Musiker in ihrer Umwelt.* In *Jüdische Lebenswelten. Essays zur Ausstellung,* ed. Andreas Nachama, Julius H. Schoeps, Edward van Volien. Berliner Festspiele. 1991.

Haywood, Charles. The Gentile note in Jewish music. *Chicago Jewish Forum,* 1946.

Idelsohn, A.Z. *Jewish Liturgy.* New York, 1934.

———. *Jewish Music in Its Historical Development.* New York, 1929.

Holde, A. *Jews in Music from the Age of Enlightenment to the Mid-20th Century.* New York, 1974.

Landau, Paul. "Das Orientbild des modernen Europa." (MS)

Lang, Paul Henry. *Music in Western Civilization.* New York, 1946.

Lauko, D. *Die jüdische Musik.* Pressburg, 1926.

Levy, S. *Das Judentum in der Musik.* Erfurt, 1930.

Moscati, Sabatino. *Geschichte und Kultur der Semitischen Völker.* 2. Aufl., Zürich/Wien, 1955.

Rothmüller, Aron Marko. *Die Musik der Juden.* Zürich, 1951.

Runes, Dagobert D., ed. *The Hebrew Impact on Western Civilization.* New York, 1951.

Sachs, Curt. *The Rise of Music in the Ancient World East and West.* New York, 1943.
———. *The Commonwealth of Art.* New York, 1946.
———. *The History of Musical Instruments.* New York, 1940.
Salesky, G. *Famous Musicians of a Wandering Race.* New York, 1927.
Saminsky, Lazare. *Music of the Ghetto and the Bible.* New York, 1935.
Sendrey, A. *Bibliography of Jewish Music.* London/New York, 1951.
Shiloah, Amnon. *Jewish Musical Tradition.* Detroit: Wayne University Press, 1994.

CHAPTERS ONE TO THREE

(Quotations from books and articles which are documented in footnotes are not necessarily repeated here.)

Ackermann, A. *Der synagogale Gesang in seiner historischen Entwicklung.* Trier, 1894.
Arends, L.A.F. *Über den Sprechgesang der Vorzeit.* Berlin, 1867.
Avenary, Hanoch. Magic, symbolism and allegory of the old Hebrew sound instruments. In *Collectanea Historiae Musicae* 2. Florenz, 1956; Jüdische Musik. In *Musik in Geschichte und Gegenwart.* Kassel, 1958.
———. Reflections on the origins of the Alleluia-Jubilus. In *Asaph: Studies in Art: Orbis Musicae,* ed. Judith Cohen; No. 6, 1978.
Bayer, Batya. The titles of the Psalms. In *Yuval,* Vol. 4. Jerusalem, 1982.
Binder, A.W. *Biblical Chant.* New York, 1957.
Cohen, Judith. Jubal in the Middle Ages. In *Yuval,* Vol. 3. Jerusalem, 1974.
Cook, Stanley. *An Introduction to the Bible.* London, 1945.
Delitsch, Franz. *Physiologie und Musik in ihrer Bedeutung für die Grammatik, besonders die Hebräische.* Leipzig, 1868.
Engel, Carl. *The Music of the Most Ancient Nations, Particularly of the Assyrians, Egyptians and Hebrews.* London, 1864.
Finesinger, S.B. Musical instruments in the Old Testament. *Hebrew Union College Annual,* 1926.
Friedländer, Arthur M. *Facts and Theories Relating to Hebrew Music.* London, 1924.
Friedmann, A. von. *Der synagogale Gesang.* Berlin, 1904–1908.
Gerson-Kiwi, E. Musique dans la Bible. In *Dict. de la Bible,* 5. Paris, 1956.
Gressmann, H. Musik und Musikinstrumente im Alten Testament. In *Religionsgeschichtliche Versuche und Vorarbeiten,* 2. Giessen, 1903.
Hemsi, A. *La Musique de la Torah.* Alexandria, 1929.
Heskes, Irene. Miriam's sisters: Jewish women and liturgical music. *Notes,* June 1992.
Hooke, S.A. *The Origins of Early Semitic Ritual.* Schweich Lectures, London, 1935.

Idelsohn, A.Z. Der jüdische Tempelgesang. In *Handbuch der Musikgeschichte*, ed. Guido Adler. Berlin, 1922.

Imber, Naphtali Herz. The music of the Psalms. *Music Magazine*, 1894.

Lachmann, Robert. *Jewish Cantillation and Song in the Isle of Djerba*. Jerusalem, 1940.

———. *Musik des Orients*. Leipzig, 1929.

Leitner, F. *Der gottesdienstliche Gesang im jüdischen und christlichen Altertum*. Freiburg, 1906.

Löhr, Max. Israel und die Kultur des Alten Vorderasien. *Der Morgen*. Berlin, 1926.

Pfeiffer, A.J. *Über die Musik der alten Hebräer*. Erlangen, 1779.

Praetorius, F. *Die Herkunft der hebräischen Akzente*. 1901.

———. *Die Übernahme der frühmittelalterlichen Neumen durch die Juden*. 1902.

Pulver, Jeffrey. Israel's music-lesson in Egypt. *Musical Times*. London, 1915.

———. The music of ancient Egypt. *Musical Society Proceedings*. London, 1921.

Reese, Gustave. *Music in the Middle Ages*. New York, 1940.

Rosowsky, S. The music of the Pentateuch: The tropes and their musical analysis. *Musical Society Proceedings*. London, 1934.

———. *The Cantillation of the Bible*. New York, 1957.

Saalschütz, Joseph Levin. *Geschichte und Würdigung der Musik bei den Hebräern*. Berlin, 1829.

Sachs, Curt. Musik der Antike. In *Handbuch der Musikwissenschaft*, ed. Ernst Bücken. Potsdam-Wildpark, 1928.

———. *Musik des Altertums*. Breslau, 1924.

———. The orient and western music. *The Asian Legacy and American Life*, ed. A.E. Caristy. New York, 1945.

———. *The Rise of Music in the Ancient World*. New York, 1943.

Schneider, P.J. *Biblisch-geschichtliche Darstellung der hebräischen Musik*. Bonn, 1834 (with a very valuable discussion of the early musicological literature on the subject).

Sellers, Ovid R. Musical instruments of Israel. *The Biblical Archaeologist*.1941.

Stainer, John. *The Music of the Bible*. London, 1879; new edition ed. F.W. Galpin, 1914.

Til, Salomon von. *Dicht-, Sing- und Spielkunst sowohl der Alten als insbesonders der Hebräer*. Frankfurt, 1706.

Wagner, Peter. *Einführung in die gregorianischen Melodien*, 1–3. 1901–1923.

Weiss, J. *Die musikalischen Instrumente des Alten Testaments*. Graz, 1895.

Werner, Eric. *The Sacred Bridge*. London/New York, Vol. 1, 1959; Vol. 2, 1984.

———. The doxology in synagogue and church, a liturgico-musical study. *Hebrew Union College Annual*, 1946.

————. Leading motifs in synagogue and plain song. *Papers of the American Musicological Society, Detroit Congress,* 1946.

————. The oldest sources of the synagogal chant. *Proceedings of the American Academy for Jewish Research,* 1947.

————. Preliminary notes for a comparative study of Catholic and Jewish musical punctuation. *Hebrew Union College Annual,* 1940.

————. Musical aspects of the Dead Sea Scrolls. *The Musical Quarterly,* New York, 1957.

————. Musical tradition and its transmitters between synagogue and church. In *Yuval,* Vol. 2. Jerusalem, 1971.

Wiley, Lulu Rumsey. *Bible Music.* New York, 1945.

CHAPTERS FOUR TO SIX

Abrahams, I. *Jewish Life in the Middle Ages.* London, 1932.

Adler, Israel. The rise of art music in the Italian ghetto. The influence of segregation on Jewish musical practice. In *Jewish Medieval and Renaissance Studies,* ed. Alexander Altmann. Cambridge, Massachusetts, 1967.

Anglès, Msgr. Iginio. Jewish music in medieval Spain. In *Yuval,* Vol. 1. Jerusalem, 1968.

Burstyn, Shai. The Arabian influence theory thesis revisited. *Current Musicology* 45/47. Festschrift f. Ernst Sanders, New York, 1990.

Badt, Bertha. *Die Lieder des Süsskind von Trimberg.* Berlin, 1920.

Berliner, A. *Aus dem Leben der deutschen Juden im Mittelalter.* Berlin, 1900.

Birnbaum, Eduard. *Jüdische Musiker am Hofe von Mantua von 1542–1628.* Wien, 1893.

Chase, Gilbert. *The Music of Spain.* New York, 1941.

Ecker, Lawrence. *Arabischer, provenzalischer und deutscher Minnesang. Eine motivgeschichtliche Untersuchung.* Bern, Leipzig, 1934.

Elbogen, I. *Geschichte der Juden in Deutschland.* Berlin, 1934.

————. *Der jüdische Gottesdienst.* Berlin, 1913.

Eisenstein, Judith. Medieval elements in the liturgical music of the Jews of southern France and northern Spain. *Musica Judaica,* Vol. 1. New York, 1975/1976.

Farmer, H.G. *A History of Arabian Music.* London, 1929.

————. *Maimonides on Listening to Music.* Bearsden, Scotland, 1941.

————. Medieval Jewish writers on music. *Music Review,* Cambridge, England, 1942.

————. *The Organ of the Ancients: From Eastern Sources.* London, 1943.

————. *Sa'adyah Gaon on the Influence of Music.* London, 1943.

————. *Studies in Oriental Musical Instruments.* London, 1931 and 1939.

Gradenwitz, Peter. Musik des Ghetto. *Monatsschrift für Geschichte und Wissenschaft des Judentums.* Breslau, 1937.

————. An early instance of copyright. *Music and Letters.* London, 1946.

————. Zur Herkunft, Charakter und Verbreitung der Jiddischen Volkslieder. In *Zeitschrift fur deutsche Philologie*, 100. Band, 1981.

————. *Die schönsten jiddischen Liebeslieder*. Dreieich, 1988.

Güdemann, M. *Geschichte des Erziehungswesens und der Kultur der Juden in Italien während des Mittelalters*. Wien, 1884.

————. *Das jüdische Unterrichtswesen während der spanisch-arabischen Periode*. Wien, 1873.

Harrán, Don. Salomone Rossi, Jewish musician in Renaissance Italy. *Acta Musicologica*, 1987.

Henriques, Rose L., and Herbert Loewe. *Medieval Hebrew Minstrelsy*. London, 1926.

Imber, Naphtali Herz. Music of the ghetto. *Music Magazine*, 1897/1898.

Jacobson, Joshua R. The choral music of Salomone Rossi. *American Choral Review*, 30:4, 1988.

————. A possible influence of traditional chant on a synagogue motet of Salomone Rossi. *Musica Judaica*, Vol. 3, 1989.

Kahn, Máximo José. Chant populaire Andalou et Musique Synagogale. *Cahiers d'Art*, Nos. 5–10. Paris, 1939.

Kinkeldey, Otto. A Jewish dancing master of the Renaissance. *Freidus Memorial Volume*. New York, 1929.

Leo da Modena. *Historia de gli riti hebraici*. Paris, 1637, Engl. transl., 1650.

Naumbourg, S., and Vincent d'Indy. *Cantiques de Salomo Rossi hebreo*. Paris, 1877/1885.

Nettl, Paul. *Alte jüdische Spielleute und Musiker*. Prag, 1923.

————. Some early Jewish musicians. *Musical Quarterly*, 1930.

Prior, Roger. Jewish musicians at the Tudor Court. *Musical Quarterly*. New York, 1983.

Ribera y Tarago, Julian. *Music in Ancient Arabia and Spain*. Stanford University, 1929.

Rikko, F., and Hugo Weisgall, eds. *Salomone de Rossi: HaShirim asher lish'lomoh*. New York, 1967.

Roth, Cecil. *L'Academia Musicale del Ghetto di Venezia*. Firenze, 1928.

————. *History of the Jews in Venice*. Philadelphia, 1930.

————. *The Jewish Contribution to Civilization*. Oxford, 1943.

Sachs, Curt. *World History of the Dance*. New York, 1937.

Salmen, Walter. *Das Lochheimer Liederbuch*. Leipzig, 1951.

————. *Denn die Fiedel macht das Fest. Jüdische Musikanten und Tänzer vom 13 bis 20 Jahrhundert*. Innsbruck, 1991.

Schudt, S. *Jüdische Denkwürdigkeiten*. Frankfurt, 1714.

Shmueli, Herzl. *Higgajon Bechinnor des Jehuda ben Joseph Arie Moscato*. Tel Aviv, 1953.

Sola, D.A. de, and Aguilar, E. *The Ancient Melodies of the Spanish and Portugese Jews*. London, 1857.

Werner, Eric. Die hebräischen Intonationen in B. Marcello's *Estro poetico-armonico*. *Monatsschrift für Geschichte und Wissenschaft des Judentums*. Breslau, 1937.

Werner, Eric, and Isaiah Sonne. The philosophy and theory of music in Judeo-Arabic literature. *Hebrew Union College Annual*, 1941.

Wolf, Albert. *Fahrende Leute bei den Juden*. Leipzig, 1909.

Zoller, J. Theater und Tanz in den italienischen Ghetti. In *Mitteilungen zur jüdischen Volkskunde*. Wien, 1926.

Zunz, M. *Die Synagogale Poesie des Mittelalters*. Frankfurt, 1920.

CHAPTERS SEVEN TO NINE

Bekker, Paul. *Gustav Mahlers Sinfonien*. Berlin, 1921.

Braham, John, and Isaac Nathan. *A Selection of Hebrew Melodies Ancient and Modern: the Poetry written by Lord Byron*. London, 1815–1822, rev. 1840.

Chase, Gilbert. *America's Music*. New York, 1955.

Drew, David. *Kurt Weill. A Handbook*. London, 1987.

Eggebrecht, H.H. *Die Musik Gustav Mahlers*. München, 1982.

Einstein, Alfred. *Music in the Romantic Era*. New York, 1947.

Faris, Alexander. *Offenbach*. London, 1980.

Gradenwitz, Peter. Jews in Austrian music. In *The Jews of Austria*, ed. Josef Fraenkel. London.

————.The religious works of Arnold Schoenberg. *The Music Review*, 21/1. London, 1960.

————. Gustav Mahler and Arnold Schoenberg. In *Yearbook of the Leo Baeck Institute*. London, 1961.

————. Schönbergs Streichquartett Nr. 4, op. 37. In *Meisterwerke der Musik*. München, 1986.

————. Ludwig van Beethoven und die hebräische Liturgie. In *Menora. Jarhbuch für deutsch-jüdische Geschichte*. München, 1991.

Gray, Cecil. *A Survey of Contemporary Music*. London, 1924, 1938.

Hensel, Sebastian, ed. *Die Familie Mendelssohn*, 2 vols. Leipzig, 1879.

Kapp, Julius. *Meyerbeer*. Berlin, 1920.

La Grange, Henry-Louis de. *Mahler*. New York, 1973, following.

Landau, Anne L. *The Contribution of Jewish Composers to the Music of the Modern World*. Cincinnati, 1946.

Mäckelmann, Michael. *Arnold Schönberg und das Judentum*. Hamburg, 1984.

Mitchell, Donald. *Gustav Mahler*. London, 1958, following.

Newlin, Dika. *Bruckner—Mahler—Schönberg*. New York, 1947, 1978.

Phillipps, Olga Somech. *Isaac Nathan*. London, 1940.

Redlich, H.F. *Bruckner and Mahler*. London, 1958.

Reis, Claire. *Composers in America*. New York, 1948.

Ringer, Alexander L. *Arnold Schoenberg. The Composer as Jew*. Oxford, 1990.

Rufer, Josef. *Das Werk Arnold Schönbergs*. Kassel, 1959; London, 1962.

Sanders, Ronald. *The Days Grow Short* (biography of Kurt Weill). New York, 1980.

Sharntte, Reinhold, ed. *Offenbach in America*. Berlin, 1957.

Schereba, Jürgen. *Kurt Weill. Eine Biographie in Texten, Bildern und Dokumenten*. Mainz, 1994.

Schoenberg, Arnold. *Style and Idea*, ed. L. Stein. New York, 1975.

Schoenberg, Arnold. *Letters*, ed. E. Stein. London, 1964.

Schoenberg, Nuria Nono-, ed. *Arnold Schönberg. Lebensgeschichte in Begegnungen*. Ritter, Klagenfurt, 1992.

Stuckenschmidt, H.H. *Schoenberg, His Life, World, and Work*. London, 1977.

Sward, Keith. Jewish musicality in America. *Journal of Applied Psychology*, 1933.

Werner, Eric. *Mendelssohn. A New Image of the Composer and His Age*. New York, 1980.

Werner, Jack. Felix and Fanny Mendelssohn. *Music and Letters*. London, 1947.

Wörner, Karl. *Schönberg's Moses und Aron*. London, 1963.

CHAPTER TEN

Avenary, H., ed. See Sulzer (below).

Baer, A. *Ba'al Tefillah oder der practische Vorbeter*. Leipzig, 1877; 1901.

Breslaur, Emil. *Sind originale Synagogen- und Volksmelodien bei den Juden nachweisbar?* Leipzig, 1898.

Cohen, Francis L. *The Rise and Development of Synagogue Music*. London, 1888.

Friedmann, A. *Der synagogale Gesang*. Berlin, 1904, 1908.

———. *Lebensbilder berühmter Kantoren*. Berlin, 1927.

Idelsohn, A.Z. Songs and singers in the synagogue in the 18th century. In *Hebrew Union College Annual Jubilee Volume*. Cincinnati, 1925.

Nambourg, S. *Semiroth Yisrael: chants religieux des Israélites*. Paris, 1847, 1867, 1874.

Schönberg, Jacob. *Die traditionellen Gesänge des israelitischen Gottesdienstes in Deutschland*. Erlangen-Nürnberg, 1926; reprinted with preface by Eric Werner, 1971.

Singer, L. *Die Tonarten des traditionellen Synagogengesanges*. Wien, 1896.

Sulzer. *Schir Zion, gottesdienstliche Gesänge der Israeliten*, 2 vols. Wien 1839, 1865.

Sulzer, ed. Avenary, H. *Kantor Sulzer und seine Zeit. Eine Dokumentation*. Sigmaringen, 1985.

Werner, Eric. *A Voice Still Heard. The Sacred Songs of the Ashkenazic Jews*, Pennsylvania State University Press, 1976.

Chapter Eleven

Antecedents of Jewish music. *Musical Courier*, 1913.
Brod, Max. Jüdische Volksmelodien. *Der Jude*. Berlin, 1916–1917.
Heskes, Irene, Ed. *The Historic Contribution of Russian Jewry to Jewish Music*. New York, 1967.
Hofman, Shlomo. The music of the Jewish Petersburg composers and its impact on the music renaissance in Israel. In *World Congress on Jewish Music, Jerusalem 1978, Proceedings*, ed. Judith Cohen, 1982.
Kaufmann, F.M. *Die schönsten Lieder der Ostjuden*. Berlin, 1920.
———. Jüdische Volkslieder. *Der Jude*. Berlin, 1916–1917.
Parkes, James. *An Enemy of the People: Antisemitism*. New York, 1946.
Sabaniev, L. The Jewish national school in music. *Musical Quarterly*, 1929.
———. *Die national jüdische Schule in der Musik*. Wien, 1927.
Stutschewsky, J. *Mein Weg zur jüdischen Musik*. Wien, 1935.
Weisser, Albert. *The Modern Renaissance of Jewish Music*. New York, 1954.
Yiddish folksong. See also bibliography for Chapters Four to Six.

Chapter Twelve

(For bibliography on various important composers, see also Chapters Seven to Nine.)

On Leonard Bernstein
Gradenwitz, Peter. *Leonard Bernstein. Unendliche Vielfalt eines Musikers*. Zürich/Mainz, 1995, 4th ed. Also in English, Spanish, and Japanese.
Gottlieb, Jack. Leonard Bernstein's Kaddish Symphony. *Perspectives of New Music*, Fall/Winter, 1965.

On Ernest Bloch
Gradenwitz, Peter. Ernest Bloch. In *Swiss Composers in the 20th Century*, ed. Andres Briner. Pro Helvetia, Zürich, 1990.
Tibaldi-Chiesa. Ernest Bloch. *Musica Hebraica*, Vol. 1. Jerusalem, 1938.

On Darius Milhaud
Milhaud, Darius (autobiographies). *Notes sans Musique*. Paris, 1949, 1963. *Notes Without Music*. London, 1952. *Ma Vie heureuse*. Paris, 1973.

On Mordecai Sandberg
Brotbeck, Roman. Völkerverbindende Tondifferenzierung. Mordecai Sandberg—ein verkannter Pionier der Mikrotonalität. *Neue Zeitschrift für Musik*, 1991, No. 4.
Heller, Charles. Mordecai Sandberg: his compositions and his ideas. *Journal of Synagogue Music of the Cantor's Assembly*, 1984.

On Schoenberg
See Chapters Seven to Nine. See also *Journal of the Arnold Schoenberg Institute*, University of Southern California, 1976–.

The Bible in Music

Gorali, Moshe. *The Old Testament in Music*. Jerusalem: Maron, 1993. Lists 5748 compositions on Old Testament poetry and prose—liturgical plays, mystery plays, oratorios, operas, psalms, songs, and instrumental works— by 1665 composers of 44 nations within a millennium of western music history.

In Memoriam

Adler, Hans-Günther. *Theresienstadt 1941–1945. Das Antlitz einer Zwangsgemeinschaft*. Tübingen, 1960.

Allende-Blin, Juan, ed. *Musiktradition im Exil*. Köln, 1993.

———. *Erich Itor Kahn*. Munich, 1994.

Dümling, Albrecht, and Peter Girth, ed. *Entartete Musik. Eine kommentierte Rekonstruktion zur Düsseldorfer Ausstellung von 1938*. Düsseldorf, 1988.

Fénelon, Fania. *Sursis pour l'Orchestre*. Paris, 1976.

———. *Das Mädchenorchester in Auschwitz*. Frankfurt/M., 1980.

Heister, Hans-Werner, Claudia Maurer Zenck, and Peter Peterson, eds. *Musik im Exil. Folgen des Nazismus für die internationale Musikkultur*. Frankfurt/M., 1993.

Heister, Hanns-Werner, and Hans-Günter Klein. *Musik und Musikpolitik im faschistischen Deutschland*. Frankfurt/M., 1984.

John, Eckhard. Musik und Konzentrationslager. Eine Annäherung. *Archiv für Musikwissenschaft*, 48, Heft 1, 1991.

———. *Musikbolschewismus. Die Politisierung der Musik in Deutschland 1918–1938*. Stuttgart, 1994.

Karas, Joža. *Music in Terezín 1941–1945*. New York, 1985.

Langbein, Hermann. *Menschen in Auschwitz*. Europa-Verlag, 1972.

McCredie, Andrew. *Karl Amadeus Hartmann*. Wilhelmshaven, 1981.

Migdal, Ulrike. *Und die Musik spielt dazu. Chansons und Satiren aus dem KZ Theresienstadt*. Munich, 1986.

Pass, Walter, Gerhard Scheit, and Wilhelm Svoboda. *Orpheus im Exil. Die Vertreibung der österreichischen Musik von 1938 bis 1945*. Vienna, 1995.

Prieberg, Fred K. *Musik im NS-Staat*. Frankfurt/M., 1982.

Strauss, Herbert A., ed. *International Biographical Dictionary of Central European Emigrés 1933–1945*. Munich/London/New York/Paris, 1983.

Weber, Horst, Ed. *Musik in der Emigration 1933–1945. Verfolgung, Vertreibung, Rückwirkung*. Stuttgart, 1994.

Wildauer, Monica, ed. Österreichische Musiker im Exil. *Beiträge '90*, Kassel, s.d.

Wulf, Joseph. *Musik im Dritten Reich, Eine Dokumentation*. Gütersloh, 1963, 1983.

A series on the lives and works of composers who perished in concentration camps during the Nazi period is published by von Bockel Verlag, Hamburg, beginning in 1994, under the title *Verdrängte Musik*. As of 1995, monographs and reports on colloquia about Viktor Ullmann, Erwin Schulhoff, and Pavel Haas have been published. The same series includes a book on the composer and conductor Berthold Goldschmidt. Born in 1903, Goldschmidt lived in exile in England and was "rediscovered" in Germany in the 1990s; at more than ninety years of age he was able to conduct some of his operas and instrumental works.

Chapters Thirteen to Fifteen

Composers

Bahat, Avner. *Le Rencontre Orient-Occident dans la musique Israélienne*. Thèse de doctorat, Université de Paris, Sorbonne, 1974.

Brod, Max. *Die Musik Israels*. Tel Aviv, 1951, 1976; with Cohen, Yehuda Walter, *Werden und Entwicklung der Musik in Israel*, Part 2, Kassel, 1976.

Gradenwitz, Peter. Composers of modern Palestine. *Musicology*, 1947.

———. Composers of Palestine. *Monthly Musical Record*. London, 1948.

———. *Music and Musicians in Israel*. Tel Aviv, 1978.

Hirshberg, Yehoash. *Paul Ben-Haim. His Life and Works*. Jerusalem, 1990.

Keren, Zvi. *Contemporary Israeli Music*. Ramat Gan, Israel, 1961.

Quarterly of Israel Music Institute, Tel Aviv. Published since 1990, this publication contains biographies of Israeli composers in almost every issue, in English and Hebrew, with lists of compositions.

Early Musical Life in Palestine

Notes, 1948–1949. This journal published an extensive bibliography on Near-Eastern and early Palestine music.

Philipsen, Carl Bernhard. Musik in Palästina. *Anbruch*. Wien, 1922.

Popular music of Palestine. *Musical America*, 1909.

Sachsse, L. Palästinensische Musikinstrumente. *Zeitschrift des Deutschen Palästina-Vereins*, 1927.

Saminsky, Lazare, and P.J. Nolan. Governor Storrs and Jerusalem School of Music. *Musical America*, 1923.

Storrs, Ronald. *Orientations*. London, 1923.

Folk Music

Binder, A.W. *New Palestinian Folk Songs*. 1926–1933, 1942.

Cohen, Dalia, and Ruth Katz. The Israeli folksong: a methodological example of computer analysis of monophonic music. In *Yuval*, Vol. 6. Jerusalem, 1977.

Schoenberg, Jacob. *Shire Eretz Yisrael (Palestinian folksongs)*. Berlin, 1935.

Shiloah, Amnon, and Erik Cohen. The dynamics of change in Jewish oriental ethnic music in Israel. *Ethnomusicology* 27(2), May 1983.

History

Bohlman, Philip V. *The Land Where Two Streams Flow: Music in the German-Jewish Community of Israel.* Urbana, Ill., 1989.

——. *The World Centre for Jewish Music in Palestine 1936–1940.* Oxford, 1994.

Gradenwitz, Peter. *Music and Musicians in Israel.* Tel Aviv, 1978.

Hirshberg, Yehoash. *Music in the Jewish Community of Palestine (1880–1948).* Oxford, 1995.

BOOKS AND ESSAYS IN HEBREW

Bronsaft, M. *The National-Jewish School in Music.* Jerusalem, 1940.

Cohen, Yehuda. *Ne'ime'i Zemirot Yisrael (The Heirs of the Psalmist).* Tel Aviv, 1991.

Edel, I. *The Palestinian Folk Song.* Tel Aviv, 1946.

Gerson-Kiwi, E. *The Music of the Orient—Ancient and Modern.* Tel Aviv, 1949.

Geshuri, M. *Essays on Hassidic Music.* Jerusalem, 1931.

Gradenwitz, Peter. Compositions by Israeli composers. In *World of the Symphony, Chamber Music, World of the Pianist.* Tel Aviv, numerous editions, since 1945.

Idelsohn, A.Z. *Jewish Music.* Tel Aviv, 1926.

——. The song of the Yemenite Jews. *Reshumot.* Odessa, 1914.

Kühn, J. *Music in the Bible, the Talmud, and the Cabala.* Vienna, 1929.

Loewenstein, H. (Avenary). Jewish music in manuscripts before 1800. *Kiryat Sefer.* Jerusalem, 1942.

Loewenstein, H. The science of music in the sources of the tenth to the seventeenth century. *Kiryat Sefer.* Jerusalem, 1944.

Portaleone, Abraham ben-David. *Shiltei Haggiborim.* Mantua, 1612.

Ravina, M. *Jewish Musicians.* Tel Aviv, 1941.

——. *Letters on Jewish Music.* Tel Aviv, 1947.

——. *Yoel Engel and Jewish Music.* Tel Aviv, 1947.

Stock, J. *M. Gusikov.* Tel Aviv, 1947.

Stutschewsky, J. *Jewish Music.* Tel Aviv, 1945.

TENDENTIOUS AND ANTI-SEMITIC PUBLICATIONS (SELECTION)

Blessinger, Karl. *Mendelssohn, Meyerbeer, Mahler: Drei Kapitel Judentum in der Musik als Schlüssel zur Musikgeschichte des 19. Jahrhunderts.* Berlin, 1939.

Eichenauer, R. *Musik und Rasse.* München, 1932.

Gerigk, H., and Th. Stengel. *Lexikon der Juden in der Musik.* Berlin, 1940.

Heuss, Alfred. Arnold Schönberg, Preussischer Kompositionslehrer. *Neue Zeitschrift für Musik*, 92(10), 1925, translated and publ. in Ringer, Alexander L., *Arnold Schoenberg. The Composer as Jew*, Appendix A. Oxford, 1990.

Judentum und Musik. In *Mit dem ABC jüdischer und nichtarischer Musikbeflissener*. Herausgegeben von Christa Maria Rock und Hans Bruckner. München, 1936.

Kahl, Willi. Mendelssohn und Hiller im Rheinland. Zur Geschichte der Judenemanzipation im deutschen Musikleben des 19. Jahrhunderts. *Die Musik*. Berlin, 1938.

Lorenz, Alfred. Musikwissenschaft und Judenfrage. *Die Musik*. Berlin, 1938.

Die Musik. Sondernummer. Berlin, 1936.

Wagner, Richard. *Das Judenthum in der Musik*. Leipzig, 1850, 1869.

Wünsch, Walter. Der Jude im balkanslawischen Volkstum und Volkslied. *Die Musik*. Berlin, 1938.

Characteristic anti-Semitic writings of the Nazi period are extensively listed in the books of Fred K. Prieberg, *Musik im NS-Staat*, Frankfurt/M., 1982, and Eckhard John, *Musikbolschewismus. Die Politisierung der Musik in Deutschland, 1918–1938*, Stuttgart, 1994.

INDEX

Italic page numbers refer to illustrations.